INTERNATIONAL ARBITRATION
FROM ATHENS TO LOCARNO

BY

JACKSON H. RALSTON

LATE AMERICAN AGENT PIOUS FUND CASE; UMPIRE OF THE ITALIAN-
VENEZUELAN CLAIMS COMMISSION; EDITOR OF "VENEZUELAN
ARBITRATIONS OF 1903"; AUTHOR OF "THE LAW AND
PROCEDURE OF INTERNATIONAL TRIBUNALS"

THE LAWBOOK EXCHANGE, LTD.
Clark, New Jersey

ISBN 978-1-58477-396-2

Lawbook Exchange edition 2004, 2016

The quality of this reprint is equivalent to the quality of the original work.

THE LAWBOOK EXCHANGE, LTD.
33 Terminal Avenue
Clark, New Jersey 07066-1321

*Please see our website for a selection of our other publications
and fine facsimile reprints of classic works of legal history:*
www.lawbookexchange.com

Library of Congress Cataloging-in-Publication Data

Ralston, Jackson H. (Jackson Harvey), 1857-1945.
    International arbitration from Athens to Locarno / by Jackson H.
  Ralston.
        p. cm.
    Originally published: [Stanford] : Stanford University Press, 1929.
  (Stanford books in world politics).
    Includes bibliographical references and index.
    ISBN 1-58477-396-0 (cloth: alk. paper)
    1. Arbitration, International. I. Title. II. Stanford books in world
  politics.

KZ6115.R35 2004
341.5'22—dc22

                                                    2003061851

Printed in the United States of America on acid-free paper

INTERNATIONAL ARBITRATION
FROM ATHENS TO LOCARNO

BY

JACKSON H. RALSTON

LATE AMERICAN AGENT PIOUS FUND CASE; UMPIRE OF THE ITALIAN-
VENEZUELAN CLAIMS COMMISSION; EDITOR OF "VENEZUELAN
ARBITRATIONS OF 1903"; AUTHOR OF "THE LAW AND
PROCEDURE OF INTERNATIONAL TRIBUNALS"

1929

STANFORD UNIVERSITY PRESS
STANFORD UNIVERSITY, CALIFORNIA

LONDON: HUMPHREY MILFORD
OXFORD UNIVERSITY PRESS

FOREWORD

We are often told, and with truth, that the modern era of international arbitrations began with the year 1794 when the Jay Treaty between the United States and Great Britain was signed. Except, however, for the Geneva award of 1872, the matters arbitrally decided usually have been until recently of minor importance. In fact little of permanent and far-reaching judicial character has taken place until within the past forty years. True it is, of course, that procedure was slowly evolving during the entire period and a better understanding of the subject-matter was gradually being reached.

During the last two-score years, however, advances have proceeded very rapidly. To realize their imposing character we shall enumerate some of the most salient events.

In 1889 the first Pan-American Conference met in the city of Washington and declared itself in favor of broad arbitration of international disputes. This was followed at intervals by five successors, all working in the same general direction. The last meeting was at Havana in February 1928 with an adjourned meeting, now in session, devoted to the consideration exclusively of arbitration and conciliation.

There followed in 1899 and 1907 the two Hague Peace Conferences, the first initiating and the second perfecting the Permanent Court of Arbitration as well as the procedure of International Commissions of Inquiry, the second conference also taking a decided stand against the forcible collection of national contract debts.

Again in 1907 was installed the Central American Court of Justice, which lasted for ten years and possessed a jurisdiction which, for extent of power, though operating within a narrow radius, has not since been equaled.

Even as brief a summary as the present should not omit reference to the Bryan Peace Treaties, providing as has so often been said a "cooling off" time for nations ready to rush at each others' throats, during which there might exist an inquiry as to the nature and facts of any supposed grievances. These treaties date from 1913 and have been so generally adopted in their original or developed form as to constitute a real addition to the subject of international relations and arbitrations.

The World War for the time checked all idea of progress under the rule of law; but at its close the long pent-up forces of pacific civilization, restrained during hostilities, brought forth the League of

Nations with its inauguration of the Permanent Court of International Justice. Scores of individual treaties between the nations have since enlarged and confirmed its jurisdiction, till now only study and casuistic skill can enable any bellicose country connected with it to find a loophole of escape from the orderly processes of the court, other means of settlement failing.

Our next and last great step is represented by the pending Kellogg-Briand Treaty, which the world, with no material exception, seems ready to accept. The corollary to this treaty is reference to the Court of International Justice or to some similar judicial body of all disputes otherwise escaping solution.

Today it is almost impossible for any nation to resort to war—euphemistically called a "method of self-help" or of "self-redress" —without incurring the condemnation of the whole body of civilized public opinion. This opinion indignantly demands why world peace and repose should be disturbed by the bad temper of an associate in the family of nations or that of the rulers of such associate, when there exist commissions to investigate as to the reality of injuries and courts to dictate proper remedies in cases of actual wrong-doing.

Despite the importance of the judicial settlement of international disputes, there has been little attempt so far to consider the subject comprehensively. Treating detached segments of the whole theory and history of international tribunals, there have been works upon arbitration among the Greeks and during the Middle Ages; reports of special arbitrations; books upon the general subject covering a great deal of ground, although imperfectly, and antedating for the most part the significant events of the past forty years. In addition, special treatises have described the Hague Conferences, the formation of the League of Nations, and the work of the Permanent Court of International Justice, as well as many other matters of lesser moment. The nearest and most recent approach to a work of broad scope is *La justice internationale,* by M. Politis, but this lacks much of completeness.

The only book containing in detail pronouncements of arbitral and other international courts of justice remains *The Law and Procedure of International Tribunals* by the present author. To this the following volume furnishes, it is believed, a natural complement, covering ground thought heretofore inadequately considered by any author. Doubtless many of its chapters could with advantage to the deeper student have been largely extended, but the writer has had consideration for the patience of the general reader.

The author desires to express his sincere acknowledgments to Dr. Arthur D. Call, Secretary of the American Peace Society, and Mr. Denys P. Myers, Director of Research of the World Peace Foundation, for careful proof reading; to Professor A. T. Murray of Stanford University for aid as to Greek nomenclature; to Miss Kate Pinsdorf for translations from the German Archives; and to Professor William Hawley Davis, Editor of the Stanford University Press, and his able assistants for aiding in the proper preparation and presentation of this book.

JACKSON H. RALSTON

PALO ALTO, CALIFORNIA
January, 1929

CONTENTS

PART I

GENERAL PRINCIPLES OF JUDICIAL SETTLEMENT BETWEEN NATIONS

CHAPTER I

THE LAW OF INTERNATIONAL TRIBUNALS

1. Natural law as applied to international situations.—By way of preface and as conducive to a broader understanding of the subject-matter which we design to treat, it seems well to make a few observations of a general character as to the nature of law, and particularly of law as applied by international tribunals.

Of late years we have been assured by many writers that there is no such thing as natural law, and in a sense often given the term it will be recognized, save by a very small minority, that natural law has no existence. Thus if we mean by natural law that in each instance a special providential interference determines the course of events, the vast majority of intelligent people will reject the idea. If, on the other hand, by the term we mean that certain governing principles which control the action of men in their individual relations still rule when they are aggregated into nations, the evidence in its favor seems overwhelming.

We find that in the material world all nature is under the control of law. The universe is built up by and through the laws of nature. It is argued that when we pass from the material world into the world of relations between human beings and unities of them known as nations, natural law no longer has any effect and that to speak of it stamps one as hopelessly medieval. Nevertheless, we find books regarded as sensible treating of human qualities and of the effects of their display by one human being upon another. We are taught that such display almost inevitably brings about certain reactions. These reactions are so universal as to indicate a law governing them. If this be true as to individuals considered singly or in small groups, at what point does it cease to be true as the groups enlarge their numbers? The fact is that so long as human beings are human beings, and governments and nations represent but aggregations of human beings, the whole cannot lose the basic human qualities of the units; and just as the individual is controlled by laws governing the consequences of the display of his characteristics, so are governments likewise limited.

From the beneficial or harmful results to the man or to his associates of the actions of the individual we deduce that such actions should be treated either as commendable and to be encouraged by us as in conformity with law, or injurious and to be so recognized by our declarations of law. The natural law back of all this was antecedent to our discovery of its existence, only waiting to be made manifest when the occasion arose.

With the individual we see that love, hatred, suspicion, contempt, jealousy, injustice call forth well-understood responses. These responses constitute expressions of natural law. Decrees against them are unavailing. Human declarations cannot prevail when opposed to deep-seated laws of nature, or natural laws.

When we turn from the individual to the nation we have not abandoned natural law but rather have widened its operations. The qualities which when displayed in the individual have been demonstrated to be anti-social and as such contrary to law are equally anti-social and infinitely more dangerous and contrary therefore to natural law when given development by the nation.

International law and international tribunals take little note of anything approaching the natural law of which we speak. Infinite violations of natural law, proved to be violations by their deleterious consequences, have as yet made scarcely any impression upon the minds of writers on the law of nations. All have been obsessed with the idea that the state is an entity beyond the reach of law, human (except as backed by superior force) or natural. We have not studied the law of nations from a psychological point of view, as we are commencing to study the natural law surrounding individuals.

Some illustrations may be given of the kind of natural law we have in mind. There is no provision in the law of nature which recognizes the right of an individual upon overpowering his opponent, irrespective of which one may have been the aggressor, to take the goods of the unsuccessful contestant or his liberty or it may be his life. We know this to be true through centuries of experience within the nation of the anti-social effects of such conduct. We have discovered that a natural law prohibits the invasion by one man of the rights of another in the manners spoken of. This prohibition we have largely embodied in our codes. We call it a natural law because we find certain results of an evil character naturally proceeding from its violation.

The law of which we speak holds equally good whether there be one or a dozen or one hundred persons engaged in its violation. In each instance the reaction of an injurious character punishes the violator of the law. When, however, we advance to the size of a nation and the original small group becomes multiplied by a thousand or a million, we imagine that the natural law, the effects of which we could see readily

on a small scale, has ceased to operate. We believe the injurious consequences proving the wrong character of the act may now be ignored.
Such is not the fact, although international tribunals treat it as such, as
is illustrated by the solemnity still alleged to belong to treaties imposed
after conflict by the victor upon the vanquished opponent and which
may involve the virtual slavery of unborn generations of members of
the vanquished nation. If we recognize that in the case of the individual
or the small group the hatred and degradation to both parties involved
in the submission of the loser to the power of the winner means the
violation of natural law, are we justified in ignoring the fact when
similar conditions exist in the case of nations? Should a court be called
upon to enforce the will of the victor in carrying out—not law in any
true sense but—the power of violence which in itself may breed further
violence in exchange thereafter?

Other instances might be given to an indefinite number, but our
present purpose is merely to call attention to the fact, and not to develop
the idea in full. We assume, therefore, with such brief argument as has
been presented that there is a natural law governing individuals, and
that, because nations are merely aggregations of individuals, there is a
like natural law extending to them. Its enforcement in international
tribunals has been, to say the least, scanty.

2. Method of trial and error as applied to law.—When we are
seeking to discover certain at any rate of the laws of nature, we do it
through the medium of what is known as "trial and error." Turning to
international law and its operations, the student has scarcely discovered
that the "trial and error" system applies equally well to this science as
it does to others. He overlooks the fact that for hundreds of years,
even in an international way, men have been unconsciously resorting to
the "trial and error" system, and that as a consequence there has been
accumulated a vast amount of data which, when studied from the standpoint of cause and effect, would furnish even the poorest philosopher
with keys to many of the principles of natural law governing the affairs
of nations. This study would develop that the laws operative between
nations, and so disclosed, are merely enlarged illustrations of what had
long before been recognized as natural and proper laws as between individuals. When this study[1] has been properly pursued we shall further

---

[1] Many of the ideas heretofore and hereafter expressed in this chapter are more
or less developed in Ralston's *Democracy's International Law* (1922), Edmunds' *Lawless Law of Nations* (1925), and Lauterpacht's *Private Law Sources and Analogies
of International Law* (1927).

find that many of the so-called principles applied even in international courts of justice are not principles at all, but are perversions of natural law and are pregnant with evil consequences.

3. Recognition of existence of natural law.—We have spoken of the fact that authors have frequently, superciliously it seems to us, disregarded the existence of anything approaching natural law as affecting the affairs of nations or even human beings. This is not, however, universally true. Cicero in his *De Officiis* says:

True law is right reason, conformable to nature, extending over all, eternal. It prescribes duty, forbids fraud. It is not one thing in Rome, another in Athens, one thing now and another later. It should cover all nations and all times. It is unique, eternal, unchangeable.[1a]

Hautefeuille says:

Divine or natural law is the only basis and the sole source of international law. It is in going back to it that one exactly determines the law of nations. Any other way leads infallibly to error.[2]

Murder was no less a crime because not denounced in the codes.[3]

William Ladd says:

The same moral laws which ought to govern individuals ought to govern nations. What is wrong for an individual is wrong for a nation. In the intercourse of these moral persons disputes will arise, injuries will be done, retaliation and revenge will follow, and unless some other means of terminating their disputes by amicable and rational methods are devised, war will be the consequence.[4]

We may also quote Revon:

The independence of the tribunal, someone has said very justly, is but a practical consequence of the proposition of legal theory that the law itself is not simply a product of the state but a distinct principle in the life of nations.[5]

So Bluntschli remarks that international law is only obligatory because it is necessary and does not depend upon the good pleasure of anyone.[6]

Dr. William A. White says:

Social laws are as much natural laws as is the law of gravity, and legislators can no more make natural law than could Newton make the law of

---

[1a] Cited by Dreyfus, *L'arbitrage international*, 12.

[2] *Des droits et des devoirs des nations neutres,* approvingly quoted by de Roquefort, *De la solution juridique,* 38.   [3] *Ibid.,* 36.

[4] *An Essay on a Congress of Nations,* 4.   [5] *L'arbitrage international,* 482.

[6] *Le droit international codifié,* I, paragraph 3.

falling bodies. . . . . We need to find these laws and work in harmony with them, not against them.[7]

Upon the basis of what has already been said, we may assert with confidence that there is such a thing as natural law. This will apply internationally to those natural relations which may be regarded as simple enlargements of such as exist between man and man. When states are fully organized and deal with each other as individuals there may well be a natural law also applicable to them and discoverable in the same manner as the natural law between individuals acting in a purely private capacity, that is to say, by the disagreeable reaction attendant upon its violation and the pleasurable reaction following upon its observance.

All law possessing the character of permanence must be natural law. Its only variations in appearance will arise not in itself but in the greater or less weight attached to some inhibitions because of the changing ideas of men as to the relative importance of given conditions. The thing will be permanent; the angle of vision will vary.

4. Kinds of law.—Let us next consider briefly, as bearing upon the jurisdiction of international tribunals, other of the various kinds of law which may exist. For it is true that law takes many phases and many things are known as international law which are merely practices and do not rise to the dignity of law in any sense of the word.

Under the head of law are also included a great variety of rules of lesser urgency than those which may be based upon natural laws. These are laws of convenience and laws merely expressive of customs which have arisen as between nations, having only such authority as may be conveniently given them.

In the conduct of human affairs there is necessarily a very great variety of acts entirely indifferent in themselves and which might with absolute propriety be carried out in any one of a variety of ways. In the sphere of law within the state we may illustrate this by our very numerous regulations with regard to the control of automobiles. A large proportion of these present approved solutions for problems which might have been with equal propriety decided in exactly the opposite sense. There was, however, a necessity for the existence of a rule which should be of binding force upon all, and this rule is laid down by the superior power. So in international law the same situation arises. These rules are, internationally speaking, given the title of law and in

---

[7] *American Bar Association Journal,* October 1927, 553.

so far as they regulate human conduct, may deserve the title. In a juster sense, however, they are no more laws than are the ordinances of a city council.

As the laws of the class referred to merely represent the more approved practices among nations, they may be arrived at by a study of treaties or of treatises on international law.

5. Fictions in international law.—In the law within the nation there are many so-called fictions. It is also true that international law has its fictions. These might possibly be treated as working hypotheses, having the sanction of convenience, and useful within strict limitations in the treatment of international affairs, but not to be given absolute weight under all circumstances because after all they are fictive in nature.

Perhaps the first fiction we shall encounter, one which has been observed in many respects as if it were law by international tribunals, is that which creates an independent individual—a corporation or moral person, as it is known in the civil law—out of the whole body of citizenship of a country. The fact, of course, is that a nation is simply an aggregate of individuals, not to be distinguished in essence from its component parts, although we treat it as a moral, or in other but truer words an unmoral, creation.

Another fiction recognized internationally is that of the equality of nations. In a sense, of course, this is a fiction upon a fiction, being equivalent to saying that, first granted the artificial creation known as a nation, such creations whenever occurring are to be treated as equal. Of course, the only sense in which nations can approach equality in a strictly international sense is in their equal capacity to bargain with one another or in their equal treatment before an international tribunal. In other words, the equality supposed to prevail among nations bears certain manifest analogies to the equality which is supposed to prevail among human beings. It is by no means an absolute inherent quality, nor could there perhaps be a quality of such a nature in things that are in themselves absolutely artificial creations like nations.

Another fiction which, like the fiction last referred to, is itself built upon the prior fiction, is that of sovereignty, by which we may assume that we mean the undisputed right of a nation without legal challenge to take such course as seems to it best. This, however, is not a fiction to be carried very far. True sovereignty is of necessity confined to a circle circumscribed by the limits of national jurisdiction. In other words the artificial entity known as a nation may possess power only within the limits of the nation. The moment it proceeds beyond national lines, it finds itself in the presence of the fiction, above referred to, of the equality of nations. Says Woolf:

> Practically everyone, from Foreign Secretaries to public-house politicians, is obsessed by the mysterious sovereignty of sovereign Powers. The ordinary view is that the action of a nation is to be determined solely by its own ideals and desires. In a sense, therefore, any international question is not international, but domestic, and a sovereign Power always has to consider only two things— what it desires and whether it is strong enough to enforce its desire.[8]

If all nations are to be treated as equal, the sovereignty of each must be limited by the equality of the nation with all other nations. These fictions, however, despite their several weaknesses, constitute law, so-called, to be observed by international tribunals.

In the fullness of time our descendants may even discover that the nation itself, which we now call sovereign internationally, is after all a fiction; that national limits create only geographical invisible barriers to the free development of mankind; that there is no reason why people on opposite sides of an imaginary line should regard themselves as potential enemies in peace and in war or deal at arm's length. If in the course of the centuries these things are learned, then men will know that national existence serves no longer any international purpose, and the law of nations will be given no more respect than the code of dueling or the rites of the Amphictyons. It will be cast upon the scrapheap of the ages.

6. Division of law into written and unwritten.—Let us pass next to other points of view of the word "law." We encounter the titles of written or unwritten law. By the unwritten law we signify the pronouncements of judges, including in this sense international tribunals, as to what the law is. These opinions often declare what has been the practice of nations in given instances, or, after the manner of lawgivers, indicate what it should be for the future. As part of the unwritten international law there might well be added the observations of international law writers.

The written law of the nation, broadly speaking, includes simply legislative statutes. Of written international law there is probably nothing of universal application, although treaties do constitute the written law as between their signatories. According to Article 38 of the Permanent Court of International Justice, the court is obliged to apply

[8] *International Government,* 39.

1. International conventions, whether general or particular, establishing rules expressly recognized by the contesting States;

2. International custom, as evidence of a general practice accepted as law;

3. The general principles of law recognized by civilized nations;

4. Subject to the provisions of Article 59, judicial decisions and the teachings of the most highly qualified publicists of the various nations, as subsidiary means for the determination of the rules of law.

This provision shall not prejudice the power of the Court to decide a case *ex aequo et bono,* if the parties agree thereto.

7. Laws of war.—In the international field and before international tribunals we meet with much that is called law and which is not law in any proper sense of the term. This is true of those practices extensively written about in works of international law under the title of "Laws of War." These supposed laws are merely a summing up of the practices usually followed during a state of war and possess none of the attributes of law whatsoever. They are not born of any rules of nature since they largely defy them. They are not laid down by any superior and of necessity obeyed by the inferior, following the spirit of the old Blackstonean definition. They are not universal and not truly obligatory. They are not the result of right reason. It is only on rare occasions that they are called into play in any degree by any international tribunal. They are rules which are supposed to be followed when nations enter the realm of anarchy, without any obligation upon nations to follow them, and without an appreciation of the absurdity of rules to govern a state of affairs which is the negation of all rule. The books describing these so-called "laws of war" are not law books, but are simply narratives of practices which nations with more or less uniformity have indulged in when at war with one another. Even when dignified with the title of "Hague Conventions" they are nevertheless with scant moral sanction and no physical sanction is provided.

Woolf says:

What should we think of a State in which there were no laws to prevent riot and murder and violence, and no police to enforce the law, but yet there were very detailed and complicated laws governing the conduct of persons engaged in riots, murder, and violence? To appeal to force is to appeal to the opposite of law; and it is natural that nations should be far more ready to break the rules of International Law during war than during peace. The Laws of War should be not the first, but the last, to be made in the Society of Nations.[9]

Said Voltaire more than two centuries ago:

[9] *International Government,* 29.

The code of murder seems to me a strange creation. I hope that soon some one will give us the jurisprudence of highway robbers.[10]

Nevertheless international tribunals are not at complete liberty (given our present restricted and imperfect civilization) entirely to ignore these alleged laws of war, however contrary to right reason and natural law and the development of law within the nation they may be. For instance, if in a siege or so-called legal bombardment the property of a neutral in the assailed city should be destroyed, he may not recover, the loss being incidental to governmental operations in the carrying on of a legally justifiable act, that is, war. So if a neutral violating blockade loses his vessel, he may not recover, though the act he was committing was perhaps in the highest degree righteous. In neither case, nor in many others which might be enumerated, would the international judge be justified in granting damages, though under analogous circumstances the individual plaintiff would recover against the individual defendant. Despite the fact that often judges are law-givers as well as administrators, they are under serious limitations and often compelled to follow unrighteous rules.

8. Substantive and adjective law.—International tribunals administer for the most part what is known as substantive law and are themselves controlled in their operations by adjective law, the latter concerning itself largely with the mechanics of the law. Procedural adjective law as we shall find is to be discovered in the treaties creating the tribunal and in the practices which have grown up in numerous international courts. Substantive law will be treated under many heads.

9. Codification of international law.—Various attempts have been made to codify the law to be followed by nations and particularly by international tribunals, and much discussion has ensued as to the possibility of the establishment of international courts before the creation of a code designed to lay down the law they are to follow. It would be useless to deny the value of the work which has been done and is in process of accomplishment in the matter of the codification of law, and yet, bearing in mind what has already been said, it must be equally manifest that codification is not of the highest present importance.

We are justified in anticipating that knowledge of international law will grow in much the same fashion as has that of law within the nation. We find that Rome existed for hundreds of years without having anything approaching a codification. Nevertheless knowledge

---

[10] *Dialogues*, Kepl's edition, xxxvi, 213.

of the law in its fundamentals, and facility in the determination and application of non-fundamentals, grew throughout all the centuries. During this period countless instances of a sort of trial and error test enabled the Romans to find the fundamentals of human law. Meanwhile the work of the praetors assisted by lawyers succeeded in reaching, as to non-fundamentals, working bases for the conduct of the Roman citizenry. It was thus only after hundreds of years and innumerable millions of cases with much legislation that the Roman law became codified into a working system. The history of the law of England has been quite similar and has not yet reached the code stage of development. For a thousand years English courts have worked over the problems of law and have made many declarations and discoveries beneficial to the English public, and legislators have done their work, but to this day there has not been any effort to codify the work of thousands of men.

Nations in the modern sense of the term have had but a few hundred years of existence. They have scarcely begun to learn the essential principles governing them. Writers of international law have largely confined themselves to the recording of acts rather than to the analysis of laws governing the acts. The preliminary steps to the formation of a real code of action in the shape of an examination of cause and effect, action and reaction, trial and error, are yet to be taken. True it is that the remark just made does not apply to the lesser rules of convenience and of courtesy which have found their way into international practice and to which we give the high-sounding name of law. These have been codified to a considerable degree, and their further codification may lead to the prevention of minor difficulties among nations.

There is great danger in carrying the principle of codification beyond the limits of merely formal matters, internationally speaking. It is true that in almost every field of science the wisdom of today becomes the foolishness of tomorrow. There seems no reason to think that by some interposition of Providence or otherwise this rule of almost universal application should find its exception in the field of international law. An attempt, therefore, to tie down future generations to the opinions of those now living may prove to be an exceedingly dangerous experiment, bearing in mind our narrow limitations of knowledge with regard to the workings of international affairs.

As was said by Sir John F. Williams,

If we assume that we can solve the overwhelming difficulty of the method of the enactment of an international code, advocates of the codification of international law have to meet the argument that international law as it now stands is in a very early stage of development and is very far from covering the whole of the international field. To inclose so young a thing—young if the periods of man's past and probable future existence on the earth are borne in mind—in the limits of a code is to stereotype what is essentially transitory and to stunt what most needs growth.[11]

Nor does the fact that up to the present time international law has not spoken on a given point indicate that an arbitral tribunal should not be resorted to, for as Politis says,

one does not wait till all individual relations have been regulated by law to impose resort to justice. The national judge should decide even in the absence of a law.[12]

Malauzat[13] inclines to the same view.

Says Balch:

As concerns juridical cases which may arise for the solution of which rules of the law of nations are not already established by the consent of nations, why should not international judges be authorized—if the nations in conflict do not agree upon a collection of rules to control the particular case—to construct and develop by their decisions the law of nations exactly as national judges in the absence of rules of national law applicable to the case brought before them have often constructed and developed the national law?[14]

Even within the sphere of law within the state—the product of several thousand years of experimentation and observation—there are comparatively few principles which may be regarded as so firmly established as to be beyond controversy or development. What, therefore, is to be expected of a science (even if it today deserved the name of science) which has but commenced its growth and as to which we have not yet learned our true method of approach? Dr. James Brown Scott cites the publicist Dubs, the president of the first federal tribunal of Switzerland, to the effect that

Experience shows that in almost all countries judicial development begins rather by determining what is right than by the appointment of a judge. In the beginning the judge is a kind of priest who conceives his knowledge of the law by direct divine revelation which he merely proclaims. He is likewise, by virtue of his oath, mysteriously bound to the divinity which speaks to him through the voice of conscience as well as by an appeal to reason.[15]

11 *Thirty-third Conference, International Law Association,* 449.
12 *La justice international,* 74.
13 *Cour de justice arbitrale,* 21.
14 *Revue générale de droit international public,* XXI, (1914), 182.
15 *Proceedings, Society for the Judicial Settlement of International Disputes,* 1912, 116.

Of course this theory implies that the law antedates the appointment of the judge and is ready to come into full force and effect upon his determination of differences between parties. This is true as to the fundamental natural laws of which we have spoken, but is not and cannot be true with regard to rules of convenience as to which the judge may himself be the lawgiver, and which he determines to be in existence because he considers such determination to be in the interest of the welfare of the community.

The principles enunciated in one case thus become the recognized law controlling another, even though the first judge can refer to no authority for his action except his own reason and has indulged in the assumption that the law has always existed though never before reduced to words.[16]

After all, the establishment of a court is of greater importance than the institution of a code. But of very great and lasting importance is it to bridge over the divergence between law within the nation and what is called international law, and to study the ethical bases of national action as against our neighbors, without which much of the more important parts of the law of nations must continue to rest upon an uncertain and shifting foundation.

10. National law as source of international law.—It will appear often enough in the course of our examination that the source of all that is truest in the law surrounding international tribunals is to be found in the universally accepted principles of law within the several states. It may be said that there are few questions of international law which have arisen or may arise between states which have not their counterpart in disputes which have been settled within the nation. It is doubtful if international law in the truest sense is or rather should be treated otherwise than is the law governing disputes of an individual character. There is no special mystery which should surround it if we will forget the exaggerated claims of nationalism and sovereignty.

Article 38 of the Statute of the Permanent Court of International Justice, heretofore referred to, recognizes the right of appeal to the "general principles of law recognized by civilized nations" and to judicial decisions as well as to the opinions of writers. All these sources have been abundantly recognized by arbitral tribunals. The common origin of all law being the same, we may understand how it has happened that a number of commissioners and umpires rendering very

---

[16] Eugene Wambaugh, *Proceedings, Society for the Judicial Settlement of International Disputes,* 1910, 140.

satisfactory or even eminent service in these capacities have been lawyers of experience in the ordinary work of the courts but without special training in the field of international law.

The decisions of arbitral tribunals themselves have furnished to later tribunals and to writers upon the subject of international law evidence of its teachings. We may note, however, that at a meeting of the Society for the Judicial Settlement of International Disputes[17] an eminent Harvard professor declared that after a careful search in treatises on international law, he had failed to find in the text or in the footnotes any citation of any decision by an international commission. Certainly this remark could not be made at the present time. Without undertaking to cover the field, we have only to refer to the recent works of Hyde (*International Law*), Fenwick (*International Law*), and Borchard (*Diplomatic Protection of Citizens Abroad*), as illustrations affording numerous citations of cases decided by umpires, illustrative of the present state of international law. In addition, according to Moore's *Digest of International Law,* in case of uncertainty as to the law, resort is to be had among others "to the decisions of international tribunals, such as Boards of Arbitration." This is further shown by the many citations Judge Moore finds it necessary to make from them.

11. Meaning of the terms "justice" and "equity."—Protocols of arbitration frequently require that the arbitrators should follow the rules of international law, justice, and equity. Considerable confusion surrounds this entire subject. What is meant by the rules of international law we may understand fairly well from what has already been said. These rules are sometimes vaguely supposed to be founded upon justice and equity and, in fact, occasionally are. When, however, the arbitrators are given power to adjudge in addition according to the rules of justice and equity or *ex aequo et bono*, something is supposed to be implied going beyond the law as ordinarily written in books of international law, and a freer field is given. Even without the use of these words, arbitrators usually consider themselves privileged to judge according to the principles embodied in them, always, however, within the limits of their jurisdiction, and not, unless otherwise authorized, as *amiables compositeurs.*

It seems to have been the opinion of Mérignhac that the giving to the arbitrators of the power to judge *ex aequo et bono* is equivalent to a full power of amiable composition. He says that "this vague formula ends in leaving to him an absolute liberty."[18] This view cannot be accepted. We share the opinion of Stoykovitch[19] to the effect that it would remove every solid basis from arbitration.

Aristotle is cited as defining equity as "a just finding by which one corrects whatever is found defective in the law because of the too general terms in which it is conceived." This reminds one somewhat of the old definition of equity under the law of England as being for the correction of that wherein the law by reason of its universality is deficient. Nevertheless, it will not be understood that there is any possible relation between the word equity as used in protocols and the same word as used in English and American law in apposition to the term "common law." In the English and American law the word has reference to a distinct branch of jurisprudence, whereas in the protocols it has reference only to the general ideas common to humanity but not reduced to the condition of working rules. Perhaps in its practical illustrations it resembles the common law definition of "equity" only in that it strives to arrive at the essence of things rather than to allow itself to be halted by the technical differences often created by municipal law. This we shall hereafter see by some examples.

Let us consider further the meaning of these words as far as they are capable of definition. "Justice," we are told by Cicero, "is the disposition of mind which gives to each person what belongs to him." Similarly it is defined by Ulpian as the constant and perpetual will to give to everyone what belongs to him.[20] A happier expression is used by Plumley, umpire, when he says

the way is equity, the end is justice . . . . If a question arises, not readily to be apprehended, wherein equity and justice differentiate, then the former must yield because the obligation of a prescribed oath is the superior rule of action.[21]

It was ruled by the umpire in the case of the Norwegian Shipping Claims that

the majority of international lawyers seem to agree that these words (law and equity), are to be understood to mean general principles of justice as distinguished from any particular system of jurisprudence or the municipal law of any state.[22]

---

[18] *L'arbitrage international*, 297.

[19] *De l'autorité de la sentence arbitrale*, 85.

[20] Ernest Nys in *Revue de droit international et de législation comparée*, second series, XII (1910), 632.

[21] Ralston, *Law and Procedure of International Tribunals*, 55.

[22] *Ibid.*, 53.

Under the protocols of 1903 between Venezuela and various powers, the commissioners and the umpire being empowered to decide all claims upon a basis of absolute equity without regard to objections of a technical nature or the provisions of local legislation, the words we are discussing were interpreted to mean equity unrestrained by any artificial rules in its application to a given case.[23]

In the Landreau Case, Lord Finlay decided that "equitably" meant "in justice and fairness."[24]

According to Grotius, Barbeyrac's translation, 1729, Book III, chap. xx, sec. xlvii, one could speak of as "equitable" that which it was well to do even if not obliged by the rules of justice so called.

It is said by Moore with reference to the Permanent Court of International Justice that

Article 38 of the Statute ends with the provision that its prescription of the rule of decision shall not prejudice the power of the court to decide a case *ex aequo et bono*, if the parties agree thereto. It has been suggested that this provision may empower the Court to exercise extra-judicial functions. It has on the other hand been surmised that, as a decision by a judicial magistrate *ex aequo et bono* is not inherently either extra-judicial or non-judicial, the design may have been merely to assure the ordinary application of legal rules. As there is no precise and all-inclusive general agreement as to what are in a strict sense rules of law, and as there often is room, in the domain of private as well as of public law, for wide differences of opinion as to whether judges may not have been influenced in a decision by considerations of what they conceived to be just and good, it may be admitted that the precise meaning and effect of the clause remain to be determined by the Court. Meanwhile, there probably is little ground for the apprehension, which has sometimes been expressed, that a disappointed litigant might find in the clause a colorable excuse for declining to abide by an adverse judgment by alleging that the Court had decided the case *ex aequo et bono* without obtaining the parties' consent.[25]

Mérignhac argues that one cannot see why equity

which constitutes one of the bases of the positive internal law of nations should not constitute also one of the bases of international law and should not be taken into consideration in a reasonable manner in the application of the latter law; so much the more so as in one part of its meanings the law of nations is taken as synonymous with natural law, consecrating the principles of morals and justice accepted by all people and setting itself against the positive law of the several states.[26]

It was the view of Goldschmidt that it was inexpedient to authorize an umpire to decide *ex aequo et bono*, the distinction between law and

---

[23] *Ibid.*, 54.   [24] *Ibid.*, 56.
[25] Moore, *International Law*, chap. iv, 119.   [26] *De l'arbitrage international*, 291.

equity being peculiar to Anglo-American law, and that such powers were too vast; that the umpire should be required to pronounce according to positive law which as official judge he could apply equitably.[27]

It is, of course, true, as indicated by Kamarowsky, that notions of justice and equity often differ not only among various peoples but even among individuals of the same nation.

> Following their personal nature, or sometimes following the degree of their mental development, men, when appreciating the same fact, give preponderance sometimes to strict and formal law, sometimes to equity. It is very difficult to reconcile the contradictions resulting from this. References to public law or international law or stipulations of treaties are equally insufficient. As a consequence of the vague character and the large extent of these notions, interpretation is susceptible of too great a latitude and to too much that is arbitrary.[28]

This might be called true but unavoidable, given the facts of human nature and human society. It is not, however, an argument against an effort to do equity in international tribunals, or at least approach it as nearly as may be.

As we have indicated, it is not, however, proper to go too far in the pursuit of equity and exceed the limits of the *compromis* or resolve the arbitration into a gathering of *amiables compositeurs*. This has been done sometimes, however. For instance, the Caracas Commission of 1869 considered itself as an international court of equity and did not trouble itself over principles of law. It decided according to the rules of justice and equity and even of morals and courtesy.[29] The mixed commission of London of 1870 refused to be a severe tribunal of justice.[30]

12. Exercise of equitable powers by commissions.—Pursuant to the power of judging equitably or *ex aequo et bono* it has been repeatedly decided that commissions had the power of determination without reference to the restrictive provisions of local law, and this has been true even where the commissions were not authorized, as in the Venezuelan cases in 1903, to decide on a basis of absolute equity without regard to objections of a technical nature or provisions of local legislation. This has undoubtedly been true because, being international tribunals and deciding according to international law, they were not under obligation to apply national laws when an international wrong would be the result of such application. This was the case notably when

---

[27] Kamarowsky, *Le tribunal international,* 340.

[28] *Ibid.,* 179.

[29] Stoykovitch, *De l'autorité de la sentence arbitrale,* 84.

[30] *Recueil des arbitrages,* II, 570, 578.

Lord Finlay refused to follow the Peruvian law relative to technical requirements as to notification to a grantor of the rights the grantee might convey to his assignee. A like rule was made in the Orinoco Shipping Company case before the Hague Tribunal.[81]

An approximation to the Anglo-American point of view as to equity, whereby the party beneficially interested is treated as the real owner, has been afforded by several cases before arbitral tribunals.[82] So also have governments been held responsible for acts resulting beneficially to them even in the absence of formal contract.[83]

13. Power of arbitrator when *compromis* is silent.—Mérignhac asks what principles should guide an arbitrator when the *compromis* is silent, and concludes that he might be invested with

absolute power of appreciation; but this idea which would be exceedingly danger-ous has never triumphed in the matter of arbitration; the idea in itself would be dangerous because the arbitrator, delivered to his own likes, would be easily exposed to deceiving himself. Nothing is in effect more vast than the field of equity, and a too free appreciation could often be transformed into the arbitrary.

We believe that even in the absence of any power such as just spoken of, his duty is, as stated by Mérignhac, "to apply international law with equity."[84] In other words, what we may regard as equity, understood in an international sense, can not be avoided whether the word is or is not employed.

It is the view of Politis that in the case of silence in the *compromis*

the arbitrator should adhere to the rules of law, however rigorous they might appear to him, for if the parties had intended to permit him to decide equitably, they would not have failed to say it, as they have done so often.[85]

The fact is, however, that rigorous rules of international law are the rare exception, however clear may be the duty of the arbitrator to adhere to them where they exist and the protocol limits his powers to them. In truth where the rules may be at all rigorous it is so because they are founded upon some thoroughly equitable principle. Otherwise the rules are simply of the moment and without firm foundation except they be especially relied upon in the *compromis* itself.

As illustrating a disposition on the part of arbitrators to exceed their just powers, we have the much-cited instance of the Northeastern

---

[81] *Law and Procedure of International Tribunals,* 100.

[82] See, for instance, *ibid.,* 55, 159; for a more direct application, see case of the Cayuga Indian claims, *American Journal of International Law,* XX, 574.

[83] For an illustration, see *Law and Procedure of International Tribunals,* 259.

[84] *L'arbitrage international,* 295. [85] *La justice internationale,* 83.

Boundary of the United States, decided by the King of the Netherlands; and as of the same nature, although the decision appears to have been given effect, the territorial decision of the Argentine Republic between Bolivia and Peru.[36]

14. The law of the case.—We should not leave the subject without referring to the fact that many times it is provided by *compromis* that the board of arbitration or other tribunal created shall conform its decisions to certain principles which shall be treated as binding law. The most notable instance of this was afforded by the Geneva Tribunal which was controlled by rules of liability set up in the treaty. A number of other instances have been supplied particularly by boundary commissions, the treaties creating them establishing, for example, the several criteria for determining what shall be deemed to constitute prescription.

[36] *Revue générale de droit international public,* 1910, 134, 246.

CHAPTER II

ARBITRAL TRIBUNALS AND COURTS

15. Institution of courts.—Having considered briefly the law and its sources, let us turn to the institution of courts. We have to recognize that the state is an entirely artificial body created for the purpose of carrying out through common agencies those functions of general import which it is impossible for the individual to perform in his own person. We may believe that when it becomes possible for the state, for all and in the name of all, to exercise certain powers more beneficially than they can be exercised by the individual, at that moment the duty of the state arises. It was from some experience of the fact that the individual could not in the interest of all be trusted to act as his own justiciary that the state stepped in and organized courts of justice, a purely artificial and appropriate but not necessarily exact way of arriving at the truth of matters. Bearing in mind the fact that acts which are anti-social and therefore wrongful usually carry with them their own punishment, there would have been slight need for the formation of courts were it not for the further fact that individuals vary greatly in power and the natural consequences which might fall heavily upon the more feeble could pass by the more powerful scarcely making any impression. It was, therefore, in the interest of the feeble that courts were organized to give full and undoubted effect to that natural law whose effects were minimized by the artificial power of some individuals.

16. Form and purpose of courts.—Of course, there is no particular sanctity in the form of courts. They are at best a crude way of arriving at justice, but, nevertheless, they have been accepted as offering the most advantageous way of reaching it, bearing in mind the infirmities of human nature.

It seems to have been the earlier feeling of English courts that in some way through their instrumentality Providence would interfere to protect the innocent and punish the guilty and that they were merely supervisors of this providential intent. Thus we find trial by battle and the various tests by ordeal of the guilt or innocence of witches. The more modern and more general view of courts, however, is that they are to administer justice in as large a measure as may be humanly possible. It is not to be overlooked, however, that in the beginning the preservation of order rather than the attainment of justice was the end sought and that such ideas of justice as existed were extremely crude.

It was very natural that among the Greeks in the international field their first impulse as to arbitration should have been to bring about a settlement of the difficulties between the parties rather than to insure justice, in other words, that the demand for order should prevail over the demand for justice. (The same tendency we shall find observable among the medieval arbitrations and also even down to arbitrations which have been had within the past century.)

Treating the object of courts in the first instance to be the preservation of order rather than the attainment of justice, it was recognized among the Greeks that before the merits of any international controversy were passed upon by the arbitrators an attempt should be made by them to bring the parties together, and it was only in the event of the failure of this effort that the arbitrators undertook to decide the merits of the controversy. This method must have involved difficulties, for there is an intrinsic difference between the acts of a mediator and the acts of a judge, and the mediator may suggest positions which will return to plague him if subsequently he changes himself into a judicial officer.

The attitude of Cicero with reference to arbitration (the international phase of the subject being practically unknown) was indicative, however, of the ancient position, for he said:

We come to judgment with the alternative of obtaining all or losing all. We accede to arbitration without the hope of obtaining all we have asked or obtaining nothing.[1]

In the Middle Ages the same rule prevailed as under the Greeks. Loria finds that the judgments of the Middle Ages were largely based not upon the idea of justice, but upon the prevention of a struggle, and therefore were determined largely upon the number of armed men who were ready to intervene for each one of the adverse parties. Thus "the end of judgment was not to find the truth, but to award victory to the most powerful party without the shedding of blood."[2]

Coming to a later period, it is said by Stoykovitch that

at the beginning of the nineteenth century after the rebirth of arbitration, we remark a certain wavering in the attitude of arbitrators, who often commence an award by saying "We are of the opinion," and who abstain from indicating the reasons of their decision, thus giving the award the air of a diplomatic bargain rather than of a judgment. This tendency is particularly strong among the mem-

---

[1] Dreyfus, *L'arbitrage international*, 273.
[2] *Publications de l'Institut Nobel Norvégien*, II, 84.

bers of mixed commissions, who recall their diplomatic origin and strive always to make a bargain between the opposite pretensions of the parties.[3]

He further remarks upon the fact that the Mexican members of the commission of Washington (1840–1842) expressed themselves in this wise: "We do not have to judge the disputes but to resolve the difficulties." It is, however, to be said that the American commissioners of the same commission entirely declined to accept this view, considering themselves judges.

17. *Amiable compositeur.*—In order of time in the process of development of adjustments in their general nature judicial, we should first consider the arrangement which has come in later days to be designated under the French title of *amiable compositeur.* Of course, no such expression was used to designate the very similar thing existing under the Greeks or in the very early Middle Ages arbitrations.

Sometimes the clause providing for amiable composition has been inserted in the *compromis.* This was the case with regard to the arbitration of 1875 relative to Delagoa Bay between Portugal and England and to a dispute referred in 1890 to the Czar between France and Holland. It was also true with regard to the Alsop case between the United States and Chile. When, however, the committee to whom the latter case was referred by the King of England reported the principles upon which it acted, this language was used:

> Your Majesty is acting as *amiable compositeur* and is free to look at the essence of things without too strict a regard to technicalities, and from that point of view, also, it appears to us that the claim put forward under this head is one which should be approved by your Majesty.[4]

Again the committee remarked:

> The duty which your Majesty has been pleased to undertake is one of pronouncing an award which shall do substantial justice between the parties without attaching too great an importance to the technical points which may be raised on either side. This is what we conceive to be the function of an *amiable compositeur.*[5]

Of course, it is evident that the Alsop case gives a more limited meaning to the locution than was understood practically by ancient tribunals.

In a dispute between Switzerland and France relative to the refunding of certain duties, the arbitrators seemed to have been influenced in some degree by the idea that they were in fact, if not in name, *amiables*

[3] *De l'autorité de la sentence arbitrale en droit international public,* 6
[4] *American Journal of International Law,* V, 1097.
[5] *Ibid.,* V, 1081.

compositeurs, for the commission, after having given a sufficient reason for its action, declined to pass upon the question of indirect damages and loss of property because

friendly and cordial relations existing between the contesting parties make it desirable not to deduce rigorously all the juridical consequences which might result from the considerations developed.[6]

The treaty referring differences between the United States and England relative to the Northeastern boundary failed to give the King of the Netherlands, named as arbitrator, any power of amiable composition. Nevertheless, he undertook to lay down a boundary not within the minds of the parties when the protocol was signed and not contemplated by the *compromis.* As a result, the United States declined entirely to accept the award and, England recognizing the justice of this view, the differences were afterwards adjusted. It is undoubtedly true, as stated by Politis,[7] that the clause providing for amiable composition has made progress especially with regard to territorial disputes, but it is also correct to say with Stoykovitch[8] that without the authorization of the *compromis* the tribunal cannot conduct itself as an *amiable compositeur.*

18. Arbitration or mediation.—To treat the powers of an arbitrator as anything less than those of a judge with corresponding duties is to reduce the arbitrator from the judicial rank to a position of a mediator and would destroy all the sanctity and authority which properly belongs to arbitration. We reach the position described by de Roquefort where

the mediator, as one sees, is a conciliator rather than a judge. The solution that he gives has nothing of an obligatory character; the conflict rests in suspense; the parties were always free to resort to violence without violating any engagement and from a juridical point of view mediation is far from offering the same interest as arbitration. If in certain delicate hypotheses mediation alone appears possible, its action is insufficient in current practice. While one may find in it a happy palliative, it should be recognized that it cannot serve as basis for an efficacious system of common law.[9]

Again, the true end of arbitration and the true functions of the arbitrator have been confused by the fact that sometimes the cause referred to arbitration was one in its nature more readily handled by

---

[6] *American Journal of International Law,* VI, 1002.

[7] *La justice internationale,* 81.

[8] *De l'autorité de la sentence arbitrale en droit international public,* 254.

[9] *De la solution juridique,* 194.

diplomacy than by legal judgment. In other words the matters passed upon were in point of fact of a nature appealing rather to the feelings than to matters of law or fact. This has been true even as to one or two arbitrations referred to The Hague. We may mention the Casablanca case, in which the differences between France and Germany were such as should have received diplomatic settlement and were amply capable of it, but could not be stated in such a manner as to call for usual judicial action. So we may believe of another case in arbitration where the award was that the flag should be saluted.

While, however, the form of arbitration is derived from the Roman law, the substance of the idea as practiced at the present time, as we shall endeavor to show, is judicial rather than purely a matter of compromise as in the Roman applications. This difference is pointed out by Stoykovitch, who finds that in internal law

resort is had to arbitration because it is sought to avoid the application of positive law which ordinary tribunals are obliged to apply. To the contrary, international arbitration is an institution of common law for the juridical solution of international conflicts and if the party resorts to arbitration, it is not to avoid but precisely to demand the application of law.[10]

So de Roquefort[11] recognizes the judicial character of the arbitral tribunal.

19. Arbitral tribunals contrasted with courts.—Let us consider at this point a difference of opinion which has arisen with regard to the functions and operations of arbitral tribunals as compared to those of formal courts of law. It has been charged with regard to arbitral tribunals that they offer a field for bargaining, and that their findings are the result of compromise rather than·of adherence to the principles of law. It is said, for instance, by Nys that

a danger in arbitration is the tendency of political men to give it the character of a bargain and to consider it as an expedient which allows the giving of satisfaction to two parties. The cause of justice and of law cannot fail to suffer from such practices.[12]

Many articles have been written on the theory that there is a subtle distinction between international arbitration and international judicial settlement. The writers have in centuries past had ground for their contentions. We have referred to Greek and medieval practices.

[10] *De l'autorité de la sentence arbitrale en droit international public,* 64.
[11] *De la solution juridique,* 9.
[12] *Revue de droit international et de législation comparée,* second series, XII (1910), 612.

There are other cases which could be enumerated and in which the umpire of a claims commission may have been unconsciously influenced by desire to placate both parties. It is equally probable that quite as numerous cases proportionately can be cited from courts of law where consciously or unconsciously the judge has been influenced by similar desires, but such cases could scarcely be cited as illustrations of the general failure of courts to comply with their judicial duty.

A further source of confusion in the minds of writers with regard to arbitrations arises from the fact that many arbitrators have been authorized to act in the capacity of *amiables compositeurs,* and so acting have felt at liberty to disregard the strict rules of law and arrive at a determination which would at least satisfy their consciences as inflicting no material wrong upon anybody.

Again there are cases where from the very nature of things judicial determination is necessarily excluded, as, for instance, the determination of boundary lines when there are no precise rules or indications to govern. The writer has in mind a case of international arbitration of this nature in which an American umpire sat with the representatives of two foreign powers in dispute over a long boundary. After going over the matter with the representatives of the disputants and finding no agreement possible, he said, "Very well, let us commence at the north end and take it up section by section. (This was accepted.) Now the first section will be from A to B and I favor a line going in this direction" (indicating it). The direction impinged upon the territory of one of the disputants, and the other disputant as to that line sided with the umpire and so much was settled. The next line suggested by the umpire impinged upon the party which had originally lost, and the opposing party agreed. In this manner, step by step, a line was established which was accepted by both parties, because practically every other step in it had been accepted by one or the other; but it cannot be said that the settlement was in any sense judicial, although arbitral.

It appears, therefore, that so far as arbitrators have of late departed from legal bases for their awards, it has been due, (a) to the fact that they have been expressly authorized to do so; (b) to the nature of the controversy as not admitting admeasurement of either law or facts. Other difficulties confronting umpires not necessarily inherent in arbitration will be adverted to later.

Subject to the exceptions which have been indicated, there can be no doubt of the duty of arbitrators to act under the guidance of law, and that they usually do so. The writer's experience confirms him in this opinion, having in mind close personal association with arbitrations affecting ten countries determined in Venezuela in 1903, as well as certain arbitrations at The Hague.

Nor is the language of several writers at all different from our present expression of belief. We are told in a decided fashion by Judge Moore

arbitration is and always has been considered in international law as a judicial process. While the mediator recommends, it is the function of the arbitrator to decide. The term "arbitration" has been applied to the judicial process in international relations because in the absence of a tribunal with a fixed personnel it remained for the parties in each case to choose the judges who were to decide the dispute.[13]

Again he remarks:

By arbitration we mean the determination of controversies by international tribunals judicial in their constitution and powers. Arbitration is not to be confounded with mediation. Mediation is an advisory, arbitration a judicial, process.[14]

Mérignhac[15] finds that there is no distinction to be made between mixed commissions and what he styles true arbitral tribunals, and that they must both judge according to the principles of international law.

According to Kamarowsky publicists agree in seeing in arbitration not a mediation or an attempt to conciliate but a juridical means of solving differences between the parties. "If this is true with relation to civil law, there is no reason not to recognize this proposition in international law."[16]

Also Stoykovitch says that

at the present time a clear distinction is made between the two methods of pacific settlement of international disputes, the first purely diplomatic—good offices and mediation—and the other purely juridical arbitration. The arbiter should lay down the law and should settle according to the rules of law the conflict between the parties. The sentence that he pronounces is a true judgment obligatory between the parties and having the authority of *res adjudicata*.[17]

Again, Thomas Willing Balch says:

Mediation in international relations is the attempt to settle a dispute between nations which seems to furnish a favorable basis for compromise. On the contrary arbitration is an attempt to regulate a difference between nations by a decision based strictly upon justice, that is to say, upon juridical reasoning. And

---

[13] *International Law*, chap. iv, 96.
[14] Moore, *American Diplomacy*, 200.
[15] *L'arbitrage international*, 226.
[16] *Le tribunal international*, 309.
[17] *De l'autorité de la sentence arbitrale en droit international public*, 7.

if the judges of an international court of arbitration do not endeavor in the best possible manner to base their decisions upon the facts and evidence, that is to say, international law, they do not fulfill as they should the functions of their judicial charge.[18]

The Hague Conventions say that arbitration is "the settlement of differences between states by judges of their own choice, and on the basis of respect for law." This language was quoted by the Court of International Justice as conveying the "common and more limited conception of arbitration.[19]

Of late years there has been much consideration—and this we shall discuss later—as to the advantages of a regular judicial tribunal settling the affairs of nations over casual boards of arbitration. We are aware of the fact that despite all that has been said there are authorities of eminence who are inclined to believe that from the standpoint of judging according to law, a distinction is to be drawn between courts and boards of arbitration. We may mention the instructions of the Secretary of State to the American delegates to the second conference at The Hague. He said:

It has been a very general practice for arbitrators to act, not as judges deciding questions of fact and law upon the record before them under a sense of judicial responsibility, but as negotiators effecting settlement of the questions brought before them in accordance with the traditions and usages and subject to all the considerations and influences which affect diplomatic agents. The two methods are radically different, pursued under different standards of honorable obligation, and frequently lead to widely different results.

The Secretary of State therefore advocated

a permanent tribunal composed of judges who are judicial officers and nothing less and who will devote their entire time to the trial and decision of international causes by judicial methods and under a sense of judicial responsibility.[20]

Chief Justice Taft has remarked:

I have no doubt there has been already emphasized the difference between a court and an arbitration. The Supreme Court of the United States illustrates that difference. It decides questions according to law. It is not the end of a mediation or negotiation. It is not the climax of a diplomatic effort to reach some solution that will prevent people from fighting each other. It has the authority to decide questions according to right and justice, and it does. And that is the difference between a court and an arbitration, as arbitrations are generally carried on.[21]

[18] *Revue générale de droit international public*, XXI (1914), 137.
[19] Advisory Opinion No. 12, Lausanne Treaty.
[20] Scott, *The Hague Peace Conferences, American Instructions and Reports*, 79.
[21] *Proceedings, Society for the Judicial Settlement of International Disputes*, 1916, 102–103.

It is sufficiently evident from what has already been said that however great an amount of truth there might have been in the remarks of the Secretary of State and the Chief Justice as to ancient and medieval arbitrations and as to certain occasional ones in comparatively recent times, and from what we have said as to territorial arbitrations which were of necessity meetings of compromise, it is true today that the arbitrator regards himself as controlled by law and not in any sense of the word a negotiator.

The advantages to be derived from the existence of a permanent international tribunal are to be found in other directions.

Some of the real weaknesses of boards of arbitration may be summed up as follows: The ordinary board consists of an equal number of representatives of the parties in controversy, with an odd man to settle the differences. Sometimes the odd man sits in the first instance with his associates in judgment and sometimes he settles their differences on appeal, his function in this respect being determined by the *compromis* creating the board. In either event under the circumstances named, the odd man is likely to become the sole ultimate judge, this because of the difficulty a national arbitrator has in doing anything which may be contrary to the assumed interest of his own nation. This difficulty arises from the fact that he is bound to be influenced by national prejudices and therefore disposed to give the benefit of any possible doubt to his own nation and because in some instances he fears the results upon his own fortunes if he goes contrary to the contentions of his own nation. Bearing in mind the personal effect of his decisions, he thus becomes really a party in interest. In no sense, at least not often, is he a free agent acting in a capacity enabling him to determine judicially the questions before him.

Ernest Nys[22] comments, as upon a weak point, on the tendency of the arbitrator in both public and private arbitrations to decide in favor of the party choosing him.

Nor is the position of an umpire at all free from difficulty under such circumstances. Whether he be regarded as a member of the court in the first instance or as acting in an appellate capacity, it is impossible for him to say to his associates that they may not discuss with him the questions at issue and bring to bear upon his judgment outside influences and appeals. The umpire is therefore in a much less free position than if he were an independent judge approachable only in

---

[22] *Revue de droit international et de législation comparée*, second series, XII (1910), 599.

open court and by legitimate argument addressed to him by the agents or counsel of the several parties. There is reason to believe that in some instances the conclusions of the umpire have been warped by appeals of the nature indicated and have not represented what might well have been his free and independent judgment.

When one man virtually determines a question, as is the case in the sort of tribunal we are now describing, the issue is subject to his personal prepossessions and idiosyncrasies. These are not properly checked up by association with others of presumably equal intelligence and disinterestedness, who might, perchance, have balancing peculiarities of view. The arbitral board becomes a one-man court, with no appeal and possessing all the evils incident to such a tribunal.

A further difficulty with arbitral tribunals is that their membership is to a large degree chosen haphazard and without due regard to the qualifications of either commissioners or umpire. In addition to this, the membership, called together in an occasional and casual way, is not able to develop or in a proper degree aid in the development of what may be regarded as an international jurisprudence. We say this not for a moment forgetting the fact that arbitral tribunals, taken as a whole, have done much to develop and regularize such science as has so far been discovered to exist in international law. This general subject we discuss at large later.

Some of the evils above spoken of have been escaped by the manner in which arbitral courts have been selected. We have in mind particularly as a notable illustration of its kind the tribunal at The Hague which passed upon the case of the Pious Fund. This consisted of a Russian and an Englishman named by the United States, two Hollanders named by Mexico, and a Dane selected as the presiding officer by these gentlemen upon coming together. The entire court was of men of distinction in the international field and free from all the influences which might prejudically affect the judgment of arbitrators. Nevertheless, it is true that each country sought to name men, who, if not prejudiced in favor of the nation naming them, were at least not prejudiced against it.

CHAPTER III

DISPUTES CAPABLE OF REFERENCE TO INTERNATIONAL TRIBUNALS

20. Independence as non-arbitrable.—Considerable differences of opinion exist among writers and statesmen relative to the disputes which are capable of being submitted to adjudication internationally. Innumerable treaties providing for future arbitrations have excepted, as non-arbitrable, differences involving the independence, honor, and vital interests of the parties to the treaty, and writers have been found in numbers to sustain the conception of the statesmen. The subject deserves examination. Let us first consider the exception of independence.

True it is, as said by Pillet, that "it is impossible that any difference should exist between states without affecting in some manner their independence."[1] But of course in the reservation of independence no extreme meaning is intended to be given to the word. We must assume that the expression means some interference with the right of the nation as such to life, in other words some proposition which means either its death or its subservience in greater or less degree to the will of some other nation. Of course, in the extreme sense indicated by Pillet the order of a court directing one nation to pay money to another nation in settlement of a claim would be construed as limiting the entire independence of the nation so ordered to pay.

We must, however, take another view as to the meaning of the word. In this view a reservation of independence seems useless although not perhaps harmful. The very fact of a reference to arbitration assumes independence, based upon (unless otherwise specified) the equality and the independence of each other of the nations entering into the contract. Independence can no more be put in jeopardy, so far as a nation is concerned, by a treaty calling for arbitration or judicial settlement than can the independence of an individual by submitting himself to arbitration or to the judgment of a court. By the very submission the right to live is impliedly reserved in his case as well as in the case of the nation.[2]

---

[1] *La cause de la paix*, 41.

[2] "International arbitration, in the strict sense, presupposes the existence of independent and autonomous states recognized as resting on a basis of juridical equality." (C. Phillipson, *The International Law and Custom of Ancient Greece and Rome*, II, 127.)

"D'ores et déjà nous affirmons que les États doivent conserver intactes leur autonomie et leur indépendance, et nous prétendons que l'établissement de l'ordre

Neither the nation nor the individual can be assumed to bargain away life. We may therefore dismiss the reservation of independence as unnecessary even though harmless, incidentally referring to it later.

21. Reservation of honor and vital interests.—We next come to the reservation of honor and vital interests. The two may be treated together, as they are commonly joined in many treaties of arbitration.

Calvo is often cited for having said that

arbitration can settle every species of difference except those in which honor and national dignity are directly in play and which arise from a personal sentiment which no third state can properly judge, each nation being the sole judge of its dignity and the rights which guarantee its safety.[3]

To like effect are cited by André[4] a large number of writers on international law including among them Bonfils, Despagnet, Geffcken, Rolin-Jaequemyns, Renault, and others.

So far has this idea carried that the writers upon this and other points argue that a *compromis* relative to the independence, integrity, the power and the honor of a country is completely null.[5] It is pointed out by André[6] that this doctrine so carried to its extreme would nullify treaties of perpetual neutrality or of annexation, as, for instance, the Treaty of Frankfort of May 1871, which affected very considerably the sovereignty of the states touched by it.

It is to be noted, however, that there is an increasing number of writers who regard the claim on the part of the government of exemption from arbitration because its vital interests or its honor may chance to be involved as entirely baseless and deceptive. Thus we find Bokanowski saying that the idea of honor is modified according to the times and places.[7] It is based upon customs more or less honest and upon a morale susceptible of change. It is subject to the caprice of climates, temperaments, and susceptibilities. An insult to a diplomat would be considered at certain epochs as reaching the state he represents, and no excuses or regrets would prevent war from starting. The same author finds[8] that reserves of honor or essential interests are hypocritical façades masking the worst instincts and the basest covetousness.

---

juridique est parfaitement compatible avec la notion que nous avons posée de l'Etat, quelque soit d'ailleurs le régime politique auquel il puisse être soumis." (Mougins de Roquefort, *De la solution juridique*, 82.)

[3] *Le droit international*, III, § 1756.

[4] *De l'arbitrage obligatoire*, 193.

[5] Acremant, *La procédure dans les arbitrages internationaux*, 28.

[6] *Op. cit.*, 194, note.

[7] *La commission internationale d'enquête*, 46.   [8] *Ibid.*, 101.

We are interested to read in the preliminary report of Professor Philip Marshall Brown and N. Politis to the Institute of International Law that

One must admit that the classic reservation concerning independence, vital interests, honor, etc., so often employed in treaties of arbitration has the effect of neutralizing every honest attempt to insure the judicial settlement of international disputes.[9]

Similar language is used by Politis on another occasion.[10]

André finds that any restriction as to sovereignty or dignity is simply a loophole for nations to escape arbitration and renders arbitration purely optional.[11]

The uncertainty as to the meaning of the word "honor" can scarcely be better shown than by the instance of the *Alabama*. After Great Britain had protested very vigorously that her honor forbade reference of the difficulties between herself and the United States to arbitration, she finally agreed to the step, and discovered in the end that honor rested only in paying the award found justly due for the errors of which she was found guilty. Again honor was assumed to be involved in the affair of the war vessel *Forte* when in point of fact there was nothing in the world involved except a dispute caused by drunken naval men. Further in the matter between France and Germany of the deserters of Casablanca, it seemed likely for a time that the "honor" of the two countries could only be properly defended by war, but it was found that trivial provisions in an award met all the necessities of the case.

22. Vital interests.—As to disputes involving the "vital interests" of a nation, often reserved from arbitration, the question is of course also open as to what interests are or are not vital, this being determined by the nation charged with the responsibility. The words, like the word "honor," have no settled meaning; the thing which appears vital at one time turning out at another to be a matter of no possible consequence, depending largely upon the weight attached by government opinion or by the whims of statesmen to the particular act in question at the time the dispute arises, or it may be dependent upon the relative strength of the nations involved.

It must never be lost sight of that vital interests more often than otherwise signify nothing save the commercial interests of an infinitely small section of the nation involved, the section in question, however,

[9] *Annuaire*, 1922, 47.
[10] *La justice internationale*, 75.
[11] *De l'arbitrage obligatoire*, 109.

being regarded as extremely important from a political point of view in the government of the nation.

To say, therefore, that the vital interests of a few are the vital interests of the nation is to ignore entirely the fact that the vital interests of the vast majority rest in the preservation of peace rather than in the prosecution of war under practically any circumstances.

But it may be that the term "vital interests" to be reserved from judicial examination means what are styled the political interests of a nation, which is to say its prestige among nations or its ability to take advantage of particular situations for its territorial or other advancement. In this sense "political" is used in apposition to the word "juridical." There is an abundance of opinion, however, that even questions denominated political are subject properly to judicial examination. Let us quote the saying of Cavour cited by Judge Baldwin, to the effect that

> Every political problem involves an economic problem, and every economic problem a moral problem. If the assertion may be too broad as applied to the government of a nation, it is not as applied to international relations.[12]

Again we may refer to the opinion of Lord Russell cited by Kamarowsky,[13] to the effect that he was unable to find in the last century a single legitimate question which it was impossible to resolve without recourse to arms if the parties were sufficiently endowed with moderation.

Revon[14] accepts the view that, like juridical questions properly so-called, political questions enter usefully within the arbitral competence whenever they do not touch in any manner the automony of states. We have already pointed out sufficiently that independence is a postulate of arbitral action and not the subject of it and, of course, autonomy in this particular sense is synonymous.

23. Treaty limitations upon "honor" and "independence."— Recognizing apparently the uncertainty of the words "honor" and "independence," and seeking to define and limit them, it is interesting to note that a treaty of obligatory arbitration between the Argentine Republic, Bolivia, and others, declares that neither the national independence nor the national honor shall be considered as imperiled in any dispute over diplomatic privileges, boundaries, rights of navigation, or the validity, interpretation, and fulfillment of treaties.[15] It is also

---

12 *Proceedings, Society for the Judicial Settlement of International Disputes,* 1912, 9.

13 *Le tribunal international,* 292, note.   14 *L'arbitrage international,* 505.

15 *American Journal of International Law,* I, 209.

noticeable that by treaty the very question as to whether the reserved rights of the nation are or are not involved in the dispute is sometimes made the subject of preliminary arbitral inquiry.[16]

24. Difference between juridical and political questions.—It is true that the last few years have seen much discussion relative to the feasibility and propriety of referring to arbitration questions which are called juridical rather than political, and sundry attempts have been made to define these words. Thus, according to Westlake

A juridical difference between states is one which can be regulated by means of known rules having behind them that force which proceeds from the general consent of the international societies.[17]

Of course, this definition leaves many things open. Is or is not the rule known? Has it or has it not behind it the general consent of the international societies? May it not be so clear and proper in itself as to deserve universal recognition even though such recognition has not yet been manifested in any manner? If so, may not the rule, till then unknown, be of as much natural force as if it had been pronounced upon by a score of writers? Is it not true that in so far as they are based on justice, the rules of international law find their precedents in what is generally recognized as law within the state? If, therefore, a given rule be universally recognized among the sovereign states of the world in their interior affairs, why may it not, though it has never been called into force internationally, be accepted immediately upon its statement in international courts? If so, of what necessity is prior consent to a given rule in determining the nature of the controversy?

A definition given by T. W. Balch is as follows:

The expression "juridical cases" should be considered as designating those questions which arise between nations and which, while being a cause of conflict between two or more sovereign states, do not menace by their solution in favor of one party or the other, the independence or any vital interest of one of the parties. Besides, the expression "juridical cases" should be considered as including all the questions which do not affect vital interests of the nations in dispute whether there are or are not rules of the law of nations upon which the majority of the great powers of the world are in agreement ready to be applied to these questions to the end of reaching a judicial decision which settles them. The expression "political cases" should be considered as designating questions arising between states which by reason of the facts and interests involved in the case menace in the future any attempt which may be made to resolve them by a

---

[16] See Treaties of 1905 between Sweden and Norway, *American Journal of International Law*, Supp., I, 169, and between Sweden and Italy in 1911.

[17] *International Law*, second edition, 1910, I, 357.

judicial decision or affect or modify favorably or unfavorably the political power and the influence of one or more of the nations in dispute. Further, the expression "political cases" should be considered as applying to all the questions which affect the vital interests of the rival nations, even though they may be rules of international law generally recognized by the nations of which the application to a case would permit strict determination upon juridical bases in favor of one party or the other.[18]

Like the definition above cited by Westlake, this remark by Balch leaves also much unanswered. In addition to the criticism already made, we may inquire, what are the vital interests of a nation and who is to determine them? Why should a nation claiming something to be of vital interest to it be permitted to triumph over all juridical rules? Is not this fact a negation of all law?

An attempt is made without more real success to draw the line between justiciable and non-justiciable cases by the Institut de Droit International.[19] The apparent consensus of opinion was, after all, that the difference was subjective as to the nations at issue; that the dispute which today was recognized as justiciable might tomorrow be treated as non-justiciable and vice versa. But the determination of the character of a dispute cannot rest in the mind of the party. We cannot permit that disputes of an international character are to be determined by the state of mind of one party and not by an international tribunal.

The only political questions suggested, for instance, by the reporters on the subject in the *Annuaire* (p. 32) as non-judicial are the migration of peoples, the Monroe Doctrine, armaments, birth or disappearance of states, recognition of new governments, and generally penal responsibility. It is to be said that with the consent of international law the domestic law controls the admission of foreigners; that the Monroe Doctrine came into being because Continental nations in the day of its origin knew only the *lex talionis* now being discarded, and that the other questions are now and naturally determined by the individual governments, save that if the expression "penal responsibility" refers to war guilt this cannot exist until war is made a crime.

A more successful effort to define the limitation of international judicial power is made by inclusion instead of exclusion in the Statute of the Permanent Court of International Justice wherein the competence of the Court is extended under certain circumstances to

(a) the interpretation of a Treaty; (b) any question of International Law; (c) the existence of any fact which, if established, would constitute a breach of an

---

[18] *Revue générale de droit international public*, XXI (1914), 181.
[19] *Annuaire*, 1922, 23–58.

international obligation; (d) the nature and extent of the reparation to be made for the breach of an international obligation.

The entirely unnecessary character of a limitation upon any reference to an international tribunal for a settlement of international disputes may be illustrated by consideration of the fact that from the standpoint of international law the several states of the Union are separate nations, and all disputes between them without exception are determined by the Supreme Court of the United States. This extends to territorial disputes, disputes as to rights in flowing water, and a great variety of other matters; but, although nothing is said upon the subject in the Constitution of the United States, it does not extend to anything in any wise affecting the independence or the autonomy of a state. While of late the doctrine has been called in question, it is not believed to extend to the enforcement of any duty which should be performed by the state toward its fellows. It has further been considered sufficient that the Supreme Court should have made its findings, leaving the enforcement of such findings to a natural respect for law and the workings of such penalties as would naturally be attendant upon the repudiation of the solemn judgment of the highest court of the land.

It remains true as said by André that

It may be in effect that beneath questions in appearance juridical are concealed political interests sufficiently considerable so that states, if they feel themselves strong, refuse to seek solution in arbitration.

He continues:

This it is, for example, that explains the attitude of the delegate of the United States at the Hague Conference when he declared that his government could not agree to submit to obligatory arbitration, monetary conventions, and those relative to the navigation of international rivers and interoceanic canals.[20]

It is undoubtedly this sense of power which accounts for the fact that almost uniformly the great nations of the earth have refused to submit to arbitration all disputes which may arise between them and other powers, while the smaller nations have, to a very large degree, agreed to send to the Hague Court of International Justice any difference of whatsoever nature.

The position taken by Kamarowsky may not be ignored:

Once an international jurisdiction shall have been created it will draw within the circle of its jurisdiction a constantly increasing number of differences, even political, since the law laid down by it will present general principles enabling

[20] De l'arbitrage obligatoire, 200.

the impartial examination of differences, envisaging them from all sides and as they really are. But a difference, whatever it may be, private or public, put to the test of law, loses force; for the points of view, excessively subjective, and the pretensions of the parties are softened by judicial criticism based upon strict justice and vanish as the fog before the sun.[21]

We will not forget that there is no inherent quality attaching to political questions and forbidding reference to arbitration. Many a protocol has without any effort converted a supposed political difference into a juridical issue.

It is noteworthy that even before the League of Nations was created there were in existence treaties of arbitration, created largely between the nations of northern Europe but not exclusively so, providing for reference to arbitration of every question which might arise between them, without any reserve whatsoever. Since the formation of the League, the majority of the smaller nations have agreed to obligatory reference to the Hague Permanent Court of International Justice of nearly every possible future dispute between themselves and other nations recognizing a reciprocal obligation. Sometimes these agreements have been without limitation of time and sometimes for the period of five or more years.

If treaties of such a nature may be signed between small nations, so may they also between large ones, and this has proved to be the case through the signing of the Locarno Pacts governing practically all possible disputes between their signatories.

Dr. James Brown Scott says:

A justiciable dispute is one which in the ordinary course of events can be presented to a court of justice—that is, presented to a court of justice and decided by a court of justice. What a justiciable dispute is, is a legal question, and is a question for a court to settle. If you discuss this question with European jurists or publicists, they will tell you very frankly and very honestly from their standpoint that the nations themselves must decide what is or what is not justiciable, and that a court cannot decide properly what is or what is not justiciable, and that nations would not be justified in submitting a question as to the nature of a justiciable dispute to an international tribunal.[22]

Not in opposition but in comment upon this statement, it may be said that not all European jurists have taken the stand attributed to them with great truth by Dr. Scott. This is evident by the fact already pointed out that certain nations have referred to court the question as to whether their vital interests were or were not involved in a given

[21] *Le tribunal international,* 317.
[22] *Proceedings, American Society of International Law,* 1915, 88.

controversy, and still more have determined to refer to court all disputes of every nature. The second reference is absolute, and the first indicates a disposition to give the court power to determine whether or not certain classes of disputes were justiciable.

Because a reference is permissible to a court, it does not follow that since the court may entertain it a remedy must be given. Even though it recognizes the jurisdiction to pass upon the question it may internationally as well as within the nation determine that, however the complainant may have been injured, there is not a legal right of recovery. This, of course, is known in our common law system as *damnum absque injuria*.

Even though a dispute between nations be found as between private individuals to constitute a grievance for which there is no remedy, such a finding in itself will make for peace. If told by the court that a nation must submit to a particular grievance without being afforded a remedy, the nation which so suffers cannot well go to war under such circumstances, because a declaration to the effect that a wrong is without a remedy is nothing more than a statement that as members of a common society the person injured must himself bear his injuries. It certainly affords no license to undertake to redress by force of arms the loss to which he has been subjected.

It is quite likely also that when references by nations to international tribunals grow more numerous, a doctrine will arise similar to that expressed by the national courts and covered by the expression *de minimis non curat lex*. In other words the offense may prove so small that to give a remedy would not be worth the time of the court. Offenses which might properly be considered as falling under this title have before now afforded provocation to war; but in the face of a declaration before the world that the offense is too small to deserve the attention of the law, it is scarcely to be thought that any nation will have the temerity to engage its opponent in battle.

25. Political and judicial questions further discussed.—Something is to be added with regard to questions which are assumed to be political rather than judicial in nature. We may call attention to the fact that under the Constitution of the United States the judicial power extends "to controversies between two or more states" and provides that "in those in which a state shall be party, the Supreme Court shall have original jurisdiction." In the face of these provisions and in the face of the further fact that cases in which states have been defendants have gone to the Supreme Court to be there dismissed because involving political questions, it is evident that the very general terms of the Constitution are really limited by the circumstances of the case. Controversies to which nations are parties may before an international tribunal be likewise subject to like limitations. Let us by analogy to cases before the Supreme Court consider what would be regarded as a political question before an international tribunal.

Almost or quite exclusively, when the Supreme Court has considered whether a question was political or not it has had reference to the authority or want of authority of the court to recognize a particular state government. This was true as to the cases of Luther *vs*. Borden, 7 Howard, 1, and Taylor *vs*. Beckham, 178 U.S. 548. In principle the same idea was involved in Cherokee Nation *vs*. Georgia, 5 Peters 1, Duncan *vs*. McCall, 139 U.S. 449, and Pacific States Telephone and Telegraph Company *vs*. Oregon, 223 U.S. 118. So also the United States Supreme Court, recognizing division of powers between the different branches of the national government, has refused to interfere with a co-ordinate department.

We have just seen that under the Federal Constitution, the recognition of the authorities of a state government created a political question and not a judicial one, and, therefore, was not to be taken into account by a court, even though the powers of a court were of the broadest possible character. A corresponding situation internationally would arise if the question before the court was as to the recognition or non-recognition as a sovereign power of some government coming under consideration before the judicial body. It would seem under such circumstances that the court would have the right to determine the fact as to whether other governments had or had not recognized the particular party as an equal in sovereign power with themselves. The determination of this one fact would settle the course to be taken by the court.

The fact that nations are, at least within certain limits, to be regarded as sovereign would also have an important influence upon the action of the court. If, for instance, an international court were called upon to direct the internal course of action to be taken by a nation, it might well refuse to do so because asked to invade the sovereignty of a nation.

A nation should be held responsible only for the results of its acts, its freedom in all other respects existing. There is a certain similarity between this position and the condition of affairs with respect to private individuals. The private individual is not to be held responsible for the workings of his mind or for actions pertaining merely to himself. It is only when he does something prejudicial to his neighbor that any responsibility exists.

We yet lack a definition of "political questions" between nations, which we are told are not suitable for judicial settlement. What they are as indicated by specific illustrations in the opinion of Admiral Mahan and Andrew D. White we shall see. Yet in our view all practically of the given instances do not offer political questions at all.

Let us consider that the prime duty of the state is to further the well-being of its citizens and not its own aggrandizement. If this be granted and, consequent upon it, the exclusive right of states to control the destinies of the people under their jurisdiction, almost the whole congeries of political questions disappears from the horizon. There remains only the matter of national recognition—internationally after all only a minor matter of fact, to be ascertained from the actions of fellow-nations at the moment—and boundary questions, universally recognized as the proper subject of arbitration or other peaceful adjustment.

Outside of the topics named, the alleged political questions then become attempts of one nation to control another—in fact national aggressions. These should be recognized for what they are, and not sanctified as political questions.

Any other possible political question becomes merely a domestic question to be hereafter discussed.

26. The contentions of Admiral Mahan.—A word is to be said with regard to the position of Admiral Mahan, he holding certain questions to be not appropriate for determination by judicial tribunals. He contends that it is not possible

to refer all disputes to arbitration because under any classification there cannot but remain always cases in which the right is one of morals and expediency—in other words, of policy—not susceptible of legal definition, because the preciseness of these deprive them of the elasticity necessary to successful international adjustments; which elasticity diplomacy possesses.[23]

It is perfectly manifest from the perusal of Admiral Mahan's work that he regarded diplomacy from a practical point of view as being merely the power of the diplomat to enforce his wishes by the strength of his nation, and that the thing which is outlawed by arbitration is the power of the nation to express its demands by force. As illustrating what he conceived to be the evil attendant upon unrestricted arbitration, we cite from his work:

[23] *Armaments and Arbitration*, 78.

The action of Italy in Tripoli; that taken by France, England, Spain and ultimately Germany, in Morocco; the case of the United States with reference to Colombia, Panama, and the Panama Canal Zone; all these may be cited as instances in which previous arbitration stipulations might have—it is claimed in some quarters actually have—seriously fettered, if not prevented, the national measures, because the national independence of action, which is the corner-stone of international law, had been mortgaged in whole or in part.[24]

We may say quite frankly that the justification of arbitration is to be found in the fact that it serves to prevent just such assertions of "independence" as appealed to Admiral Mahan. It is because by the use of arbitration the independence of the smaller nations may find protection against the tyranny of the larger that arbitration exists. The independence of the small nation is quite as vital as the independence of the large one. At another point Admiral Mahan argues that

A danger in the path of arbitration, of legal decisions as opposed to diplomatic arrangements, is that existing political differences will be brought to the bar, not merely of laws applicable but outworn, but of legal tenures based on antiquated or obsolete conditions formerly suitable to times and circumstances but which no longer are so. Law lacks elasticity, not merely because of the time needed to pass new legislation, but because it itself, at least in international relations, may be correct as a general proposition, yet cannot always be applied satisfactorily to a particular case. In such instances a different instrument is required. A political *impasse* must be met by a special provision, by measures which shall proceed on a basis not of strict legality, but of evident necessary expediency; in short, by diplomacy rather than by law.[25]

We have pointed out the strict association made by the Admiral between diplomacy and force. The rest of his argument is to the effect that international law, since all international appeal must be made primarily to it, is an antiquated science—something far from the fact. In so far as the argument holds good at all it is in favor of international legislation, something which will further tend to diminish the application of that force which was so agreeable to Admiral Mahan.

27. Ideas of Woolf.—Leonard S. Woolf contends that

International Law is so fragmentary and incomplete that it does not touch at all a number of very important international relationships, and a dispute arising

[24] *Op cit.*, 4. It is said in the *Autobiography of Andrew D. White* (II, 353) that "obligatory arbitration on all questions would enable any power, at any moment, to bring before the tribunal any other power against which it has, or thinks it has, a grievance. Greece might thus summon Turkey; France might summon Germany; the Papacy, Italy; England, Russia; China, Japan; Spain, the United States, regarding matters in which the deepest of human feelings—questions of religion, questions of race, questions even of national existence—are concerned."

[25] *Ibid.*, 99.

from such relationships could not at present be decided according to law. Take the dispute between Russia and Austria at the beginning of this war, or between Spain and the United States at the beginning of the Spanish-American war. No human being could possibly decide either case by determining the legal rights and obligations of the parties, because the rights and obligations actually defined by International Law were so few and so unimportant.[26]

With exactly as much truth might one have said but a few years ago that there was no law applicable to the management of automobiles, or, to come to a more modern period, the radio. Nevertheless before statute law existed in anywise affecting their conduct, the courts found no trouble in discovering sufficient analogies from the law in other respects to control very largely the movements of automobiles, certainly in every case where their directors injured the rights of other people. It is only because we find international law obscured by false conceptions with regard to sovereignty that we are at all justified in considering that it is fragmentary. When the moment of application comes with regard to any particular problem, we find ourselves instinctively turning to the law within the nation and giving it international application.

All this is not to say that there is not a broad field to be usefully covered by legislation of an international character.

Mr. Woolf advises us that there are certain classes of differences within the states which are never referred to judicial tribunals. He remarks, for instance:

No sane man would suggest that the home rule question could find a satisfactory solution in a court of arbitration, and the reason is obvious—the interested parties could not possibly feel that it was rational to expect that the settlement would be just and, therefore, to accept it.[27]

We have to repeat that there is and must always be a broad field for legislation, and that such questions as Mr. Woolf has in mind, if they are encountered, will not be taken jurisdiction of by any international court. For such a court would recognize its incompetency and decline jurisdiction just as we have seen, in certain cases, jurisdiction has been declined by the Supreme Court of the United States. It remains, therefore, true that when all is said and done, the most that any court can do is to determine its own power of action. A finding by the court that it is without jurisdiction because the question presented is not of a judicial nature, is equivalent to saying that the appropriate remedy must

[26] *International Government,* 66.
[27] *Ibid.,* 70.

be sought elsewhere, and so saying the generality of the language of reference is no more impinged upon than is the case in like language applicable to the jurisdiction of the Supreme Court of the United States.

28. Domestic questions.—Of late there has arisen in the United States and perhaps elsewhere, a disposition to exclude from the consideration of proposed courts of arbitration what are called "domestic questions." Without a definition at least, the exclusion seems superfluous. By the very conditions of its existence, an international court deals with international questions and not with those which are domestic.

International law has even now progressed far enough to indicate at least some of the questions to be regarded as domestic and excepted from international jurisdiction. We have already instanced that of admission to the country. So it has been with regard to internal taxation in a dispute between Sweden and Spain cited by Stoykovitch.[28]

It may be true in certain instances that it will be difficult to say when a question is domestic and when international, just as it is true that certain questions are one or the other according to the point of view, as for instance, contentions relative to nationality. If, however, it be considered in any degree necessary to make such a reservation as we speak of, it should be accompanied by a strict definition. As a suggestion, we offer the following:

A domestic question relates to the sovereignty of the state within its territorial limits and not involving illegal deprivation of a foreigner submitting to its laws of his rights of life, of liberty, or of duly acquired property.

It is believed that this definition would leave all questions outside its purview as within the international field. It is true that the definition would not contemplate the continued existence of the Monroe Doctrine, but this doctrine, considering the original reasons for its proclamation and the Latin-American attitude toward it, is without essential vitality.

29. Obligatory arbitration: its development.—In addition to what has already been said, it seems well to add something with regard to the manner in which the idea of obligatory arbitration has received development. We started with occasional reference of comparatively insignificant matters to one or more arbitrators. Even this was done with considerable reluctance as involving infringement upon the sacred right of sovereignty. No especially deleterious results happening, the field enlarged and minor classes of subjects were made the material of

---

[28] *De l'autorité de la sentence arbitrale,* 14.

reference. Gradually the classifications were enlarged so as to include practically all varieties of disputes, even political and domestic, when exigency called for it, since, after all, territorial difficulties may be classed as both political and domestic.

Gradually the institution of *clauses compromissoires* became more common. This ground was entered upon with much hesitation and trepidation and with a feeling that it must be hedged about with limitations, such as respected "honor," "independence," "vital interests," and, of late, "domestic questions," leaving broad loopholes of escape at the option of either of the parties interested and offering nothing of a compulsory character. The hesitation may be well shown by reference to the language of some of the authors.

Thus Malauzat contends that states cannot without lessening their independence submit in advance for all time and in all cases to a fixed magistrature.

But since the states can submit a litigation to the decision of arbitrators chosen by them without infringing upon their sovereignty this sovereignty would not be diminished any more in case the states should solemnly take an engagement to submit to an international tribunal for a certain length of time one or certain categories of affairs.[29]

Féraud-Giraud argues that as the laws do not permit a citizen to refer for the future, under circumstances that he cannot know or anticipate, the judgment of differences, the importance and gravity of which he cannot suspect, to a third person who at the moment of acting could be in a very deplorable condition so far as rendering a judgment is concerned, so it is still more rigorously forbidden to the head of a state. He cannot thus blindly compromise the future and the destinies of his nation, when, to safeguard them, he ought to fail to comply with his given word. The author while considering himself a partisan of arbitration protests vigorously against present day tendencies toward the extension of arbitration through treaties binding nations in a general and permanent manner.[30]

The subject considered by M. Féraud-Giraud did not pass unnoticed by Kamarowsky, who quotes Goldschmidt to the effect that the Roman law, differing from certain contemporary law, gave effect to an agreement of arbitration upon disputes to arise in the future, and who argued that if the clause in question restrained considerably the liberty of

29 *Cour de justice arbitrale,* 21.
30 *Revue de droit international et de législation comparée,* XXIX (1897), 334.

states, it was not at the expense of ordinary jurisdiction but, on the contrary, supplemented jurisdiction where wanting.[31]

In the mind of André the objection to the use of a broad form of obligatory arbitration rests in the ability of a power to employ force. He contends that the states, being sovereign and having power to do as they please, naturally employ force whenever, there being sufficient interest in play, they consider that they have no chance of obtaining success judicially, while on the contrary their power allows them to hope for success. "This is," in his opinion he says "the true reason which in the present international situation often forbids giving to arbitration an absolutely general competency."[32]

Meanwhile the institution of courts of arbitration took on new forms and enlarged powers. The possibilities of a wide jurisdiction being given to courts of arbitration, though still hedged about with restrictions and perfectly optional, was shown by the Hague Conventions of 1899 and 1907. Some slight additional impetus was given to the general idea by the institution of the Central American Court of Justice in 1907, having jurisdiction over all disputes between the countries of that region. This, however, received its quietus at the hands of the United States ten years later, although this country was responsible for its formation. This was the first great instance of absolute compulsory arbitration agreed upon in advance of the existence of any dispute. A possible evil, attendant upon it as an international court, was that it might be invoked in certain cases not alone between governments but by private individuals against governments.

Meanwhile a number of countries discovered that they could as between themselves agree in advance to send to arbitration all or certain classes of difficulties which might arise between them, sometimes without any equivocal reservations whatsoever.

We thus by natural steps reach the point where under the League of Nations certain categories of disputes are customarily sent to a permanent Court of International Justice. Following closely upon this, and inspired by the League of Nations, we discover that certain of the great powers of Europe are willing, as illustrated by the Locarno Pacts, to refer all justiciable questions to a court. At the same moment we find an increasing number of countries by agreements between themselves ready to have practically all their differences, on conditions of reciprocity, determined by the Court of International Justice. We may

[31] *Le tribunal international,* 315.
[32] *De l'arbitrage obligatoire,* 196.

therefore regard Admiral Mahan as something of a prophet when he declared that "There is, then, a clear tendency in arbitration to progress from a means to be used voluntarily to one that shall be more compulsive."[33] This he regretted as interfering with national freedom of action, or, in other words, with the use of force to carry out the will of the one esteeming itself the strongest.

That it is always possible to sign treaties of obligatory arbitration is in fact made manifest on slight consideration from the position occupied by those nations which have become neutralized. It is never permissible for neutralized nations, as for instance Switzerland, to engage in war except when their territories are invaded. They are, therefore, compelled to arbitrate on all questions within judicial jurisdiction, and likewise all other nations are forced to arbitrate with them. What, therefore, may be done as to a neutralized country is also capable of happening to all other countries. As to those nations in the League of Nations, speaking in the broadest sense, it is remarked by Politis that, while arbitration is not, properly speaking, obligatory, still

It is not exact to say that arbitration remains in the League of Nations purely optional. There is a certain obligation which in place of being direct is indirect. This results from the obligation imposed upon members of the League to submit their differences to one of two procedures—arbitration or inquiry instituted by the Pact.[34]

After all, in diplomacy as in many other things, there are fashions. The use of the terms "honor" and "vital interests," even the reservation of "independence," are going out of style along with "national dignity." Their immediate successor in the newest mode is "domestic questions," with some stress on the part of the United States on "Monroe Doctrine," which remains undefined if not non-existent. One day statesmen may learn that their nations can with healthfulness be exposed to the direct rays of the sun of the law, the better so when divested of the stifling protection of reservations. Meanwhile courts will recognize as of course that there are matters necessarily reserved for legislative and executive action among the nations.

[33] *Armaments and Arbitration*, 4.
[34] *La justice internationale*, 234.

CHAPTER IV

INITIATION OF ARBITRAL OR JUDICIAL PROCEEDINGS

30. Exchange of notes.—The simplest manner in which arbitral or judicial proceedings may be inaugurated at the present day is through the exchange of notes between the respective powers, without further or other formality. Many arbitrations have been based upon such exchanges, among which may be enumerated disputes between: Switzerland and France concerning the interpretation of a regulation of a commercial convention; Brazil and Great Britain, relative to claims of Count Dundonald; Great Britain and Peru in the matter of the claim of Thomas M. White; and Spain and the United States as to claims in 1871, and the extension of this original agreement. After the formation of commissions, exchange of notes has been resorted to on several occasions with reference to relatively minor matters, as, for instance, the extension of the time for the organization of the British-American Commission of 1915 and a like situation arising between France and the United States. The protocol between Mexico and Venezuela having referred to arbitration claims presented by the citizens of Mexico against Venezuela, and it appearing possible that counter claims affecting Mexican demands might be offered for consideration, the two governments exchanged notes allowing the arbitral commission to examine them. So also in the case of Oberlander and Messenger, by exchange of notes between the United States and Mexico, the time for the presentation of claims before the mixed commission was limited and this limitation was embodied in the commission rules.[1]

It is said by Judge John Bassett Moore, touching senatorial control, that

the first case submitted to the Permanent Court of Arbitration at The Hague under the convention of 1899—the well-known claim presented by the United States against Mexico on behalf of the Pious Fund of the Californias—was submitted under a simple executive agreement. Other examples might readily be given; but it suffices to say that, where the settlement embraced claims against the foreign governments alone and not against the United States, twenty-seven of our international arbitrations up to 1908, were held under simple executive agreements as against nineteen treaties.[2]

It may be added as a matter of current history that at the time of signing of the Pious Fund Protocol, Secretary Hay consulted with Senator

[1] *Law and Procedure of International Tribunals*, 5, 6.   [2] *International Law*, 87.

Allison, chairman of the Senate Committee on Foreign Relations, as to the necessity of submission of the protocol to the American Senate. It was the Senator's opinion that as the protocol involved no possible award against this country, senatorial advice and consent were unnecessary. The Mexican Senate gave formal ratification.

31. The *compromis*.—Before entering into a discussion of its nature and contents, a word of explanation should be made with regard to the *compromis,* the instrument commonly laying the foundation for any international tribunal, the word itself being derived from the French civil law governing private arbitrations. The *compromis* may be so designated in its title although often given the name of convention, treaty, or protocol. It may be a document complete in itself, or it may form part or the entirety of a preceding general treaty or special treaty providing for the invocation of an arbitral tribunal whenever the occasion should arise. When forming part of a former treaty and couched in general terms, the portion providing for the formation of an arbitral tribunal is known as the *clause compromissoire.*

32. *Clause compromissoire*.—Clauses of this description have been in existence from the earliest time, many instances being discoverable among the ancient Greeks. They may be viewed from several different aspects. Often they are limited to the question of the interpretation or application of the clauses of the treaty of which they form a part, all questions arising thereunder being referred to an arbitral tribunal. Thus at the session of Zurich in 1877, the Institute of International Law approved unanimously a declaration favoring the insertion in all future international treaties of a clause stipulating for recourse to arbitration in case of dispute upon their interpretation and application.

The *clause compromissoire* may also be part of a general treaty, referring to arbitration all or particular classes of differences which may arise between nations. Viewed from the point of efficacy, it may provide in detail for the immediate formation of a court upon difficulties arising, or it may amount to nothing more than a naked promise to arbitrate differences which may thereafter arise.

The question as to the proper application of a *clause compromissoire* arose under the Treaty of Commerce between Spain and Sweden and Norway of 1883, renewed in 1887, by which it was stipulated that in consideration of a customs tax of a certain amount per actual liter, the alcohols of each country should not pay in the other any right of excise or of consumption greater than rested upon similar national merchandise. Relying upon this text the Swedish and Norwegian merchants protested against the mode of the collection of the impost with regard to alcohol manufactured in Spain. The Society of Carlesheim, having an important business in alcohol with Spain and finding its revenue affected by the measure, submitted the case to several eminent publicists of Europe, asking if there was not occasion to resort to arbitration as provided by the protocol. These gentlemen were of the opinion that the question related to the interpretation and execution of the treaty of commerce and should consequently in virtue of the articles of the treaty be settled by arbitration. This case was referred to arbitration, but the demands of Sweden and Norway were rejected.

Another question arose between Switzerland and Italy. Italy by a decree of 1893 decided that the customs impost should thereafter be paid only in metallic money, and that payment in Italian paper money should no longer be permitted. In consequence of the rarity of metallic money this measure advanced the customs duties about ten per cent, which led the Swiss Federal Government to contend to the Italian Government that the context of the Treaty of Commerce of 1892 was abrogated by the Decree of 1893 and that Switzerland most certainly would not have signed the treaty in 1892 if such conditions had been imposed in the first instance. Italy rejected the Swiss contentions, alleging that the Decree of 1893 was a matter of interior order, not implying any interpretation of the application of the treaty, and therefore she was free from the arbitral jurisdiction. This involved necessarily, of course, that the arbitrators had no right to pass upon their own jurisdiction, since in order to give the *clause compromissoire* its practical operation the arbitration should begin to function as soon as a question was raised and the question of interior character should be passed upon by the judges. In other words, the board of arbitration should of itself have the power to determine whether the case in question was one of those where arbitration should be exercised; otherwise the *clause compromissoire* would be but a vain promise.[3]

We advert elsewhere to the fact that the agreement of arbitration may give the court power to create for the parties rules of future action as well as to pass upon disputes which have already arisen. In other words, the arbitrators may become legislators as well as judges.

It is a common defect of the *clauses compromissoires* that they do not provide with sufficient clearness for the manner in which they should be executed. They leave open generally the definition of the

---

[3] *Recueil des arbitrages*, t. I, 105.

differences to be referred to an arbitration or inadequately describe them, and they fail to state the manner in which the board of arbitration shall be selected and function or how its awards shall be carried out. The usual clause thus amounts to very little more than a pious wish.

33. Essentials of a *compromis*.—Let us now consider the general nature and requisites of a *compromis*. The *compromis* is in itself a matter of the highest importance with relation to the subsequent arbitration or judicial settlement. It is the law of the parties and of the case, and every provision becomes important.

Usually after setting forth the names of the contracting parties, the *compromis* should state clearly the nature of the difference or differences which have arisen and are to be determined. This statement will bind and limit the jurisdiction of the judicial body. We next reach the matter of the formation of the court. This may consist of a single person, who may be the head of a government, the occupant of any office, or a private individual. More often under present day practice there are from three to five persons created into an arbitral court. Each party names one or two as the case may be, and these coming together may select a third or a fifth man. Sometimes the third or the fifth man who acts as the umpire is named by mutual agreement. Not infrequently he is named by some entirely neutral power. Thus, for instance, with regard to the Venezuelan Arbitrations of 1903, by agreement between the several powers, the president of the United States named the umpires of the English, German, Italian, and Dutch commissions, while the Queen of Holland named the umpire of the American commission, and Spain the umpire of differences between Venezuela and Mexico.

The umpire may be chosen as a president of the commission, sitting with it and hearing in the first instance with his fellows the matters brought before the commission. In this event the court is to be considered as a complete body of three or five men as the case may be. Such is the manner of procedure laid down by the Hague Conventions. On the other hand, as is very frequently the case, the umpire may be called upon to act only after the commissioners or representatives of the two countries have differed in opinion, in which case the difference is referred to him for determination. The situation in this respect and all others is controlled by the exact language of the protocol. Other methods of reference will be described later.

The protocol will also provide usually for the oath to be taken by the commissioners or umpire. This is a matter of no little importance as controlling the jurisdiction of the court, for, naturally, the officials named cannot exceed the obligation imposed upon them by their oath of office. The oath, therefore, becomes not merely a solemn promise to do their duty but the boundary of their jurisdiction.

It will be found that many protocols provide either in the oath or otherwise the law to be followed by the arbitrators, often directing that the decision shall be in conformity with the rules of international law or according to equity and justice, or follow the decisions as to international law laid down by other like tribunals.

The protocol will also lay down any other special rules of procedure designed to control the arbitration. These rules usually govern the time within which the case, so-called, of the complaining government shall be presented and the time allowed for reply and rebuttal. They may also control the manner in which proof may be taken, and, if there be a large number of individual claimants whose rights are to be passed upon, the time within which the complaints or memorials are to be filed and the manner in which proof may be made, together with what shall be considered as constituting proof. A limitation is also usually fixed upon the time for the completion of the work of the commission.

Other provisions may relate to the form of the award and subsequent action thereon. The question of interest upon the award may also be considered as well as other details with reference to its time of payment and execution.

It is not without precedent for nations to provide in the protocol special rules to control the judgment of the tribunal. Thus, for instance, the Geneva commission was controlled by the Three Rules of Washington, as they were styled, which laid down the law under which the case was to be decided. Again, the treaty between Venezuela and Great Britain relating to the settlement of conflicting boundaries between British Guiana and Venezuela established the principles to be invoked as governing prescriptive rights to territory, as was also the case under a boundary convention between Honduras and Salvador.[4]

Protocols frequently provide that the determinations when reached constitute an end of the matters in question, absolutely binding upon the parties to the controversy. It is not believed that provisions of this kind add anything to the sanctity of an arbitral finding—of course, the effect of such finding being inherent in and of itself without additional words in the protocol.

---

[4] *Law and Procedure of International Tribunals,* 316.

In the case of claims commissions the *compromis* may also provide that all claims not presented within a specified time shall be thereafter barred, and this agreement is valid although made by the government and not by the individuals affected, the government being presumed to be the agent for its nationals.

The protocol may likewise make suitable provisions for the costs incident to the procedure. These are usually divided between the parties, each paying the costs of its agent or counsel. In many cases each party very improperly pays the cost of the commissioner or commissioners named by it. We say "improperly" because such a provision detracts from the impartiality and independence of the court. The commissioners on both sides should be paid from a common fund and at a like rate and should not owe any obligation to the country naming them.

Exceptional protocols have given what were virtually legislative powers to arbitral boards. We have referred to the Fur Seal Arbitration, which laid down rules concerning the pursuit of seals, and the North Atlantic Fisheries Arbitration promulgating fishery regulations. We add the arbitrations of the ambassadors at Constantinople in 1902.[5]

It is pointed out by Dreyfus that it is incorrect to say that, the protocol being signed,

the parties are only bound by honor; the bond that unites them is more intense. There is not only between them a national obligation founded on good faith, but a juridical obligation founded on law.[6]

34. Violations of *clauses compromissoires*.—Indirectly a *clause compromissoire* may be violated as well as directly; for instance, when, in the instance given before, Italy refused to submit to arbitration a question with Switzerland on the theory that the matter in dispute was a domestic one. Italy undertook to be the judge in her own case and to such extent violated her treaty. A number of cases of direct ignoring or violation of clauses of this description are enumerated by Bonfils.[7] It is to be noted that these clauses were usually couched in the most general terms, leaving the details entirely open for subsequent arrangement, and therefore subject to many differences of opinion on minor matters and uncertain of operation.

35. Heads of governments as arbitrators.—Some details are properly to be added, expanding discussion of the provisions usually contained in the protocol.

[5] Stoykovitch, *De l'autorité de la sentence arbitrale,* 106.

[6] *L'arbitrage international,* 359.

[7] *Droit international public,* 4th edition, § 969.

Perhaps it was natural in the earlier arbitrations of the modern period that the head of a neutral government, almost invariably the monarch, should be chosen as the arbitrator. A reason for this lay in the fact that, the contest being between two states claiming to be themselves sovereign, it was felt by them that reference to any power of less importance was derogatory to their dignity. This condition of affairs has lasted down to the present time, and even the past fifty years have witnessed many such references.

After the War of 1812, England and the United States referred a matter in dispute to the Emperor of Russia. Again the same nations referred their differences, arising out of a contest relative to the Straits of Haro, to the Emperor of Germany. Many differences between South American countries have been sent to the arbitrament of the Spanish Crown. The Emperor of the French determined the claims of the United States against Portugal relative to the destruction of the American brig, *General Armstrong.* Italy and Colombia referred to President Cleveland the settlement of the Cerruti case. President Grant arbitrated the dispute between England and Portugal relative to the island of Bulama, and Victor Emanuel settled a contest between England and Brazil. Chile and the United States sent the Alsop case to the King of England for arbitration.

Comparatively common as have been references to the head of a foreign country, such a choice is by no means to be favored. To begin with, the reference may result in accusations of partiality on the part of the head of government as between nations, and therefore the award may be conducive to international agitation. Again, it is to be borne in mind from the standpoint of justice that the monarch does not act on his own judgment and is not expected so to act. He affixes his name to a report prepared by a committee in whom he or his ministers have personal confidence. His award, therefore, becomes in fact the award of persons of perhaps inferior ability and under all circumstances persons who act under an incomplete sense of responsibility. As to their selection, we may refer to the fact that in the dispute relative to the Straits of Haro the Emperor of Germany selected as his advisers a geographer, an international lawyer, and a diplomatist.

Some of the difficulties attendant upon the choice of a head of a state are pointed out in a letter from Dr. Francis Lieber to Secretary Seward, published by the New York *Times,* September 22, 1865.[8] As

---

[8] Cited approvingly by Kamarowsky in *Le tribunal international*, 207.

expressed by Dreyfus a reference to a sovereign

is not without danger; sovereigns rarely judge in person; they delegate their powers and sign prepared awards. If they wish to judge themselves their crown is not a guaranty of competence. It would be better to have a tribunal less august and more enlightened.[9]

Where a reference is made to the chief magistrate of a country who dies before his work is completed, his successor in office is recognized as having the right to perform the duty. Thus upon the decease of Alfonso XII, King of Spain, the Queen Regent became arbitrator in the boundary conflict between Colombia and Venezuela in 1869. Emile Loubet, President of France, executed the duties of arbitrator between Colombia and Costa Rica, who had confided the rôle to his predecessor in office, M. Felix Faure.[10] Of course, if the reference had been strictly to Faure by name it could have been successfully argued that upon his death the arbitration fell to the ground, the trust being personal and not to the head of a nation. This would be true even though the reference described him as President of France, such being merely a personal description.

36. Other special references.—On many occasions, an early one going back to the famous division of the world between Spain and Portugal in the sixteenth century, the Pope has served as arbitrator between nations. Reference to the Pope continues up to the present time, particularly as to disputes between the Catholic South and Central American states, although the Pope passed upon the difference between Germany and Spain as to the Caroline Islands. In the earlier cases the Pope spoke *ex-cathedra* and without any obligation to give reasons for the decision. At the present time the opinion of the Papacy should, like all other arbitral opinions, be fortified by reasoning.

Exceptional modes of reference have been to the Senate of Hamburg, to committees of the Royal Geographical Society or of the French Academy of Sciences, and to named private individuals, often the diplomatic representatives of neutral nations.

A number of disputes between nations have been referred to the judicial authorities of other countries. Chief Justice White and Chief Justice Taft, for instance, have acted as arbitrators, the first of a dispute between Panama and Costa Rica and the second of a dispute between Costa Rica and Great Britain. Nicaragua and France united in a reference to the French Court of Cassation.

[9] *L'arbitrage international*, 358.
[10] *Law and Procedure of International Tribunals*, 34.

A reference of an unusual character was made by Great Britain and the United States in sending the difference as to the Alaska Boundary to a board consisting of six, three named by each country. Other joint commissions have been formed to settled boundary questions between the United States and Canada and the United States and Mexico. A joint high commission arranged the terms of the Treaty of Washington of 1871 between the United States and Great Britain.

37. Reference to mixed tribunals.—We come now to the selection of members of mixed tribunals, which have played a most important part of late years in arbitrations strictly so called, as distinguished from tribunals of a more judicial form. Laying aside, because of having failed to accomplish anything, a tribunal under one clause of the Jay Treaty which sat at Philadelphia, the first of the modern mixed tribunals was formed under the same treaty, a very distinguished one sitting in London, of which the American members were William Pinkney and Christopher Gore. These gentlemen with two excellent English associates, together with an umpire, constituted the commission. The umpire, chosen by lot, was an American. This commission decided many important propositions, perhaps the most valuable of which was with relation to the right of an arbitral tribunal to pass upon its own jurisdiction. While we believe that the decisions were generally just and always well-fortified by reasoning, nevertheless the manner of the appointment of the umpire was essentially vicious.

From the formation of the Jay commission down to the time of the *Alabama*-Geneva commission, the practice was quite uniform that each of the parties in interest should name its representative upon the commission and they in coming together would select the umpire either by agreement or by lot, or he would be selected by the joint action of the two governments. After the Geneva commission and down to the present time, it may be said, subject to later observations, that the same process has been followed. (An exception was the Venezuelan Arbitrations of 1903, when neutral nations named the umpires.) The manner of the selection of the Geneva commission was, however, distinctive. The United States appointed one representative on the tribunal and England one, while the heads of the governments of Brazil, Italy, and Switzerland were asked each to name one commissioner. When they assembled, the Italian nominee was made president of the board. The attitude of the disinterested members of the commission toward the representatives of the two countries in dispute is illustrated by a remark of Mr. Moorfield Storey:

In the paper just read, the Geneva tribunal was mentioned. Mr. Charles Francis Adams told me that when the Geneva tribunal met there was a dais on which the three neutral arbitrators had seats and a long table in front with a single seat at each end, the seat at one end being assigned to Sir Alexander Cockburn, the English member of the tribunal, that at the other to Mr. Adams, the American member. As they entered the hall, Sir Alexander Cockburn said, "You see, Mr. Adams, they perfectly well understand our relations to this arbitration." And so he assumed the attitude of counsel and understood that as his position.[11]

An exceptional case and by no means a precedent was that of the British-Venezuelan commission to settle the boundaries of Venezuela and British-Guiana, in which England was directly represented on the tribunal and the United States took the place of Venezuela on that body.

We have noted elsewhere the fact that these several tribunals have differed as to the powers of the odd man, he sometimes sitting, as is the case with references under the Hague Conventions, as president of the tribunal and forming an integral part of the judging body; and sometimes not called into action until the commissioners, sitting separately, have failed to come to an agreement, so that in the latter instance the umpire virtually becomes a one-man court of appeal.

There is little to be said in favor of the usual methods of selecting a mixed tribunal. We have adverted to the fact that the commissioners were apt to regard themselves and be regarded by others as simply the representatives of the nations in dispute and therefore serving in no judicial function. This has been so as to the national representatives even where the majority of the commission were of neutral nations, as illustrated by the position of the contestants' commissioners at the Geneva tribunal. It fortunately was not true of the Venezuelan-American commission of 1903, the recent British-American commission, the existing German-American commission, and perhaps a few others.

To avoid the position we have suggested as common, in selecting the tribunal which adjudged the case of the Pious Fund of the Californias, the United States and Mexico agreed that no national of either country should sit upon the court. In this as well as in other cases where no national was chosen to adjudge under the Hague Conventions, unanimity was attained; but in other cases, as for instance the Japanese House Tax case and the Norwegian Shipping case, a case between the United States and Norway, in which nationals were permitted to sit, the unsuccessful national vigorously dissented.

[11] *Proceedings, Society for the Judicial Settlement of International Disputes,* 1910, 147.

CHAPTER V

SOME JURISDICTIONAL QUESTIONS

38. General considerations.—A number of questions have been or may be raised with regard to the jurisdiction of international tribunals. The general observation may be made that jurisdiction must be ample to cover that of the person, usually the state, and of the subject-matter, with authority to grant the particular relief. Questions of this nature are determined in the first instance by resorting to the protocol, beyond which the tribunal has no right to go even in the name of equity. This jurisdiction as between them may extend as far as may be agreed upon by the parties, and contemplates any kind of remedy to which they may consent. The tribunal itself must and does have power to pass upon its own jurisdiction.

If a jurisdictional question be not raised by the parties it may be raised by the court, which, if it finds itself justified in so doing, will refuse jurisdiction.[1]

A troublesome question may arise as to whether and when an international court has exceeded its jurisdiction. As to this there is no completely satisfactory answer applicable on all occasions, if no appellate tribunal be provided. Even then its determination may be called into question. About all one can say is that, a final judgment being arrived at, the party deeming itself aggrieved may make representations to the successful one relative to the errors complained of and seek a settlement out of court or the establishment of a new reviewing tribunal. If these are refused, nothing remains. The case is in no wise different from that arising from errors of other sorts, as for instance from error in the application of the facts presented. Meanwhile the award has to be met.

An illustration of an award finally in large measure held erroneous for want of jurisdiction is afforded by the case of the Orinoco Shipping and Trading Co. In this the original award was made by an umpire and in part confirmed and in part set aside by the Hague Permanent Court of Arbitration.

The general power to set aside the action of arbitral courts will be further discussed under the head of Awards.

39. Jurisdiction over the person.—Doubt upon this sort of jurisdiction can rarely arise in international tribunals, usually created as they are by *compromis* or its equivalent, which involves the consent of

---

[1] *Law and Procedure of International Tribunals*, 38, 208.

the parties to their appearance before the court. Nevertheless it has been touched upon several times, as for instance by the Central American Court of Justice in a dispute between Costa Rica and Nicaragua, and by the Permanent Court of International Justice in a case in which Russia refused to submit to the advisory jurisdiction of the court, not being a party to the treaty of submission. So again, the Central American Court, holding its jurisdiction to relate strictly to cases of violation of treaties or conventions or other cases of international character, refused to recognize the right of a private individual as a claimant before it, no international question being involved.

Ordinarily when cases are presented before an arbitral tribunal the presentation is made under protocols giving jurisdiction only over claims of nationals of one or both of the contending parties. It is, however, quite possible for the governments to agree that claimants who are citizens of neither nation may appear before the tribunal. Again, in the Venezuelan Arbitrations of 1903, the language of the Italian protocol allowed the presentation of "Italian Claims," with certain exceptions. Jurisdiction was therefore taken without challenge over a claim arising out of the Postal Treaty for an amount specifically due by the Venezuelan Government to the Italian Government. The language in its implications was much broader than if it had been simply confined to claims of subjects of Italy.

40. Jurisdiction over the subject-matter.—Of more importance are questions relating to the jurisdiction of arbitral tribunals over the subject-matter. In the beginning, questions submitted for the judgment of such a tribunal must mean contentions in some respect of an international character. Thus it was said in a case before the British-American commission of 1853[2] that the fact that the claim came nominally within the letter of the convention did not settle the question of jurisdiction, and that if any class of claims had not theretofore been regarded as matters of international adjustment the court was not necessarily bound to regard them as included within the provisions of the convention.

Some differences of opinion have arisen among commissions relative to their power to take jurisdiction over claims against the nation arising from non-payment of public bonds. There seems to be, however, no reasonable doubt that the commissions have a perfect right to pass upon claims of this nature, provided at all events it is perfectly clear that

---

[2] *Law and Procedure of International Tribunals*, 44.

the ownership of the bonds has at all times remained in the hands of citizens or subjects of the claimant country.

Some of the matters which have been recognized as properly subject to international tribunals are: breach of contracts and of concessions; the infliction of personal injuries, including imprisonment and death; denial of justice in the courts; notorious injustice affecting the claimant; forcible expropriation of property or its destruction; rental for the use of property; violations affecting individuals of certain so-called laws of war, etc. Some of these headings call for further development.

It has been held under certain protocols that there can be no right of recovery internationally until an effort to obtain justice has been made in the courts of the defendant nation. If, however, in the pursuit of justice before such courts the claimant has endeavored to carry his case to the highest court of appeal and met with denial of justice or notorious injustice, such fact would put his right to relief before an international tribunal beyond question. The same rule has been applied when the title to real estate was involved, the international court taking jurisdiction if it became apparent that the real estate claimant had been denied justice in the local courts.

The question has arisen as to what constitutes denial of justice, and we are told that it includes

not only refusal of a judicial authority to exercise its function, and notably to pass upon petitions submitted to it, but also persistent delays on its part in pronouncing its decrees.[3]

In another case it was said:

It is only in cases where justice is refused, or palpable or evident injustice is committed, or when rules and forms have been openly violated, or when odious distinctions have been made against its subjects, that the government of the foreigner can interfere.[4]

Even when the international courts have taken the view that local remedies should be exhausted before an appeal to them there have often been circumstances excusing its application. For instance, it has been declared "Justice may as much be denied when it may be absurd to seek it by judicial process as if denied after being so sought."[5]

It must not be overlooked that the rule requiring the assertion of remedies before resorting to an international tribunal is for the most part a rule of convenience of foreign offices in determining whether or

---

3 *Law and Procedure of International Tribunals*, 86.
4 *Idem.*
5 *Ibid.*, 87.

not they shall interpose to secure special relief for their nationals rather than an imperative rule controlling the jurisdiction of international tribunals, for the latter have held repeatedly and with propriety that their courts had been substituted for national forums which otherwise might have had jurisdiction over the subject-matter.[6] So the Calvo clause has been held repeatedly as of no moment once a commission has been appointed.

Commissions have repeatedly declined to recognize any jurisdiction for the enforcement of demands based upon intangible things affecting, if they affect anything, the government of the claimant nation. Under this heading jurisdiction has been declined for supposed insults or indignities to the government, the individual foreigner not being affected. Again it is true, as stated in one case, that

all the considerations for or against a claim which appeal to the diplomatic branch of a government have not necessarily a place before an international commission.[7]

41. Jurisdiction to grant particular relief.—In other connections we have referred to the fact that in various cases international tribunals have undertaken to go beyond the fair import of the language of the *compromis* appointing them and have undertaken to act on their own ideas of fairness and justice, something entirely beyond their powers. Anything, of course, done in this respect would be beyond the jurisdiction to grant the particular relief the tribunal can give and therefore void.

Something, however, remains to be added. It would be beyond the power of international tribunals to grant relief, as has been stated, for something which might be claimed to be a national insult, although these words themselves are incapable of satisfactory definition. Beyond this, however, unless expressly stated otherwise the ordinary jurisdiction of an international tribunal extends only to the claimant of ordinary relief customarily given by such body. For instance, a tribunal of this nature would have no right to decree specific performance of a contract, something which requires action of a more positive character than the direction of the payment of debt. The same would be true with regard to enforcing a duty by way of mandamus. This has been so declared under the Federal Constitution of the United States in a case brought by Kentucky against the Governor of Ohio requiring him to deliver up a fugitive slave. The Supreme Court declined to act, remarking that

---

[6] *Ibid.*, 66, 363.   [7] *Ibid.*, 231.

"indeed, such a power would place every state under the control and dominion of the general government, even in the administration of its internal concerns and reserved rights."[8] Similarly when an attempt was made to enforce the laws of Wisconsin upon a foreign insurance company, Mr. Justice Gray said, "This court has declined to compel performance of obligations which if the states had been independent nations could not have been enforced judicially, but only through the political departments of their governments."[9]

42. Calvo Doctrine.—What is generally known as the Calvo Doctrine, under which controversies arising under a concession can only be passed upon by the courts of the nation granting it and can not be made the subject of international claim, has been a frequent source of conflict in international tribunals. The prime question has been whether in the face of an agreement on the lines of this doctrine it was proper for an international tribunal to take jurisdiction. It is not part of our intention to review at large the decisions upon this point, but it does seem important to indicate the jurisdictional aspect of the controversy.[10]

The Calvo Doctrine was illustrated to its fullest extent by a clause of the Grell concessions, assigned to the Orinoco Shipping and Trading Company, which read as follows:

Disputes and controversies which may arise with regard to the interpretation or execution of this contract shall be resolved by the tribunals of the republic in accordance with the laws of the nation, and shall not in any case be considered as a motive for international reclamations.[11]

We may consider two questions: Do these clauses in themselves establish as beyond controversy the right of the local courts to pass finally and conclusively upon all questions which may arise under the contract? And is an appeal to an international tribunal under any circumstances permissible? The governments of concessionaries have been very slow to admit the absolute and complete right of the defendant governments to require under all circumstances submission of the controversy to the local courts. They have claimed the right, superior to that of the citizen, to protect his interest even despite his own prior action. Nevertheless certain principles appear obvious even though they have been the subject of considerable debate. The first is that under a

---

[8] *Proceedings, Society for the Judicial Settlement of International Disputes,* 1916, 150.

[9] *Ibid.,* 1916, 98.

[10] For a review in detail of the controversies about the so-called Calvo Clause, see *Law and Procedure of International Tribunals,* 58–72.

[11] *Ibid.,* 59.

clause of the concession it is ordinarily the duty of the concessionary to apply to the courts of the nation granting this concession for such relief as he may think appropriate. Next it seems equally obvious that, provided the courts are in a position to render ordinary justice, it is only upon an application on the ground of denial of jurisdiction or gross injustice or some other violation of international law that the clear right exists, despite the Calvo Clause, of appeal to the home government for diplomatic assistance. The Calvo Clause will not bar responsibility therefore for what would otherwise be a ground for diplomatic and subsequent arbitral action.

Appeal to arbitral tribunals may further be made when the arbitral agreement provides for the settlement of all controversies between the nationals of one nation against the government of another. A provision of this kind has been held to supersede the powers of the national courts and to control, despite the wording of any concession placing apparently unlimited powers in national courts.

Other questions have arisen where the defendant country has undertaken by executive decree to declare null and void or set aside a concession once entered into, and cases of this nature have been held entirely proper to be passed upon in the first instance and relief granted by international tribunals. They have been regarded, not as instances of dispute or controversies "with regard to the interpretation or execution of the contract," but as creating an independent substantive offense clearly coming within the jurisdiction of the later tribunal, without any necessity of appeal to the national courts.

An unusual case arose before the United States and Chilean Commission under the Convention of 1892, in that of the North and South American Construction Company against Chile. The contract provided for the appointment of a board of arbitration to settle all disputes as to the interpretation and execution of the contract. Subsequently Chile suppressed the tribunal of arbitration, and the majority of the commission held that by suppression the memorialist had recovered "its entire right to invoke or accept the mediation or protection of the government of the United States," although by another clause of the agreement it had been provided that in all matters and things relating to the contract the Company was to be treated as a citizen of Chile, and that in relation to such matters and things it would neither invoke nor accept the mediation or protection of the United States.[12]

---

[12] *Law and Procedure of International Tribunals*, 63.

43. Decisions of prize courts.—Broadly speaking arbitral courts have no power over decisions made by local tribunals, there being no such thing as an appeal in the usual sense of the term from the local to an arbitral court. Nevertheless, directly and indirectly, that is to say, by special power given to arbitral courts or by their interpretation of their own jurisdiction, the judgments of local courts have been called into play and in effect reversed or confirmed by arbitral tribunal. This we shall find illustrated in prize and other decisions.

A prize court is a local court in the sense that it operates within the jurisdiction of a nation. In a larger sense a court of prize is a court presumably instituted to enforce the dictates of international law. We have pointed out in an earlier chapter that international law, as affecting the rights of neutrals, dealt with in prize courts, is not true law, being founded upon the power of the belligerents to enforce their will *nolens volens* upon a more or less morally innocent neutral. Nevertheless, such as it is and with all its imperfections on its head, it is the duty of a prize court, if it can discover the meaning of this pseudo-international law or create a meaning for it in this regard, to administer such law. Thus the tribunal becomes, at least in a conventional sense, a court of international law. When, therefore, its decisions are called into play in an international tribunal and are there reviewed, it is but the passing upon a question of international law by the last tribunal having any jurisdiction over the subject, and the conclusion of the prize court becomes in effect merely an opinion and not a final judgment, and as such it is subject to reversal.

In addition it often is the case that decisions are pronounced in prize courts in the absence of the parties beneficially concerned, this because of their residence within one of the belligerent nations or for other adequate reason. In such event the judgment of the prize court becomes merely a judgment *in rem*. As a judgment *in rem* it is sufficiently valid to carry with it the title to the thing (the vessel or cargo which is before the court for adjudication) and therefore convey to a purchaser through its decree a complete and unqualified ownership in the thing bought by him. Nevertheless the parties in interest, not being before the court, are not to be considered as in anywise bound by the decision; and they may therefore, if they can, obtain a reversal of the findings of the local court sitting as a prize court without touching the title to the vessel or cargo, but condemning the defendant government to repay them the value of the property lost through invalid judicial proceedings.

It was upon reasoning such as we have outlined (except so far as our remarks are concerned affecting the integrity of prize law as a branch of international law) that the American commissioners under the Seventh Article of the Jay Treaty of 1794 maintained the invalidity in that commission of the findings of the British prize courts, and their contentions were sustained by the umpire. Since then no material doubt has remained with regard to the general thesis that a prize court is a court of international law, and that its findings offer questions of international law coming fairly within the powers of an arbitral tribunal to review. This was the holding of the Anglo-American Commission of 1853 as well as of a like commission in 1871, the latter commission in a number of instances reversing the findings of the Supreme Court of the United States.[18]

44. Review of the action of local tribunals in other cases.—We have had occasion to refer to the fact that an appeal to an international tribunal from the decisions of national courts is always allowable, even in cases involving the Calvo Clause, whenever there has been a denial of justice or notorious injustice. The international tribunal will pass upon the question as to whether these conditions exist. This has been often illustrated. A peculiarity of the White case between England and Peru, is that the senate of Hamburg recognized the fact that rules of procedure followed by the courts in any country were to be judged solely and alone according to the legislation in force there, and no fault was to be found with the proceedings under review since they were fully justified according to Peruvian procedure. In this particular case mere existence of circumstances of hardship were held not to justify a finding against the defendant country.

45. Necessity of appeal to local courts.—We have had occasion to note the fact that over certain classes of cases the jurisdiction of local courts is absolute, except at any rate where there is denial of justice or notorious injustice. In many classes of cases[14] it has also been held that an appeal should be made to the local court and carried to the

---

[18] *Law and Procedure of International Tribunals,* 114. In cases of this description it has been generally held that where it was possible for the neutral to enter an appeal from the findings of the prize court it was his duty to prosecute such to the highest court of the country seizing the property so that there might be shown before the arbitral tribunal an exhaustion of legal remedies before the complaint was brought to it. Various circumstances, however, have been held to excuse the want of such an appeal (*ibid.,* 112–13).

[14] It is to be noted that when the complaint is against governmental action, as distinguished from that of individuals, no question of exhaustion of legal remedies arises. *Law and Procedure of International Tribunals,* 95.

highest possible court before any action should be asked from an international tribunal.

This is not, however, ordinarily the rule before arbitral tribunals, which are intended to take their place in cases where but for their existence the local court would possess full power. Even where appeal to local courts would otherwise have been regarded as essential it has been held to be avoided by various circumstances, as for instance the fact that because wrongdoers had been given special judicial authority an appeal to them would be entirely unavailing.

CHAPTER VI

PARTIES

46. Nation or individual as party.—In a broad and important sense the parties to a proceeding before an international tribunal are the governments in dispute. This is obvious enough when the dispute relates to some matter directly affecting sovereign jurisdiction or matters which may be regarded as touching the operations of government. Naturally this is the case in all territorial disputes or questions of diplomatic privilege and the like. It exists likewise when the property of the individual is affected. In the view of the sovereign, treating the matter from the international point of view, whatever affects the citizen affects the power over him, as constituting a possible though shadowy infringement upon the sovereign's authority, and thereby lessening the importance of the nation. Hence it is that even without any express authorization from the citizen the nation may, or claims the right to, act through the government *sua sponte*.

Of course as Stoykovich points out

It is by virtue of a fiction that one considers the injustice done to an individual as in reality an injustice done to the state to which he is subject. The intervention of the state gives to a claim which had in its origin a judicial character, a political shade, introducing in the affair the notion of national interest and honor.[1]

47. Control of nation over grievance of national.—Internationally the nation assumes the right to barter away the rights of its subject or enforce them or change the forum of enforcement in any way pleasing to it. Thus the nation may, as in the case of the *Alabama* claims, agree with another for the establishment of a tribunal determining the primary question of right or wrong and broad questions of damage. It may, as in that case, the first points being settled, create another court determining the share of each individual in the award, and, as in other cases, actually diminishing the amount that in right he should have received.[2]

Without consulting with the parties really in interest, it is within the power of the government, and it therefore assumes as its right, to

[1] *De l'autorité de la sentence arbitrale,* 27.

[2] The action of the state depends often upon considerations of a political order, and if his government refuses to act, the individual is without any recourse. The clear right of the individual can be thus sacrificed for political reasons and reasons of convenience (Stoykovitch, *De l'autorité de la sentence arbitrale,* 28).

create rules for the settlement of claims of its nationals which can be unjust to the individual. Whatever may be the rule thus created, if embodied in a *compromis* it is the duty of the tribunal to accept and follow it.

Sometimes the nation or state in its representative capacity speaks for a great but indefinite number of its citizens. This may be illustrated by the case of Missouri *vs*. Illinois as cited by Judge Taft, he saying that under the circumstances of the case the right to sue

treats Missouri as the parent of her people, and as entitled to represent them. This is departing from the technical idea of representation. Missouri is not a trustee in the property sense, but in view of the fact that it is international jurisdiction which the court is exercising, it permits the state to assume that relation toward her citizens.[3]

48. Right of national before an international tribunal.—When the nation creates with another an international tribunal for the purpose of passing upon the claims of its nationals against that other, the individual wronged has not therefore the right to appear and be heard. He may only appear in the name of his nation, and, as far as permitted by it, ordinarily acts through its agent, who files his memorial in the name of the nation. The agent has the right at any time to dismiss the claim or to compromise with regard to it. This is consistent with the fact that it is the nation which acts and not the individual.

Because the nation espouses the claim of its national it does not follow that the tribunal will take or retain jurisdiction over it. It will be recognized that the national rather than the nation is the ultimate beneficiary, and hence arise many questions of citizenship and of interest in the subject-matter. Conflicts of law relative to citizenship are frequent. Disputes arise over the transfer of ownership from the citizens of one country to those of another. These matters are all within the jurisdiction of an international tribunal to determine, but it is foreign to the purposes of this book to follow up or discuss them.

An exception to the rules we have been indicating may be found to have existed in the Central American Court of Justice which under Article 2 of the Treaty of Washington creating it had jurisdiction to hear and determine questions which an individual of one of the nations might raise against another nation because of violation of treaties and in other cases of an international character, whether or not supported by his own government, provided he had exhausted remedies afforded

[3] *Proceedings, Society for the Judicial Settlement of International Disputes,* 1916, 100.

by the laws of that country for such a violation or under claim that justice had been denied.

It remains substantially true as stated by Sir John F. Williams that

An individual cannot "violate International Law." All he can do is (a) to violate the law of his own State by doing something which is a contravention of that provision (if any) of the municipal law of the State which enjoins individual conduct in harmony with the rules of International Law; or (b) so to behave that he involves his State in responsibility for his acts, and thus makes it in its turn and on its own behalf violate International Law. In the former case, he is justiciable by the Courts of his own country; in the latter, not he, but his State, is amenable to such sanctions as International Law may impose—and the sanctions of International Law are more readily applicable to violation of the law of peace than to violation of the law of war.[4]

49. Intervention of other interested parties.—Not alone the original parties in interest in a dispute but also in certain cases other parties claiming an interest may be heard before the tribunal.

The rules of the Permanent Court of International Justice provide that application for intervention must be communicated to the registrar at the latest before the commencement of the oral proceedings, though the court may in exceptional circumstances consider an application submitted at a later stage. The application specifies the case, a statement of law and fact justifying intervention and documents in support. By the Statute (Article 62) controlling the court, any state considering that it has an interest of a legal nature which may be affected by the decision may submit a request to intervene as a third party; and by Article 63, when the construction of a convention to which states other than those concerned in the case are parties, is in question, the registrar shall notify such states forthwith, but the intervening state is bound by the judgment.

It was pursuant to the foregoing provisions that the Hague Permanent Court of International Justice allowed the intervention of Poland in the *Wimbledon* case.

When, however, Russia, not a party to the Covenant of the League of Nations, refused to submit to the jurisdiction of the court in the matter of the Eastern Carelia dispute, the court refused its advisory opinion in the matter as the parties in interest would not be bound. The position of the Central American Court of Justice was not governed by the same rule as to the interpretation of a treaty to which the United States was a party, probably on the theory that the rights to be passed

---

[4] *Report, Thirty-third Conference of the International Law Association,* 445.

upon antedated the rise of the interests of the United States, and this nation took a position subject to the former situation.

Article 84 of the Hague Convention of 1907 provides that

When it concerns the interpretation of a convention to which parties other than those in dispute are parties, they shall inform all the signatory powers in good time. Each of these powers is entitled to intervene in the case. If one or more avail themselves of this right, the interpretation contained in the award is equally binding on them.

CHAPTER VII

PLEADINGS, PROCEDURE, AND EVIDENCE

50. Preliminary observations.—It will be well to distinguish between certain varieties of international commissions and tribunals. We may first consider those in which the governments are distinctly the parties most concerned. In a number of these cases there is difficulty in determining which party, if either, is to be considered plaintiff and which defendant, the governments being joint claimants to the subject-matter in dispute and each seeking the recovery of something which may be regarded as of political interest. Illustrations of what we have in mind are afforded by the Alaska Boundary convention, the Northeastern Boundary dispute and a number of other cases largely relating to territorial limits. As touching the difficulty of settling which may be regarded as plaintiff and which defendant, we refer to the Venezuelan Preferential case at The Hague, wherein the question was evaded by allowing the several parties in interest to present and discuss their respective propositions in alphabetical order. In disputes of the general character of those we are now discussing, it is ordinarily provided in the *compromis* that the "case," as it is termed (the meaning of which we shall discuss later) shall be served by either party upon the other within the same limit of time, with a similar provision as to the counter-case and any subsequent pleadings.

There are, of course, certain other classes of commissions as to which governments ought to be regarded as the prime and most important factors although private interests are at the bottom of the dispute. Illustrations of what we have in mind are afforded by the Geneva Tribunal determining the *Alabama* case and the Atlantic Fisheries case. In these and in like instances, so great a number of its nationals are affected by one common principle that the government is justified in regarding the controversy as peculiarly its own.

Again there may be cases like those of the Pious Fund of the Californias and the Orinoco Shipping Company, decided at The Hague, in which the amount or principle involved may be regarded by the government as important, and therefore the proceedings are entirely between the governments; and the individual claimant receives only incidental attention, notwithstanding the private origin of the case, retaining his interest in the results. In all of the foregoing instances, the cases are peculiarly governmental.

By way of contrast to the illustrations we have given we may distinguish those where the government, although acting ordinarily in its own name, proceeds for the separate benefit of a large number of individual claimants, who present their several complaints in the manner hereinafter indicated and who are the ultimate beneficiaries of possible awards.

51. Challenge.—We may consider, as properly coming either before the meeting of the court or at the time of its convening, the matter of challenge of a member of the court. This subject, while it has received little attention, is nevertheless one of potential importance if it be considered that a tribunal should be not only just but recognized as just by the parties at issue. The Hague Conventions are silent upon the point, and therefore under them an arbitrator may be named by one of the parties who is under broad suspicion of unfairness, personal prejudice, or being interested in the subject-matter. By the convention establishing the Central American Court of Justice, this point was amply covered. Again in the General Arbitration Treaty between Bolivia and Brazil it was met by a provision that "each of the high contracting parties shall propose an arbitrator whose nomination shall become definitive only with the consent of the other."[1] These agree upon the third man. A similar provision is contained in the general arbitration treaty between Brazil and Peru.[2]

The Central American Treaty of Arbitration of 1923 provides for challenge of arbitrators for named causes and of the umpire absolutely as to the two who may be the first so appointed.

It is remarked by Bustamante that as to the Statute under which the Hague Court of International Justice was formed,

the proposal that it should be possible for a litigant to challenge one of the judges was the subject of considerable discussion; it was not adopted, and the provision for national judges is in a way a substitute for it. Nevertheless the Statute provides, in Article 24, that if one of the judges considers that for some special reason he should not take part in the discussion of a particular case, he is to inform the president of the fact; or if the president considers that for some special reason a judge should not sit, he is to give him notice accordingly. If the president and the judge do not agree, the question is to be settled by the court.[3]

This does not cover, of course, all the reasons for which a right of challenge should exist in the ordinary arbitral tribunal. The Statute

[1] Manning, *Arbitration Treaties,* 443.
[2] *Ibid.,* 451.   [3] *The World Court,* 222.

rather looks forward to the formation of a court on which both parties should be represented, a condition not at all in accord with the concept we have of courts like unto those within a state. In a discussion of the subject-matter by Malauzat he says:

> It would have been the reasonable thing to exclude them [the representatives of the parties on the court] or at least to give each party the right to challenge the judge of the adverse party without risking an infringement upon the free choice of judges by the parties, since the parties would voluntarily carry their disputes before a court where they could not have representatives.[4]

Perhaps it would be more correct to say that the parties should be willing to carry their disputes before a court upon which they have no representative. In point of fact the parties have been usually unduly solicitous to have a representative among the judges on the court, a condition which has brought much evil to the cause of international arbitration.

52. Case, counter-case, and memorial or other pleadings.—In all instances where the government acts peculiarly in its own interest or under the very special circumstances we have above illustrated, the contentions of the government are presented by means of a "case." The case, as it is termed, is a statement devoid of technical form, developing in a narrative way the claims of either country with reference to the subject-matter of dispute, and either in its body or by way of annexes setting forth all documentary proof upon which reliance is placed. This is not under oath, the good faith of the government being a sufficient voucher as to the truth of the matters presented by it. The Continental practice appears to favor the presentation of the argument along with the development of the facts; but the American practice, which seems to be more clear-cut, makes an absolute distinction between the development of the facts in the case and the development of the law or argument in the brief. The latter is not usually presented until the court meets, although the protocol may provide for an earlier exchange of briefs or argument.

The rules of the Permanent Court of International Justice at The Hague provide as follows as to what the case shall contain: (1) a statement of the facts on which the claim is based; (2) a statement of law; (3) a statement of conclusions; (4) a list of the documents in support; these documents shall be attached to the case. By the conclusions we are to understand a statement of the relief sought to be

---

[4] *Cour de justice arbitrale,* 102.

obtained. This sometimes becomes a matter of importance; for instance, the Central American Court of Justice found in one case that its jurisdiction was limited to the granting of the relief prayed for and it would give none other.[5]

As stated, in those cases where it is doubtful whether one side or the other may be classed as plaintiff or defendant the case is usually served on either side within the same fixed limit of time. The parties are, therefore, under the disadvantage of not knowing until the cases are exchanged what the contentions of the opponent may be, and can, therefore, only meet them directly by means of the next step in the proceedings, which is the counter-case. The observations already made with reference to form and effect of the case may be repeated. We add, however, that according to the rule of the Permanent Court of International Justice

the counter-case shall contain: (1) the affirmation or contestation of the facts stated in the case; (2) a statement of additional facts, if any; (3) a statement of law; (4) conclusions based on the facts stated; these conclusions may

---

[5] *American Journal of International Law*, XI, 729.

According to the practice of the United States, at least in recent years, the case and counter-case are to be regarded more or less as true pleadings, although expanded so as to give a complete, though succinct, statement of the facts relied on to establish the various contentions of the respective parties. The case states the facts as persuasively as possible, ordinarily in narrative form, points out the conclusions which it is conceived should be drawn from these facts, and is accompanied by documentary evidence which is relied upon to support the facts therein related, by way of appendix. The counter-case performs a similar function as regards the facts relied upon in answer to the case of the other party. But when, as in perhaps the majority of instances, case and counter-case are to be followed with either written or oral argument, or perhaps by both, it has not been the American practice to argue, or even to any considerable extent to marshal, the law or the facts in the case or counter-case.

Continental and Latin-American practice, in which even the British occasionally join, is otherwise. The case and counter-case are made use of for argument as well as statement. The Continental method has the practical advantage when opposed to the American method that under it the members of the tribunal take their places upon the bench fully acquainted with the strength of the side employing it while the strength of the other side is as yet undeveloped. In other words, the Continental method secures the first favorable impression with the tribunal, which, as everyone knows, may be lasting. On the other hand, it has the practical disadvantage at all times, that it is likely to result in the wasting of a great deal of ammunition in establishing contentions which are conceded and attacking positions which are undefended, and may result in compelling those who follow it to change their position during the course of the argument. It is submitted that the American method is more in accordance with the provisions of the protocol when these call for a case, counter-case, and argument, and is more conducive to a logical and orderly presentation of the questions at issue. (Speech of William Cullen Dennis, *Proceedings, Society for the Judicial Settlement of International Disputes*, 1912, 166–67.)

include counter-claims, in so far as the latter come within the jurisdiction of the court; (5) a list of the documents in support; these documents shall be attached to the counter-case.

What we have said as to the time of service of case and counter-case is, of course, modified when there is a party naturally plaintiff or defendant, as for instance was the United States in the Pious Fund case, when the order of service of pleadings followed in the sequence naturally appropriate to ordinary judicial proceedings.

The case, and sometimes also the brief or argument, is served within the specified time upon the foreign office of the opposing party, although a different method of service may be provided for. After proceedings are once under way, service may be had upon the subsequently appointed agent.

Before the Hague Court of International Justice when proceedings are instituted by means of an application, in the absence of a contrary agreement the documents are: the case by the applicant; counter-case by the respondent; reply by the applicant; and rejoinder by the respondent.

It must not be overlooked that the only documents in the way of pleadings receivable by the court, except motions and other incidental matters, are those particularly provided for in the *compromis*.

We have next to note certain differences in situation between that prevailing when the government as a political power speaks and when there are private individuals interested who to a greater or lesser extent speak for themselves. In the latter event the claimant, using the name of the government and acting under its aegis, prepares a memorial setting forth the grounds of his claim and the relief asked, which memorial with the consent and approval of the agent of the government is submitted to the tribunal. To this memorial the opposing government through its agent submits such reply or other pleading as may seem to it appropriate.

The general remark may be made that in all instances the relief ultimately granted must be that asked for in either case or memorial.

Of course other pleadings and motions may be found appropriate to the circumstances of the particular case. Among these may be, in addition to case and counter case, memorial and answer, replications (when permitted by the *compromis*) and pleas, such as those of prescription, motions to dismiss, demurrers or exceptions, pleas to the jurisdiction, etc.

53. Agent and counsel.—Before international tribunals the government is represented by an agent and generally in no other way. The agent may sign the original case, although frequently he does not appear until case and counter-case have been exchanged between foreign offices. When he is appointed the management and direction of the affair rests in his hands. According to the language of the Hague Conventions it is the right of the parties to appoint agents to "attend the tribunal to act as intermediary between themselves and the tribunal." They are further authorized to present and support claims before the tribunal and to make all necessary answers or explanations. Sometimes their powers are set forth quite at length in the protocol under which they are appointed.

Undoubtedly so far as the management is concerned, the counsel are of lesser importance than the agent, and act under the direction of the latter. As their name indicates they render such advice as they may outside of court and present the argument within the tribunal.

We should not, however, fail to observe the distinction in powers before the court sometimes made between agent and counsel. Bokanowski, speaking of international commissions of inquiry, says that

> It would be unhappy to give the counsel a situation subordinate to the agents. The former are the procureurs of governments, the latter are the attorneys. The first are the defenders of the special cause in litigation; they question the witnesses and address the court. The agents [attorneys] watch over the maintenance of the *compromis* and the regulation of the procedure; they represent the public interests of states in the suit. The political competence of the one and the judicial competence of the others, exclude all interference. To the diplomats one confides the rôle of agent and to jurisconsults in international law that of counsel.[6]

Some color is given to the view of Bokanowski by proceedings before the Fur Seal Arbitration, the president of which said, "We will not recognize the agents as arguing the matter. We recognize them as representing the government. Counsel will argue the matter and we will dispose of it." Nevertheless, if the agent be the intermediary between parties and the court as stated by the Hague Conventions, it is very difficult to find cause for limiting or diminishing his power before the tribunal.

54. Rules of procedure.—Like all other courts international tribunals possess the inherent right to establish rules governing pleadings and proceedings before them. Naturally these rules must themselves be subordinate to the provisions of the *compromis* and cannot by any scheme of interpretation extend or modify its provisions. While

---

[6] *Les commissions internationales d'enquête,* 98.

the power to make rules is inherent, nevertheless many protocols have expressly conferred upon the tribunal the power of establishing them. This is true even under the Hague Convention of 1907, although itself containing many articles controlling procedure in the absence of provisions in the *compromis*. Article 74 of this Convention declares that

The tribunal is entitled to issue rules of procedure for the conduct of the case, to decide the forms, order, and time in which each party must conclude its arguments, and to arrange all the formalities required for dealing with the evidence.

Article 30 of the Statute governing the Hague Permanent Court of International Justice provides: "The court shall frame rules for regulating its procedure. In particular, it shall lay down rules for summary procedure." These rules at great length cover the workings of the court and the duties of ordinary judges and of the Registrar, as well as govern pleadings and proceedings before the Court, providing also for petitions of intervention and the form of the judgment, applications for revision, summary and advisory procedure, and the power of the Court to correct errors from slips or accidental omissions.

The rules of mixed commissions have included among other things the time and place of hearings, form of dockets and records, filing and docketing of claims, pleadings, including memorial, answer, reply, and amendments to pleadings, printing and copies of pleadings, notices to parties, motions to dismiss or reject, taking of written and oral testimony, hearings, awards, duties of the secretary, computation of time, amendments to rules, and silence of rules. While the establishment of rules is important and necessary, care nevertheless has to be taken that justice is not defeated because of a rule the existence of which is intended to further justice.

55. Memorial and answer.—We have referred to the fact that before mixed commissions the claims of individuals particularly are usually presented by means of what is called a memorial. This is usually required to be drawn in accordance with forms prescribed by the rules, although often it is received in very informal shape. It should be under oath and is usually required to be. If, however, it is rejected for informality, such rejection is without prejudice and permission is given to present a more formal document.

Of course the memorial should contain a recital of such facts as may serve to indicate clearly that the court has jurisdiction over the case, this observation referring particularly to allegations with regard to citizenship as well as anything else bringing the claim within the purview of the *compromis*. It must specify the relief sought.

The memorial is properly presented by and under the authority of the agent of the government, although signed and sworn to by the claimant or his authorized representative.

The response to the memorial may come in the shape of an answer, plea, motion to dismiss, or exception. In the informal practice of some commissions the defendant nation is considered in the absence of other pleadings to have entered a general denial.

56. Language.—The *compromis* may itself determine what should be the language of the tribunal or it may confer power upon the tribunal itself to fix the language. The protocol in the case of the Pious Fund of the Californias was silent upon this point and the judges presiding afterwards commented upon the circumstance as one to be thereafter settled by the *compromis*. In accordance with this suggestion the treaty covering the Venezuelan Preferential case provided that the proceedings should be carried on in English, but arguments might be permitted to be made in any other language. In the Pious Fund case, however, the tribunal, while directing the minutes to be kept in French, permitted the use of French and English before it. The court determining the Venezuelan Preferential case allowed the protocols of the proceedings, decisions, and sentence to be drawn up in English and French, the oral discussion to be in either of these languages, and written and printed matter to be in English and accompanied by translation in the language of the power by which they were filed. This the court declared to mean that the English language was recognized as the official language and French as subsidiary.

In the Japanese House Tax case before a tribunal of The Hague, French was recognized as its language with a right to present any communications in French or English. In the Muscat case, French was determined to be the language of the tribunal although in argument French and English were both allowed. In the Cerruti case, heard at Rome, by the protocol documents were put in evidence in Italian, Spanish, and French, and Italian and French were employed in the oral discussion. French was the language of the Timor arbitration between Portugal and the Netherlands and of that relative to seized property between Portugal and Great Britain, Spain and France. French and English are the languages of the Hague Permanent Court of International Justice, "but the court may at the request of the parties authorize another language to be used. The Court has permitted coun-

sel to address it in a language other than English or French."[7] At the
Geneva Arbitration the languages of the arbitrators, other than
the English and American, were Italian, Portuguese, and German,
although the Italian Count Sclopis spoke and wrote English and the
Swiss Mr. Staempfli read it. However, all the arbitrators knowing
French well, this language was admitted, and we had the curious sight
of a tribunal employing a language which was not that of any of its
members.

57. Evidence.—When the common law lawyer enters the field of
practice before an international tribunal he finds that his trial training
means very little. The case of the civil law practitioner is quite different and he is much more at his ease, having less to unlearn, for such
rules of evidence as have any existence are derived from the civil law.
In a general way it may be said that the objections to evidence which
constitute a large part of the work of the trial of cases at common law
resolve themselves into objections, not to the form of evidence at all,
but solely to its weight, which is passed upon by the court, practically
everything being receivable. Thus we find hearsay evidence presented
and unsworn documents of various kinds and even unproven scraps of
paper and papers the signatures to which are not established. Of course
these general observations are modified in particular cases by the provisions of the *compromis* or by the rules established by the tribunal
itself.

To begin with, the papers attached to the case and counter-case go
on the faith of the governments presenting them. Under the general
rule that the commission is to consider all that may be submitted to it
by the respective governments no other principle could be adopted. This
is not to say that they are to be given an improper weight and may not
be opposed by countervailing evidence, but until so opposed they receive
full and proper credence as to authenticity.

Of course an unsworn paper will not receive the same attention
granted to an affidavit or deposition, and in many tribunals an affidavit
taken without notice to the adversary party has even been suppressed
from consideration, though as to this the practice has not been uniform.

Guided by the ideas above expressed, there have been received in
evidence letters, current price lists, consular certificates, ex parte affi-
davits, proclamations, telegrams, printed volumes giving accounts of
proceedings touching the matters in issue, receipts, maps, etc.[8]

---

[7] Moore, *International Law*, chap. iv., 112.
[8] *Law and Procedure of International Tribunals*, 215.

Usually the tribunal has confined itself to the consideration of written evidence, but on rare occasions the witnesses have been produced in person. There usually seems no reason why this should not be done except for limitations in the *compromis,* for if a deposition is receivable surely the man himself may be produced.

Judgments of a national tribunal have been received in evidence, not as conclusive of the law and the facts but for their evidential value, when their findings were sufficiently clear.

Commissions have been very positive in refusing awards upon the sole testimony of the interested parties, the only exception being when the countervailing proof was in the possession of the defendant nation and not produced.

Frequently the various cases of claims have been treated as one with regard to the use of evidence, that given in one being referred to in another before the same body.

Secondary evidence has been received when the destruction of the original has been proved.

When objections to the presentation of evidence have been made on the ground of interest or relationship, under local law such objections being well-founded, the commission has refused to regard them, considering such objections to be of too technical a nature to deserve consideration in an international tribunal.

Where the umpire sits on appeal from differences between the commissioners he may not hear evidence not submitted first to the commissioners.

58. Presumptions arising from the evidence.—As in the case of local courts, so in international commissions certain presumptions may arise from evidence. There is, for instance, one as to the regularity and necessity of governmental acts and that the conduct of the government will not be reckless and careless. This is nothing more than a presumption of innocence till the contrary be shown. It is also to be presumed that public officers perform their official duty and act in accordance with law. These and other presumptions may be rebutted by proof of the actual facts. In one case the umpire found it necessary to say that he could indulge in no presumption lowering to either of the governments in dispute and was bound to presume equality of position and equality of right.

We have already alluded to the presumption arising from the fact that the party possessing evidence fails to produce it.

Presumptions of payment may arise in favor of the government and against a claimant who delays too long in the presentation of his claim, though, once presented, no mere lapse of time will excuse its non-payment. Many questions have arisen as to the sufficiency of the presentation, but we may say generally that when the government is through its official head once put on notice of the non-payment its responsibility in this respect is complete.

As to other points of evidence, we refer to *Law and Procedure of International Tribunals*.

CHAPTER VIII

INTERIOR LAW OF INTERNATIONAL TRIBUNALS

59. Common and civil law in international tribunals.—It has often been argued that great difficulty would be experienced within commissions between nations governed by various systems of law because of contradictions and confusions which might arise between them. For instance, it has been assumed that because the civil and the common law have had different origins it would, therefore, prove impossible that a tribunal settling differences between countries under the two systems could reach conclusions which would be acceptable to both. This belief has no foundation in practice. We will note in the beginning as we have stated elsewhere, that nearly all the so-called international questions are simply national questions viewed from another standpoint and offer comparatively little that is novel to the experienced lawyer. Nor are the differences between Roman and common law so wide, where they exist at all, as to be unbridgeable. The remark of Judge Riddell has great substance:

> I am perfectly safe in saying that in nine hundred and ninety-nine cases out of a thousand the decisions, based upon principles—outside of the limit of petty technicalities—will be precisely the same whether you take the principles from Justinian, or whether you take the principles from Blackstone. There is no great difference between the laws of the civilized nations if you leave aside the accidents.[1]

As to the effect produced by bringing together judges trained under different systems, we quote the opinion of Dr. Hammarskjöld, Registrar of the Permanent Court of International Justice:

> One thing is certain, namely, that the shock which does take place between opinions based on different systems and on different legal training is the source of a great completeness of consideration and a guaranty for the all-sided and impartial character of the final decision or opinion. Of course, this situation may lead to difficulties. It is obvious that it is far easier to agree between people who, by reason of their very education and their very origin, are likely to hold the same views; but if this Court were to be composed in a manner offering such facilities, it would be immensely impoverished as compared with what it is today. ("Sidelights on the Permanent Court of International Justice," *Michigan Law Review,* XXV, 327.)

60. Points of division.—Experience shows that there are not more than three points as to which the two great systems of law

---

[1] *Proceedings, Society for Judicial Settlement of International Disputes,* 1910, 309.

materially differ. The first of these is as to the manner in which proof is made. Owing largely to the jury system, the common law has evolved an intricate and often cumbersome theory of evidence. This is, of course, often departed from in equity practice. By contrast to this, we find a much more simple and direct system pertaining to the civil law and yet a system which is under similar conditions quite as likely to bring about a just decision. In the matter of evidence the civil law in international tribunals has already triumphed over the common law, technicalities of the latter being quite universally rejected, and the result of this has been on the whole to further the ends of justice.

Another point of division not however universal between the two systems, is with regard to the law of descent and particularly with reference to the question as to whether or not the law of the place where an inheritance is situated or the law of the country of citizenship of its owner shall prevail. Under the common law system, the law of the locality prevails, while under civil systems the rule is by no means uniform. This becomes of some moment occasionally in public international tribunals as well as in the realm of private international law, and yet it does not offer a question of first-class importance. Very naturally the tendency of umpires of English or American extraction has been to follow the practice of jurisdictions with which they were most familiar, and probably the like tendency prevails with civil law arbitrators. Assuming this, however, the result arising from the different conclusions reached by umpires will not be more important than that which arises from the different decisions of the highest tribunals of the civil courts of the United States.

A third point upon which different rules of law prevail as between nations relates to citizenship. The observation just made with regard to differences of practices among umpires will undoubtedly hold good in this regard. There will be a greater tendency on the part of English and American arbitrators to give preference to the law of the domicile as determining citizenship, whereas the usual continental European inclination will be to give greater weight to the law of the nationality of the persons concerned.

61. Stare decisis.—The doctrine of *stare decisis,* as is well known, leads the English or American judge to adhere to the principles of a decision once laid down, with the idea thereby of giving stability to the law. On the contrary the idea of the Continental jurist is that each case should be decided of itself and without reference to what the court may have done in other instances. This difference between the Continental system and the common law system, however, is more apparent than real; and to a much greater extent than he usually acknowledges the civil law judge does aim to adhere to the prior decisions of controlling courts. The fact that he does this through the intermediation of law writers does not affect the substance of the situation. However, treating the subject internationally, many arbitral tribunals have decided expressly that they did not consider themselves bound by the prior decisions of other arbitrators and have acted accordingly; nor are they bound, as they have repeatedly declared, by their own decisions. Neither is one umpire of a commission bound by the decisions of his predecessor in the same commission. This is on the theory that each separate commissioner or umpire has for himself taken his oath to adjust the matters in controversy according to his own conscience and not according to that of another man. Notwithstanding the foregoing, the arbitrators have frequently referred for their rules of action to the decisions of prior international tribunals.

"The fact, moreover," says Judge Moore, "is to be observed that a certain weight is given to judicial decisions, and a certain law-establishing force, whether the principle of *stare decisis* be or be not accepted as an obligatory rule. Students of jurisprudence know that the difference is not so great as is commonly supposed."[2]

The tendency of Continental jurists to adhere to theory (despite the reality for the most part of a contrary practice) is shown by the *Annuaire de l'Institut de droit international,* it appearing that only the minority of the commission considering the subject thought that an interpretation once given a treaty should be adhered to in future cases.[3]

62. Local laws.—It is frequently a matter of importance in commissions to determine to what extent, if at all, they are controlled by the local laws of the countries in dispute. Undoubtedly certain local laws have no place whatever in international tribunals. It has been decided, for instance, with regard to local laws of prescription that they relate exclusively to the domain of the civil law and cannot be applied to an international dispute.[4] Nevertheless the fundamental idea of prescription has received repeated application before international tribunals, and this has been given without any reference to national laws upon the subject. In other words, the international tribunal has determined whether under all circumstances of the case the great principles of

---

[2] *International Law,* 118.

[3] *Annuaire,* etc., 1897, 115.

[4] Pious Fund case; see *Law and Procedure of International Tribunals,* 375.

repose and the theory of laches, to both of which prescription bears true relation, should under all the circumstances of the particular case be invoked. This is true, notwithstanding the language in the Alsop Case stating too broadly that "as against or between sovereign states this rule does not apply." The rules followed upon this particular subject are excellently summed up in a report to the Institute of International Law made at The Hague in August, 1925:

GENERAL RULES IN THE MATTER OF LIMITATIONS OF ACTIONS
IN INTERNATIONAL RELATIONS

I. Practical considerations of order, of stability and of peace, long accepted in arbitral jurisprudence, should include the limitations of actions for obligations between states among the general principles of law recognized by civilized nations, which international tribunals are called upon to apply.

II. In the absence of a conventional rule in force in the relations of the litigant states, fixing the limit of the prescription, its determination is a question left entirely to the decision of the international judge, who, in order to admit the plea based on the lapse of time, should recognize in the circumstances of the case the existence of one of the reasons which impose the prescription.

III. Among the elements to be taken into consideration by the international judge, are the following:

a) The public or private origin and the contractual or tortious character of the debt which forms the object of the litigation. As a general rule it is more difficult to admit prescription for public debts than for debts of a private origin, for contractual debts than for tortious debts;

b) Whether the delay in the claim applies to the original presentation or simply to its renewal, as prescription ought to be excluded in the second hypothesis except if it is established as a fact that the subsequent inaction of the claimant state is not imputable to the adverse party or to a case of *force majeure*.

IV. The prescription of a debt of private origin, in conformity with competent internal law, renders inadmissible the international claim, unless the grounds of this prescription itself can be put in issue according to the rules of international law.

V. The international judge can not apply prescription unless it is pleaded.[5]

So also international tribunals have refused to be bound by local laws requiring the giving of a formal technical notice consequent upon the assignment of a concession, and have refused to hold a country liberated because of the failure of such notice to be given.[6]

Furthermore local laws which have placed upon witnesses arbitrary

[5] *American Journal of International Law*, XIX, 760; see *Law and Procedure of International Tribunals*, 383.

[6] Landreau case, and Orinoco Shipping Company case; see *Law and Procedure of International Tribunals*, 100.

limitations arising out of their presumed interest in the subject or because of relationship or employment, have been disregarded as not to be recognized in an international forum.

On the other hand, in large classes of cases local laws have of necessity been given their full operation, as, for instance, those affecting marriage, partnership, corporations, and other legislation determining social status; also laws controlling the rights and obligations of holders of real estate, including questions of heirship and succession, and those controlling fishing. So also the local admiralty law has been recognized internationally,[7] while a vessel navigating the ocean has been considered to carry with her the laws of her own country.

Local laws are not to be maintained as against international law and are limited in their operation to local territory, except as regards a nation's own citizens.

By the Venezuelan Arbitral Agreements of 1903, it was provided that claims before the commissions should be determined "upon a basis of absolute equity without regard to . . . . provisions of local legislation."[8] This provision was held to prevent the operation of all Venezuelan laws which might in any way interfere or restrict an attempt on the part of a foreigner to obtain relief before the commissions, but did not affect laws controlling such matters as marriage, partnership, corporations, and taking of proof, except as to certain technical requirements.

Commissions have not been uniform in their holdings as to the acceptance of local law as determining when and to what extent, under certain circumstances, damage had been inflicted. For instance, some commissions have inquired into the state of local law in determining the question of the amount of damages either for attacks on liberty or seizure of property, and also determining damages in respect of a profit of which the individual had been deprived. In other words the local test of damages in local cases has been applied as determinative of the international measure of damages.[9] However, this position has not been universally taken, and awards have been given for damages and in cases of death according to principles laid down by the commission and without reference to local law.

In the case of the Norwegian Shipping claims, the Hague Tribunal declared that it was not bound by certain sections of the Revised Statutes

---

[7] *Law and Procedure of International Tribunals,* 103.
[8] *Ibid.,* 98.
[9] *Ibid.,* 102.

and other laws of the United States "nor by any other municipal law, in so far as these provisions restricted the right of the claimant to receive immediate and full compensation, with interest from the day on which the compensation should have been paid *ex aequo et bono*."[10]

63. Technical objections before commissions.—With or without provisions in the protocol covering the matter, commissions have undertaken to decide questions before them without regard to objections of a technical nature either based on local legislation or otherwise. This is, of course, evident from illustrations already given. This leaves open, however, the question as to what objections are or are not technical, and it would seem to us, and there are arbitral decisions sustaining this position, that if the objection goes to the right of recovery it may not be classed as technical, whatever it may be based upon. In the opinion of Professor Rolin the arbitrator in the *Macedonian* case rejected what had been theretofore regarded as American law in favor of a rule protecting private property on land which was in his opinion more up to date and which, as it happened, served the interests of the United States against what had been theretofore its position.[11]

64. International law as of the date of the acts complained of.—In several cases tribunals have been instructed to find what was the state of international law at the time of the acts complained of and to make their decisions accordingly. This was true in the Pelletier case between the United States and Haiti in 1884 and again in the cases of the *Cape Horn* and another between the United States and Russia.

65. International law as following national decisions.—The student of the decisions of international tribunals may be surprised to find to how large an extent these tribunals follow principles of law which have been established by national judges and how little there is of law as developed before such tribunals which does not have its firm foundation in the results of prior studies by national judges. This must have been manifest to a degree from all that has gone before; but without in anywise undertaking to declare that the enumeration we are about to give is conclusive, it will serve to show the large degree of dependence of international judges upon the law as expounded within the nations. National law has been followed among others upon the doctrine of *res judicata* and the competence of a court to pass upon its own jurisdiction. The fundamental principles of prescription, both of an acquisitive (usucaption) and an extinctive nature, and the doctrine

---

10 *Ibid.*, 105.
11 *Recueil des arbitrages*, II, 220.

of laches have been widely followed. Interest has been determined according to the ideas of national judges whose investigations as to the measure of damages, direct, indirect and consequential, have instructed many umpires. The same is true as to the matters touching the burden of proof and the nature of property.

States have been held responsible for the acts of their agents under analogies furnished by the decisions of national judges, and so have been determined responsibilities under contracts and concessions. The local conceptions of the liabilities of partnership have been carried into international forums. The idea of what we would call a common law lien has received recognition whether rightfully or not in the Venezuelan Preferential Case. Rules of interpretation have been adopted from local forums, and while a difference has been recognized between Roman and common law on the subject of the merger of prior negotiations into the completed contract or protocol, the civil law theory admitting them has received recognition. From the local forum the international judge has taken the law of trespass, estoppel, and subrogation, as well as that of servitudes, and has found a definition for equity.

From the standpoint of the views of national judges, for international law as such is silent on the subject, the arbitrator has considered various matters affecting evidence, such as the burden of proof, the effect of admissions, the recognition of assignments on a judicial theory of equity even against local laws and of *force majeure*, the effect of compromises and various presumptions, the admissibility or weight of proof which might have been offered, and what might be evidence of due diligence or the lack of it.

On the procedural side the law within the nation has furnished precedents affecting the right of revision or new trial.

66. Evil of departure from national law.—It is true that it has only been when international tribunals have found themselves obliged to depart from the teachings of law within the states and to follow what is proclaimed strictly as international law that they have failed to display the high degree of justice they should have been able to exhibit. This has been illustrated by their very general failure to recognize duress as invalidating contracts entered into by nations. Upon this point they have felt compelled to follow the doctrines of writers instead of the dictates of natural law as discovered by national courts. This is also illustrated by their recognition as lawful of interferences with the rights of neutrals, which ought never to be limited by belligerents, any such limitations being a denial *pro tanto* of equality between nations.

Again international courts pursuant to such doctrines, which cannot be justified by any true law, have denied responsibility toward neutrals for a variety of acts of war—acts for which as between two individuals responsibility would be undoubted.

Similarly international tribunals have recognized the entire propriety of the arbitrary acts of princes or *faits du prince*, whereas often such acts, although justified by so called international law, have involved a direct and improper interference with the rights of individuals, and are justified only by superiority of force.

It would seem a fair inference from the foregoing that whenever and as far as international courts have undertaken to follow state laws they have at least sought to reach justice in their conclusions, while often when making alleged international law pure and simple their mentor, they have departed from any approximation to justice.

CHAPTER IX

INTERNATIONAL AWARDS

67. Power of majority to act.—An award, very commonly called sentence, should be signed by all the arbitrators taking part therein, at least by all, not less than a majority, who concur in the conclusions.

Three copies of the awards of The Hague Permanent Court of Arbitration are customarily made, one for each of the parties and the third to remain in the archives of the court.

It is true as Acremant said: "You do not have to consider if it [the award] is by a majority or unanimously. It is the tribunal which decides."[1]

The question as to the sufficiency of an award in which only the majority concur has several times arisen and as many times been decided in favor of the power of the majority. For instance, the American commissioner in the case of the Reserved Fisheries claims with Great Britain declined to sign the award under the treaty "except with the unanimous consent of its members." The American Secretary of State argued in the same line. But after the English reply the award of the majority was carried out.[2] The Supreme Court has recognized the power of the majority to act for the commission.[3] In the *Alabama* case the British arbitrator refused to sign the award, but its entire validity was recognized notwithstanding, and the payment made.

Article 78 of the Hague Convention of 1907 provides that "all questions are decided by a majority of the members of the tribunal."

68. Reasoning set forth in awards.—A question which has received much attention relates to the necessity for setting forth the reasoning upon which an award is based. Says Politis:

Without being yet obligatory, usage establishes the custom of giving reasons in sentences. It is introduced under the influence of the mixed Anglo-Saxon commissions where the commissioners, conforming to the custom of their country, give separately their opinion indicating the reasons upon which it is based. To the contrary the sentences of sovereigns are refractory to this usage.[4]

A number of writers have said or indicated that an award which did not contain the reasoning leading to the conclusions was of necessity null. For instance, Darras[5] and Bureau[6] go so far as to contend

[1] *La procédure dans les arbitrages internationaux*, 136.
[2] *Law and Procedure of International Tribunals*, 109.
[3] Columbia *vs.* Cauca Company, 190 U.S. 524.   [4] *La justice internationale*, 87.
[5] "De certains dangers de l'arbitrage international," *Revue générale de droit international public*, VI, 547.   [6] *Le conflit Italo-Colombien.*

that when the arbitrator fails to give the reasons for his decisions he has exceeded his powers and his sentence is null. Acremant[7] quotes Fiore as holding in his *Droit international codifié* that the complete lack of reasoning in fact and law is one of the causes of nullity in the award.

Notwithstanding the citations so far given it cannot be accepted that an award is null simply because of the failure of the arbitrators or umpire to assign reasons or because they or he assign an insufficient one. Certainly no award has ever been refused execution on such a ground, and the precedents of fulfillment are entirely too numerous to justify the statement that because of such lack the award is incompetent.

It will be borne in mind that the arbitrations of the Middle Ages were very generally given without any statement of reasons. Coming to a later period we find that in the Portendick affair between France and Great Britain, the arbitrator, Frederick William IV, King of Prussia, gave no reasons for his award. Baron Bülow said rather naïvely that to give reasons would expose the king to disputes and criticisms scarcely compatible with a supreme and final decision.[8] Baron Roenne, umpire of the Mexican Claims Commission under the Treaty of 1839, gave no reasons for his opinions, and the Prussian government by which he had been named repeatedly declined to state the reasonings upon which he based his conclusions, although he had furnished the government with them. In the Derbec case before the French-American Claims Commission, it was stated by the majority of the Commission that

International commissions do not usually give the reasons for their decisions except when the decision stands upon some principle of law which they think ought to be made known.[9]

The commission, therefore, reserved for itself the most ample power of giving or refusing to give its reasons. The award of President Cleveland in the Cerruti case between Colombia and Italy gave no reasons and was criticised severely therefor, but the award, nevertheless, stood. Other cases of a like description which may be added are those of the award of Queen Victoria in a dispute between France and Mexico in the year 1844 and the award of the Czar Alexander II in the dispute between Peru and Japan relative to the *Maria Luz* in 1875.

Of course, it may be readily understood that the giving of reasons is scarcely approved or is entirely unnecessary in cases where the dispute does not rest upon any clear-cut question of law or fact. This is often

---

[7] *La procédure dans les arbitrages internationaux*, 143.
[8] *Recueil des arbitrages*, I, 543.
[9] *Law and Procedure of International Tribunals*, 108.

the case in boundary disputes or when the arbitrators virtually serve as *amiables compositeurs* or when the differences of fact are of too slight importance to justify cumbering the record with long discussions.

It nevertheless remains true that even though there is no rigorous rule requiring the giving of reasons sufficient to support the conclusion, yet, in a large majority of the cases, reasons should be given. This is necessary to satisfy the parties that their contentions have received consideration and to justify the action of the court in the event of criticism. Undoubtedly monarchs have shrunk from the giving of opinions, not desiring that the sufficiency of their reasoning should be called in question by people of lesser dignity in their eyes. However this feeling may have actuated them, it has no part in the workings of courts which must always by reasoning be ready to justify their conclusions.

M. de Martens at the first Hague Peace Conference fought strongly against the idea that arbitral sentences should set forth the reasoning on which they were based; perhaps because as it is said by Stoykovitch[10] he had a purely political conception of arbitration; but very probably because his award in the *Costa Rica Packet* case was criticized as based on insufficient reasons, and as having been of the nature of a compromise. However, the Hague Peace Convention of 1899 provided (Article LII) that "The award given by a majority of votes is accompanied by a statement of reasons," and the Convention of 1907 is to the like effect.

As to the practice before the Hague Permanent Court of International Justice, we quote Moore:

> Every judgment is required to state the reasons on which it is based and to contain the names of the judges who have taken part in it. If the judgment is not unanimous, dissenting judges are entitled to deliver separate opinions. Judgments must be rendered in open court after due notice to the agents of the parties. If the meaning or scope of the judgment is disputed, the court, on the request of any party, is to construe it.[11]

The Hague Convention of 1899 provided (Article LII) as to the award that "those members who are in the minority may record their dissent when signing." The Convention of 1907 is silent on this point, though providing that all decisions are to be made by a majority. M. Acremant[12] adheres to the view that the minority to avoid confusion should not be permitted to present their reasons for dissent. This view

---

[10] *De l'autorité de la sentence arbitrale,* 93.

[11] *International Law,* chap. iv, 112.

[12] *La procédure dans l'arbitrage international,* 144.

does not commend itself to us. This right on the part of a minority must operate to compel greater care and study by the majority.

69. Terms of award.—A word should be said as to the terms of the award. This, of course, is rigidly limited by the conditions of the reference, which may not be exceeded. Usually the award calls for the payment of money, except of course in the cases of boundary disputes or disputes as to territorial possessions. Occasionally, the sentence is of a different character. This was true in the Muscat case between France and England involving the right to fly the French flag.[18] In one or two cases the punishment of the offenders by the defendant government has been required.[14] In the Casablanca case in which the judgment of the court more nearly resembled the action of an *amiable compositeur,* the various parties considered in default were given a gentle chiding, this taking the place of a cold-blooded award of damages.

70. Reservations and protests.—A practice which has been resorted to a number of times is that of making reservations against an award and its validity. Usually, if not always, this action leads to nothing. On several occasions the United States has filed protests. This was true as to the Reserved Fisheries Claims award to which reference has been made. It was true also as to the Chamizal award in an arbitration between the United States and Mexico, which award still remains unsettled, and in the Norwegian claims. It will be noted, however, that the Reserved Fisheries Claims and the Norwegian Shipping Claims were both paid by the United States notwithstanding its protest, in the first instance based upon want of unanimity among the arbitrators, and in the second based upon an alleged excess of power on the part of the umpire.

Reservations or protests were also quite largely indulged in before the Venezuela commissions which met in Caracas in 1903. No objection was there made to their filing, but no action was ever taken in any way to meet their contentions.

In a dispute, however, between Austria and Hungary, the arbitrators denied the right of the representative of Austria to make a reservation. His authority, it was held, related only to the solution of the litigation. Apart from this, however, the tribunal held that it ought not to admit the reservation as being injurious to its prestige and to the authority of *res judicata* by way of arbitration. It held further that a reservation was in contradiction to the purpose of the *compromis,* which was that

---

[18] *Law and Procedure of International Tribunals,* 307.
[14] *Ibid.,* 122.

the matter of the frontier should be determined definitely and not temporarily.[15]

It has, however, been repeatedly recognized that the arbitrators have the power to correct any arithmetical error they may make in the award, and only to this extent may protests be regarded as being effective.[16]

71. Error as vitiating award.—We come now to the important question of error in the award of such character as may vitiate it. Upon this point much has been written. We may open the discussion with a reference to Article 1010 of the French Code of Civil Procedure, a provision which has had its influence upon thought on this general subject. This law says that an appeal against a judgment of arbitration may be for the following reasons: (1) if the judgment has been rendered without a *compromis* or beyond the terms of the *compromis;* (2) if it has been rendered upon a *compromis* which was null or expired; (3) if it has been rendered by some arbitrators not authorized to judge in the absence of the others; (4) if it has been by a third (umpire) without his having conferred with the arbitrators in division; (5) if it has been pronounced upon things not demanded.

According to Bluntschli, the award can be considered null:

(*a*) In so far as the arbitral tribunal has exceeded its powers; (*b*) in case of disloyalty or denial of justice on the part of the arbitrators; (*c*) if the arbitrators have refused to hear the parties or have violated some other fundamental procedure; (*d*) if the arbitral decision is contrary to international law (but the decision of the arbitrators cannot be attacked on the pretext that it is erroneous or contrary to equity). False calculations remain reserved.[17]

Mr. Goldschmidt[18] enumerates some ten different reasons for attacking the award of arbitrators, while Calvo[19] gives a half-dozen. It is to be borne in mind that these and other authors have virtually transferred to international arbitrations the principles which they have found observed in private arbitrations, and they have done this without very great regard to their probable application to international affairs and without the ability to point to instances as to many of their suggestions in international practice sustaining their theories or making them of real value.

---

15 *Law and Procedure of International Tribunals,* 120.
16 *Ibid.,* 208.
17 *Le droit international codifié,* Art. 495.
18 *Revue de droit international,* etc., 1874, 447.
19 *Le droit international,* § 1774.

De Card[20] more wisely limits himself to saying that the decision of the arbitral tribunal is only to be considered as non-obligatory when in violation of the mandate, and for evident injustice or material error.

Confining itself more closely to the bounds of experience, the Institute of International Law sitting at The Hague in 1875 provided by Article 27 of its rules that

The arbitral sentence is null in case of a void *compromis* or excess of power or proved corruption of one of the arbitrators or essential error.[21]

Let us consider some of these grounds.

M. Weiss says truly that it has been remarked that the nullity of a *compromis* can rarely be invoked against the validity of the award, because the party interested should make the objection in the course of the procedure, in the absence of which objection the nullity of the *compromis* will be considered as effaced by the tacit ratification of the parties.[22]

Again, as Lesboa remarks:

May the nullity of a *compromis* of a treaty of arbitration which has been solemnly concluded with all the formalities required to complete international acts be recognized only after the arbitral sentence has been pronounced? This seems to us impossible. To admit such an hypothesis would be to admit it for all sorts of international treaties after they had been ratified and put into execution. During all the time of the negotiation of the treaty of arbitration and as well during the debates of the arbitral tribunal there is plenty of time to examine if the *compromis* be legitimately concluded.[23]

The objection of want of jurisdiction in the commission appears to have been raised in a dispute between the Canton of Tessin and the Canton of Uri and to have been based upon a want of power in the representatives of Tessin to agree to submit the dispute to a commission. The matter was subsequently arranged between the parties.[24] A like case occurred as to the diamond deposits dispute between the Transvaal and indigenous tribes in 1871. The arbitrator gave his award in favor of the tribes and the Volksraad criticized severely the government, in consequence of which the President and his associates resigned. The intermediate President, Erasmus, protested against the sentence, declared that President Pretorius had not the authority to sign the

20 *L'arbitrage international*, 53.
21 *Revue de droit international*, etc., VII (1875), 282.
22 *Revue générale de droit international public*, 1910, 122.
23 *Revue de droit international*, etc., 2nd series, IV (1902), 63.
24 *Recueil des arbitrages*, I, 275.

compromis alone, and that the procedure was null therefor and the award without value. But the arbitrator declared that he had no reason to take notice of the conflict arising within the representative Republic between the executive and the legislative power and intended to have his award respected. Nevertheless, we are told that the sentence remained unexecuted for reasons foreign to its juridical value.[25]

It must be recognized that an award which goes beyond the terms of the *compromis* is, to such extent, null and void. It was the belief of the United States in the case of the Northeastern Boundaries that the King of the Netherlands exceeded his power as an arbitrator and undertook to act as a mediator. The United States, therefore, refused to carry out the decision as a departure from the powers of the arbitrator, and Great Britain disregarded the award. A like assertion was made by the United States with reference to the award in the Chamizal case with Mexico. Again, the United States contended that in the Orinoco Shipping and Trading Company case the umpire between the United States and Venezuela at Caracas had been guilty of exceeding his jurisdiction. With this contention the Permanent Court of Arbitration at The Hague in part agreed, holding that

excessive exercise of power may consist, not only in deciding a question not submitted to the arbitrators, but also in misinterpreting the express provisions of the agreement in respect of the way in which they are to reach their conclusions, notably with regard to the legislation or the principles of law to be applied.[26]

Other awards have not escaped criticism from writers, at least on the ground of having exceeded the terms of the *compromis,* as for instance, the Cerruti award of President Cleveland and the boundary award of the Argentine Republic in the dispute between Bolivia and Peru.

It is, of course, to be conceded as beyond argument that fraud or corruption on the part of the umpire will vitiate an award. Cases of this description are so rare that from a practical point of view they might even be called non-existent. Nevertheless, there is the case cited by Barbeyrac between the Emperor Maximilian and the Doge of Venice, who reciprocally tried to corrupt the Pope, Leo X, who was chosen as arbitrator of their difference. An instance of actual fraud is to be cited in the arbitrations of the United States and Venezuela under the Protocol of 1866.[27] In this instance Venezuela promptly protested

---

[25] Stoykovitch, *De l'autorité de la sentence arbitrale,* 192.
[26] *American Journal of International Law,* 1911, 233.
[27] Moore, *International Arbitrations,* 1660.

against the awards, charging fraud. After several years Congress made full investigation, finding the charges sustained, consequent upon which a new arbitral board was provided for, which revised the findings of the discredited commission.

Awards have also been set aside because of fraud in their procurement. This has been true of a number of cases cited in the *Law and Procedure of International Tribunals.*[28]

A much more difficult question, but one which nevertheless has been raised in a practical way as to the nullity of an award, has been when it involved what is often termed "essential error." While the writers are in agreement as to the fatal character of essential error, it is not easy to define it. It is, of course, error to pass the limitations of the *compromis,* whether we call it excess of power or give it some other title. It cannot be, however, that every wrongful appreciation of the facts produced before the arbitrator constitutes error, notwithstanding the opinion of Savigny who said that "Error is the inexact notion that we have of a thing. It consists in believing true that which is false and false that which is true." If this language were given its broad and natural application it would be practically impossible ever to reach finality, for continually the thing which might seem obvious to one would seem inexact to another, and the purpose of all judicial action is to settle finally just such differences. In recognition of the impossibility of reviewing an arbitration because of a want of proper appreciation of the facts, at least in the opinion of one of the parties, the Permanent Court of Arbitration in the Orinoco Shipping and Trading Company case found that, as to certain items which it was asked to reconsider because of essential error in the determination of the umpire, his award was

based on a consideration of facts and on an interpretation of legal principles which are subject neither to re-examination nor to revision by this tribunal, the decisions awarded on these points not being void.[29]

It would seem that the question as to what is or is not essential error usually involves jurisdiction and is to be approached from this point of view. Three questions are to be asked: (1) Had the court jurisdiction over the parties to the controversy? (2) Had it jurisdiction over the subject-matter as to which it acted? (3) Had it jurisdiction to pass the particular award or sentence it granted? If these

---

[28] On page 118.
[29] *American Journal of International Law,* V (1911), 234.

three questions are answered in the affirmative, then it would seem to us almost impossible to conceive of the existence of essential error no matter how grossly the court may have erred in its appreciation of the facts adduced before it. If error in such appreciation exists it is to be met by an application for revision or review, a subject to be hereafter discussed. We advance the foregoing as the true meaning of essential error, at the same time recognizing the truth of the statement made by Audry:

> In internal law the difficulty of characterizing essential error does not appear because it is possible to determine it in a precise way with the aid of the law and a constant jurisprudence, but in international law there is neither text nor jurisprudence permitting the definition of essential error.[30]

It is the opinion of the writer, as it was when acting as American Agent in the Pious Fund case,

> the point being considered by him, no authority believes that the award of arbitrators may be attacked because of erroneous appreciation either of the facts or of the law as applicable to them. We have seen that upon this point Bluntschli argues that a decision may not be attacked on the pretext that it is erroneous or contrary to equity save for errors of calculation; while Heffter finds that errors which may be alleged against the sentence, when they are not the result of a partial spirit, do not constitute a case of nullity. Kamarowsky quotes Chrabro-Vassilewsky as contending that the effect of an arbitral sentence cannot be lost on account of reasons affecting its substance. Vattel declares that the parties may not say "it is manifestly unjust, since it is pronounced on a question which they have themselves rendered doubtful by the discordance of their claims, and which has been referred as such to the decision of the arbitrators." Calvo is of the opinion that the decision of arbitrators cannot be attacked on the pretext that it is "erroneous or contrary to equity or prejudicial to the interests of one of the parties."[31]

Demolombe is cited as having said: "Ignorance does not know; error believes it knows and deceives itself." This may be a correct definition of error, but not of essential error, which, as we have endeavored to point out, means something fundamental in character.

Nys cites the words of Count Nigra at the Hague Conference of 1907 to the effect that "error is always possible, and if there is truly an evident error in the eyes of public opinion why require that it should be consecrated? Why not revise it?[32] But it will be noted that an error of such a description, while affording an excellent reason for the forma-

---

[30] *La révision de la sentence arbitrale,* 71.
[31] *American Agent's Report,* 222.
[32] *Revue de droit international,* etc., XII (1910), 623.

tion of a new tribunal of revision, at least if it be of sufficient gravity, is no proof of essential error in itself vitiating the award *ipso facto*.

A line between what may be regarded as excess of power and essential error has apparently never been clearly pointed out. The same act viewed from different standpoints may come under either denomination. The words, "excess of power," having in mind illustrations given already, will seem to speak for themselves. Suppose, however, a tribunal directed an award after having refused to hear one of the parties. It would seem that such action on its part would entirely invalidate the award, and it might be considered that the tribunal had exceeded its powers in so acting or that it had been guilty of an essential error in not having laid down the foundation upon which judicial jurisdiction must rest.

It is the fact that there is no tribunal capable of determining whether the award of an arbitration is infected with excess of power or essential error, and, except by subsequent agreement, the nations are left to claim as they see fit existence of a wrong of this character. Unfortunately, therefore, the way is open for international differences arising anew even out of an attempt to settle them. What has been done in this regard by the allowance of revision, we shall hereafter consider.

72. Effect of award on third parties.—Something should be said as to the effect of an award upon the rights of third parties. As M. Politis remarks,

> Respect for the rights of third parties goes of itself. It is, however, sometimes formally indicated in the award. Thus it was in the affair of Guiana between Great Britain and Venezuela where the arbitrator reserved the rights of Brazil as to the contested territory.[33]

Again, in the case of Costa Rica and Nicaragua before the Central American Court of Justice, that court, while indicating its jurisdiction as of the broadest character between Central American states, limited itself "to a determination of the juristic relations existing between Central American states engaged in controversy and to a declaration of the law with respect to them"; but refrained "absolutely from cognizance [of] conditions of fact and law which their acts have created with respect to other nations not under the jurisdiction of the court."[34] In the case of Salvador against Nicaragua the same court followed this rule but declined to refuse jurisdiction simply because a nation foreign

[33] *La justice internationale*, 89.
[34] *American Journal of International Law*, II, 212.

to the Central American government possessed interests connected with the controversy.[35]

The Permanent Court of International Justice refused to take jurisdiction to interpret a treaty to which Russia, a party interested in the dispute, was not a party and had refused to subject herself to the jurisdiction of the court.

73. Execution of the award.—The award once pronounced, we arrive at the stage of its execution. It is true, as said by Stoykovitch, that

> The state cannot invoke an obstacle of interior order to refuse the execution of an award. It is obligated by the award to the full plenitude of its sovereignty, and its execution is imposed upon the legislative and judicial powers which are but a part of the sovereignty and cannot consequently place themselves above it.[36]

So it is said by Politis that

> While excess of power renders legitimate a refusal of execution, it is necessary that it be certain and indisputable and that there be some interest favoring it, a double condition which explains why refusal of execution is in fact exceedingly rare.[37]

Thus it has been that while the English representative on the Geneva tribunal protested its injustice, England paid the award; and while the United States in the Norwegian Shipping Company case likewise protested, the award was paid promptly by the action of the Executive and legislative departments. Again, while Mexico protested with justice, as later events showed, against the Weil and La Abra awards, they were, nevertheless, paid when due, although the money was subsequently returned to Mexico.

74. Award as *res judicata*.—What is the effect of an arbitral award as *res judicata?* If there be identity of parties and identity of subject-matter there is no reason why the doctrine of *res judicata* should not have as great a bearing internationally as it has in internal law. The civil law attached the authority belonging to *res judicata* to the decisions of arbitral tribunals.[38]

This doctrine was invoked on behalf of the United States in the case of the Pious Fund of the Californias, the first case heard at The Hague,

---

[35] *American Journal of International Law*, II, 692.

[36] *De l'autorité de la sentence arbitrale*, 255.

[37] *La justice internationale*, 92.

[38] "Les sentences arbitrales sont de véritables jugements; elles sont donc investies de l'autorité de la chose jugée." (*Répertoire générale de jurisprudence*, IV, "Chose jugée," § 204.)

and the Permanent Court of Arbitration decided that the rule applied "not only to the judgments created by the state but equally to arbitral sentences rendered within the limits of the jurisdiction fixed by the *compromis*," and also that "this same principle should for a still stronger reason be applied to international arbitration."

The precise limits of the subject-matter covered by the term *res judicata* is indicated by the opinion in the Pious Fund case, it being said that

all the parts of the judgment or the decree concerning the points debated in the litigation enlighten and mutually supplement each other, and that they all serve to render precise the meaning and the bearing of the *dispositif* (decisory part of the judgment) and to determine the points upon which there is *res judicata,* and which thereafter cannot be put in question.[39]

In this instance the court held in effect that the various steps necessary to bring about the result were themselves to be regarded as part of the decision, as, for instance, the prior decision of Sir Edward Thornton, which the court regarded as *res judicata,* gave a round judgment for a sum which represented the annual payments due from Mexico multiplied by the number of years for which the payments were in default. The determination, therefore, of the principal sum involved the determination of the annual amount which should be paid by Mexico.

The same tribunal, however, did not treat the prior award as *res judicata* with regard to the method of payment, declaring that the "question of the mode of payment does not relate to the basis of the right in litigation but only to the execution of the sentence." Therefore, although Sir Edward Thornton had directed in the first place payment to be made in Mexican gold dollars, the Hague Court required it "to be in money having legal currency in Mexico," it having been demonstrated that the currency of Mexico was silver and not gold. The same result might have been reached if the court had proceeded upon the ground that the original wrong having been committed in Mexico and the obligation resultant upon the wrong being payable in that country, the currency of the country would necessarily have been the medium of payment.[40]

[39] *Law and Procedure of International Tribunals,* 50.

[40] We refer to the footnote on page 57, *Law and Procedure of International Tribunals,* relative to the question as to whether the calculation of the Hague Court ought not have been on the theory of what the Mexican dollars should have produced on the day when the respective installments were payable if at that time exchanged into the money of the demanding nation. Upon this point the note refers to the Montano case before the Peruvian commission (Moore, 1620–1638), the Cerruti

75. Attacking prior awards.—Sometimes prior awards of an umpire between nations have been called in question in later commissions; but never, it is believed, successfully. For instance, the commissioners under the Mexican-American Treaty of 1849 declined to review the action of the umpire of the Mexican Claims Commission of 1839, holding that his decision was final and conclusive. Umpire Plumley in the Fabiani case[41] held, following a Supreme Court decision, that a prior award was conclusive and final. It is to be noted that in addition the award possesses the quality of verity, and

it is the source of all inhering presumptions, and, of course, pertains to all awards alike—to the negative as well as to the positive—i.e., to those rejecting as well as to those allowing claims.[42]

76. Power of interpretation of commission.—Questions of interpretation may arise in connection with an arbitration and its award in two ways: first, the interpretation of the protocol under which the court acts, and this interpretation, of course, is carried out into, and forms, in a sense, part of the award; and, second, the interpretation to be given to the award itself. Let us first consider that aspect of interpretation which is summed up in the award as the necessary result of all antecedent proceedings. Calvo indicates that under all circumstances where the arbitral tribunal entertains doubts concerning the extent of the *compromis* it should interpret it in the largest sense.[43] Rolin-Jaequemyns is equally generous in his view, and declares that the question of jurisdiction should not be resolved by strict interpretation of the *compromis* "but it is necessary in all cases of doubt to settle it affirmatively." In this conclusion he finds himself following Anglo-American jurisprudence, which recognizes even in civil arbitration the principle that "a fair and liberal construction is allowed in its interpretation."[44]

Mérignhac found that the *compromis* was to be interpreted by the arbitrator as covering what it gave him, if not expressly at least

---

case between Italy and Colombia (*Revue générale de droit international public*, XIX [1912], 273), a decision of the German-Belgian Commission under the Versailles Treaty (*Recueil des décisions des tribunaux arbitraux mixtes*, etc., 1924, 300), the Spadaforo case (Descamps and Renault, 1904, 820) before an Italian-Colombian commission.

[41] French-Venezuelan Commission under the protocol of 1902, Ralston's Report, 81, 141.

[42] *Law and Procedure of International Tribunals*, 117.

[43] *Le droit international*, § 1757.

[44] *Revue de droit international*, etc., IV (1872), 137.

impliedly, including the accessories, the things dependent upon the subject of litigation which were regarded as incorporated in it; further that he should prefer an extended to a narrow interpretation, which might risk leaving out of the award certain points that could lead to new conflicts, while the intent of the parties had been to the contrary.[45] A different course was pursued by the Franco-Chilean Tribunal of 1882 which believed its powers under the protocol were of strict law and defined in express terms, the exercise of which was virtually and necessarily required not to be extended by interpretation beyond its terms.[46]

The right of an international tribunal to pass upon its own jurisdiction is in itself an affirmation of its right to interpret the protocol under which it is appointed. This view was taken by the American commissioners under the Seventh Article of the Jay Treaty and maintained by the English Lord Chancellor.[47] Similarly in the Pious Fund case the Hague Permanent Court of Arbitration held that the convention of 1868 between the United States and Mexico "had accorded to the mixed commission named by these states, as well as to the umpire to be eventually designated, the right to pass upon their own jurisdiction."[48]

Notwithstanding the fact that in the absence of any convention on the subject, arbitral tribunals have the right to pass on their own jurisdiction, treaties have undertaken particularly to invest them with this power, as for instance, one of 1902 between the Argentine Republic, Bolivia, and other nations.[49]

77. Interpretation of awards.—Let us now consider the matter of the interpretation of the award itself. Arbitral courts have been very slow to interpret or reconsider in any way the award once rendered, preferring to have it stand of itself. This general feeling is sustained by the language of the Permanent Court of International Justice in Advisory Opinion No. 8, (Delimitation of Jaworzina) in which it was said broadly that

in the absence of an express agreement between the parties, the arbitrator is not competent to interpret, still less modify his award by revising it. . . . . And even leaving out of the question the principles governing the authoritative interpretation of legal documents, it is obvious that the opinion of the authors of a document cannot be endowed with a decisive value when that opinion has

45 *L'arbitrage international,* 181.
46 *Ibid.,* 292.
47 *Law and Procedure of International Tribunals,* 46.
48 *American Agent's Report,* 17.
49 *American Journal of International Law,* 1907, Supplement, 299; Manning, *Arbitration Treaties,* 307.

been formulated after the drafting of that document and conflicts with the opinion which they expressed at that time.

Except for the powers particularly conferred by the *compromis* the arbitrator has no power of interpretation of the award once it has passed beyond his control, save at least pursuant to the joint request of the parties in interest and even then he may refuse.[50]

78. Further as to review of awards.—It is the opinion of Stoykovitch that causes of nullity should be admitted with great precaution and no one should be authorized himself to pass upon the validity of an award, but that this power should be reserved to an impartial tribunal which could be created following a new convention concluded by the parties.[51] We have spoken above, however, of the power of interpretation exercised by the Permanent Court of Justice at The Hague. In other connections, we discuss the various reasons invalidating an arbitral award. We may, however, refer at this time to the discovery of a situation which, while not invalidating the award fundamentally, nevertheless operates to justify a review of the facts or situation upon which the award was based. This point is illustrated by the provisions of certain treaties, notably between South American countries. For instance, that between Bolivia and Brazil provided that

if, before the complete execution of the sentence, either of the two interested parties should have knowledge of the falsity or spuriousness of any document that may have served as a basis for the award or should establish that the sentence in whole or in part was based on an error of fact, such party may then take steps to have the decision reviewed before the same arbitrator or tribunal.[52]

Naturally not every fact of the prohibited nature will justify an application for such review. It must have been of a nature to serve as basis for the award in whole or in part, and this was recognized in the rules of the Franco-German Commission of 1922, which established that the new fact in order to open a way to revision must be of a nature to exercise a decisive influence upon the sentence, and that this condition

---

[50] "Il en résulte enfin que si la sentence a besoin d'être interprétée, elle ne peut l'être que par l'accord des parties, qui peuvent y procéder seules ou en s'adressant ensemble à l'arbitre pour l'y autoriser. L'arbitre ne peut pas intervenir d'office, ni à la demande d'une seule partie. A moins d'être saisi par les deux à la fois, il doit s'y refuser. C'est ce que fit le roi de Prusse, lorsque le gouvernement britannique l'invita à fixer le sens de sa sentence dans l'affaire de Portendick. Il refusa de fournir une interprétation officielle. Il se borna à donner un avis officieux." (Politis, *La justice internationale*, 89.)

[51] *De l'autorité de la sentence arbitrale*, 256.

[52] Manning, *Arbitration Treaties*, 445.

could be recognized by the commission when it related to a fact unknown to the tribunal and to the demanding party, and applied for within a year from the closure of the discussion in the case.[53]

During the early Middle Ages, as stated by Stoykovitch, the arbitral sentence was always conclusive and there were no known cases of appeal, the arbitrators being through with the affair when the judgment was rendered.[54] On the other hand, however, there were cases where the arbitrators, being unable to pass upon all the questions, reserved the right of rendering a second award to settle points not decided; and they reserved often the right of interpretation and of correction of the award, which Stoykovitch thought was but a natural extension of their powers. However, the commissions of modern times have assumed no such authority.

79. **Rehearings and revisions of awards.**—We have heretofore considered the power of a commission over an award once rendered. We must now examine under our present heading the matter of rehearings and revision. It was the position of Count Löwenhaupt of the Spanish-American Claims Commission that

if a petition for rehearing is submitted by the arbitrators the duty of the umpire to examine the points submitted is the same as if the case had never been before the umpire, and he has to give a decision; but if one of the arbitrators refused to certify the disagreement the case cannot again come before the umpire under the agreement of 1871.[55]

The same umpire refused to consider a petition for a rehearing transmitted to him by the secretary of the commission, being limited by the agreement to questions upon which the arbitrators did not agree and which they had submitted to him for decision.

The protocol referring the case of the Pious Fund to arbitration permitted revision under Article LV of the Hague Convention, provided demand should be made within eight days after announcement of the award, proofs thereunder submitted within ten days after revision being allowed, and counter-proofs within the following ten days unless further time should be granted by the court; it also provided for a period within which other proceedings should be had. Article LV of the Hague Convention of 1899 provided that revision could only be asked for

[53] *Recueil des décisions des tribunaux arbitraux mixtes*, etc., I, 55.
[54] *Le compromis et les arbitrages internationaux*, 29.
[55] *Law and Procedure of International Tribunals*, 208.

on the ground of the discovery of some new fact calculated to exercise a decisive influence on the award, and which, at the time the discussion was closed, was unknown to the tribunal and to the party demanding the revision.

After providing that such proceedings could only be instituted by a decision of the tribunal expressly recording the existence of the new fact and of its character and the declaring of the demand admissible on this ground, it was left to the *compromis* to fix the period within which demand for revision should be made. No demand was made in the Pious Fund case for revision, and members of the tribunal determining the case subsequently commented upon the inadvisability of such provisions.[56]

Application for revision is contemplated as possible by Article 66 of the rules of the Permanent Court of International Justice. This application must contain reference to the judgment impeached; the facts on which the application is based; and a list of the documents in support which are to be attached. It is made the duty of the Registrar to give immediate notice of the application to the other parties concerned, who may in turn submit observations, within a time limit to be fixed by the court or president. If the judgment be pronounced by the full court, application must be made to it; if by one of its chambers, the application may be dealt with by the same chamber.

80. Allowance of interest.—Questions as to the right of arbitral tribunals to grant interest, and, if granted, the rate at which this should be done, have been matters of frequent occurrence. Before going into them in detail, we should advert to the decision of the Hague Permanent Court of Arbitration in the case of Russia versus Turkey, in which the general nature of interest was discussed.[57] The court was of the opinion that

all interest-damages are always reparation, compensation for culpability. From this point of view all interest-damages are compensatory, whatever name they may be given . . . . It is certain, indeed, that all culpability, whatever may be its origin, is finally valued in money and transformed into obligation to pay; it all ends, or can end, in the last analysis, in a money debt. The tribunal, therefore, cannot possibly perceive essential differences between various responsibilities. Identical in their origin—culpability—they are the same in their consequences—reparation in money.

A large number of tribunals have granted interest in the award, at rates varying from three to six per cent, and in one instance eight per

56 *American Journal of International Law*, V, Supplement, 77.
57 *Ibid.*, VII, 191.

cent, dependent sometimes upon the rate paid on government obligations and sometimes upon the then financial situation of the world.[58]

The time from which interest should date has received repeated consideration, and the general rule is that interest on all contract obligations at least is to be dated from the time when the defendant government was first put upon notice of the existence of a claim against it.[59] If, however, the conduct of the claimant has been such as to indicate an intention not to demand interest, it is to be considered as waived.

The general rule has been, subject to the language of particular protocols, that interest could be allowed only to the time of the conclusion of the labors of the commission, although in certain instances, under protocols at least not forbidding it, interest has been permitted to the day of payment of the award. The usual theory of commissions has been that they lacked power to extend an obligation and keep it running at a time when they were themselves *functus officio*.

International tribunals have continually refused to compound interest, finding no power in themselves to do so. Sometimes interest has been refused because the lump sum awarded was considered as having included a sufficient allowance for interest. This was true in the case of the Norwegian Shipping Claims.

It is practically the universal rule that in damage cases interest is refused, the award itself being assumed to be sufficient to cover all loss.

Elaborate rules governing the granting or refusing of interest were laid down in the United States and Germany Mixed Claims Commission.[60]

---

[58] *Law and Procedure of International Tribunals,* 129 ff.
[59] *Ibid.,* 132.
[60] *American Journal of International Law,* XVIII, 603.

CHAPTER X

SANCTIONS OF INTERNATIONAL AWARDS

81. Necessity of sanctions.—So accustomed are we to the usual methods of administering and enforcing judgments within the state that the question most commonly asked with regard to international awards and judgments is, "How can they be enforced?" It is not alone in private discourse but also in the proceedings of international bodies that the question is asked; and many schemes of enforcement, from the cessation of diplomatic relations up to war, have been suggested and urged. A kindred question arises as to the method of enforcement of any principle of international law. We find Moore enumerating in the *Digest of International Law* modes of redress as being (1) negotiation; (2) good offices and mediation; (3) arbitration; (4) withdrawal of diplomatic relations; (5) retorsion or retaliation; (6) display of force; (7) use of force; (8) reprisals; (9) peaceful blockade; (10) embargo; (11) non-intercourse. There seems no appropriate place in the text-books for the all-pervasive and all-powerful influence of international public opinion.

Dr. Harry Pratt Judson, discouraged by what he considered recent violations of rules of international law in defiance of the world public opinion, declared that these

have not the weight of a farthing. All nations are bound by their own immediate, countervailing interests, and they disregard any of these rules that get in their way, merely because they get in the way of what they believe to be their interests.[1]

But the Doctor overlooked the fact that the great interest of every state internationally is to stand well with its fellows, and any departure from a course of conduct sanctioned by mankind generally carries punishment of some sort. There is further much greater reason for observing an award than there is for paying obeisance to an abstract principle of law.

Experience, both private and public, when given full consideration, seems to demonstrate that the question of sanctions is one of very minor importance in practice. In our private intercourse we discover that the obligations which are most generally enforced and are most effective are in no wise dependent upon force as a sanction. The man who gambles pays his debt of honor, as he regards it, with greater certainty than he will meet an obligation enforced by execution. Similarly, taking the

[1] *Proceedings, American Society of International Law*, 1915, 111.

civilized world at large, we find that the purely moral obligation upon the child to support an aged parent is observed in like manner. In each instance the breaking of the obligation would materially lower the standing of the man in the community and among his associates. The power, therefore, of public opinion proves to be greater than any writ in the hands of a sheriff.[2]

From this humble but assuredly suggestive beginning, let us proceed to situations more closely resembling these we are considering. The Constitution of the United States was formed between states of equal dignity. These states agreed that between themselves a Supreme Court should determine all differences. At the same time, feeling their own dignity and independence, they did not provide in any wise for any method of enforcement of the orders and decrees of the Supreme Court, and to this day none exists. On only one occasion has the Supreme Court indicated that, necessity existing, it would find a way to make its orders effective, and this suggestion it was unnecessary to carry out, if, indeed, there was any possible way in which it could have been done. The mere fact that the Supreme Court reaches a certain conclusion is sufficient to make that conclusion respected by the state against which it is directed.

Turning from the United States to the international field, we find that the awards of international tribunals have practically without exception met with immediate acquiescence and fulfillment. The honor of the nations entering into a *compromis* has been engaged and the results have been accepted, though often with regret and protest.

It may be argued with great force that, granting at least civilization at its present stage, the addition to courts of a power of enforcement of their decrees has weakened the moral sanctity of their conclusions and has changed to a legal obligation, having only such sanctity as the force of the state may give it, the moral obligation which might otherwise have existed in full force and virtue. In other words, we may be told with a certain degree of truth that the power of execution attached to courts has had the effect of lowering the moral standard of the community at large which would have been maintained had the element of force been excluded. It seems only natural to believe that force incites to evasion, whereas there is little escape from a moral condemnation,

---

[2] The tremendous force of world opinion in causing compliance with the dictates of international law, compelling reference in many cases to arbitration, and insuring compliance with the orders of international courts, has never been more clearly pointed out than by Secretary Root. (*Proceedings, American Society of International Law*, 1908, 14.)

resting upon the public opinion of the community for its sanction. So again, turning to the international field, we may conclude that just as force as against individuals is believed to lower the moral tone of the community, so likewise would the application of force in any degree as between nations have a similar tendency.

It is, of course, hard to dissociate the existence of a court from the idea of force. This is shown even by the opinion of as eminent a man as Ruy Barbosa, who at the Second Hague Conference in arguing against an international court of justice assumed that it would enforce its decrees by force. He said,

> If you create international powers it is necessary to arm them with efficacious instruments against revolt. There are rebel nations. Repression then should be resorted to. Upon whom will this duty rest? Assuredly upon the strongest nation or upon the concert of the strongest. What in the end will be the result? Simply to legalize the domain of force and substitute it for that of the equilibrium of sovereignty. And this is how peace at all hazards, in seeking to embrace justice in the place of arbitration, will finish by putting force in the place of right.[3]

We venture to say consequent upon our reasoning that there is no more reason for requiring the conclusions of a court of international justice to be backed up by force than there is for attaching a similar requirement to the orders of a court of arbitration.

It has been argued that while the orders of a court of arbitration are obeyed, this is because the court is ordinarily named by the express consent of the nation for the determination of a narrow question or range of questions, and that the same sanctity will not attach to the orders of a court created by virtue of a general agreement that all questions or a considerable range of questions shall be in advance of their origin referred to such a court. The argument, of course, does not hold good when tested by such an institution as the Supreme Court of the United States, nor does there seem to be any reason to believe that the force of public opinion of the world will operate in any less degree to sustain the findings of a duly constituted court than it will to sustain the conclusions of an ephemeral board of arbitration. In the case of the World Court the penalty for disobedience to the consensus of opinion of the entire world will assuredly be more severe than anything which might result from disobedience to the order of a tribunal of arbitration, having its existence only as between two nations in dispute.

82. Some opinions of writers.—The conclusions to which we

---

[3] *Actes et documents*, II, 661.

have come lead us into accord with those entertained by several writers. Commenting upon the general subject, Professor William I. Hull says:

The apparent helplessness of the Supreme Court in its summons to the states and in the enforcement of its judgments against them, would be paralleled in the World Court. The lack of a police power or military force, for the coercion of a sovereign state, would be the most astounding defect of both, in the minds of the thoughtless or of those obsessed with the war-born assumption that there is no real power among men except that of national armaments or an alliance of national armaments.[4]

He found as sanctions for the opinions of the Supreme Court and for a court of nations when formed,

the oaths of the state, or national, officials to sustain the Constitution under which each court is created; this covenant with God and their own consciences, and the good faith and honor arising from it; the majesty of the Supreme Court and the even more majestic World Court; the character and reputation of the judges, and the irresistible appeal of the reasonableness upon which their judgments are based; above all the enlightened and organized public opinion, within each state and within the Union, in the case of the Supreme Court, and within each nation and within the entire family of nations, in the case of the World Court.[5]

Again, it was said by Westlake that

abundant experience of international arbitrations has proved that the awards given in them are generally carried out. Logic may reiterate the warning that there is no security for their being carried out, but the theoretical imperfection of arbitration arising from this cause is not felt to be practically a great deduction from the value of the service which they can render to peace.[6]

Malauzat inquires if it would be desirable or possible to constrain by force states to execute condemnations pronounced against them, and he answers, citing Pillet (*Lettre sur l'arbitrage adressée à M. Straud, 3*) as follows:

The only authority upon which one could rest in international relations is the authority of justice and reason, and this authority is not completely illusory as one might think, for if nations love to triumph by force they detest being reputed to sustain an unjust cause.[7]

Mr. Horace G. Macfarland finds that the great forces operating as sanctions for international law in general are "the necessity of intercourse between states; the conscience of the individual state; and the *sittlichkeit* of the society of nations." He asks,

---

[4] *Proceedings, Society for the Settlement of International Disputes*, 1916, 199.
[5] *Idem.*
[6] *International Law*, II, 352.
[7] *Cour de justice arbitrale*, 153.

Are, or are not, the three above named forces a sufficient sanction to prevent such a glaring act of bad faith as the repudiation of the judgment of the proposed court by a nation that has voluntarily in the most solemn manner submitted to the court's jurisdiction? This must, I think, be answered in the affirmative.[8]

Experience proves the correctness of an affirmative answer.

The lack of a sanction in permanent treaties of arbitration did not seem to Revon a matter of great importance. The essential is, he says, "that an arbitral tribunal be created; once its judgments are rendered the sentiment of national honor can suffice to ensure it respect."[9]

Of similar character were the ideas of William Ladd, who, writing a hundred years ago, said: "Physical power to enforce the laws of our Congress, or the decrees of our Court, forms no part of our plan."[10]

Kamarowsky summarizes Laveleye to the effect that all support of the awards of the (proposed) tribunal by armed force would have as a result the deprivation of nations of their sovereignty. This, he points out, would inaugurate a universal right of intervention and all differences, even insignificant, could light the fires of a general war. We would find ourselves confronted by a new and magnified Holy Alliance, which would offer little guaranty for the ulterior development of liberty.[11]

The experience of the ancient world and of the Middle Ages shows the great importance attached to the making of an oath in connection with international obligations. Today the obligation can no longer be personal to the signer, and the oath is unknown. The obligation is transferred from the individual to the mass, but the duty of good faith becomes not attenuated but extended.

[8] *Proceedings, Society for the Judicial Settlement of International Disputes,* 1913, 325.
[9] *L'arbitrage international,* 495.
[10] *An Essay on a Congress of Nations,* 76.
[11] *Le tribunal international,* 398.

PART II

INFLUENCES WORKING TOWARD JUDICIAL SETTLEMENT

CHAPTER XI

IDEALS OF INTERNATIONAL TRIBUNALS AS DEVELOPED BY THE WRITERS

83. Preliminary observations.—During the long decline of the Roman Empire no attention was paid, so far as history informs us, to any systematic study of the relations between states, for in the modern sense they had no existence. In truth, up to about the year 1800 there was little useful, and practically no effective, thought bestowed upon the judicial settlement of disputes between nations save by a handful of persons. Of course from time to time appear individuals possessed by dreams upon the subject. Even when we discover them their ideas will seem usually very general and always vague.

While once perhaps in a generation some one more advanced than his fellows may have written against war and for arbitration, it will be found that usually his contemporaries knew him not; or if they did, they ignored his preachments in this direction. It has been left to the literary antiquarian of the present day by accident or design to stumble upon his productions, with a tendency on the part of the discoverer to exalt their importance. For to have been really significant they should have had a contemporaneous influence or directed later followers. The fact is that, vague and uncertain though they were, they were too much at variance with their times to move any of the leaders of their day and generally passed speedily into oblivion.

We may venture to believe that if no one of the authors, even Grotius (except those writers within the past one hundred and fifty years whom we shall introduce to the reader), had ever lived, the cause of international judicial action would have been in no wise retarded. The subject was latent till there came about the right conjunction of growth of civilization, softening of manners, general diffusion of intelligence (even though this be yet rudimentary), and a certain rigidity in the structure of nations. There had to be bodies capable of contracting and being contracted with and whose constituents felt responsibility for their actions.

True it is, as we have found elsewhere, that during all the years now under examination there were from time to time arbitral settlements of disputes. Each tribunal was, however, an isolated fact, not a regular proceeding based upon the ideas of authors or pursuant to any theory or predetermined plan.

Many writers attach overmuch importance to the sayings of the earlier authors. We may remind ourselves that about sixty-five years ago Wendell Phillips in one of his orations spoke of the mysterious and as yet unknown powers of the air which mankind would submit to its uses. It will, nevertheless, scarcely be said that the orator was the discoverer of radio. Similarly, we shall not place too much emphasis upon the casual or even planned utterances of men living in a dreamland of their own and exercising scarcely the slightest influence in this regard upon the thought of their day.

Let us now turn to the work of some of those to whom we have referred, more in disparagement after all of their times than of their labors.[1]

84. Early writers on the subject of international justice.—The earliest was Dante, whose conception was of a supreme monarchy capable of disposing of all differences between princes. Says he:

> Between two princes whomsoever, if one is not subject to the other, it is evident that a dispute is possible either by their own fault or that of their subjects. Then there should be a judicial power to settle the conflict. And since no one can judge the other because the latter is not subject to him—for an equal has no jurisdiction over his equal—there should be a third possessing a vaster jurisdiction which by the extent of his right is superior to both. And this is the monarch or the emperor. Thus the monarchy is necessary to the world.[2]

But universal monarchy never prevailed and his words were lost.

We come to Pierre Dubois, a French contemporary of Dante, and a greater master of the judicial idea, for he rejected at once the idea of a universal monarchy. His suggestions have been compared to those embodied in the Hague Conventions, though the resemblance is but superficial and incomplete. According to his plan, there should be a Council of the Christian nations, which should designate men to select three judges from among the prelates. Three should also be named by each of the parties to a dispute, who were not likely to be corrupted, and at a proper place should receive pleadings and proofs, with depositions, and be assisted by assessors, the costs to be defrayed by the two parties. After the decision an appeal might be taken to the Sovereign Pontiff, who could, if it were just to do so, amend or change it. If he did not, it was to be confirmed and registered. Many needed and important details are lacking in this plant, among others as to the selection and numbers of the Council, and the manner of naming the representatives of the parties. Other

---

[1] For much contained in this chapter, at least to the time of the Treaty of Westphalia in 1648, we are indebted to Lange, *Histoire de l'internationalisme*.

[2] Dante, *De Monarchia*, X.

faults are obvious. But of course it accomplished nothing and Dubois himself was forgotten till recently resurrected by the antiquarians.

The next plan, if we may so denominate it, having in mind, like that of Dubois, a sort of union between nations called Christian, was that of George Podiebrad, king of Bohemia. About the year 1462, influenced it is believed by the ideas of Antonius Marini, a French merchant born in Grenoble, he had presented to King Louis XI of France a proposed treaty for the union or federation of Christian nations against the Turk. Crimes committed by the subjects of the powers were not to involve peace, but to be referred to a sort of court or consistory or parliament of all. If one state were to be attacked by an outside power, the federal "congregation" was to send delegates to a suitable place for the purpose of electing arbitrators or persuade the offending party to have the difficulty resolved by a competent judge or the judicial power of the federation. If peace could not be re-established, the members of the federation should aid their associate. The proposition came to nothing, but it seems to us to be a treatment of the subject made by an author rather than an abortive treaty.

Several authors may be dismissed with a few words. We find that Erasmus of Rotterdam was an advocate of conciliation between nations. He declared that it was the duty of a power in the event of difficulty with a neighbor to conciliate or appeal to judicial determination. His exhortations were general, but his plans, if any, took no shape. "Why," he asks, "should not the puerile quarrels of princes be resolved by arbitrators?"

We turn to the writings of two Spaniards who are credited with being at least among the first students of the law of nations in a time when in its human relations it was not far from being barbaric—Francisco de Vitoria (born 1480) and Francisco Suarez (born 1548). While the first urged that the prince should examine carefully into any cause in which he was concerned, yet "Francisco does not suggest the award of an arbiter."[3] Suarez recognized the need of law in an association of states. If the prince were in doubt the matter might be referred to arbitration. As to the prince being bound to make such a reference, he was of the opinion that "the affirmative side is very probable."[4]

We come to Gentile (born 1552). He noted with emphasis the idea, oft repeated later, that wars were necessary because of the lack of a superior jurisdiction. "War," he said, "is introduced of necessity, that

[3] James Brown Scott, *Spanish Origins of International Law*, 90.
[4] *Ibid.*, 83.

is to say that there cannot be litigation between sovereign princes or peoples not subject to a jurisdiction except by their free will, because they have no judge or superior . . . . There is no judge for a prince on this earth, or otherwise stated he is not prince over whom another holds primacy . . . . Then between princes judgment by arms is necessary."[5]

85. Crucé, Sully, and Grotius.—We arrive at a time when three authors almost entirely contemporaneous addressed themselves in some measure to the problem before us—Crucé, Sully, and Grotius. Let us consider the first from the order of publication though not of birth (1590), Eméric Crucé. In 1623 he published *Le nouveau Cynée ou discours d'Estat représentant les occasions et moyens d'establir une paix générale et la liberté de commerce par tout le monde.* His proposition contemplated a permanent congress composed of representatives of all the sovereigns, which should regulate the differences between them. The gravest questions touching sovereignty and independence were to be referred to arbitration, and he thought that, once admitted for them, the court could not be rejected for disputes of lesser importance. The arbiters for grave questions he believed should be princes.

We cannot spend more time over Eméric Crucé. Interesting as is his little volume, it remained without visible influence, and until resurrected recently by some industrious antiquarians it remained practically unknown to later centuries. There is no conclusive evidence that Grotius profited by this particular work or that Sully followed it, though both Sully and Crucé recognized the necessity of giving an economic basis to the political federation proposed.

We have next to consider Grotius (born 1583), whose work, *De jure belli ac pacis,* published in 1625, had so great an influence in regularizing the irregular practices of war. Grotius devotes one section of a single chapter to the discussion of arbitration as a means of settling a dispute before war between those nations which have not a common judge. His whole discussion is decidedly brief and is as follows:

Christian kings and states are above all obliged to resort to arbitration to prevent resort to arms. For if formerly the Jews and Christians, to avoid being judged by those who were not of the true religion, established among themselves amiable arbitral judges, as St. Paul expressly ordered, how much the more should one thus act to escape war, which is a much greater evil. Tertullian, to prove that a Christian should not bear arms, makes use of this argument, which he was not even permitted to plead.

For the reason I have just given and for several others, it would be useful

[5] Lange, *Histoire de l'internationalisme,* 301.

and in some fashion necessary that the Christian powers should make between themselves some sort of body in whose assemblies the troubles of each should be determined by the judgment of others not interested, and that there should be sought means of constraining the parties to come to an agreement under reasonable conditions.[6]

Thus runs his entire argument upon this most important topic.

Grotius again discusses the nature of arbitrations,[7] but having in mind arbitrations succeeding a war and determining conditions of peace, a form today unknown.

We now note the Grand Design of Henry IV, much cited as a precursor of present-day schemes of international governments and of arbitration, and as having influenced the writings of Bentham and others who have materially developed the ideas of the hour. And yet a reading of the Design[8] will fail to develop much of value.

Sully ascribed to the king the intention of uniting all of Christian Europe except Russia against the house of Austria, and taking from it by treaty or by force all of its continental possessions except Spain. These, it is said, were to be divided up equitably among the seizing nations except England, and, though this is not absolutely clear, France. Thereupon a general council was to be called into existence formed on the model of the ancient Amphictyons of Greece, and in the opinion of King Henry IV to consist of four commissaries each, named by the Emperor of Germany, the Pope, the Kings of France, England, Denmark, Sweden, Lombardy, Poland, and the republic of Venice, and of two from the other republics and inferior powers, making a total of about sixty-six persons, to be re-chosen every three years. It was left open as to whether this might not be divided for purposes of convenience into three bodies of twenty-two each, and also was unsettled the question whether there might not be councils of inferior degree. In the event of inferior councils being called into existence an appeal would lie to the general council.

The general duty of the supreme council was "to deliberate on any affairs which might occur; to discuss the different interests; pacify the quarrels; clear up and determine all the civil, political, and religious affairs of Europe, whether within itself or with its neighbors."

Once established, the Grand Design of Sully (or Henry IV) was not flexible in that new arrangements of states were not provided for or any method of amendment indicated.

---

6 Grotius, *De jure belli ac pacis*, II, xxiii, 8.   7 *Ibid.*, III, xx, 46–47.
8 Sully's *Grand Design of Henry IV*, Grotius Society Publications.

All this, while beyond its time, was but a dream, and even as such contained little suggestion of judicial settlement of any difficulties.

86. Fénelon.—A little later, in 1698, came the published utterances of a man—not at all an author on what was then considered the law of nations—Fénelon, Archbishop of Cambrai, who appreciated the subject we discuss as did no other writer of his day. When he wrote *Telemachus* for the benefit of his royal pupil, he argued with eloquence and at great length the righteousness and advisability of arbitration. We quote but a few words:

> A private individual who possesses a field, inheritance from his ancestors, can only maintain himself by the authority of law and the judgment of the magistrate; he would be very severely punished as a disturber if he sought to preserve by force what justice has given him. Do you believe that kings can employ at first violence to sustain their pretensions without having tested all the ways of softness and humanity? Is not justice more sacred and more inviolable for kings with relation to whole countries than for families with relation to cultivated fields? . . . . If the king agrees to some arbiter to settle a difference he shows his equity, his good faith, his moderation. He makes known the solid reasons upon which his cause is founded. The arbitrator chosen is a mediator and not a rigorous judge. One does not submit blindly to his decisions, but one has a great deference for him; he does not pronounce a judgment as a sovereign judge, but makes propositions, and by his counsels one sacrifices something to preserve the peace.[9]

While it is true that Fénelon confused the functions of mediator and arbitrator in his *discours,* we may excuse this as being a matter as to which men presumably more learned in the law have been guilty down to the present day.

87. Penn, Abbé de Saint Pierre, Rousseau, and Vattel.—As a devoted advocate of peace the subject under discussion did not escape the observation of William Penn, who in the last decade of the seventeenth century wrote an *Essay on the Peace of Europe.* He planned the organization of an international tribunal, desiring to form the sovereigns of Europe into a permanent Diet. Disputes escaping settlement by diplomacy were to be laid before it and by it referred to a section of ten members. Refusal to refer by one party or refusal to respect the decision subjected the offender to the exercise of force by the others.

The next step in order of time was by Charles Irénée Castel, Abbé de Saint Pierre, who desired that differences between powers should be presented to a Senate composed of representatives of twenty-four

---

[9] Fénelon, *Telemachus,* Garnier edition, Book XVII, 458.

powers, who were to act as mediators and if necessary as arbitrators. Failure to carry out its conclusions, reached by a three-fourths vote, would result in a declaration that the defaulter was an enemy of the Society of Nations and war against it would be declared. While commented upon and criticized by Leibnitz, as containing the germs of fundamental ideas, it owes its greatest meed of fame to Rousseau.

The plan of the Abbé de Saint Pierre was extensively reviewed by J. J. Rousseau,[10] who broached a modified plan of his own, based upon that of the Abbé, involving five articles: (1) a perpetual irrevocable alliance between the contracting powers, meeting by plenipotentiaries, where all differences were to be terminated by arbitration or judgment; (2) details of the number and method of control of the Diet; (3) confederated guaranty of the possessions and government of each state and renouncement of all anterior pretensions, future disputes to be regulated by arbitration, without violence being resorted to under any pretext; (4) cases under which a violator would be put under the ban of Europe as a common enemy, as, for instance, when it refused to execute judgments, made warlike preparations, negotiated treaties contrary to the federation, or took arms to resist it or to attack one of the allies, with details governing enforcement of its rights by the confederation; (5) the majorities necessary to reach the conclusions of the Diet, but the five fundamental articles not to be changed without the unanimous consent of all parties.

At the time of the formation of the American Union no writer upon international affairs was held in higher repute than Vattel,[11] who showed himself a strong advocate of arbitration and who says much as to the construction, interpretation, and application of the *compromis*. Doubtless in concluding as he does that arbitration is "a very reasonable method and conformable to natural law" he was largely influenced by the Swiss practice of providing for it in all treaties with neighboring powers, whenever differences could not be adjusted amiably.

88. Immanuel Kant.—We come next to the ideas of the great German philosopher, Kant.[12] Referring only to such of his positions as are of present-day interest in the consideration of our text, we find that he considered that "the civil constitution in every state shall be republican," and that "international right shall be founded on a federation of free states." He explained war by saying that "the method by

---

[10] *Les œuvres complètes,* edition of 1823, V, 405 ff.

[11] *Le droit des gens,* edition of 1777, Book II, chap. xviii, § 329.

[12] *Perpetual Peace,* first published in 1795, Trueblood's translation.

which states prosecute their rights cannot under present conditions be a process of law, since no court exists having jurisdiction over them, but only war. But through war, even if it result in victory, the question of right is not decided." However, his main theme was that of international federation, and no scheme for the working out of courts under it was evolved.

89. Bentham and Ladd, and Jay.—We come now to the consideration of the plans of two authors who because of certain fundamental resemblances should be linked together in this discussion. Bentham's *Plan for an Universal and Perpetual Peace,* though written in 1789, was not published till 1838 (republished in *Grotius Society Publications,* No. 6, 1927). After laying down a number of propositions, calculated to insure peace among the nations but foreign to our present purposes, he says:

that the maintenance of such a pacification might be considerably facilitated by the establishment of a Common Court of Judicature for the decision of differences between the several nations, although such Court were not to be armed with any coercive powers.

Bentham argued:

Establish a common tribunal, the necessity for war no longer follows from difference of opinion. Just or unjust, the decision of the arbiters will save the credit, the honour, of the contending party.

Rejecting apparently any necessity for force to insure the performance of judicial awards, Bentham placed force as last among the sanctions of the orders of the Congress or Diet he planned, relying preferably and almost exclusively upon public opinion.

Let us consider an American author, William Ladd, who in 1840 wrote for the American Peace Society, *An Essay on a Congress of Nations for the Adjustment of International Disputes without Resort to Arms.*[18] Without examining, as foreign to our purpose, his plan for a congress of ambassadors for "the purpose of settling the principles of international law by compact and agreement, of the nature of a mutual treaty, and also of devising and promoting plans for the preservation of peace, and meliorating the condition of man," he proposed "a court of nations, composed of the most able civilians in the world, to arbitrate or judge such cases as should be brought before it, by the mutual consent of two or more contending nations."

[18] Reprinted by the Carnegie Endowment for International Peace, edited by Dr. James Brown Scott, 1916.

Touching the enforcement of its decrees, Ladd said: "Physical power to enforce the laws of our Congress, or the decrees of our Court, forms no part of our plan."[14] Again he remarked that he believed "even now, public opinion is amply sufficient to enforce all the decisions of a Court of Nations, and the 'schoolmaster is abroad,' and public opinion is daily obtaining more power."[15]

We have grouped together Bentham and Ladd, not alone because of closeness in point of time of their utterances, but also because they were apparently the first great thinkers who recognized the world's public opinion as offering the surest sanction for the decrees of an international court of judicature. Even William Penn was ready to resort to force to sustain such adjudications.

The writers just mentioned were speedily followed by William Jay.[16] Jay desired that the nations of Europe should erect a court for the trial and decision of their respective differences. Public opinion was to give it power.

90. A period of lassitude.—During the ensuing thirty years little progress in the direction interesting us was made among writers of international law, while, as we see elsewhere, the general idea grew among statesmen. The few writers touching the subject do not seem to have exercised large influence. We only reach a period of real activity consequent upon the reference of the *Alabama* claims to arbitration. Then for the first time men opened their eyes to the possibility of wide application of judicial methods to the settlement of international disputes and commenced to devote volumes to its history and theory. Perhaps we should make passing mention of the work of Bara[17] published in 1872, though written long before. He found one of the greatest needs of the times to be the establishment of an international jurisdiction as alone being capable of leading states to general disarmament, holding that until organized the nations had the right and sometimes the duty to take to arms. "War," he wrote, "will more than once save liberty and peace." Even judicial control, he contended, should be preceded by the promulgation of international law. In fact, his complete tripod consisted of the law, the court, and a federal union.

In the same year was published the work of Goblet d'Alviella[18] of

---

[14] *Op. cit.*, 91.

[15] *Ibid.*, 92.

[16] *War and Peace: The Evils of the First and a Plan for Preserving the Last*, 1842; reprinted by the Carnegie Peace Endowment in 1919, with introductory note by Dr. James Brown Scott.

[17] *La science de la paix.*   [18] *Désarmer ou déchoir*, 1872.

which from our point of view we need say only that it contemplated the gradual establishment of international tribunals, without speaking of their organization or working.

Lorimer, writing a little later, in several essays proposed a court of justice with two sections, civil and criminal. He suggested fourteen judges, six of whom were to be named, one each by the great powers. In civil affairs there was to be but one court of all the members, who would decide by a majority. To the court were to be referred all questions of public international law involving pecuniary or territorial claims, rectification of frontiers, and so forth, dependent upon interpretation of existing treaties or legislative acts of the international government. Questions could be referred by the parties themselves, or sent by an international bureau. Questions of private international law could be raised only on appeal authorized by the government of the state to which the parties belonged.

Lorimer recognized a distinction between juridical disputes, properly so-called, and political questions. The latter went to an international assembly composed of a senate and chamber of deputies. Purely national questions were excluded, but this body determined whether they were national (as we say today, domestic) or international.

The character of civil wars as distinguished from rebellions was to be determined by this body, and whether civil wars came within its jurisdiction. Colonial questions were excluded, in this respect Lorimer doubtless being influenced by the propensity of his native land for colonies. Attempts to enlarge or change frontiers came within the jurisdiction of the assembly, and could be settled directly or upon judicial reference.

The criminal side of the court was to be provided with a public prosecutor.

In 1873 Emile de Laveleye[19] discussed arbitration somewhat as his minor topic. He counted much upon the approval and acceptance of a code, and therefore a system of permanent arbitration with a high court of nations, without favoring force to carry out its decisions, this involving danger to the public peace.

In view of citations already made, it is not strange that, as if by way of preparation in some sort for the coming day when courts would at least be influenced by it, in several places draft codes sprang into existence. We refer to the two leading ones of the time by David

---

[19] *Des causes actuelles de la guerre et de l'arbitrage.*

Dudley Field[20] and Bluntschli.[21] To these may be added those of A. P. Sprague, in *Internationalism* (1876), Fiore and a number of others cited by Darby, *International Tribunals*.

We have to refer to the work of Rouard De Card.[22] This book briefly reviewed the history of arbitration and the views of writers upon the subject. His conclusions point to the advantage of codification of international law, melioration or lowering of tariffs, extension of international conventions.

A book of real importance from the modern standpoint was that of Kamarowsky.[23] In this the Moscow professor discusses methods of solution of conflicts between states, the origin of the idea of an international tribunal, and its theoretical development, the fundamental principles of its organization. This was the first serious attempt on anything like a complete scale to cover the whole subject from both theoretical and practical standpoints. The various propositions of the authors are examined and summed up.

M. Kamarowsky himself proposed the establishment of a court of sixty, two named by each of the eighteen European and twelve American states, members to be chosen from academies or faculties of law, who should make the nominations to the government. When an international congress was organized it should name the judges rather than the separate governments. The judges should be irremovable but invited to resign at sixty-five or seventy years of age. The tribunal, by virtue of the principle of sovereignty, should be voluntary; but reference once made the parties were obliged juridically to submit to its decision rendered within the limits of international law. The voluntary principle would not prevent obligatory conventions to appeal to the tribunal. Domestic questions were excluded from jurisdiction and only juridical international questions were to be considered. In a fashion the author describes juridical questions to be those which by virtue of positive international law or conventions between the parties were capable of objective and juridical appreciation.

Kamarowsky would divide his tribunal into four parts, dependent upon the character of the dispute to be determined—diplomacy, war and navy, private international law, and what he described as social international law. He also expected the court to co-operate in the codifi-

---

20 *Draft Outlines of a Code*, 1872.
21 *Le droit international codifié*, 1869 and 1872.
22 *L'arbitrage international dans le passé, le présent, et l'avenir*, 1877.
23 *Le tribunal international*, 1887.

cation and promulgation of international laws. A number of provisions affecting procedure were provided, among others that the whole body of the court could review the decision of a section.

The work of Kamarowsky was followed in 1889 by that of Mougins de Roquefort.[24] This book, while containing much useful discussion, fails sometimes to differentiate in principle between mediation and arbitration.

An able, interesting, and unusually eloquent work is that of Revon.[25] This embodies an excellent history of the subject, including accounts of the various elements making up its progress, whether individuals, societies, international bodies, the press, parliaments. In his description of the struggle toward peace he stresses very much the necessity for economic unity.

There soon followed the work of Professor Mérignhac.[26] This still remains one of the most useful handbooks on the practice of international arbitration, and is oft cited in the operations of tribunals of this nature. After the historical part, as good as then available data permitted, the author discusses acutely the contract of *compromis* from all points of view—the selection of arbitrators, organization and workings of the tribunal, and in detail procedure before it—with examination as to the nature and enforcement of the award. The formation of the great international court of the future is envisaged from the standpoint of broad principle rather than in detail, and the work closes with a discussion as to the obstacles in its way.

We now reach a period of greater political activity and less speculative writing affecting international courts. The year 1899 was marked by the first Hague Peace Convention and the year 1907 by the second. Between these dates was published *Les sanctions de l'arbitrage international* by Jacques Dumas. This work goes beyond the title and discusses the subject from the broadest point of view. The sanctions proposed by the various theorists are examined in the light of their main theses. Sanctions are classified as moral, material, civil, penal, and political, and all from their historical aspect.

Before much further attention could be given to our subject came the long night of the World War when all thought of agencies of peace

---

24 *De la solution juridique des conflits internationaux.*

25 *L'arbitrage international,* 1892.

26 *Traité théorique et pratique de l'arbitrage international* with the subtitle, *Le rôle du droit dans le fonctionnement actuel de l'institution et dans ses destinées futures,* 1893.

was suspended, only to be resumed with the signing of the Treaty of Versailles, and followed by the institution of the Permanent Court of International Justice. Of the workings of this court have been written several excellent compendiums, of which we mention *The World Court*, by Señor Antonio S. de Bustamante, and *The Permanent Court of International Justice*, by Professor Manley O. Hudson.

We conclude this branch of our discussion with a reference to the last volume treating the subject of international tribunals in anything like a broad way—*La justice internationale*, by Professor N. Politis. As the work of an experienced internationalist, it commands our respect, being a fundamental though not exhaustive treatise upon the theory as well as the history of international tribunals. In scope and method of treatment in many ways it suggests the approach of Kamarowsky and Mérignhac, though more philosophical and less concerned with the details of arbitration; and, of course, being later in date, it treats largely of the present Permanent Court of International Justice.

CHAPTER XII

LEGISLATIVE EXPRESSIONS TOUCHING JUDICIAL SETTLEMENT

91. General observations.—Much of the progress and development of arbitration from a practical point of view has come from the executive rather than from the legislative side of government. We may illustrate this by reference to treaties of arbitration from the time of the Jay Treaty to the latest agreement to arbitrate filed with the League of Nations. In all these the legislature, while under certain constitutions taking a final part, as in the case of the Senate in the United States, has usually played, at least directly, a relatively unimportant rôle. The active moving instrumentality has been universally the executive. Nevertheless it is true that the state of feeling prevailing in the legislature may have had its influence upon the executive, while, when necessary, the ratification or non-ratification of pacts submitted by the executive is a matter of the most vital importance.

Let us now consider legislative reports and debates bearing upon the question.

92. United States.—The earliest legislative attention to the general subject was given by the legislature of Massachusetts. The American Peace Society on February 6, 1835, urged upon the legislature "that some mode of just arbitration should be established for the amicable and final adjustment of all international disputes instead of an appeal to arms," and that "such steps may be taken in relation thereto as may appear best adapted to promote the end in view." The committee to which reference was had prepared an extended favorable report on which no final action was taken.

In 1837 the representative of the American Peace Society again petitioned to like effect, and the legislature so resolved.

Based doubtless upon the petitions mentioned and others, both privately signed and by the Massachusetts Peace Society, the legislature by resolution approved April 25, 1838, called for the "institution of a Congress of Nations for the purpose of framing a code of international law, and establishing a high court of arbitration for the settlement of controversies between nations." The governor was requested to send a copy of the resolutions and report to the President and to the other state governors for the co-operation of their legislatures.

The American Peace Society, the Vermont Peace Society, and others

in 1837 petitioned Congress to accede to a proposition of the Mexican
Congress for reference to arbitration by a friendly power of claims
which the two countries now or hereafter could not compromise. The
petitioners further prayed that Congress adopt the principle of reference
to a third party on disputes not amicably adjusted, as an invariable and
not an occasional rule of action. This latter proposition was reported
upon unfavorably by Mr. Legare of the Foreign Affairs Committee,
who attacked it at great length and who found as an objection entirely
fatal that

The unanimous consent of nations, in the actual state of the world, to such a
proposal, is—as anyone will be convinced who reflects a moment upon their political relations, or who will but cast his eye over a map of Europe—entirely out of
the question; and the refusal of a single great power to acquiesce in it, would
alone render it abortive.[1]

The report, however, agreed in "recommending a reference to a third
power of all such controversies as can safely be confided to any tribunal
unknown to the constitution of our own country. Such a practice will
be followed by other powers, already inclined . . . . to avoid war
and will soon grow up into the customary law of civilized nations."

Other petitions submitted about this time received similar treatment.[2]

In 1850, the Peace Society again petitioning, Senator Foote of
Mississippi reported from the Foreign Relations Committee a resolution
to the effect that it would be proper and desirable for the United States,
whenever practicable, to secure in its treaties a provision referring to
umpires all future misunderstandings not capable of amicable negotiation before resort to hostilities. This was allowed to lie on the table.

The same committee through Senator Underwood on February 22,
1853, by the smallest majority reported a resolution to much the same
effect as that reported by Senator Foote, urging treaty provisions for
adjustment of misunderstandings and controversies by disinterested and
impartial arbitrators to be mutually chosen. This was never debated in
the Senate.

On January 22, 1872, John B. Storm of Pennsylvania introduced in
the House of Representatives a resolution advocating arbitration as a
substitute for war in settling national differences, and Senator Charles
Sumner did likewise in the Senate on May 31 of the same year. On
June 9, 1874, Senator Hamlin of Maine presented a resolution from the
Committee on Foreign Relations embodying part of the Sumner Reso-

[1] Ladd's *Essay on a Congress of Nations*, Appendix, 137.
[2] *Arbitration and the United States*, 488.

lution. On the last day of the session the Senate passed the resolution, which simply recommended "the adoption of arbitration as a just and practical method for the determination of international differences, to be maintained sincerely and in good faith, so that war may cease to be regarded as a proper form of trial between nations."

Meanwhile, on June 17, 1874, Stewart L. Woodford of New York had moved a concurrent resolution in the House of Representatives, requesting the President to negotiate with all willing civilized powers for the establishment of an international system of arbitration, and this was adopted by the House. Immediately afterward in the same body, Godlove S. Orth of Indiana reported from the Committee on Foreign Affairs a House resolution looking to the use of the treaty-making power of the government to secure adjustment of "all alleged causes of difference by impartial arbitration."

The Woodford resolution was not acted upon by the Senate, which contented itself with the Hamlin resolution above referred to.

Bills were introduced in the Senate by James F. Wilson of Iowa in December 1887, and by William B. Allison of the same state in April 1888, the first calling for an international tribunal to settle disputes between nations, and the second specifying Great Britain and France as the states to be negotiated with.[3] On June 13, 1888, a resolution favorable to arbitration introduced by John Sherman, Chairman of the Committee on Foreign Relations, was passed. This was afterward (December 9, 1889) introduced as a concurrent resolution and adopted by both houses. It requested the President to invite at opportune times any foreign nation with which we had diplomatic relations to agree to reference to arbitration of any differences or disputes which could not be adjusted by diplomatic agency. Meanwhile, various bills to like ends were introduced in the House by Messrs. McKinley, Yardley, and Kerr.

Let us now touch in a summary way upon treaties of arbitration receiving the attention of both the executive and legislative treaty branches of our government—the Senate.[4]

In response to the expressions on the part of both branches of the American Congress, the British House of Commons and as well the French Chamber of Deputies, Secretary of State Gresham took up the matter with the English Minister, but his death interrupted the discussion. Later, in 1896, Lord Salisbury reverted to the matter in a long note to the British Minister, submitting a detailed plan for an arbitral

---

[3] *Arbitration and the United States,* 498.
[4] For full information we refer to *Arbitration and the United States.*

board, but not giving it jurisdiction over any "difference which in the judgment of either power, materially affects its honor or the integrity of its territory . . . . except by special agreement." The result of long negotiations between Lord Pauncefote and Secretary Olney was a proposed treaty submitted to the Senate. This, however, came to no final vote during Cleveland's administration.

President McKinley resubmitted the treaty, and it was reported to the Senate with modifications. Important amendments were proposed by the minority of the committee, and after much debate the treaty was rejected, a two-thirds majority being lacking—43 yeas, 26 nays.

The subject was renewed by President Roosevelt. In 1903 an arbitration treaty was concluded between Great Britain and France, and this induced activity in this country in which the President took part, in the first place by the submission of the proposed treaty mentioned to the members of the Senate Committee on Foreign Relations, all but one of whom encouraged him to proceed. Accordingly Secretary Hay invited other nations to enter into like treaties with the United States, and such were signed with a number of them. The Senate advised and consented to the ratification of the French treaty with an amendment which provided that, before appealing to the Permanent Court of Arbitration, the parties should conclude a special *treaty* instead of *agreement* as originally provided. This, of course, reserved the powers of the Senate as fully as if there had been no arbitration treaty at all. Ratifications were never exchanged.

Later, however, the President negotiated with France an arbitration treaty for reference to the Permanent Court of Arbitration of difficulties of a legal nature or relating to interpretation of treaties not settled diplomatically, and not affecting vital interests, independence, or honor of the contractants, and not concerning the interests of third parties. This, however, contemplated an agreement in each case to be ratified by the Senate, and in France constitutionally. The Senate thus won its fight for its claimed prerogative of control over all treaties, and exchange of ratifications followed. At this time twenty-five treaties were negotiated, three of which never went into effect, and eleven were allowed to lapse, though one was later renewed.

In 1911 President Taft negotiated treaties with France and England which illustrated a considerable advance over previous efforts. These referred to the Hague Court justiciable questions not possible to adjust by diplomacy, but by special agreement to be advised and consented to by the Senate. The treaties provided for a joint high commission of inquiry, to which, upon request of either party, a controversy could be referred for investigation before submission to arbitration. This commission should be composed of three nationals of either nation unless otherwise constituted by exchange of notes. The question as to whether a dispute was subject to arbitration under Article 1 of the treaty was to be submitted to the commission.

The proposed treaties were the subject of extended debate in the Senate, which took away the power given to the joint commission of determining if a controversy were subject to arbitration, and added a resolution withdrawing from arbitration questions affecting admission of aliens to the country or to educational institutions, affecting territorial integrity, indebtedness of any state, or the Monroe Doctrine, or other purely governmental policy. With this condition of affairs President Taft declined to proceed with exchange of ratifications.

We need not do more than briefly refer to some recent events still comparatively fresh in the mind of the reader. We mention first the Covenant of the League of Nations, approval of which, after the making of reservations, failed to receive a two-thirds majority in the Senate. It will be recalled that, among other points of difference, President Wilson considered its Article X "the heart of the Covenant," and only in an objectionable sense did the opponents agree with him. Experience seems to have shown that Article X had much less importance than either side attributed to it.

The Senate in 1926, subject to certain reservations not necessary for us to consider, agreed to accept contingently the jurisdiction of the Permanent Court of International Justice. The fifth reservation was so worded as to make its literal acceptance difficult and further consideration as to its meaning and application is pending.

93. Great Britain.—On June 12, 1849, Richard Cobden[5] moved in the House of Commons that the British Government should conclude with other powers treaties by which they should agree to resort to arbitration between themselves of differences not arranged through diplomatic negotiations. While he was not a partisan of a supreme court of nations he thought his plan would render wars more just and more legitimate. This motion provoked a lively debate, one member styling it as inopportune and ridiculous.

Lord Palmerston opposed Cobden's motion, not disapproving of the principle but declaring that for England it would be injurious and for

---

[5] Kamarowsky, *Le tribunal international*, 281.

other states inadmissible. Without a sufficiently large army, the arbitral tribunal would be no more than a mediation. Private individuals as judges would be incompetent.

After a long debate Cobden's motion was rejected—176 nays to 97 yeas.

Twenty-four years later, July 8, 1873, Henry Richard again raised the question in the House of Commons, moving an address to the Queen for the purpose of charging the foreign minister to enter into communication with other powers to ameliorate international law and institute a permanent and general system of international arbitration. This he supported in a long and brilliant speech.[6]

Gladstone as Prime Minister responded, finding the motion premature and therefore more injurious than useful. He did not think the idea had as yet penetrated sufficiently public opinion and the European cabinets. Others responded and the motion for previous question prevailed—98 to 88—the Richard motion being adopted without division.

The response of the Queen promised whenever occasion presented itself to seek to extend the settling of international differences by the impartial judgments of friendly powers and the adoption of international rules. This means mediation rather than arbitration, yet it had its influence on the Continent.

In 1887 William Randal Cremer circulated a memorial in the British House of Commons, which was signed by 232 members and presented to the President and both Houses of the American Congress by a delegation of members of Parliament. This, backed up by measures introduced in Congress, induced the United States to conclude with Great Britain a treaty to refer to arbitration disputes not adjusted by diplomatic agency. It received the hearty consideration of the President and was shortly followed by the steps recited in speaking above of the course of our Senate and House of Representatives. In England these events inspired great popular activity, petitions being signed by nearly 1,300,000 persons, and led to the adoption of a favorable resolution by the House of Commons. President Cleveland took pleasure in commending it to Congress.[7]

94. France.—On January 12, 1849, M. Bouvet asked the French Assembly to take steps for the convocation of a congress looking toward disarmament and the establishment of arbitral tribunals to take the place of war.[8] While the examining committee found the propositions

---

[6] *Ibid.,* 288.   [7] *Arbitration and the United States,* 500.
[8] Kamarowsky, *op. cit.,* 304.

reasonable, they declared against French initiative in view of the then unrest in Europe.

In 1879 a number of the inhabitants of the department of the Rhone petitioned the Chamber of Deputies to come to an understanding with the governments of other countries upon the establishment of an arbitral tribunal. This the examining committee, while agreeing with the sentiment of the petitioners, found premature. It said:

The idea is making way among intelligent people; it is up to the press, to meetings, to associations to propagate it more and more. Such is the conclusion of the committee.[9]

In 1887 Messrs. Passy and Boger[10] submitted to the Chamber of Deputies resolutions relative to the creation of a general arbitral tribunal and an extension of processes of mediation and arbitration. The committee found they could not be taken into consideration when all nations, even neutralized ones, were on a formidable war footing. However, the French Chamber of Deputies on July 8, 1895, invited the government as soon as possible to negotiate a permanent treaty of arbitration with the United States.[11]

95. Italy.—Italy was early among modern nations to give considerable application to the compromissory clause and advancement of international arbitration. In 1871 Signor Morelli proposed in parliament a motion in favor of an international amphictyonic tribunal. In 1873 Signor Mancini proposed[12] that the chamber resolve that the government should strive in its foreign relations to render arbitration a more accepted and frequent method of resolving according to justice international litigation; that when occasion arose it should introduce in treaties a clause directing that difficulties over their interpretation and execution should be referred to arbitrators. This was unanimously carried.

According to Bluntschli,[13] Italy was the first to introduce the compromissory clause in treaties of commerce and navigation, and a long series of such treaties is cited by Mérignhac (p. 203).

In the month of June, 1890, in both houses of the Italian parliament the subject of arbitral treaties was raised. The prime minister gave scant encouragement in view of the increasing armaments, but the

---

[9] Kamarowsky, *Le tribunal international*, 305.
[10] Mérignhac, *L'arbitrage international*, 370.
[11] *Arbitration and the United States*, 500.
[12] Mérignhac, 375.
[13] *Le droit international codifié*, 489.

following month both houses authorized their negotiation with other powers.

96. Spain.—In 1890, on the motion of Señor Marcoartu, the Senate adopted a resolution authorizing the government to proceed to the negotiation of general and special treaties of arbitration with civilized countries whose independence and authority were recognized. The Minister of Foreign Affairs, declaring that Spain had several times resorted to arbitration and would continue to do so as much as possible, thought that to be useful the movement should extend to all countries. On June 12, 1893, Señor Marcoartu and others[14] followed up the matter by presenting a draft of a law declaring that hereafter no international convention should be ratified if it did not contain a clause submitting to arbitration questions which might arise as to the interpretation and application of the treaty. The preamble recites that the Academy of Moral and Political Sciences had November 21, 1883, expressed its desire for such a clause, and other bodies had done likewise.

97. Netherlands.—On November 26, 1874 (Mérignhac, 376), the second chamber carried a motion inviting the government to use all its efforts to make arbitration the method of settling disputes between civilized people, and that meanwhile the compromissory clause should be inserted in all treaties concluded between Holland and other states.

98. Sweden and Norway.—The second chamber of the Swedish diet in 1874 and the Norwegian parliament in 1890 (Mérignhac, 376) asked the king on all suitable occasions to use his efforts to bring about the establishment of an arbitral tribunal, permanent or special, to settle international differences.

99. Belgium.—On January 20, 1875 (Mérignhac, 377), the chamber of representatives invited the government to seek when occasion offered the establishment of procedure for the creation and working of international arbitrations, and when convenient to seek in treaties settlement by arbitration of differences under them. The senate concurred the following month.

100. Denmark.—In March 1875 (Mérignhac, 377) a proposition was brought before the Rigsdag asking the government to work for the establishment of a European arbitral court to decide international disputes. In March 1888, the lower house of the Danish parliament expressed its sympathy for an address signed by five to six thousand

---

[14] *Revue de droit international et de législation comparée* (1893), 409.

Danes demanding the establishment of a permanent court of international arbitration, especially for the Scandinavian nations. In November 1890, the Minister of Foreign Affairs said that, while willing to accept the propositions made him, the innovation would have the great powers against it.

101. Roumania.—The chamber of deputies in the commencement of the year 1893 voted urgence upon a proposition asking the government, in its foreign relations, to strive to make arbitration an accepted and common method of resolving according to justice international controversies as to matters susceptible of arbitration, and to take advantage of opportunities to introduce into treaties a clause referring to arbitrators difficulties arising out of their interpretation and execution.

102. Germany.—In 1878 (Mérignhac, 380) Herr Zimmerman vainly proposed to the Reichstag a resolution relative to the establishment of arbitral tribunals, and on February 8, 1893, a like proposition coming from Herr Bebel met the same fate.

CHAPTER XIII

COLLECTIVE AGENCIES WORKING FOR ARBITRATION AND JUDICIAL SETTLEMENT

103. Peace societies in the United States.—The general subject of which we write has commanded a very considerable support in the United States even from an early period. The first organized movement resulted in the formation of the New York Peace Society in August 1815. This was followed during the same year by similar societies in Ohio, Massachusetts, Pennsylvania, Maine, New Hampshire, Vermont, Rhode Island, Connecticut, Georgia, and North Carolina. In 1828 these various organizations were gathered into a national body known as the American Peace Society, which exists to this day and during all these years has regularly published an official organ. For many years it has had as a part of its platform the furtherance, among other things, of commissions of inquiry, councils of conciliation, arbitration of differences, international courts of justice with obligatory jurisdiction, and the enlargement of the obligatory jurisdiction of the Permanent Court of International Justice by the framing of rules of international law.[1]

In 1895 was organized a voluntary association meeting annually at Lake Mohonk, New York, for the purpose of conferring upon the subject of arbitration. Its conferences were kept up for twenty years and the reports of its proceedings are entitled to large respect, active participants having included many of the most prominent international lawyers of the United States.

In 1907 occurred the first meeting of the American Society of International Law, which had been in process of formation during two preceding years. Its main purpose was and is to further the study of international law, but it has given large attention to all matters of arbitration and judicial settlement of disputes.

In 1910, largely under the efficient leadership of Dr. James Brown Scott, there was organized the American Society for the Judicial Settlement of International Disputes, the prime purpose of which was to secure settlement of disputes through an international judiciary rather

---

[1] For a full history of this Society and of the development of peace propaganda in the United States and abroad, see *The American Peace Society—A Centennial History*, by Edson L. Whitney.

than to further the more limited field of arbitration. This lasted actively until 1915, and during the period of its existence gathered together many eminent advocates of the peaceful settlement of international troubles.

On October 12, 1912, there was organized, chiefly through the labors of Dr. James Brown Scott, the American Institute of International Law, the purpose of which was to unite in one organization the most eminent authorities on international law to be found in the Western Hemisphere and to codify the law of nations. This society has exercised a wide influence on international thought within the sphere of its operation. Its *Recommendations of Habana Concerning International Organization* (published under this title with other valuable matter by the Carnegie Peace Endowment) called for arbitration of non-justiciable disputes, and a court of justice when justiciable and assuming political importance.

Contemporaneously with discussions in Congress and in the several legislatures of which we speak elsewhere, organizations of importance, such as the Bar Association of the State of New York, have worked actively for the cause of a permanent international court, this association having, in resolutions passed in 1896, asked the President of the United States to prepare a plan for the organization of a permanent international court.

In the month of January 1915, a meeting of prominent women of the United States was held at Washington to further measures in the interest of peace, and particularly to attack the economic causes of war. This resulted in a larger gathering a year later, which brought about the formation of the world-wide Women's International League for Peace and Freedom.

104. Organizations abroad.—A number of peace conventions have been held in the various countries of Europe, as for instance, London in 1843 and 1851, Paris in 1849, Brussels in 1848 and 1873, Frankfort in 1850, and at Geneva as late as 1926. At all of these meetings the subject of arbitration and international tribunals has played a prominent part. These conventions were in part at least the outgrowth of the work of the London Peace Society, organized in 1816, La Société des Amis de la Morale Chrétienne et de la Paix, organized in Paris in 1821, and the Geneva Peace Society, established in 1830. Back of recent European congresses has been largely the Bureau International de la Paix, for many years located at Berne but now at Geneva. We should add that twenty-four congresses, beginning with that of Paris in 1889, have been held under an initiative beginning with the International League of Peace and Freedom.[2]

In 1867 the League of Peace and Freedom was founded at Geneva, aiming at the codification of international law and the establishment of an international court. Its labors have continued to the present time. It is now known as Association de la paix par le droit.

In 1873 there was formed at Ghent by leading internationalists, largely European, the Institute of International Law. The subject of arbitral procedure received especial attention early in its career, and proposed rules governing it were adopted by this Institute August 28, 1875. These rules were based upon a report by Mr. Goldschmidt, who had been theretofore directed by the Institute to prepare a report upon the subject. Later, at its session at Zurich in 1877, the Institute urged the adoption of the compromissory clause as applicable to the interpretation and application of all future treaties. In 1904, at its Edinburgh session, it expressed the opinion that in all cases of divergent interpretation of international conventions resort should be had to the Permanent Court of Arbitration at The Hague. In its session at Christiania in 1912, it endorsed strongly the desire expressed by the second Peace Conference for the establishment of a court of arbitral justice.

In October 1873 there was formed at Brussels, the International Law Association, the inception of which appears to have been due to Dr. James B. Miles, Secretary of the American Peace Society. It was at first given the name of "Association for the Reform and Codification of the Law of Nations," that title being changed later. The membership of this organization differs widely from that of the Institute of International Law, and is unlimited. Its appeal is not alone to lawyers or specialists in international law, but to all persons interested in any phase of the subject from a practical point of view. Its labors have been directed to private international law as well as public. It has favored an international code, particularly in the beginning of its career, on the theory that a code must precede any general resort to arbitration, and that the want of one obstructed the substitution of arbitration for war. In 1895 it adopted rules of procedure for international arbitration and in 1901 discussed the treaty of arbitration between Great Britain and France.

Latterly several organizations have been formed deserving at least mention, as for instance, the Federation of the League of Nations Societies, brought into existence in 1919, and L'Union juridique internationale, organized in Paris in 1919.

2 Whitney, *The American Peace Society—A Centennial History*, 168.

In 1888, at Paris, several French and English parliamentary members, upon the insistence of William Randal Cremer, of the British House of Commons, presided over by M. Passy, had the idea of grouping together the parliamentary representatives of various countries in an interparliamentary union where questions relative to peace and especially arbitration could receive attention. An earlier attempt in this same line dates back to 1870. The first meeting, however, as the Interparliamentary Union, took place in 1889. The most important step taken by it in its early history was at the Hague meeting in 1894, at which the principles were laid down upon which a permanent court of arbitration should be organized. These principles declared that national sovereignty must be maintained, the adhesion to the court must be voluntary, all nations must enjoy complete equality, and its decisions must have the form of executory judgment. Its draft for the organization of a permanent court of arbitration, submitted by Senator Descamps of Belgium in 1895, contributed materially to the convention on the subject adopted by the Hague Conference of 1899. The resolutions of this body gathered at St. Louis in 1904, presented to President Roosevelt, resulted later in the calling of the Second Hague Peace Conference. This organization has been actively maintained to the present time.

At the Paris Peace Conference, held in 1919, there were submitted several plans having national endorsement.[3] The first of these was submitted by the Italian Government and proposed an international court of justice composed of judges, one from each contracting state, appointed for a term of six years. The German delegation also presented a draft somewhat analogous to the Italian draft. The Austrian delegation came forward with a note based on suggestions made by Professor Lammasch calling for a tribunal of fifteen judges and eight deputy judges elected by the general assembly of the League, so that no state had more than one member. As early as 1917 the Scandinavian countries had begun to work out a plan for world organization, one part of which dealt with international judicial power. Later these nations, together with the Swiss Federal Council and also the Netherlands, drafted plans for the organization of the court, which were submitted to the advisory committee of jurists, to which was referred the formation of a statute to control the Permanent Court of International Justice.

---

[3] Bustamante, *The World Court,* 33.

CHAPTER XIV

LATIN AMERICA'S WORK FOR ARBITRATION

105. Conferences and congresses.—We shall see from a cursory glance that Latin America, through its congresses and conferences either among the nations of Central and South America or in conjunction with other countries, has taken many steps toward international arbitration. While one is compelled to recognize that many of these efforts have failed in their beginnings, nevertheless the cumulative effect even of failures has been marked in advancing the cause of juridical settlement. At the same time the successes have been marked and have created most important precedents and examples.

From a period in the midst of the struggles between the Spanish colonies and Spain, Bolívar indicated his devotion to international union and peace. In 1815 he asked:

> Why should remote climes, diverse situations, opposing interests, dissimilar characters, divide America? How beautiful it would be if the Isthmus of Panama could be for us what the Isthmus of Corinth was for the Greeks! Would to God that some day we have the fortune of installing there an august Congress of the representatives of the republics, kingdoms, and empires, to treat and discuss the high interests of peace and war with the nations of the other three parts of the world.[1]

Resulting undoubtedly from Bolívar's influence we find that a treaty between Colombia and Peru, dated July 6, 1822, looked to the settlement of all difficulties and disputes by a general assembly of the American states which should act as an arbitral judge and conciliator. This was followed by similar provisions in treaties between Colombia and Mexico and Colombia and Chile.

In 1822, Bolívar invited the presidents of Colombia, Mexico, Peru, Chile, and Buenos Aires to send their plenipotentiaries to the Isthmus of Panama for the purpose of forming an assembly which could be useful "in great conflicts and be a point of contact in common dangers and faithful interpreter of our public treaties when difficulties should arise and as conciliator of our differences."[2] Nothing, however, came of this at the time, and on December 7, 1824, his formal call to the governments of the American republics was issued. In doing this he reverted to his earlier language, indulging in prophecy:

> When after a hundred centuries posterity may seek the origin of our public

---

[1] Urrutia, *La evolución del principio de arbitraje en America*, 18.
[2] *Ibid.*, 27.

law and recall the pacts which have solidified its destiny, it will register with respect the protocols of the Isthmus. In them it will discover the plan of the first alliances, which will trace the march of our relations with the universe. What will then be the Isthmus of Corinth compared with that of Panama?[3]

Bolívar looked forward with confidence to Great Britain's joining with the Latin-American countries, thus offering a confederation superior to that of the Holy Alliance. From this union he anticipated advantages to England and to all the world.

With high expectations the representatives of Colombia, Central America, Peru, and Mexico met on June 22, 1826, and adjourned on July 15, expecting to gather later in Mexico at a similar congress. The United States was not represented, delegates named by it not arriving in time. Great Britain and Holland were represented by observers.

Sundry treaties were signed, our interest, however, being confined to Articles 16 and 17 of the Treaty of Union and Perpetual Confederation, which attempted to establish a general assembly of the confederated powers as a supreme tribunal. This treaty was ratified only by Colombia, and that at a time when Bolívar was dissatisfied with the results of his work and considered it a failure. The proposed gathering in Mexico never took place.

Another attempt was made at Lima toward the end of 1847 to unite the Spanish-American countries through a congress of plenipotentiaries of the American republics of the Pacific, including Chile, Peru, Bolivia, Ecuador, and Colombia. A treaty was signed at this congress on February 8, 1848, for the determination among other things of boundary questions, which were to be submitted to an arbitral tribunal. The use of good offices was also provided for, and the arbitration suggested, while attenuated, was considered, nevertheless, a step in the development of public international law. Nothing, however, appears to have come of it.

A further congress was held at Santiago in September, 1856, without reference to arbitration, however.

In 1864–1865, a congress was held at Lima, including representatives of Chile, Bolivia, Colombia, Ecuador, Peru, El Salvador, and Venezuela, at which a treaty was signed, providing for reference to the decision of an arbiter when difficulties could not be otherwise arranged. This, however, was never ratified.

A conference held in Caracas in 1883, attended by various American

3 Urrutia, *op. cit.,* 29.

plenipotentiaries, resolved in favor of the establishment of arbitration as the sole solution of all controversies upon rights and interests which might be in dispute. Otherwise than as the expression of a desire it resulted in nothing.

We come now to the first active steps taken by the United States in association with the Latin-American countries and looking toward closer universal relations.   In 1882 Secretary of State Blaine sent a circular letter to all the American republics, inviting them to assemble at a congress which it was proposed should take place in Washington. Because, however, of disturbed conditions in South America, nothing came of this project until 1889. Then the invitation was renewed, and the first Pan-American Conference was held in Washington from October 2, 1889, to April 19, 1890. On its agenda was a proposition for the formulation of a definite plan for the arbitration of international disputes. There was much difference of opinion among the delegates as to how far arbitration could go. The plan, so far as it might be called one, which the delegates adopted contemplated arbitration as a principle of American international law for the solution of differences and disputes between two or more of them, and declared that arbitration was obligatory in all questions of diplomatic or consular privilege, limits, territories, indemnifications, rights of navigation, and validity, interpretation, and execution of treaties. This plan, however, was never ratified. The conference marked, nevertheless, a step in advance as it provided for the creation of the International Bureau of American Republics.

A second Pan-American Conference was held at Mexico City from October 22, 1901, to January 31, 1902, with the question of compulsory arbitration the chief subject of discussion. One of the results of the conference was the signing of a treaty, ratified finally by Salvador, Guatemala, Uruguay, and Mexico, providing for arbitration of all disputes not affecting national independence or national honor. A further result was the signing of another treaty, finally ratified by Guatemala, Salvador, Costa Rica, and Colombia, providing for the submission to the Hague Permanent Court of Arbitration of all claims for pecuniary damage of sufficient importance and not adjusted. A commission of five jurists to prepare a draft code of public and private international law was also authorized.

The third Pan-American Conference was held at Rio de Janeiro from July 21 to August 25, 1906. This resulted in extending the treaty providing for reference to The Hague signed January 30, 1902, until December 31, 1912. It was resolved

To recommend to the governments represented therein that they consider the point of inviting the Second Peace Conference at The Hague to examine the question of the compulsory collection of public debts, and, in general, means tending to diminish between nations conflicts having an exclusively pecuniary origin.[4]

The fourth Pan-American Conference was held at Buenos Aires from July 12 to August 30, 1910. This resulted in little, so far as arbitration was concerned, beyond the preparation of a new convention with reference to pecuniary claims. To this was added that the decision in arbitration "shall be rendered in accordance with the principles of international law," of course, changing in no respect the principle usually followed in arbitrations.

The fifth Pan-American Conference was held at Santiago, Chile, from March 25 to May 3, 1923. This conference declared its general approval of the extension which had taken place in recent years in the application of conciliation, judicial settlement, and arbitration as means of deciding controversies between the nations of the continent, and expressed the hope that progress of these methods of settlement might continue and their application in the near future be as general and broad as possible.

The Costa Rican delegation presented a project for the establishment of a permanent American Court of Justice, which proposition was referred to the Committee of Jurists for study.

The most important work of this conference was with relation to a proposition submitted by Señor Gondra of Paraguay looking to the extension of commissions of inquiry. This we sufficiently discuss in chapter xxvii, entitled "International Commissions of Inquiry."

The sixth Pan-American Conference was held at Havana, Cuba, January 16 to February 20, 1928. At this conference an attempt was made to bring about a change in the Gondra Convention; but this was postponed while that convention was under consideration by the states which had not yet ratified. This conference passed a resolution which reads as follows:

WHEREAS the American Republics desire to express that they condemn war as an instrument of national policy in their mutual relations; and

WHEREAS the American Republics have the most fervent desire to contribute in every possible manner to the development of international means for the pacific settlement of conflicts between states:

1. That the American Republics adopt obligatory arbitration as the means

4 *Report of Delegates of the United States,* Senate Document No. 365, 59th Congress, 2d Session, 116.

which they will employ for the pacific solution of their international differences of a juridical character.

2. That the American Republics will meet in Washington within the period of one year in a conference of conciliation and arbitration to give conventional form to the realization of this principle, with the minimum exceptions which they may consider indispensable to safeguard the independence and sovereignty of the states, as well as matters of a domestic concern, and to the exclusion also of matters involving the interest or referring to the action of a state not a party to the convention.

3. That the Governments of the American Republics will send for this end plenipotentiary jurisconsults with instructions regarding the maximum and the minimum which they would accept in the extension of obligatory arbitral jurisdiction.

4. That the convention or conventions of conciliation and arbitration which may be concluded should leave open a protocol for progressive arbitration which would permit the development of this beneficent institution up to its maximum.

5. That the convention or conventions which may be agreed upon, after signature, should be submitted immediately to the respective Governments for their ratification in the shortest possible time.

Certain other congresses call for attention. One was held in September, 1856, at Santiago, which, while doing nothing for arbitration, prepared a treaty called "Treaty of Continental Union." It contained this provision:

The Congress of plenipotentiaries will have right and representation sufficient to offer mediation by means of an individual or individuals from its midst operating in case of differences between the contracting states, and none of them shall have power to refuse to accept such mediation.

On November 9, 1856, a like treaty was signed at Washington between Mexico, New Granada, Venezuela, Guatemala, Salvador, and Costa Rica. Neither treaty was ratified.

In 1892, a juridical congress was held at Madrid, composed of representatives of Spain, Portugal, and the Latin-American countries. Arbitration cut a large figure in its discussions. The congress resolved: (1) That arbitration is convenient in the present state of international society, to decide contentions between nations; (2) Its acceptance by Latin America, Portugal, and Spain would be very opportune at the present moment; (3) That the states represented in the congress should prepare special treaties of arbitration, taking as basis that between Spain and Ecuador of May 23, 1888, until new and desired progress in international public law may make possible the creation of a permanent tribunal destined to avoid or put an end to existing questions or questions which may arise between the states mentioned; (4) All international conflicts without exception should be submitted to arbitration. A further clause provided for additional doctrinal labors. A later congress of like character, meeting at Madrid toward the end of 1900, declared in favor of obligatory arbitration without exceptions as a norm of action between the nations named.

The treaty between Ecuador and Spain above referred to contemplated unlimited arbitration through a friendly government.

106. Latin-American legal doctrines.—Certain legal theories have been pressed by Latin-American nations upon arbitral tribunals, and even when not so presented have found their way into international law as laid down in textbooks and treaties. The special doctrines appearing before arbitral tribunals are those embodied in the Calvo Clause and the principle of *uti possidetis juris*.

The supreme idea underlying the Calvo Clause was first put into shape by Charles Calvo, an Argentinean jurist, in his great work, *Le droit international théorique et pratique*. The fundamental principle is that when a foreigner enters another country he submits himself to its laws, system, and accidents of government, forfeiting by his entry right of appeal to his home government to redress his grievances by diplomatic intervention or otherwise. Its origin undoubtedly was due to the fact that great nations had as to various claims for damages to their nationals often acted oppressively toward Central and South American states. The greatest application of the Calvo doctrine has been in connection with contracts and concessions. Calvo's position was:

> Aside from political motives these interventions have nearly always had, as apparent pretexts, injuries to private interests, claims and demands for pecuniary indemnities in behalf of subjects or even foreigners, the protection of whom was for the most part in nowise justified in strict law. . . . . According to strict international law, the recovery of debts and the pursuit of private claims does not justify *de plano* the armed intervention of governments, and, since European states invariably follow this rule in their reciprocal relations, there is no reason why they should not also impose it upon themselves in their relations with nations in the new world.[5]

Fenwick sums up the Calvo doctrine as teaching that

> Neither armed nor diplomatic intervention is justified as a means of enforcing the claims of citizens in foreign countries on account of losses sustained in time of civil war or armed insurrection.[6]

By constitutions, statutes, and special provisions of contracts, the

---

[5] *Le droit international théorique et pratique,* Vol. 5, fifth edition, 350, § 205.
[6] *International Law,* 159.

Latin-American countries have striven pertinaciously to make their action with regard to the interpretation and construction of contracts with foreigners free from foreign diplomatic interference, negativing the right of interference by express words or by making the foreigner as to the contract a citizen of the contracting nation. Nations other than those of Latin America have often refused to regard it as possible for their citizens to contract away the right of diplomatic intervention in any manner, or have claimed redress because of denial of justice to their nationals.

The general doctrine has made some progress before international tribunals. We have considered this in chapter v, sec. 43.[7]

The term *uti possidetis juris* is derived from the Roman law, in which it designated an interdict of the praetor, by which the disturbance of the existing state of possession of immovables, as between two individuals, was forbidden.[8]

The term found its way into international law as signifying that the victor at the close of a war retained territory he had taken from the enemy before the conclusion of peace, unless otherwise specified in the treaty.

In Latin America the term signifies that each country is to be considered as possessing the territory embraced within the vice-royalty, captain-generalcy, or presidency under which it was held by Spain. Usually and more properly the period to which the doctrine relates is 1910, the year of independence from Spain. Of course, with so much territory unexplored and with so many boundaries unknown, many uncertainties existed despite the doctrine.

Many treaties between Spanish-American countries rely upon the doctrine, and it has been recognized as between Brazil and several of her neighbors.

At least twice of late the doctrine of *uti possidetis* has been relied upon in arbitral proceedings where the umpire was of a non-Spanish country. The first of these was in a boundary dispute between Panama and Costa Rica, decided by Chief Justice White.[9] A later case was between Colombia and Venezuela, decided by the Swiss Federal Council in 1922.[10]

With regard to the Drago doctrine, not yet brought before arbitral

[7] See also Ralston's *Law and Procedure of International Tribunals,* 58–72.
[8] John Bassett Moore, *Memorandum on* "Uti Possidetis," 5.
[9] *American Journal of International Law,* VII, 913.
[10] Ralston's *Law and Procedure of International Tribunals,* 322.

tribunals, we have to say that it was first enunciated by Señor Luís Drago, Argentine Minister of Foreign Affairs, in a letter to the Argentine minister at Washington, December 20, 1902.[11] Its design was to oppose collection in America of public loans by military means as implying territorial occupation. Its author desired that there should be

no territorial expansion in America on the part of Europe, nor any oppression of the peoples of this continent, because an unfortunate financial situation may compel some one of them to postpone the fulfillment of its promises.

To a large degree, the Drago doctrine was embodied in the Porter resolution concerning the enforcement of public debts, included in the conclusion of the Second Hague Peace Conference and referred to herein.[12]

While it is true that the doctrine of *uti possidetis juris* has no broad international importance, limited as it is in its operations to Latin America (Spanish and Portuguese), yet the Calvo and Drago doctrines are capable of wide application and are properly the subjects of much study.

107. References to arbitration.—In the matter of referring national disputes to arbitration, the course of Latin America has been of a remarkably advanced character. Probably the first modern attempt to refer all international disputes to arbitration was between Colombia and Peru by treaty dated September 22, 1829.[18]

By the provisions of this treaty,

Whatever may be the occasions of dispute between the two Republics, on account of complaints of injuries, aggravations, or damages whatsoever, neither of them will have the power to authorize reprisals or declare war against the other without previously submitting the differences to the government of a power friendly to both.

This treaty was followed, up to July 1927, by twenty-nine like treaties between Latin-American countries and treaties between individual nations among them and other countries, including Switzerland, Belgium, Spain, Persia, Italy, Great Britain, France, but none with the United States. In some instances a *compromis* is called for. In others special reference is provided to particular tribunals.

In chapter xxii, relating to the Central American Court of Justice, we have noted this body as furnishing the high-water mark of inter-

---

[11] *American Journal of International Law*, I, Supplement 1.

[12] See *infra*, chap. xxiv, § 220.

[18] Manning, G; *Tratados Públicos y Acuerdos Internacionales de Venezuela*, 65. Date erroneously given as August 27, 1828, in *Banishing War through Arbitration*, 31, by Noel H. Field.

national submission to justice. Its present successor lacks its bold originality and progressiveness.

Manning (*Arbitration Treaties among the American Nations*) enumerates to the year 1910 two hundred and twenty-eight arbitration treaties in which Latin America has participated, among its members for the most part. Their subject-matter in this list is: General, 104; interpretation, 12; specific claims, 21; boundary, 47; certain disputes, 3; specific disputes, 2; certain claims, 31; all claims, 2; pecuniary claims, 3; questions of honor, 2; treaty violation, 1. These general headings, in view of our previous discussion, call for no special comment, save as to questions of honor, the reference being exceptional. On August 26, 1895, Peru and Bolivia, through the good offices of representatives of the Holy See, France, Colombia, and Italy, agreed to submit to arbitral decision of a South American government the question: "Were the regrettable acts committed by Peru in 1890 of the same nature and gravity as the regrettable acts committed by Bolivia during the last Peruvian civil war so as to require a like salute to the flag?"

By a further protocol dated September 7, 1895, Brazil, or in the event of its declination, Colombia, was named as the arbiter.

An early illustration approaching what we now call "outlawry of war" was afforded by a treaty between Costa Rica and Honduras of January 4, 1850. This provided that:

The two republics bind themselves never to make war against each other, nor will either give assistance in attacks that may be made on the other. If differences should arise they will always settle them by arbitration; and only in case one of them will not abide by such arbitration, will the other be permitted to make use of arms.[14]

The suggestion has been made that the sovereignty of the several Spanish-American republics has been so uncertain in character as to lead them readily to accept arbitration. This may have a certain foundation, though it is to be noted that smaller nations have been much more willing to rely upon law for their vindication than have larger ones who have very generally preferred to rest their supposed rights upon their ability to maintain them.

[14] Manning, *op. cit.*, 30.

PART III

HISTORY OF ARBITRAL TRIBUNALS

CHAPTER XV

ANCIENT ARBITRATIONS

108. Some early arbitrations.—Before taking up the more important field of arbitrations among the ancient Greeks, we may refer to scattered instances many years before Christ.

So far were the ancient Greeks affected by the idea of arbitration that they assumed its existence among the gods. Thus, for instance, we are told that Pausanias relates that, a difference arising between Poseidon (the Latin Neptune, god of the sea) and Helios (the sungod) with regard to the possession of Corinthian territory, the hundred-handed giant Briareus (known also as Aegaeon) acted as mediator, awarding to Poseidon the isthmus and its neighborhood and to Helios the height which dominated the city. From that time the Corinthians considered that the isthmus belonged to Poseidon. According to the same writer there was a legend to the effect that Inachus (the mythical king of Argos) arbitrated in the dispute between Poseidon and Hera (the Latin Juno, queen of the gods) as to Argolis, and that he was assisted by Cephisus and Asterion (two river gods). Poseidon, however, did not acquiesce in their decision, which was delivered in favor of Hera, and in retaliation caused their water to disappear.

Again in the case of the conflicting claims of Athena (protecting goddess of Athens, called Minerva by the Romans) and Poseidon as to the possession of Aegina, Zeus was the arbitrator and decided they should hold it in common.[1]

But passing from the world of gods to that of man, we find from recent discoveries of Hittite archives, that about 400 B.C. a bitter feud raged between the two Sumerian cities situated near each other on a canal; that war having failed to bring about a decision, resort was had to arbitration, and the King of Kish was called in to define the frontier between the two states. A record of the treaty of delimitation has been recently discovered.[1a]

We learn that in the year 486 B.C., after the death of Darius, conflict arose between his sons, Xerxes and Ariamenus, concerning the succession to the throne, and that they united in submitting the matter to the judgment of their uncle, Artaphernes, who decided in favor of

---

[1] Phillipson, *The International Law and Custom of Ancient Greece and Rome*, II, 129.
[1a] L. W. King and H. R. Hall, *Egypt and Western Asia*, 171.

Xerxes. As tending to weaken the effect of this decision as of an international nature, Herodotus indicates that the submission was to Artaphernes as a domestic judge and there was, of course, no international question involved.

With entire lack of detail, Xenophon informs us that Cyrus, having a difficulty with the King of Syria, referred the matter to the arbitrament of one of the princes of India. We have no knowledge as to whether anything resembling a judicial determination was involved in the conclusion of this case.

Artaphernes, governor of Sardis, Herodotus states, forced the Ionians or Greeks of Asia Minor, who were under Persian rule, to make treaties between themselves to regulate for the future their differences by judicial procedure so as to put an end to the violence which, up to that time, they had practiced. This direction hardly rises to the dignity of a precedent in international law. We have no knowledge as to whether it was carried out, but, if so, it was merely the action of an inferior under the direction of his superior.

The foregoing apparently exhausts the list of all suggestions of arbitration in the ancient world other than Greek or Roman.

109. Ancient international law.—The existence of arbitration bearing an international character depends in some degree at least upon principles of law, or through it should come the development of principles of international law. These principles may be of such character as necessarily relate to intercourse between independent states, or they may be merely the application of recognized ideas relating to private law which are given simply a new and wider application through their acceptance between nations. We might add further that they may be developed in the course of the arbitration itself and theretofore appeal for application of a judicial theory comparatively or absolutely unknown. Having this observation in mind, it may be said that, where arbitrations have been shown, the existence of international law in some way or other is recognized. Thus, when we are told by Raeder that history and epigraphical researches show that there were at least eighty-one arbitrations between Greek towns, of whose existence we have more or less complete evidence, we must believe that there was such a thing as international law among the Greeks, despite the opinion of Laurent, to the effect that

L'absence d'un véritable droit des gens entre les peuples grecs est attestée par tout leur état social.[2]

[2] *Histoire du droit des gens,* II, 118 f.

In further opposition to the idea of Laurent, we refer to the work by Coleman Phillipson,[3] devoted for the most part to illustrations of what were plainly rules of international law among the Greeks and Romans.

We refer to the oath of the hieromnemons as given by Aeschines.

I swear never to destroy any of the villages forming part of the amphictyons nor turn the bed so as to prevent the use of the running waters, either in time of peace or war, and if any people violate this rule I shall declare war against it and will destroy its towns. That if anyone pillages the property of the gods or in anywise becomes the accomplice of those who touch sacred things or aid them by his counsel, I will employ in avenging my feet, my hands, my voice, and all my strength.[4]

110. Attitude of the ancient Greeks toward arbitration.—The general idea of arbitration met with a large degree of favor among the Greeks. Some illustrations may be cited. Thucydides praised the words of Archidamus, a king of Sparta, who declared that it was impossible to attack as an enemy him who offered to answer for his deeds before a tribunal of arbitration.[5]

So Aeschines in his discourse against Ctesiphon eulogized arbitration and praised Philip of Macedonia for having shown himself ready to accept in his quarrels with the Athenians the judgment of an impartial city.

Of course, the language and conduct of all Greece was not uniform. Thus we find[6] that there were not less than three cases where Spartans refused to allow arbitration to settle differences between themselves and other states. In two of these cases, Athens was the power which sought to establish arbitration.

We would expect to find among the Grecian people with their relatively advanced condition of civilization, an inclination toward arbitration, it being true, as said by Gennadius that

we shall ascertain still more conclusively that international arbitration has its origin and has found favor among nations devoted to free institutions and in times when intellectual culture flourished; while, on the other hand, it remained unknown to barbarous nations or has proved incompatible with the conditions essential to despotism and the pursuits of conquering people.[7]

111. Universality among the Greeks.—In considering arbitration

---

[3] *The International Law and Custom of Ancient Greece and Rome.*
[4] Raeder, *L'arbitrage international chez les Hellènes*, 165.
[5] Mérignhac, *L'arbitrage international*, 21.
[6] Raeder, *op. cit.*, 142.
[7] *A Record of International Arbitrations*, Broad Views, 1904, p. 133.

among the ancient Greeks, one of the first facts with which we are struck is its universality as between large cities and small, and this during the period from the middle of the seventh to the middle of the second century before Christ. Thus we find it utilized[8] equally between the mainland and the isles of the Aegean and Ionian seas, and also upon the shores of Asia Minor. Similarly it spread to the Greeks of Sicily, Athens, Sparta, Corinth, and Thebes. The Achaean and Aetolian Leagues, together with the smallest towns, as the Laconian village of Geronthe and the Thessalian of Mondaia, all shared in its benefits. So Athens was party to various affairs from the seventh to the second centuries before Christ.

It seems to be true that the greater obligation to resort to arbitration rested upon towns of the same league, and that arbitration between towns of different leagues was more rare and less imperative,[9] but arbitration was not always confined to an isolated town or a state.[10] Thus the Aetolian League was one of the parties to a difference relating to Panormus. The Achaean League was officially a party to an affair of arbitration arising because its strategus, Aratus, had tried during a time of peace to surprise the town of Argos; and the same was the case in the differences of Athens on the subject of the juridicial situation of the Delians. We are told that in one case two leagues were, so to speak, parties in one affair touching a question of difference of frontiers between the village of Azorus, which belonged to the league of the Perrhaebians, and Mondaia, which belonged to the Thessalian League. Another was a case directly of arbitration between the Magnesian and Perrhaebian Leagues. It is considered[11] that in this latter case arbitration was brought into play, if not upon the initiative of the two leagues, respectively, at least upon their authorization.

The leading states of a league were obliged in their own interests to see that the towns belonging to their respective hegemonies should not enter into war against each other, but that differences arising were, as far as possible, arranged pacifically, whether by the direct initiative of the controlling power or by arbitral decision proposed by it. Arbitration thus played a certain rôle in each system of alliance. This application of arbitration was not entirely of an optional character, but approached obligatory arbitration.[12]

112. The *clause compromissoire*.—Treaties including what is known as the "compromissory clause" were frequent among the ancient

---

8 Raeder, *op. cit.*, 240.   9 *Ibid.*, 235.   10 *Ibid.*, 246–47.
11 *Ibid.*, 158–59.   12 *Ibid.*, 150.

Greeks. Many of the details of these treaties we shall have occasion to discuss later. A comparatively early illustration of a treaty with a clause of this nature is furnished by the year 444 B.C. in a treaty of alliance between Sparta and Athens by which the contracting parties undertook to substitute a pacific settlement for a violent solution of their difficulties.[13] In 421 B.C. the treaty between the Spartans and Athenians provided as follows:

It shall not be permissible for the Lacedaemonians and their allies to make war upon the Athenians and their allies or to inflict upon them damage in any manner under any pretext whatsoever. The same prohibition is made to the Athenians and their allies as to the Lacedaemonians and their allies, but if there should arise a difference between them they will remit its solution to a procedure according to a method upon which they will come to an agreement.[14]

In the year 418 B.C. there was concluded a treaty of peace for fifty years between Sparta and Argos, and by virtue of this treaty it was provided:

If there should arise a difference between any of the towns of the Peloponnesus or beyond, either as to frontiers or any other object, there shall be an arbitration. If among the allied towns they are not able to come to an agreement, the dispute will be brought before a neutral town chosen by common agreement.[15]

Coming down to a later period, we find that in the first half of the second century,[16] a convention was signed by the four principal towns of the Island of Lesbos referring difficulties to judges of a town to be chosen by lot, and whose mandate covered directing at first an effort to conciliate the parties; if they should not succeed, the judges had power to pronounce a judgment with executory force.

There were also examples of compromissory clauses between the towns of Crete.[17]

An elaborate method of arbitration was agreed upon by treaty between Sardis and Ephesus in the year 98 B.C.[18] If either of the parties should violate the treaty establishing peace and friendship, the other had the right to prepare a complaint, and thirty days after at the latest the two parties were to appear by special envoys at Pergamos, which would be the permanent conciliator, this by way of a prelude to an arbitral sentence. During the five following days Pergamos should proceed by lot to select a town to act as judge, this to be upon the basis of a list which the parties prepared in advance. Within sixty

13 Raeder, op. cit., 87.   14 Ibid., 180.
15 B. Sax, L'arbitrage international, 5, citing Thucydides.
16 Raeder, op. cit., 185.   17 Ibid., 162.   18 Ibid., 185.

days thereafter the parties were obligated to appear before the judges, carrying an undertaking written by their town declaring that they would respect the judgment. If one of the parties did not appear, it lost by default.

113. Form of *compromis*.—According to Mérignhac[19] the procedure in arbitration was approximately that ordinarily used, the *compromis* (protocol) designating the arbitrator and the object of the litigation. The process thereafter to be followed we shall indicate later.

According to Raeder[20] the *compromis* described the question to be decided and the tribunal could not go beyond the mandate thus given it by the parties. This rule was in concordance with that applicable under Roman law to arbitral decisions in civil affairs.

114. Subjects of dispute.—The most ordinary subject of dispute among the Grecian cities was as to frontiers. This, we are told,[21] was the case in the dispute between Mondaia and Azorus and, in fact, as Raeder remarks, the larger share of the differences are related in one way or another to questions of frontiers.[22] The same was true as we shall find with regard to such differences as were submitted by the Greek cities to Rome for determination.

But differences did not always relate to frontiers. Thus, for instance, there were the attack upon Argos through the Achaean strategus, Aratus, in the midst of peace;[23] the expedition of Athens against Oropus; the lack of proper treatment on the part of another Greek town of a neighboring village, the citizens of which were deprived unceremoniously of their property; the disagreement between Athens and Delos on the subject of the right of administering the Sanctuary of Apollo at Delos; the difference between the town of Lebedos in Asia Minor and a neighboring village with reference to the priest of Zeus; and the question whether Lepreum was always obliged to pay rent to the Temple of Zeus at Olympia.

115. The judges.—A necessarily important question concerned the selection of judges. It was the conclusion of Raeder[24] that the most habitual mode of regulation of differences between the towns of the Achaean League was through the arbitration of judges belonging to a third town which was in general a member of the League, but could, however, be taken from the outside.

Various writers stress greatly the figure played by the Amphictyonic Council in the settlement of difficulties between cities. Raeder, how-

---

[19] *Op. cit.*, 20.   [20] Raeder, *op. cit.*, 274.   [21] *Ibid.*, 158.

[22] *Ibid.*, 247.   [23] *Ibid.*, 248.   [24] *Ibid.*, 220.

ever, finds[25] that as far as we are able to know, the cases adjudged by the Amphictyonic Council related to infractions of observance of religious rites. When there were breaches of the orders of this tribunal with relation thereto, they were made by individuals and not by states so that these breaches offered no international aspect. This was, as Raeder finds, very far from creating a permanent tribunal of arbitration.[26] However, Raeder expresses himself[27] to the effect that when there was an infraction of the conventions which formed the base of the amphictyonic system or the duties imposed by it, that is to say, when one of the members of the Amphictyon had violated certain very simple rules of the law of nations or had not respected the amphictyonic divinities, their goods or their worship, there was reason for a judgment to be passed by the Council. The habitual form was to ask a city to organize a tribunal of arbitration.

As to the manner of selecting judges, it is to be noted that in default of a *compromis,* the question of nomination of a tribunal of arbitration was left to the decision of the parties between themselves.[28] Within the Achaean League it seems that the authorities of the League were content to determine the third town which should be requested to charge itself with the mission of judging, after which it would be its affair to regulate the nomination of judges. Thus it was when Megara sent one hundred and fifty-one judges in the affair of Corinth against Epidaurus.[29]

The practice as to the number of judges to pass upon difficulties was by no means uniform. While it was a very general rule that difficulties should be referred to a neutral city, the manner in which such city designated the number of judges from among its citizens who were to determine the difficulty differed very widely. Some illustrations may be given. Perhaps the largest tribunal, expressly described as the "largest permitted by law," was that of six hundred members appointed by the Milesians to pass upon a difficulty between Sparta and Mycene.[30] These were chosen by lot.[31] Three hundred and one men were named to pass upon a dispute between Paros and an unknown adversary. Tod tells us[32] of the Larissaean tribunal of three hundred and thirty-four. Two hundred and four constituted the Cnidian Court on the occasion of the dispute between Cos and Calymna, and Megara created a tribunal of one hundred and fifty-one men to judge between

---

[25] *Ibid.,* 167.   [26] *Ibid.,* 169.
[27] *Ibid.,* 173.   [28] *Ibid.,* 265.   [29] *Idem.*
[30] Tod, *International Arbitration among the Greeks,* 101.
[31] Raeder, *op. cit.,* 254.   [32] Tod, *op. cit.,* 102.

Corinth and Epidaurus.[33] A tribunal of five members arbitrated between Athens and Megara on the subject of Salamis, and a like tribunal arbitrated in other cases enumerated by Raeder.[34] Four men of Cassandria judged between Peumata and neighboring villages, and at least three others between Athens and the Boeotian League. A tribunal of three members was also named in a large number of cases given by Raeder,[35] while one judge was designated by the people of Apollonia to pass upon differences between Kalatis and a neighboring village,[36] and also acted in other cases.[37] However, as will have been noted, tribunals of three members were the most frequent, but five it is stated by Raeder[38] were also normal. The judges were often accompanied by secretaries. Again certain institutions were named, as, for instance, the Delphic Oracle adjudged one affair and was selected to judge another. The Pylaeo Delphic Amphictyon also acted and the assembly of the Council of the Greeks was chosen, but transferred its duty of judging to Argos. We are further told by tradition that the Messenians proposed arbitration to Sparta with the Argive Amphictyon or the Aeropagus as a tribunal of arbitration.

Assemblies of leagues functioned as arbitral tribunals as, for instance, the Ionian, the Laconian and the Thessalian. The tribunals of their leagues are also cited as having judged between the Boeotians and the Ionians. We may also mention the great Hellenic tribunal which Philip of Macedonia organized after the battle of Chersonesus, and which judged between Sparta and Megalopolis and between Sparta and Messina.[39]

According to Tod[40] there are at least six known instances in which the tribunal consisted of representatives of two or more states. Plutarch tells of a dispute between Andros and Chalcis, in which the question was referred to three towns, two voting for Andros and one for Chalcis. It may be inferred that the decision of the court was that of a majority of what were doubtless three panels.

On occasion the Delphic Oracle was consulted and gave answer in strict conformity with its name, as, to illustrate, about 550 B.C. a difficulty arising between the kings of the Cyrenians, it directed that an arbitrator should be found at Mantinea.[41] Private individuals were sometimes named, as, for instance, a conqueror of the Olympic Games, to decide between the Arcadians and the Eleans upon a question of

[33] Raeder, op. cit., 254.   [34] Ibid., 256.   [35] Op. cit., 256.
[36] Idem.   [37] Ibid., 249.   [38] Ibid., 256.   [39] Ibid., 249.
[40] Tod, op. cit., 129.   [41] Revon, L'arbitrage international, 85.

frontiers; Periander between Athens and Mytilene apropos of the Promontory Sigeum; Themistocles between Corinth and Corcyra on the subject of Leucadia.[42]

Sometimes the people of a town were declared to be the judges. Thus, the people of Argos were, upon the request of the assembly of the Hellenic Council, charged with the duty of judging between Melos and Cimolos, and so the people of Smyrna judged between Milotuo and Priene. In the dispute between Brycos and Carpathos, the people themselves are mentioned as having functioned as judge and in such capacity brought about a conciliation.[43]

When arbitration was organized following the intervention of a power outside the conflict, it is said to have been without doubt the fact that habitually this power suggested itself at the same time to fill the functions of arbitrator.[44]

An exceptional instance was one between Elis and Pisa, who, because of damages inflicted by the Tyrant of Pisa, Demaphon, upon the inhabitants of Elis, resorted to the arbitration of sixteen women, one from each of the sixteen towns which composed then the region of Elis.

116. Oath of judges.—It is interesting to know that as a first step in the performance of their duties, judges were frequently called upon to take an oath. That administered by the strategus of Cnidus in the case between Calymna and Cos was as follows:

> I swear by Jupiter, by the Lycian Apollo, and by the earth that I will judge in the case joined between the parties under oath as will appear to me most just. I will not judge according to one witness if this witness does not appear to me to tell the truth. I have not received any present with relation to this suit, neither myself nor any other for me, man or woman, nor by any detour whatsoever. May I prosper as I adhere to my oath, but unhappiness to me if I perjure myself.[45]

Under all circumstances in the later arbitrations, the judges made oath to the performance of their duties.

117. Representation by agents.—The parties were represented by their agents. For example, in the complaint of Athens against Megara with relation to Salamis, Solon directed the affair for Athens and Hercas for Megara. Hyperides spoke in the name of Athens before the Amphictyon Council.[46] Samos was represented before the Rhodian tribunal by six persons. In the suit between Magnesia and Priene, Mag-

42 *Idem.*
45 *Ibid.,* 132–296.
43 Raeder, *op. cit.,* 254.
46 *Ibid.,* 291.
44 *Ibid.,* 262.

nesia was represented by at least twelve men, especially chosen, upon whom she relied, with advocates as well.

118. Judges as conciliators.—It is interesting to know that at a much later period those chosen as judges often regarded themselves as in the first instance conciliators, and in such capacity sought to bring the parties together. It was only, therefore, after failure of conciliation in many instances that the usual judicial functions were entered upon. This seems to be true, although the Greeks argued that a tribunal of arbitration was in itself an institution furnished with the power of judgment and should judge. Nevertheless, frequently in the *compromis* the parties gave to the judge the mission of seeking to arrange a conciliation. In the arbitration between Paros and its adversary, it was said expressly that the proposal of conciliation of the tribunal of arbitration was accepted by the representatives of the parties and had the authority of *res judicata*.[47]

We may anticipate matters somewhat by saying that apparently, even after a hearing, a reconciliation might be sought for before the pronouncement of a judgment. Thus we are told that the Magnèsian judges in the controversy between Itane and Hierapytna, not wishing to decide the matter immediately according to strict law (according to old usages), sought to bring about a benevolent conciliation, and it was only after this effort failed that they pronounced their judgment.[48] Again, according to an inscription found in the Isle of Delos, certain towns agreed, according to the circumstances of each affair, that they would try to bring about a compromise between the parties in the event of a difference and, if this should not succeed, the judges should definitely decide the difference.[49] In one case the disputing cities agreed to resort to the arbitration of the Thessalian city of Larissa. Larissa sent three judges with a secretary to examine the neighborhood, there being a question of frontiers. The judges sought at first to determine the affair by agreement, but, only succeeding in part, the remaining portions were determined by an award.[50]

119. Procedure.—Procedure appears to have been regulated by the several tribunals, sometimes in consultation with the representatives of the parties; but certain general features appear. After the judges had taken their oath, the complaint of the plaintiff and the response of the defendant were equally supported under oath.[51] It then seems to have been entirely possible, differing from modern practice, for the lawyers to act as witnesses.[52] If the dispute related to a matter of boundary,

---

[47] Raeder, *op. cit.*, 292.   [48] *Ibid.*, 304.   [49] *Ibid.*, 91.
[50] *Ibid.*, 161.   [51] *Ibid.*, 135.   [52] *Ibid.*, 299.

the judges proceeded to examine the disputed territory as well as to examine the witnesses. If these witnesses were present in person, they were not required to be put under oath, but if their depositions had to be taken, an oath was requisite. In such cases the witnesses were heard on a fixed day in the adverse towns by the central authority of the town in question, in such a way, however, that the opposing party had the right to be represented. A deposition was then sent under official seal. The absent witnesses were obliged, conformably to the Greek practice, to testify under oath that they were prevented from being personally before the tribunal.

It was expressly determined in one case that the affirmations of witnesses should be deposited with the tribunal before the commencement of the arguments. As the depositions of witnesses are mentioned as having been read by the secretaries with the other documents in the case, it follows that cross-examination of the witnesses took place, not at the same time as their depositions, but after the first intervention of the advocates. At Athens it was expressly determined that the depositions of witnesses should be taken in writing.[53]

The time for argument was also fixed and when the water had run out the clepsydra the arguments closed.

120. Evidence.—There is much resemblance between evidence receivable under the ancient Greek arbitrations and that receivable under modern tribunals. For instance, in a frontier dispute, an old man was heard who had known the places in question as a pasture in his youth.[54] Other men of the neighboring region who knew the place well were also heard as witnesses.

Even in those early days archaeological appeals were made, if we accept as historical the tradition that in the dispute between Athens and Megara over Salamis, Solon appealed to the evidence of tombs discovered on the Island, he claiming that the Athenians buried their dead turned westward, while the Megarians buried turned toward the east. The Megarian advocate, Hereas, accepted the evidence as valid, but maintained that his countrymen also buried in a western position and that the real test lay in the fact that whereas the Athenians placed but one body in a tomb, the Megarians often interred three or four bodies together.[55]

In the suit between Itane and Hierapytna, a series of public documents were submitted to the tribunal of arbitration of Magnesia, as,

---

[53] Raeder, *op. cit.*, 301.   [54] *Ibid.*, 298.   [55] Tod, *op. cit.*, 150.

for instance, old letters, old documents relating to the frontier, maps and treaties of peace between Itane and other towns, the recital to the Senate of a Roman embassy, as well as all sorts of other documents.[56] When the Rhodians judged between Samos and Priene, there was produced a series of documents, such as ancient judgments, old decrees, appeals for aid to different kings, and citations of the works of known historians, to show the situation in ancient times.

The acquirement of title to land by what we term prescription seems to have been recognized, as may be inferred from citations already given. We find, however, special reference to "having occupied this territory" and "retained in their hands for many generations."[57] Both expressions are indicative of the recognition of a prescriptive right. So in the case of Priene and Magnesia, a judgment decided that Priene had not furnished proof that at the decisive moment she had in truth chosen the district. The Magnesians seemed to have contented themselves with proving that Priene, so far from having considered the country as its property, had pillaged it and delivered it over to flames.

121. Awards.—We reach the time of the formation of the awards and are told that when there were more than one judge all proceeded to a vote by balls to arrive at the result. The larger share of the judgments of which we have knowledge appear to have been rendered unanimously, although sometimes the judges were divided. In these cases the majority prevailed.[58] A case calling for some special note shows the various steps up to one particular award. In the dispute between Samos and Priene, the Roman envoy, Manlius Volso, was arbitrator and awarded the country to Samos. There being strong reasons to believe that he received presents from the Samians, Priene took up the affair again a short time after and the parties agreed in 180 B.C. to have the affair adjudged by Rhodes. The Rhodian people named five judges whose duty it was according to the *compromis* to review the whole affair, trace the frontiers, and either bring about a compromise or render a judgment. The judges made a minute examination of the disputed district, accompanied by the attorneys-in-fact of the two parties. These, coming before them at Rhodes, each in his own fashion, developed the difference and presented the arguments. After examining the neighborhood, the final union was had in the village of Ephesus, a neutral ground, and the judgment recognized that Priene was right in its contentions.[59]

[56] Raeder, *op. cit.*, 301.
[57] Tod, *op. cit.*, 142.
[58] Raeder, *op. cit.*, 307.
[59] *Ibid.*, 159.

The award often contained the reasoning upon which it was based. It appears, for instance, that in a dispute in which Pitane was the successful party, according to the inscription which has perpetuated the souvenir of the event, five Pergamenians were appointed and arrived at a judgment giving detailed reasons, with a résumé as to the procedure.[60]

It is interesting to know that the award, executed in duplicate, was habitually deposited in the temples or at public places and the parties engaged themselves by oath to execute it.[61] Among other illustrations of the fact just alluded to, we may add one given by Raeder,[62] the judgment being posted at Delphi as well as in the Temple of Apollo at Larissa, and expenses divided between the two contesting villages. In the *compromis* between Mytilene and Pitane, it was decided that the judges should send a copy of the judgment to each of the parties and see that it was properly published by being posted on the columns.[63] So we often find in the *compromis* clauses determining how the judgments should be made public.

Judges signed the award in their own names when individually designated, but when the tribunal was of another kind, as, for example, when the town of Cnidus gave its judgment, this was promulgated by the authorities of the town and in the name of the state.

As in some of our very recent arbitrations, questions arose as to the application of the judgment, which, perhaps, was intended merely as a guide rather than as absolutely determining the entire difficulty. In consequence, therefore, special commissions were sometimes appointed to trace out the frontiers in a final manner and upon the basis of the decisions given. This was the case between Milet and Priene decided by Smyrna.[64]

122. Sanctions enforcing awards.—The time within which a judgment should be executed was often determined by *compromis*.[65] In fact, there were many cases where the *compromis* contained an express clause to the effect that the parties would respect the award, and pay a fine if they did not respect it.[66] In one case this fine was fixed at five talents.[67] In a dispute between Paros and Naxos, it was provided that if one of the parties should not obey the orders of the tribunal, it should pay a fine of twenty talents. If a private individual did not respect a judgment, the fine was fixed at five talents. The people of Latos and the people of Olus entered into an agreement with the people of Cnosus each for the

---

[60] *Ibid.*, 202.   [61] Mérignhac, *op. cit.*, 20.   [62] Raeder, *op. cit.*, 116.
[63] *Ibid.*, 281.   [64] *Ibid.*, 160, 310.   [65] *Ibid.*, 227.   [66] *Ibid.*, 272.   [67] *Ibid.*, 116.

sum of ten talents in evidence of submission to the *compromis* and judgment. If one of the two peoples failed to comply with the *compromis* or acted against the respondents, the cosmes of Cnosus should recover and send the amount in question to the one who complied.[68] We may add with reference to this case that Cnosus was obligated to render a judgment within six months and do whatever was necessary to make it public within thirty days thereafter by inscription. The judgment was to be definitive and all differences terminated by it. Modifications could be made to the *compromis* if the two parties agreed. It was in conformity with this that a first period of six months for the pronouncement of the award was extended to twelve months.[69]

In the dispute between Hierapytna and Priene, the highest officials of the two towns were obliged to present a bond guaranteeing that they would carry out the agreement, while we may note at this time that the Cretan League of which they were both members promulgated an edict laying down certain rules of procedure for the case.[70]

123. Judgment by default.—Judgment by default was not unknown. If a fine was provided by the *compromis* in case of default, the party defaulting was subject to it. If nothing was agreed upon in advance, the judges could refuse to examine the affair and the complaint failed, if it was the complainant who defaulted, while if the one who was the object of the claim, it could be adjudged in contumacy. This rule was in force in Athens and it is at least believable that the same juridical rule may have been applied before tribunals of arbitration. It may be seen, however, that notwithstanding absence of a party, the judges examined the affair and rendered a judgment absolutely as if the interested party had been present. For instance, the arbitral tribunal of Matinea inflicted upon Aratus a fine, even though it had not appeared. Sicyon condemned Athens, which was in default, to pay a considerable sum of money in its difference with Oropus.

124. Roman association with Greek arbitrations.—Let us now turn to the association of the Romans with Greek arbitrations. The general attitude of the Roman Senate with regard to appeals to it is described by Tod, as follows:

The whole body of amphictyons might sit as a single arbitral court, but that the Roman Senate should ordinarily act as such was out of the question; it was too far distant from the scene of the dispute to be able accurately to ascertain all the facts, and its business was too great and pressing to allow it to make a detailed inquiry into each individual case. It therefore followed one of two

---

[68] Raeder, *op. cit.*, 126.   [69] *Ibid.*, 127, 162.   [70] Raeder, *op. cit.*, 124.

courses. Either it laid down the law of the case and delegated to some free community the task of adjudicating on the facts and issuing an award accordingly, or it despatched envoys, singly or in bodies, to decide such disputes, the verdict in each case being subject to senatorial ratification. These in their turn seemed to have claimed the right to delegate their functions.[71]

The indignation of Pausanias was excited (in connection with the delegation of a frontier quarrel between Sparta and Argos) by the arrogance of the Roman legate and the character of his deputy rather than by any breach of law or usage on the part of either.

The earliest appeal made by the Greeks to Rome in connection with any arbitration among themselves was in 189 B.C. when, Sparta endeavoring to occupy Las, a maritime city of Laconia, the latter complained to the Achaean League, whose head demanded the surrender of the instigators, and, failing to obtain them, made war on Sparta. The old state of property was then re-established there, the laws of Lycurgus superseded by Achaean laws and the fortifications pulled down. In 188 B.C. ambassadors arrived in Rome from Sparta to protest against these proceedings and from Athens to justify them. Roman mediation proved to be of little avail and later the Senate was invited by all parties to arbitrate the dispute. In 184 B.C. Appius Claudius Pulcher, along with other commissioners, was despatched to Greece, and in the general assembly convened at Clitorium in Arcadia caused to be canceled the sentence of death that had been passed on two Spartan emigrants, but referred the main questions at issue to Rome. The Senate again charged Appius Claudius together with others to adjudicate. The award was to the effect that Sparta should re-enter the Achaean League, be permitted to reconstruct her fortifications, and re-establish Lycurgan institutions, and that the Achaean League should no longer exercise criminal jurisdiction over the Spartans. This award was to be committed to writing and signed by both Lacedaemonians and Achaeans.[72]

Eumenes, King of Pergamum, having sided with Rome, received after war Lydia and Phrygia, Mysia and Lycaonia, the greater part of the peninsula of Asia Minor, and was under Roman protection. A dispute arising between him and Antiochus as to whether Pamphylia lay on this side of or beyond the Taurus, and therefore whether it belonged to one or the other, the controversy was referred to Gnaeus Manlius Volso, who, ceasing to be consul in 188 B.C., remained as

[71] Tod, op. cit., 98.

[72] Phillipson, The International Law and Custom of Ancient Greece and Rome, II, 156.

proconsul in Asia to complete his command. He submitted the conflict to the Senate as the only competent authority, and a special commissioner was dispatched to Asia. Apparently Pamphylia was not adjudged to belong to either of the contending parties because some twenty years later it sent ambassadors to Rome as an independent state.[73]

Gortyna having deprived Cnosus of a portion of its territory, it is probable that the two cities applied to Rome to settle their differences and that the Senate referred the question to the Roman commissioner then in Greece (184 B.C.). The decision was in favor of Cnosus, but from the words of Polybius it would seem that it was a compromise effected through the mediation of Claudius.[74] About the year 164 B.C. Sparta and Megalopolis had a territorial dispute submitted to Callicrates. His decision was not accepted by Sparta, which appealed to the Achaean League. The latter imposed a fine on Sparta, which still refused to give up the contested territory but offered to submit to a Roman arbitration. The Senate accordingly deputed two of its members to decide the cause.[75] The fine is regarded by Raeder[76] as being not so much a judgment of arbitration as a fine for the violation of the peace toward other members of the league.

A controversy arising in 159 B.C. between Athens and Delos is considered to have been of a private international character. The Roman arbitrators pronounced in favor of the League and recognized its judicial competence with regard to the various confederates. Polybius relates that after Delos had been granted to Athens, the Delians removed to Achaea, and, having been enrolled members of the confederacy, wished to have their claims against the Athenians decided according to the convention existing between the Achaean League and Athens. The Athenians denied their right to plead under that engagement and the Delians asked leave of the Achaeans to make reprisals on the Athenians. The latter dispatched ambassadors to Rome in connection with the matter and obtained a decision to the effect that judgments pronounced by the Achaeans in accordance with their laws concerning the Delians possessed juridical validity and binding force.

125. Arbitration under Rome.—The Romans, we are told, never dreamed of an impartial arbitration of their differences with neighboring nations, for almost from the earliest time they struggled for domination. There is, however, cited an award rendered between them and the Samnites.[77]

---

[73] Phillipson, *op. cit.,* II, 155. [74] *Ibid.,* 156. [75] Phillipson, *op. cit.,* 157.
[76] Raeder, *op. cit.,* 60. [77] Revon, *L'arbitrage international,* 103.

Some of the writers treat of the functions of the fetials as equivalent in some degree to those of arbitrators and as passing upon the justice of disputes with other nations. This was the conclusion of M. Weiss.[78] It is, however, the better founded belief of Mérignhac[79] that the duty of the fetials was not to undertake to see if a war entered into was or was not well founded from the point of view of law, their rôle being limited to the fulfillment of the religious formalities without which the war could not be considered as just and therefore as favored by the gods. It is thus in Mérignhac's opinion the Romans understood the expression *"bellum justum,"* these words not signifying war conformably to law but war with relation to which there had been observed the accustomed rites. This was also the view of Laurent.[80]

It is equally true, although for different reasons, that the officials who were known as recuperators cut little figure internationally. These seem to have been the representatives of foreigners within Roman communities and to have been asked from time to time to defend and look after their interests. Their functions seem to have rather resembled those of consuls of the present day and they appear to have possessed a jurisdiction which might in certain phases be considered as extra-territorial. It is said by Accarais, *Précis de droit romain*, paragraph 738, cited by Mougins de Roquefort, that

as to the recuperators, their origin relates to the differences which could arise between Roman citizens and members of a foreign nation. Some treaties stipulated that causes of this kind could be judged by the special commissioners the Romans called recuperators.[81]

At the time of the origination of the Roman people they found themselves in the presence of leagues which united into a sort of confederation in cities of primitive Italy, this the result of the primordial political unity of the race. These leagues were bound together by more or less strict bonds. That of the Etruscan, according to Mommsen, was extremely restricted. The entire nation did not figure in it and only the Etruscans of the north and the Campagna were united into special confederacies. Each one of these leagues included a dozen communities recognizing a metropolis. The Etruscan communities seem at this time to have been without dominant authority, not having any commission to

---

[78] *Le droit fécial et les féciaux,* 478.
[79] Mérignhac, *op. cit.,* 26.
[80] *Etudes sur l'histoire de l'humanité,* III, 17.
[81] Mougins de Roquefort, *De la solution juridique,* 102.

interfere with common affairs and settle differences arising between the various cities.[82]

The earliest arbitration in which Rome took part appears to have been between the Aricians and the Ardeans, 446 B.C. Aricia was one of the members of the Latin confederation. A decision in her favor caused internal dissensions in Ardea; the people were desirous of joining the Volsians, while the nobility adhered to Rome. Hence the Romans, taking advantage of this intestine strife, dispatched a band of colonists to Ardea and distributed among them the lands of those who were opposed to Rome.[83]

The action of Rome in the matter of the boundary dispute between Nola and Neapolis over two hundred years later (195–183 B.C.) was not materially different, although the historical accuracy of the accounts we have of it has been doubted. The arbitrator was Labeo, and Cicero says that, the Senate having appointed him, on reaching the contested territory, he advised the parties not to be greedy or grasping and rather to retire than to push forward. They followed his counsel, and a belt of neutral land was left between them. This he awarded to the Roman people, and his action was, as Cicero exclaimed, "surely deceit and not arbitration.[84]

In 193 B.C. the province of Emporia, the wealthiest portion of Carthaginian territory, was partly plundered and partly even seized by Numidians, encroachments and seizure of larger territory following. Carthaginian embassies were again and again sent to Rome adjuring the Senate either to allow them to defend themselves by arms or appoint a court of arbitration with power to enforce its awards or regulate afresh the frontiers. Roman commissioners sent to Africa investigated, but came to no decision, or, at most, a provisional judgment was given recognizing the fact of possession (157 B.C.).[85]

A difference between Meliteia and Narthacium (150–146 B.C.) referred to the occupation of a territory by Narthacium. The latter claimed that it was recognized in 196 B.C. by the pro-consul as belonging to Narthacium, but the Meliteians contended its occupation was established after that and that the territory had been theirs from time immemorial. An inscription found in Thessaly gives the translation of a senatusconsult relating to the claims. This contains a preamble showing the date of the decree of the Senate and its publication, a summary of claims advanced before the Senate by the deputies of Meliteia and of

---

[82] Mérignhac, *L'arbitrage international*, 356.   [83] Phillipson, *op. cit.*, 159.
[84] Phillipson, *op. cit.*, 161–62.   [85] *Ibid.*, 160.

Narthacium, and finally the senate's decision.[86] The cities of Ateste and Patavium having a territorial dispute referred it to Caecilius, the proconsul, 141 B.C., both having been allies of Rome at the time.[87]

The dispute between Sparta and Messene in reference to a mountainous district offers features of interest and is especially suggestive of the conditions which we have seen arising under certain Greek arbitrations. Both claimed the tract of land in question and cited in their support the authority of poets and annalists. As Tacitus says,

While the Lacedaemonians advanced extracts from history and passages of ancient poetry, the Messenians produced an ancient chart of the Peloponnesus showing its division among the descendants of Hercules. They alleged that this showed that the lands in dispute, where the temple of the Limnatidian Diana stood, had been allotted to the King of Messene and that there were also extant inscriptions on stone or brass tablets which confirmed their claims.[88]

"If fragments of poetry and loose scraps of history were to be admitted," comments the Roman historian, "they had a fund of evidence more ample and directly in point."

The judgment just mentioned was given in 338 B.C. by Philip of Macedonia in favor of Messene upon the finding of a court of arbitration including representatives from all Greece, and more than a century later a similar verdict was pronounced by Antigonus after he had defeated Cleomenes, 221 B.C. Later a decree of L. Mummius was in favor of the Messenians. About 140 B.C. Sparta appealed to the Roman Senate which appointed the city of Miletus as arbitrator. Accordingly, a court of six hundred judges was established and, after a hearing, it appeared that 584 votes against sixteen decided that the territory in question, having been in the possession of Messene before the arrival of Mummius, ought, therefore, to be adjudged to the Messenians. Later the conflict was revived, and the proconsul arbitrated pursuant to the instructions of the Senate. Finally, A.D. 25, both cities made a direct appeal to Rome through their ambassadors and the Senate pronounced in favor of Messene.[89]

War broke out between Hierapytna and Itanos (138-132 B.C.), over a territorial controversy. On appeal of Hierapytna to Rome, the Senate dispatched to Crete certain commissioners, and an arrangement in its favor was reached, though it is not clear whether these proceedings were in the nature of mediation or arbitration. Itanos did not acquiesce, and applied to the Senate to reconsider the question, which was there-

---

[86] Ibid., 158.
[87] Ibid., 162.
[88] Phillipson, op. cit., II, 163.
[89] Ibid., 162, 163, 164.

upon referred to the city of Magnesia with instructions embodied in a senatusconsult. Magnesia decided in favor of Itanos, but its opponent again appealed to Rome. The case was then resubmitted to Magnesia, whose assembly nominated a body of arbitration, but we have no record of their sentence.[90]

Pisae had been an ally of Rome from 225 B.C., and Luna was established in 177 B.C. as a Roman colony in the former territory of the Apuani and served to protect the frontier against the Ligurians. A dispute between the two towns arose from the assignment to colonists of Luna of lands within the territory of Pisae. The colonists maintained that the lands had been allotted to them by the Roman commissioners charged with the partition thereof, while Pisae held their occupation unjustifiable. Accordingly, the Roman government appointed five arbitrators to investigate and settle the controversy.[91]

Pompey furnished arbitrators to settle boundary disputes between Parthians and Armenians.[92]

A territorial dispute between Ateste and Vicetia (135 B.C.) was settled by the proconsul appointed by the Roman government to officiate as arbitrator.[93] The case of Genua and the Vitorii involved several questions. The first-named was an ally of Rome, and the Vitorii were in a condition of dependence with regard to Genua. A dispute arose partly as to the competence of the courts of Genua and partly as to certain land rights. The award of the arbitrators appointed by Rome determined the limits of the public and private lands and also defined the rights and obligations of the Vitorii with respect to Genua. The award provided further that the litigants should again have recourse to the same arbitral tribunal if differences of a like kind afterward arose between them.[94]

In the territorial dispute between Juba and Leptis Magna on the African coast, a decision was delivered adverse to the claims of Juba, King of Numidia.[95]

Doubtless in all cases cited the physical power of Rome back of adjudications rendered under Roman direction was sufficient to insure the carrying out of the award, and it is the opinion of Raeder[96] that the Roman Senate found that a sentence once given should be maintained by force, the two parties having granted their consent to arbitration.

The Roman arbitrations of which we have so far spoken were more

---

90 Phillipson, *op. cit.*, II, 158.
91 *Ibid.*, 162.
92 Calvo, *Le droit international*, III, 434.
93 Phillipson, *op. cit.*, II, 164.
94 *Idem.*   95 *Idem.*
96 Raeder, *op. cit.*, 320.

or less of a judicial character. They were had not between nations which were independent, as is the theory of international law usually today, but between nations which were subordinate to the superior power of Rome. In this respect they offer a certain kinship to the conditions prevailing between the several states of the American Union and the central power of the United States of America. Through the Supreme Court of the United States the differences between states are determined, and through the Senate of Rome the manner in which the differences between nations subject to Rome should be settled was determined.

At Rome, according to Phillipson,[97] there appear also to have been administrative arbitrations arising sometimes out of the payment of tribute and sometimes out of the occupation of territory. These were regarded as occurring between communities dependent on Rome and therefore within the circle of her interests, relating to cities in a state of dependence *de facto* and *do jure*. Of such are said to have been the dispute between Pergamum and Roman officials (122 B.C.) as to a tribute imposed, which was settled by a consul or praetor, assisted by a council of senators. So also as to a conflict between Oropus (on the eastern frontier of Boeotia) and Attica and the Roman tax gatherers (73 B.C.) relating to the interpretations of a decree of Sula conferring certain territory on the temple of the Amphiareum in Oropus.[98]

[97] Phillipson, *op. cit.*, II, 164.
[98] *Ibid.*, 165.

CHAPTER XVI

ARBITRATION FROM ANCIENT TIMES TO THE JAY TREATY OF 1794

126. General considerations.—Passing from the meager experiences of Rome with arbitration, we take up very briefly the long period extending to the beginning of the Middle Ages. This, in fact, furnishes us with but few examples which have survived historically of anything approaching an international tribunal.

Mérignhac informs us[1] that the barbarian world recognized the usage of arbitration. Procopius cites the example of the Gepidae who proposed an arbitration to the Lombards, declaring that it was unjust to use violence toward those who demanded a judge. Cassiodorus reports that the ambassadors of Theodoric, king of the Ostrogoths, carried letters from their master to the kings of the Heruli and the Varnes, praying them to join with them and the envoys of Gondebaud to invite Clovis, king of the Franks, to renounce war against the Visigoths and accept the arbitration of the united kings. This step was not in vain and Clovis in fact consented to an agreement.[2]

127. Influence of the church.—From a practical point of view the earliest and most important influence tending toward arbitration was that of the Papacy. Revon[3] finds that the rôle of the Papacy in the Middle Ages was superb; that while the jurist might question its methods of action, the historian was obliged to admit that the end attained was great. "The excesses, even, of the court of Rome," says Chateaubriand, "have served to extend the general principles of the rights of peoples."

Of course when the power of the church first commenced to be exercised in this direction there was no such thing as formal international law, the title itself being entirely unknown. Nevertheless, the fact that arbitration was indulged in indicates that the thing existed even though the name were unknown, for if the arbitrators were to act at all as judges it must have been on the theory either of the existence of a law of nations or of power in them to create and apply the law under the particular circumstances.

This remark, however, is not to be understood as carrying the same meaning as it would applied to the affairs of today, because the papacy

---

[1] Mérignhac, *op. cit.*, 31.   [2] *Idem.*   [3] Revon, *op. cit.*, 122.

acted not merely in a judicial capacity but also by virtue of its power as a sovereign, and this to a very considerable degree excludes all idea of law.[4] Furthermore, as is stated by Revon,

the Popes were not merely judges but also legislators; they made the law and at the same time that they made it, they interpreted it to their own fashion, leaving no remedy to the states submitting to their sentence. In fact by the political intrigues in which they were engaged, they often became judges and parties in the same cause; their sentence was not objective but subjective, thus no impartiality; above all, we have seen, they esteemed themselves sovereign; consequently they could not recognize above them any principle of justice.[5]

In his discussion of the subject, Revon declares that it may be said that

the papacy in the Middle Ages prepared the contemporary law of nations without establishing the juridical idea of arbitration. It prepared the law of nations, and in fact it was due to the papacy that there were concluded the first treaties of peace; by its legates were stifled a thousand causes of war ready to arise in the diplomatic domain; by its mediation later came the usage of addressing oneself to neutral powers to ask good offices even before a war or at the moment of signing peace. Likewise, the councils could be regarded as having been the precursors of the great modern international congresses; one saw taking part in them not alone the ecclesiastics but the representatives of Christian princes whose rank and place were in advance anticipated and defined with exactness; there were discussed grave international questions; Europe at Plaisance and Clermont for the first time became conscious of the political solidarity which should unite its various states.[6]

It is the just observation of Revon[7] that the Papacy, as afterward the Roman Empire, precisely because of its enormous importance in the world, could not conceive of the idea of arbitration as we understand it. All notion of equality between states, and consequently of common duties and rights, was absent from its politics. Thus it was that the arbitration of the Popes was not the final sentence of a judicial suit freely engaged in, legally conducted, subject to certain rules of international procedure, and determined according to the principles of an overruling law of nations.[8]

Nevertheless, we may observe that the great powers which tended to prevent war in its international relations during the Middle Ages, were the papacy and the Empire, which made themselves judges of conflicts menacing European peoples.

It is noted that, as the political force of the Papacy lessened, law

---

[4] Revon, op. cit., 118.   [5] Ibid., 125.
[6] Ibid., 124.   [7] Ibid., 118.   [8] Ibid., 122.

came forward and as the Pope ceased to be a superior whose findings were incontestable, he became a true arbitrator. From this resulted a number of interesting decisions, among them the arbitration of Boniface VIII between Philip le Bel and the King of England (1298) ; that of John XII between Philip le Long and the Flemings (1319) ; and in the fifteenth century that of Leon X between the Emperor Maximilian and the Doge of Venice.

As to the frequency with which resort was had to arbitration, Mérignhac finds[9] that there may be counted not less than one hundred in Italy in the thirteenth century between princes and communes of that country, but that when absolute monarchies were little by little erected in Europe upon the ruins of the feudal system, arbitration became more rare. Nevertheless, while this procedure was going on under the influence of religious and feudal ideas, arbitrations were much used during the Middle Ages, offering the singular spectacle of conciliation and peace advancing between populations of the most warlike character.

128. Arbitration aside from papal.—Progress during the Middle Ages in the idea of arbitration was not by any means confined to countries most markedly under churchly influence. We find, for instance, that in the very beginnings of union between the various cantons of Switzerland it was provided in the treaty of alliance between Uri, Schwytz, and Unterwald that

if any difference should arise between the confederates the wisest men among them will intervene by arbitration to appease the difficulty as it may seem to them suitable, and if one or the other of the parties violate their sentence, the other confederates will declare themselves against him.[10]

So we find according to Vattel that later the Swiss in treaties signed between themselves and with other powers took the precaution to agree in advance concerning the manner in which differences should be submitted to arbitrators in case they could not be amicably adjusted. He affirms that this measure of wisdom contributed no little to assure to the Swiss their independence and the respect of Europe. The Hanseatic League, formed in 1210, between Lübeck and Hamburg and including in 1360 fifty-two towns and in the fifteenth century eighty towns of the Baltic, the Rhine, and Flanders, regulated from 1418 by way of arbitration all differences arising between the contract towns. Lübeck designated four towns charged with the duty of settling the differences, the

---

9 Mérignhac, *op. cit.,* 38.
10 Sax, *Histoire de l'arbitrage international permanent,* 7.

sanction being the excommunication of the violators of a sentence. The League, by a special clause of the treaty of Calmar in 1289, became arbitrator for all conflicts which might arise between two Scandinavian kingdoms, its old adversaries, Norway and Denmark.[11]

The Constitution of 1495, promulgated by the Diet of Worms, forbade all war between the confederate states of the German Empire, and created to punish the violations of this fundamental law a supreme court called "Imperial Chamber," which, reorganized several times, was not put into its final form until 1530. Established in a definitive way at Spire at that time, this court was, in 1698, carried to Wetzlar, where it continued to sit until the fall of the Empire in 1806. The workings of the Imperial Chamber were not regarded with much favor by the Austrian emperors and when there was created in 1501 by Maximilian the Aulic Council, which in the first place was confined to the administration of the hereditary domains of the Emperor and the judgment of causes reserved to him, the court of Vienna extended little by little its jurisdiction to cases under the Imperial Chamber. Its interferences were given as one of the causes of the Thirty Years War.

According to Mérignhac certain Russian jurisconsults mentioned the existence in the Middle Ages of a tribunal composed of boyards belonging to the different principalities, passing chiefly upon frontiers.[12] If the tribunal could not terminate the dispute, the metropolitan designated a third person accepted by the parties, who finally decided. This jurisdiction disappeared at the time of the final establishment of the supremacy of Moscow.

The arbitration clause (*clause compromissoire*) seems to have been frequent enough in the Middle Ages, although not subject to regular rules. It further appears to have met with a certain degree of success. This remark is true according to Novacovitch,[13] notwithstanding the view of Kamarowsky denying such clauses success and Mérignhac finding them rare.

We give a few examples of treaty arbitration agreements. In a treaty of alliance concluded in 1235 between Genoa and Venice, there is to be found an article to this effect: "If there should arise between the said cities any differences which cannot be easily settled between them, it will be determined by the arbitration of the Sovereign Pontiff."[14]

---

11 *Ibid.*, 8.   12 Mérignhac, *op. cit.*, 358.
13 *Les compromis et les arbitrages internationaux du XII⁰ au XV⁰ siècle*, 20.
14 Mérignhac, 40.

In 1343 King Waldemar of Denmark and King Magnus of Sweden concluded an arbitral convention by which they decided to confide to an arbitral commission all the grave disputes which could arise between them thereafter, the convention being entitled "treaty of perpetual peace."[15] Difficulties were referred to a commission of three bishops and three knights named by each and in the event of disagreement to two among them, chosen one on each side, who were to give a final decision.[16] A treaty of alliance concluded in 1464 between the Counts Ulrich and Eberhardt of Württemburg and the equestrian order of the Society of the Shield of St. George in Upper Swabia, provided for an arbitral commission to decide differences which might arise between them either of a general character or upon the subject of the conditions of aid and division of prisoners.[17]

The kings of France and England concluded in 1475 a treaty of arbitration good for three years and renewed first in 1478 and then for one hundred years *post mortem primo nostrum decedentis* in 1479.[18]

The treaty signed in 1516 between Francis I and the Swiss Cantons, a treaty known under the name of "perpetual peace," contained the following clause:

Difficulties and disputes calculated to arise between the subjects of the king and the inhabitants of the Swiss Cantons shall be terminated by the judgment of four men of substance, two named by each party, which four arbitrators shall hear in a designated place the parties or their attorneys, and if their opinions are divided, the plaintiff may choose from the neighboring countries a *prud'homme* beyond suspicion and who will meet with the arbitrators to decide the difficulty. If the dispute be between a subject of the Cantons and leagues and the King of France, the Cantons will examine the complaint, and if they find it justified they will support it before the king; but if the king is not satisfied with it the claimants can call the king before arbitrators, who will be taken from among the judges of Coire or Valais acceptable to the parties, and whatever will then be done and concluded by said judges, by an award or amicably, shall prevail, and be observed without any question.[19]

129. Questions referred to arbitration.—We cite under other headings many instances illustrating the kind of question referred to arbitration. We may add at this point that there were during the Middle Ages questions of indemnity, of responsibility for arbitrary acts, jurisdictional questions and trespasses or excess of powers, of the division

[15] Novacovitch, *op. cit.*, 18.
[16] Acremant, *La procédure dans les arbitrages internationaux*, 49.
[17] Novacovitch, *op. cit.*, 156.
[18] Lange, *Histoire de l'internationalisme*, 122.
[19] Mérignhac, *op. cit.*, 40.

of lands or the division of prisoners. There are several examples where the arbitrator was called on to pronounce between various claimants to a succession. There were cases of disputes upon questions of damages to be paid or of limits violated or unsettled, and these were among the more numerous.[20]

130. Arbitrator as *amiable compositeur*, or mediator.—By a quite universal practice it would appear that before proceeding to adjudge, the arbitrator acted in the capacity of what subsequently became known as *"amiable compositeur"*—in other words he sought to find a basis for the composition of difficulties before considering them from the standpoint of law. As is said by De Card

the arbitrators proposed to the parties an arrangement and if an amicable settlement were impossible they rendered their sentence.[21]

So Novacovitch finds[22] that the commission composed of representatives of the parties first sought conciliation and an amicable settlement before proceeding to judgment.

The later authorities declare that the arbitrators were called without distinction "arbiters," "arbitrators," and *"amiables compositeurs,"* no distinction being made between the terms, a difference later made by the French code being too subtle and too learned for the writers of the *compromis* of the Middle Ages.[23]

Mérignhac agrees[24] that before the eighteenth century it was often very difficult, sometimes impossible, to clearly separate cases of mediation and of arbitration, either because the terminology was not yet very well defined, or because the expressions employed were equivocal, or that the difference was not clearly in the thought of the negotiators. Thus in 1334, Philip of Valois declared himself chosen judge, bargainer, and *amiable compositeur* between the King of Bohemia, the princes of Germany, and the Duke of Brabant. It is to be added that often mediation took an obligatory character by reason of the fear inspired by the mediator, who was regarded as ready to impose his point of view by arms. Again, Henry IV pronounced as mediator between the Republic of Venice and the Pope, Paul V. The Pope for his defense counting upon Spain, Henry IV, to oppose the armaments of that country, proposed to the Swiss arrangements having in view the raising of ten thousand men in such manner that the Pope was forced to accede to the wishes of the King of France.

---

[20] Novacovitch, *op. cit.,* 70.   [21] *L'arbitrage international,* 53.
[22] Novacovitch, *op. cit.,* 49.   [23] *Ibid.,* 82.   [24] Mérignhac, *op. cit.,* 41.

Nevertheless, we find in the treaty of 1467 between the Duke of Milan and the Swiss Cantons a clear reference to the difference between the functions of a judge and an *amiable compositeur*. The same was the case in a dispute between Milan, Venice, and Florence.[25] Again in 1595 the distinction between mediation and arbitration was perfectly remarked by the French minister, who interposed between the Protestants and Catholics, ready to come to conflict on the subject of the expulsion of the Catholic magistrates from Aix-la-Chapelle and their replacement by a Protestant magistrate.[26] In this case the King of France was asked to name impartial persons who could act, not as judges or arbitrators, but as mediators and *amiables compositeurs.*

In 1245 Saint Louis was called upon to pronounce on the succession of the Counts of Flanders and Hainaut, and did so with powers which enabled him to avoid a decision entirely unfavorable to one of the two parties. In 1481, in a *compromis* between Holland, Zeeland, Frisia, and several towns, the arbitrators were authorized to decide in the most useful and suitable way.[27] On the other hand, in 1319, the Duke of Brabant and the Count of Holland insisted that the Count of Juilliers should decide rigorously according to the rules of law. This difference related to the possession of the domain of Hoesden, and the arbitrator declared in his sentence that he decided *de jure,* while he should have preferred making an amicable composition.[28]

Under the peace concluded between a great number of German states in 1254 there was created a regular federal assembly, each member of the union having power to name four delegates. These delegates reunited to occupy themselves periodically with federal affairs, but besides were competent to regulate in the way of amiable composition or to judge according to the need the differences which might arise thereafter between two or more states of the union. The mixed tribunals instituted by the German treaties of arbitration were a particular form of arbitration, composed of judges of equal number of the two parties and presided over by a *gemeiner mann,* an umpire. They thus resembled the mixed commission employed in our day. If the composition of these tribunals were defective, the parties chose judges among their own counselors. Although these commissions should commence by an amicable intervention or amiable settlement before judging, nevertheless their function was also to judge and therefore there was an arbitration.

131. Arbitration to conclude peace.—We are told by Novaco-

---

[25] Novacovitch, *op. cit.,* 83.

[26] Mérignhac, *op. cit.,* 42.

[27] Novacovitch, *op. cit.,* 76.

[28] *Ibid.,* 77.

vitch[29] that in the Middle Ages resort was often had to arbitration, not to prevent a war but to put an end to one. The parties, tired of fighting, chose one or more arbitrators and gave them the duty of reconciling the parties and re-establishing peace. Also the prince who interposed himself as mediator assumed sometimes the task of arbitrator. He concluded a truce awaiting the definitive provisions of peace. In other cases arbitration was a preventive measure as we find it in many treaties of defensive alliance.

As illustrative of an arbitration after concluding a war, we have among others the case where the Duke of Lorraine and the Duke of Burgundy, desiring peace, prayed the Count of Charolais to reconcile them. He responded he would terminate their differences by an arbitral sentence.[30] The *compromis* was prepared, and the Count delegated his powers to five of his counselors and approved the treaty of peace made by them. Again in 1441 Francisco Sforza acted as arbiter between Venice, Florence, and Genoa on the one part and the Duke of Milan on the other.[31] Grotius emphasizes this sort of arbitration.

132. Choice of sovereigns or the Pope as arbitrators.—It was, perhaps, usual and natural that among the sovereigns of the Middle Ages there was little inclination to bow in any cases of arbitration to the determination of anyone occupying the rank of less than that of their peer. The exceptions to this rule we shall have occasion to review hereafter. This feeling that the recognition of the orders of anyone of inferior majesty constituted an infringement upon the rights of sovereignty made it, of course, readily possible that the decisions of the popes and of the Holy Roman emperors should be sought. Their powers, it was believed, were able to settle all questions by virtue of a superior right that they believed they held from God. They acted in truth as masters of the world.[32]

We find that Popes Alexander III, Honorarius III, John XXII, and Gregory IX were frequently chosen as arbitrators in quarrels agitating Europe, while Pope Alexander VI, by an arbitral decision remaining celebrated, traced an imaginary line from one pole to the other, dividing thus between the Spanish and the Portuguese possessions and territories discovered in the New World.[33] Even after the schism of England when the papacy had lost Teutonic and Gallo-Teutonic Europe, the prestige of the Popes was so great that it imposed itself upon the Poles and the Muscovites. We should mention also in the seventeenth

---

[29] *Ibid.*, 38.   [30] *Ibid.*, 138.   [31] *Ibid.*, 71.
[32] Rouard De Card, *op. cit.*, 12.   [33] Mérignhac, *op. cit.*, 33.

century the arbitration of Gregory IV with reference to the subject of the forts of the Valteline, and as late as the eighteenth century that of Pope Clement XI, who settled the differences between Louis XVI and Leopold I, who were created arbitrators by Article 8 of the Treaty of Ryswick.

In face, however, of the weakening of faith and of the opposition of princes, the heads of the Church were obliged to abate their pretensions as the sovereigns of the world.

Next after the popes in claims of universal supremacy were the emperors of Germany, who considered themselves as the successors of the Roman Cæsars. The struggle between the Church and the Empire, the spiritual power and the temporal power, filled the second half of the Middle Age, the two principal events being the War of the Investitures and the struggle of the Guelphs and the Ghibellines. The tendency of the Holy Roman Empire to universal domination naturally caused it to attempt to constitute itself, as had done the popes, a universal arbitrator between the kings.[34] In this effort it met with little success, facing as it did powerful princes who refused to submit to its yoke. It did not have the enormous spiritual force of the popes, and thus before the papacy it succumbed in the struggle. "The laic suzerainty of the emperors over Christianity," says Bluntschli, "was less recognized than the ecclesiastical sovereignty of the popes. They did not succeed even in preventing in Germany and Italy the lords, great and small, from troubling the interior peace by incessant struggles."[35]

Turning to the selection of kings as arbitrators, an early and much cited instance is that of Louis IX of France, who was chosen in 1263 as arbitrator by virtue of a *compromis*. In the case of the difference between the King of England, Henry III, and his barons, after having attentively heard the complaints of the two parties at Amiens (where were imprisoned the King of England and his wife), he decided that the stipulations of Oxford should be abrogated; that the king should be relieved of his oath; that the fortresses which were occupied by twenty-four barons should be restored to Henry, but that the rights of the English people embodied in the charters should remain inviolable. Making a pretext of this last restriction, the barons declined to submit to the decision.

In 1268 the same king, Louis IX, determined the conflict between the Counts of Luxemburg and of Bar. In 1334 Philip of Valois as

---

[34] Mérignhac, *op. cit.*, 35.   [35] Revon, *op. cit.*, 127.

"judge, negotiator, and *amiable compositeur*" brought about the conclusion of a peace between the king of Bohemia, the princes of Germany, and the Duke of Brabant. Again in 1444 Charles VII decided an exchange of possessions between the Duke of Anjou and Count Antoine de Vaudemont, notably with relation to the Duchy of Lorraine. In this case the king suggested himself as arbitrator. Louis XI filled several times the rôle of arbitrator, in 1463 between the kings of Castile and Aragon, in 1475 between the Duke of Austria and the Helvetian Republic.[36]

It was, however, in vain that Philip II proposed himself as arbitrator between France and England.[37] As late as 1701, pursuant to the application of the Counts of Bentheim, the King of England rendered a decision at The Hague.[38]

It is not to be assumed that in the Middle Ages any more than at present, at least as a rule, the monarch named as an arbitrator acted in that personal capacity. He seems to have referred the differences sent him to his counsellors, but the parties knew this would happen when choosing the king as arbitrator.[39] The arbitration was none the less valid because delegated in this manner.[40]

133. Other arbitrators.—Cardinals and bishops not infrequently acted as arbitrators. Appeals, for instance, to the cardinals were perhaps most frequent among the Italian territorial divisions of the Middle Ages.[41] The Treaty of Nonancourt, 1177, designated three archbishops as arbitrators between Louis the Young and Henry II of England with reference to Auvergne, Chateauroux, and other fiefs.[42] In 1276 two bishops and a man of arms were taken as judges between the kings of Hungary and Bohemia.[43] In 1441, an archbishop, a duke, a landgrave, and a prince decided between the princes of Saxony and the margraves of Brandenburg, ending a war. In 1475 the differences existing between Louis XI and Edward of England were referred to the Archbishop of Lyon and the Count of Dunois, for France, and to the Archbishop of Canterbury and the Duke of Clarence for England.[44] In 1475, national differences in which Edward VI of England was concerned were submitted to an assembly of bishops.[45]

Towns were not infrequently chosen as arbitrators, following in this respect, perhaps, the ancient Greek custom. For instance, in the

[36] *Ibid.,* 128.   [37] Mérignhac, *op. cit.,* 35.

[38] Kamarowsky, *Le tribunal international,* 186.   [39] Mérignhac, *op. cit.,* 227.

[40] Novacovitch, *op. cit.,* 86.   [41] *Ibid.,* 72.   [42] Mérignhac, *op. cit.,* 34.

[43] *Idem.*   [44] Novacovitch, *op. cit.,* 158.   [45] Revon, *op. cit.,* 128.

fifteenth century, Lübeck and a number of other Hanseatic towns coming to an agreement with Holland, Zeeland, and Frisia, selected their arbiters, each party designating in the *compromis* five towns, and among the five there had to be chosen two who should send their deputies to Campen. The deputies of the four towns thus assembled were to settle the troubles within thirteen weeks.[46] The Treaty of Westminster of 1655 restoring harmony between France and England stipulated in Article 24 (probably because of the preference of Cromwell) that the Republic of Hamburg should fill the part of final arbitrator between the two parties to determine damages suffered on one part or the other after the year 1640. There may be cited further in 1665 the arbitration of the Grand Council of Malines between Frederick William, Elector of Brandenburg, and the States General apropos of a debt, called the "Debt of Hoysfer."[47] It may not be out of place at this point to refer to the fact that differences relative to fortified places and on secondary points between France and Spain at the time of the Peace of Nimeguen, 1678, were referred to the States General of the United Provinces.[48]

The ancient French parliaments, which were not at all parliaments in the modern sense of the term but a collection of judges, also acted as arbitrators, their own sovereign not being involved in the litigation. Thus in 1240 the Parliament of Paris acted as arbitrator between Emperor Frederick II and Pope Innocent IV.

The Parliament of Grenoble under the reign of Francis I was chosen arbitrator in a conflict between two princes on the subject of the possession of the Milanais, and in 1613 and 1614 rendered two decisions in the conflict between the Archduke of Austria and the Duke of Württemburg with reference to the county of Montpellier.

Individuals were from time to time chosen as arbitrators. A difference arising after the death of Charles V in 1380 between the Dukes of Anjou, Bourbon, and Berry with reference to the formation of a Council of Regency, it was referred to Jean Desmarts, a lawyer. An award based upon his report was entered in Parliament by the Decree of October 1380. "Desmarts paid dearly," says the historian of the *Ordre des Avocats*, "for the dangerous honor of judging the quarrels of princes. Nothing could protect him from vengeance and he perished on the scaffold."

In 1570 the King of Spain and Switzerland, to put an end to disputes relative to the frontiers of the Franche-Comté, submitted to the

---

46 Novacovitch, *op. cit.*, 72.   47 Mérignhac, *op. cit.*, 36.

48 Kamarowsky, *Le tribunal international*, 185.

judgment of a counselor of the Parliament of Dijon named Jean Bégat.[49] By the Treaty of Westminster in 1655 between France and England, it was provided, among other clauses, that the damages suffered by the parties should be fixed within six and one-half months by six commissioners, three from each party, who in case of disagreement should refer themselves to the Republic of Hamburg, which would name new commissioners charged with giving a final decision.[50]

Italian jurisconsults were called on to resolve the conflict of the Dukes of Mantua and Savoy with reference to Montferrat, and the Doctors of Pérouse, Boulogne, and Padua were asked to give their opinions as to the right of the Duke of Farnese to the throne of Portugal.

We have already noted the provisions existing between the Swiss Cantons relative to the settlement of disputes by arbitration. These agreements were carried out in Switzerland from the fifteenth century to the Revolution by submission to the judges of the conflicts of the Cantons, whether among themselves or with neighboring powers.[51]

As is the general custom in arbitration, so we are told,[52] regularly arbitrators who were absent or prevented from action could be replaced, the substitute being designated by the party which had chosen the arbitrator in default.

134. Procedure.—Not a great deal is to be said with regard to procedure before arbitrators in the more ancient arbitrations. We are told that by many a *compromis* the arbitrators were given power to decide standing or sitting, on holidays or non-holidays, in the presence of the parties or in their absence.[53] As to their general power to make rules and govern procedure, we find that, according to the *compromis* made in 1441 between Holland, Zeeland, Frisia, and certain towns, the arbitrators should have power to receive demands, complaints, and allegations of the two parties and terminate the affair and everything dependent upon it in such manner as they might find useful and convenient.[54]

We are not without even early examples showing that the parties to aid the arbitrators sent their delegates and their lawyers. In 1176 the Kings of Castile and of Navarre sent before the arbitrator (the King of England) ambassadors to receive from his hands the award and also four delegates to explain to the arbitrator their points of view and arguments. In 1277 the King of France in the arbitration between the

[49] Mérignhac, *op. cit.*, 38.   [50] Kamarowsky, *op. cit.*, 186.   [51] Revon, *op.cit.*, 149.
[52] Novacovitch, *op. cit.*, 75.   [53] *Ibid.*, 78.   [54] *Ibid.*, 76.

Duke of Burgoyne and the Count of Nevers was assisted by two knights delegated by the parties to serve him as counselors.

In the dispute relative to Montferrat pending between the Dukes of Savoy and Mantua and the Marquis of Saluces, the attorneys of the litigant parties, who disputed either an entire claim to Montferrat or to special territories or rights, appeared before the persons delegated by Charles V to examine into the facts and upon whose advice he was to judge. The Emperor passed first upon the principal object of the litigation and awarded Montferrat to the Duke of Mantua. Then he ruled upon the question of the *dot* of Blanche of Savoy, which he directed to be guaranteed by particular sureties, and at last pronounced upon the question of gifts on account of marriage. The award of possession of the Duke of Mantua was subordinate to the giving of sufficient bond into the hands of the Emperor, and the parties were solemnly cited to come to the imperial court to hear the sentence which ruled finally upon the entire question.[55]

The presence of the parties upon notice was held necessary, though they might be represented by others. Sometimes it was provided, as in the arbitration of Saint Louis between the children of the Countess Marguerite of Flanders in 1245, that the arbitrators, if the parties did not come to hear the announcement of the sentence, could act nevertheless, which seems to imply that the presence of the parties was almost counted the *sine qua non* of the validity of the sentence pronounced. Besides the parties, numerous witnesses were present at the publication of the award and sometimes placed their signatures upon the act of arbitration as corroboration.[56]

The time within which arbitration should be complete was frequently regulated. Thus, according to a treaty of 1405, it was the duty of the arbitrators to determine the question within six weeks and three days. They were obliged to take an oath and send to each party a copy of the award. However, in another treaty the period was reduced to one month and it was not always considered requisite that the written award should be furnished.[57]

135. Collateral jurisdiction.—The jurisdiction of the arbitrators extended even to questions intermingled with the principal one. It concerned secondary questions and the details not touched upon precisely in the *compromis* but which by reason of their dependence upon the principal question entered into and should be resolved with it. Thus

---

[55] Mérignhac, *op. cit.*, 39.   [56] Novacovitch, *op. cit.*, 85.   [57] *Ibid.*, 50.

the arbitrators settled points not anticipated by the *compromis* but not exceeding the limits of their power. This idea seems to have been expressed in the award of the King of France in 1289 between the Duke of Brabant and the Count of Guelders.[58]

136. Sanctions.—We come now to the question of sanctions or penalties to insure the enforcement of the award. In modern times these have not been found in any sense essential, but it was quite otherwise during the Middle Ages. These were in general fixed by the *compromis,* but there were cases (as that of the *compromis* of the King of Castile in 1368) where the arbitrator enforced the guaranties stipulated in the *compromis* by new sureties, or where the arbitrator had the power to guarantee the award as he might judge best, the *compromis* making no mention of any penalties. Thus in 1440 the King of France arbitrated between the Duke of Lorraine and Count de Vaudemont, declaring a penalty of one thousand gold crowns against the one who should not observe his award.[59]

In an arbitration between the towns of Nona and Arbi, a pledge to carry out the award was required from twelve men of each city as well as its representatives; in other cases where penalties were fixed, they were modest. In 1226 in a *compromis* between Riga and Donamunde it was of but ten gold marks. The penalty was three thousand gold crowns in the *compromis* of Louis VI and Edward IV in 1475 and of one hundred thousand silver marks in 1332 between the Duke of Brabant on one side and the King of Bohemia, the Archbishop of Cologne, and their allies on the other side. There was a sanction of one hundred thousand gold crowns in 1440 between the Duke of Lorraine and the Count de Vaudemont and in 1298 the King of England undertook to observe the award of Pope Boniface VIII under a penalty of one hundred thousand silver marks and pledged all his goods. In Italy the pecuniary penalties were always large. In 1376 the treaty of peace between the Pope, the Duke of Savoy, and the Viscount of Milan was guaranteed by a penalty of one hundred thousand gold florins. The Viscounts of Milan and Florence undertook in 1392 to observe the arbitral sentence under a penalty of two hundred thousand gold florins. In the arbitration of 1433 between the Dukes of Milan and Venice, the penalty was one hundred thousand gold ducats, and in 1441 between the Duke of Milan on the one part and Venice, Florence, and Genoa on the other, the penalty reached the sum of two hundred thousand gold

[58] *Ibid.,* 80.   [59] Novacovitch, *op. cit.,* 97.

ducats.[60] There is the case of a treaty whose execution was guaranteed under a penalty of one thousand marks.[61]

It was not unusual that the sanction provided by treaty for the violation of an arbitration was excommunication. Thus we find, for instance, in the case of an alliance concluded between Venice and Genoa by virtue of which all differences arising between the cities were submitted to the arbitration of the Pope the sanction provided was excommunication.[62] The decisions of the Hanseatic Confederation formed in the beginning of the thirteenth century also claimed such a sanction.[63]

It is true that a guaranty most in use was the taking of an oath and pecuniary penalties, the oath being of great efficacy, owing to the importance attached to it in the Middle Ages and the penalty the Church pronounced against perjurers. In the arbitration rendered by Philip of Valois between the King of Bohemia and his allies and the Duke of Brabant in 1334, the parties undertook to execute the treaty under penalty of their faith and their oath, which failing they could be prosecuted in all ecclesiastical and secular courts.[64]

The influence of the church diminishing, the menace of excommunication was insufficient to induce controlling states to keep their word, and the Swiss plenipotentiaries of 1291 went far enough to admit violent enforcement.[65]

There are cases cited where the arbitrator himself undertook to join in the enforcement of an award against a recalcitrant party. Treaties were even made of this nature, obliging the authority of the arbitrator to be thrown in with the force of the party prevailing in the arbitration.[66] To this effect was an arbitration in 1391 between the towns of Italy and a treaty of peace concluded in 1435 between the Pope, Venice, and Florence on one side, and the Duke of Milan on the other.

137. Finality of award.—We come now to the question of the finality of the award under certain circumstances. It is generally conceded that through corruption in the arbitrator the award becomes void. Happily such cases have been practically unknown in the past one hundred and more years and do not seem to have cut any important figure in the period we are now treating. Barbeyrac, however, cites the case of the Emperor Maximilian and the Doge of Venice, who are each said to have tried to corrupt Pope Leo X, arbitrator of their differences.

[60] Novacovitch, op cit., 94, 95. [61] Ibid., 50.

[62] André, L'arbitrage obligatoire, 31, and Sax, L'arbitrage international, 6.

[63] André, op. cit., 31. [64] Novacovitch, op. cit., 93.

[65] André, op. cit., 32. [66] Novacovitch, op. cit., 96.

138. Interpretation of award.—A very extreme case of an exercise of the power of interpretation, one not justifiable on any principle with which the present day is acquainted, occurred in this wise: The King of France having decided in 1277 between the Duke of Burgundy and the Count of Nevers and dying shortly afterward, his son was called upon to elucidate some words of the award diversely interpreted by the parties.[67]

We have now to touch upon a point in which the medieval concept of the power of arbitrators differs very widely from that at present prevailing. Now universally the arbitrator considers his power limited and, once the decision has been reached, save it be for the correction of immaterial errors and errors in calculation, he claims no power or right over the interpretation given his conclusions. This right of correcting or adding to an award seems sometimes to have been given by the treaty itself, which also would give to the arbitrators power of interpretation.[68]

Sometimes the arbitrator in giving his award reserved the right of passing upon difficulties of interpretation and execution which might thereafter arise, as, for instance, in 1289 in the arbitration made by the King of France between the Duke of Brabant and the Count of Guelders. Generally the decision was final and without appeal, and, once rendered, except as indicated, the power of the arbitrator was gone.[69]

One or two cases which seem peculiar to our modern point of view may be indicated. For instance, the Duke Philip of Burgundy rendered in 1452 an arbitral sentence between the Duke of Anjou and the Count de Vaudemont, deciding first that Ferry, the eldest son of the Count de Vaudemont, should marry Yolande, eldest daughter of the Duke of Bar; the *dot* to be given by the Duke of Bar was fixed in detail, thus regulating at the same time certain claims of the Count de Vaudemont. The Duke of Bar should pay in addition to the Count de Vaudemont an annual charge of one hundred and twenty florins claimed by him by virtue of the succession which had fallen to him. The award contains other provisions not necessary to be noted, and the Duke of Bar being a prisoner at the moment of the arbitration was obliged to ratify the sentence and thereupon was put at liberty.[70]

According to the arbitral sentence between the Knight Jean d'Egmond and the Convent of Saint Adalbert concerning the temporal domain of d'Egmond, the knight became a vassal of the convent as to the domain and the Pope confirmed the sentence.

---

[67] *Ibid.*, 82.   [68] Novacovitch, *op. cit.*, 81.   [69] *Ibid.*, 29.   [70] *Ibid.*, 144.

CHAPTER XVII

EARLY AMERICAN ARBITRATIONS

139. Colonial and under Articles of Confederation.—We are informed that an arrangement of difficulties between the early settlements in this country was in at least one instance secured through an arbitration. This was in 1650 between the Province of New York, then under Dutch control, and the colony of Connecticut. By agreement these difficulties were referred to the colony of Massachusetts for settlement. This was done at the instigation of Peter Stuyvesant of New Amsterdam, then governor, and was the result of an active correspondence carried on between him and John Eaton, governor of Connecticut. Our information with regard to this is but meager.[1]

Article IX of the Articles of Confederation of 1777 provided that "the United States in Congress assembled shall also be the last resort on appeal in all disputes and differences now subsisting or that hereafter may arise between two or more states concerning boundary, jurisdiction, or any other cause whatever; which authority shall always be exercised in the manner" set forth in the article in question. A summary of this manner is that there should be in the end five or more persons who would be commissioners or judges determining "the controversy, so always as a major part of the judges who shall hear the cause shall agree in the determination." The judgment and sentence were to be final and conclusive and the judges were to act under oath.

Under this provision one controversy was determined. This arose in 1782 between Pennsylvania and Connecticut, each claiming the same territory in the Valley of the Susquehanna River. The court sat at Trenton and its proceedings and decisions were recorded in the *Journal of Congress*. The Commissioners decided that

the State of Connecticut has no right to the lands in controversy. We are also unanimous of opinion that the jurisdiction and pre-emption of all the territory lying within the charter boundary of Pennsylvania, and now claimed by the State of Connecticut, do of right belong to the State of Pennsylvania.[2]

A number of territorial and other disputes between the states have

---

[1] Article by Thomas Willing Balch, *Revue générale de droit international public,* XXI (1914), 139, referring to *Hoadly's Records of the Colony and Plantation of New Haven, 1638-1649,* pp. 507-36; Ebenezer Hazard, State Papers 1794, Vol. II, p. 154.

[2] *Journal of Congress for 1783,* 129–140.

arisen under the Constitution of the United States and have been decided by the Supreme Court of the United States.

140. Arbitrations under the Jay Treaty of 1794.—The modern era of arbitral or judicial settlement of international disputes, by common accord among all writers upon the subject, dates from the signing on November 19, 1794, of the Jay Treaty between Great Britain and the United States. Prior to this time arbitrations were irregular and spasmodic; from this time forward they assumed a certain regularity and system.

The treaty in question provided for three separate boards of arbitration. The first dispute according to Article 5 of the Treaty had reference to a question of boundary of the northeast portion of the United States, and concerned the determination of what river was "truly intended under the name of St. Croix mentioned in" the Treaty of Peace. This provided for the appointment of one commissioner on the part of Great Britain and one on the part of the United States named by the President "by and with the advice and consent of the Senate;" and that the two commissioners should agree on the choice of a third, or if they could not so agree, each should propose one person and of the two names so proposed one should be drawn by lot. As it happened, fortunately the two commissioners were able to agree upon the third man without resort to lot, and the report of all three in accordance with the treaty decided what river was the St. Croix intended by the treaty, with a description of it and the latitude and longitude of its mouth and source. By the terms of the Article under which they were appointed, the decision was final and conclusive, not to be thereafter "called into question, or made the subject of dispute or difference between the parties."

The sixth article of the treaty dealt with the claims of British merchants and others, reciting that debts bonafide contracted before the peace still remained owing by citizens or merchants of the United States, and that by the operation of statutes within the states recovery of the debts had been delayed and the value and security impaired or lessened, so that British creditors could not obtain or receive adequate compensation for their losses and damages. For the purpose of ascertaining the amount of such losses and damages five commissioners were to be appointed, two by the King of England, two by the President of the United States with the advice and consent of the Senate, and the fifth by their unanimous vote, and if they could not agree, the commissioners on either side were, respectively, to propose one person, and the name of one of the two so proposed should be drawn by lot in the presence of the original commissioners. The commissioners were to be sworn to decide "according to justice and equity." Three of the commissioners constituted a board and had power to do any act pertaining to the commission, provided one named on each side and the fifth commissioner were present. All decisions were to be made by a majority of those then present. In the lottery for the choice of the fifth commissioner, an Englishman then in the United States was chosen.

The commission so organized decided some cases and functioned for a considerable length of time; but difficulties arose among the members, as a result of which the American commissioners withdrew and the board was unable to act further. One of the great questions of difference was as to whether it was the duty of the English creditor to have exhausted his remedies before appealing to the board, and this question was decided in favor of the creditor by the vote of the umpire and the British members of the commission—a decision exactly contrary to that arrived at by the commissioners under the seventh article of the treaty, of the workings of which we shall hereafter speak.

As a result of what has already been said, the commission failed to function, and after correspondence between the two governments a cash sum was paid by the United States in lieu of any possible recovery.

From the point of view of its contributions to international law, the third commission formed under the seventh article of the Jay Treaty was by far the most important. The purpose of this article was to meet complaints made by citizens of the United States against Great Britain "by reason of irregular or illegal captures or condemnations of their vessels and other property, under color of authority or commissions from His Majesty" and for which "adequate compensation for the losses and damages so sustained cannot now be actually obtained, had, and received by the ordinary course of judicial proceedings." The commission had also jurisdiction over complaints by British subjects of "loss and damage sustained by reason of the capture of their vessels and merchandise, taken within the limits and jurisdiction of the States and brought into the ports of the same, or taken by vessels originally armed in ports of the said States."

Under this article commissioners were to be appointed in the manner provided by the preceding article relating to the claims of British subjects against the United States, and the umpire was selected by lot, fortune this time favoring the Americans. The American representatives on the commission were among the ablest men in the country, and their distinction and ability added greatly to the authority of the board of which they were members.

A number of questions of the highest importance were decided by the commission, perhaps the most important being one upon which the commission was nearly wrecked, that of its power to determine its own jurisdiction. Upon this, the advice of Lord Chancellor Loughborough was sought, and he declared that "the doubt respecting the authority of the commissioners to settle their own jurisdiction was absurd, and that they must necessarily decide upon cases being within, or without their competency."[8]

Other questions of importance arose as to necessity of the exhaustion of judicial remedies and when the apparent want of such exhaustion was excusable. Precedents upon these points created by the commission have since proved to be of great value.

[8] Moore, *Digest of International Arbitrations,* 327.

CHAPTER XVIII

LATER ARBITRATIONS BETWEEN THE UNITED STATES AND GREAT BRITAIN

141. As to territorial disputes.—Recognizing the Jay Treaty as marking the beginning of the modern era of arbitrations, especially between the United States and England, we note that the subject-matter of one board was that of territorial boundaries. A number of other disputes of like character were subsequently dealt with in the same general manner.

In 1814, by Article 4 of the Treaty of Ghent, there was referred to a joint commission of two members, having power in the event of disagreement to call in a third, the question of the ownership of islands in Passamaquoddy Bay and of the Grand Manan in the Bay of Fundy. This arbitration was had without calling in the assistance of an umpire.

By Article 5 of the same Treaty of Ghent a like arbitration commission was appointed to determine the northeastern boundary of the United States from the source of the River St. Croix to the St. Lawrence River. These commissioners failing to agree, the question was referred to the King of the Netherlands. His award, given January 10, 1831, assumed the form largely of a recommendation rather than of a decision. As such the United States rejected it, and England accepted the judgment of this country as to the character of the award. It was undoubtedly void as failing to follow the terms of submission. Later this particular difficulty was adjusted by voluntary action between the two countries embodied in the Webster-Ashburton Treaty of 1842.

Article 6 of the Treaty of Ghent also referred to a joint commission the determination of the boundary along the middle of the Great Lakes to the water communication between Lake Huron and Lake Superior. This resulted in an agreement between the arbitrators, which agreement was accepted by the parties.

Article 7 of this same treaty contained a similar reference covering the boundary line to the Lake of the Woods. In this case the commissioners were unable to agree and the question was settled by the Webster-Ashburton Treaty.

A further boundary dispute occurred with relation to the northwestern corner of the old United States and concerning the meaning of the convention signed at London October 20, 1818, as to the extension to the Pacific, and afterward undertaken to be covered by the boundary treaty of June 15, 1846, which carried the boundary line "to the middle of the Channel which separates the continent from Vancouver's Island; and thence southerly through the middle of the said Channel, and of Fuca's Straits, to the Pacific Ocean." After having been the subject of long-continued dispute, the matter was by Articles 34–37 of the Treaty of Washington of 1871 referred to the Emperor of Germany as arbitrator, and he sustained the American claims.

The last territorial dispute between the two countries related to the Alaskan boundary with Canada. This was in 1903 referred to a joint commission composed of an equal number of representatives of Great Britain and the United States and for the most part decided in favor of the United States, one of the British arbitrators accepting the American view.

142. Arbitrations touching pecuniary claims between the two countries.—Again taking as our point of departure arbitrations affecting pecuniary claims later than the Jay Treaty, we have to note that the first difference related as to whether under Article 1 of the Treaty of Ghent the United States was entitled to compensation for slaves in the territory in possession of the British at the time of its ratification, which territory was restored to the United States. The question of the construction of the article was referred to the Emperor of Russia by an agreement concluded in 1818. His decision was in favor of the United States. The award determined, however, only the question of interpretation, leaving open a decision as to the amount. The determination of this was referred to a board of arbitration, which before its labors had ended was rendered of no importance by a convention under which Great Britain paid to the United States a given sum in full settlement.

A convention was established between the two countries by treaty under date of February 8, 1853, for the adjudication of all claims arising against either on account of citizens or subjects of the other since the date of the Treaty of Ghent and which were yet unsettled. By this a commission of two members, one for either party, and an umpire, was created. This commission passed upon some one hundred and fifteen claims and was in a high degree successful.

A commission of minor importance was created under the treaty of July 1, 1863, to pass upon the claims of the Hudson's Bay and Puget Sound Agricultural Company for appropriations of land. This resulted in an award against the United States for $650,000.

After the conclusion of the American Civil War a large number of claims were made against the United States resultant upon the operations of war, the principal nations claimant being Great Britain, France, and Spain. The claims on behalf of Great Britain were, by Articles 12–17 of the Treaty of Washington of 1871, referred to a mixed commission consisting of one representative of either nation and an umpire. The United States was finally adjudged to pay nearly $2,000,000 to Great Britain because of the claims of one hundred and eighty-seven English claimants.

Consequent upon the decision hereafter to be referred to, and of the tribunal of arbitration concerning the judicial rights of the United States in Behring's Sea, and the right of protection of property of the United States in the fur seals frequenting the islands of the United States therein, there was created under date of July 8, 1896, a board of two commissioners with an umpire to fix damages to which the United States might be liable with respect to claims against it, including also claims for seizures of and interference with certain named British sealing vessels. Under this convention on December 17, 1897, an award was rendered against the United States for $473,151.26.

The final board of arbitration relative to individual claims between the two countries was created under date of August 18, 1910, by what was styled a "special agreement for the submission to arbitration of pecuniary claims." The tribunal provided for by this treaty, although not meeting at The Hague, was by its terms constituted in compliance with Article 87 and Article 59 of the Hague Peace Convention of 1907, and its proceedings regulated by chapters iii and iv of the Peace Convention, excepting Articles 53 and 54, as far as the tribunal might consider them "to be applicable and to be consistent with the provisions of this agreement." This agreement did not provide for a general submission of all claims, but that either party should within four months from the date of its confirmation present to the other party any claims it desired to submit to arbitration, and the claim so presented, should, if agreed upon by both parties, unless reserved as provided in the convention, be submitted to arbitration. All claims were to be decided "in accordance with treaty rights and with the principles of international law and of equity." This agreement operated under certain terms of submission attached to it, which terms provided as follows:

I. In case of any claim being put forward by one party which is alleged by the other party to be barred by treaty, the Arbitral Tribunal shall first deal with and decide the question whether the claim is so barred, and in the event of a decision that the claim is so barred, the claim shall be disallowed.

II. The Arbitral Tribunal shall take into account as one of the equities of a claim to such extent as it shall consider just in allowing or disallowing a claim any admission of liability by the Government against whom a claim is put forth.

III. The Arbitral Tribunal shall take into account as one of the equities of a claim to such extent as it shall consider just in allowing or disallowing a claim, in whole or in part, any failure on the part of the claimants to obtain satisfaction through legal remedies which are open to him or placed at his disposal, but no claim shall be disallowed or rejected by application of the general principle of international law that the legal remedies must be exhausted as a condition precedent to the validity of the claim.

IV. The Arbitral Tribunal, if it considers equitable, may include in its award in respect of any claim interest at a rate not exceeding 4 per cent per annum for the whole or any part of the period between the date when the claim was first brought to the notice of the other party and that of the confirmation of the schedule in which it is included.

The labors of this commission have now terminated.

143. Arbitrations other than territorial and of a pecuniary nature.—The first arbitration between the United States and England of the description we are now to discuss related to what was known as the Reserved Fisheries Questions. This case arose out of Article 1 of the convention between the two countries signed at London in 1818, and had for its object the exact determination of the parts of the coast reserved exclusively for the fishermen of each nationality. By a treaty signed June 5, 1854, the dispute was referred to two commissioners who chose an umpire. Its award, made in 1866, reported that "all the delimitation had been completed excepting on a small section of the southern coast of Newfoundland and a section of the coast of Virginia." By Article 20 of the Treaty of Washington, the awards of the commission were made final.

The next arbitration between the United States and England was by far the greatest of all, and related to what were known as the *Alabama* claims. These arose out of the fact as charged by the United States that the English Government during the Civil War had been guilty of many violations of the obligations of neutrality as between the United States Government and the so-called Confederate Government. After arbitration had been refused by England on the theory that it could not permit others to judge of the honor of its conduct, and after an unsuccessful attempt to arrive at a treaty of arbitration, the Treaty of Washington of May 8, 1871, referred the dispute to a high commission of five arbitrators.

We have to note the unusual manner of selection of the arbitrators. The United States and Great Britain named one each, respectively,

Charles Francis Adams and Sir Alexander Cockburn. The remaining arbitrators were Count Frederic Sclopis, named by the King of Italy, Jacques Staempfli, named by the President of the Swiss Republic, and Baron d'Itajuba, named by the Emperor of Brazil. These gentlemen selected Count Sclopis as their president.

The decision of this commission was to be governed by rules agreed upon by the high contracting parties "as applicable to the case, and by such principles of international law not inconsistent therewith as the arbitrators shall determine to have been applicable to the case." The rules were as follows:

A neutral government is bound—

First, to use due diligence to prevent the fitting out, arming, or equipping, within its jurisdiction, of any vessel which it has reasonable ground to believe is intended to cruise or to carry on war against a power with which it is at peace; and also to use like diligence to prevent the departure from its jurisdiction of any vessel intended to cruise or carry on war as above, such vessel having been especially adapted, in whole or in part, within such jurisdiction, to warlike use.

Secondly, not to permit or suffer either belligerent to make use of its ports or waters as the base of naval operations against the other, or for the purpose of the renewal or augmentation of military supplies or arms, or the recruitment of men.

Thirdly, to exercise due diligence in its own ports and waters, and, as to all persons within its jurisdiction, to prevent any violation of the foregoing obligations and duties.[1]

While the Geneva tribunal was hailed as a great triumph for the cause of arbitration and in spirit was such, it was yet a greater triumph

---

[1] It may be worth the reader's while to compare the rules of Washington with rules agreed upon by the Institut de droit international at The Hague in 1875, which were as follows:

CONCLUSIONS ADOPTÉES À LA HAYE

I. L'Etat neutre désireux de demeurer en paix et amitié avec les belligérants et de jouir des droits de la neutralité, a le devoir de s'abstenir de prendre à la guerre une part quelconque, par la prestation de secours militaires à l'un des belligérants ou à tous les deux, et de veiller à ce que son territoire ne serve pas de centre d'organisation ou de point de départ à des expéditions hostiles contre l'un d'eux ou contre tous les deux.

II. En conséquence, l'Etat neutre ne peut mettre, d'une manière quelconque, à la disposition d'aucun des Etats belligérants, ni leur vendre, ses vaisseaux de guerre ou vaisseaux de transport militaire, non plus que le matériel de ses arsenaux ou de ses magasins militaires, en vue de l'aider à poursuivre la guerre. En outre, l'Etat neutre est tenu de veiller à ce que d'autres personnes ne mettent des vaisseaux de guerre à la disposition d'aucun des Etats belligérants dans ses ports ou dans les parties de mer qui dépendent de sa juridiction.

III. Lorsque l'Etat neutre a connaissance d'entreprises ou d'actes de ce genre,

for diplomacy. The agreement around a council board between English and Americans as to the law which should govern the then future board of arbitration settled a situation much more difficult than was presented at Geneva. The prior work rendered the labors of the Geneva tribunal little more than that of a jury of award, settling the amount of damages under the eye and direction of the court.

Aside from claims made on behalf of the United States for destruction of vessels under the flag of the United States, this government in its case demanded recovery before the tribunal for national expenses to which the government had been subjected in pursuing the cruisers whose acts were complained of; loss in transfer of American commercial marine to the British flag; enhanced payments of insurance; prolongation of the war and addition of a large sum to the cost of the war and suppression of the rebellion.[2]

The presentation of claims of the nature indicated met with vigorous resistance on the part of the British, who contended that the treaty never contemplated the presentation of such demands for indirect damages. This point threatened for a time to break up the tribunal, when the commission through its president declared that without intending "to express or imply any opinion" upon the point of difference "as to the interpretation or effect of the treaty," the commission had "arrived, individually and collectively," at the conclusion that the indirect claims "do not constitute upon the principles of international law applicable to

incompatibles avec la neutralité, il est tenu de prendre les mesures nécessaires pour les empêcher, et de poursuivre comme responsables les individus qui violent les devoirs de la neutralité.

IV. De même, l'Etat neutre ne doit ni permettre ni souffrir que l'un des belligérants fasse de ses ports ou de ses eaux la base d'opérations navales contre l'autre, ou que les vaisseaux de transport militaire se servent de ses ports ou de ses eaux, pour renouveler ou augmenter leurs approvisionnements militaires ou leurs armes, ou pour recruter des hommes.

V. Le seul fait matériel d'un acte hostile commis sur le territoire neutre ne suffit pas pour rendre responsable l'Etat neutre. Pour qu'on puisse admettre qu'il a violé son devoir, il faut la preuve soit d'une intention hostile (*dolus*), soit d'une négligence manifeste (*culpa*).

VI. La puissance lésée par une violation des devoirs de neutralité n'a le droit de considérer la neutralité comme éteinte, et de recourir aux armes pour se défendre contre l'Etat qui l'a violée, que dans les cas graves et urgents, et seulement pendant la durée de la guerre.

Dans les cas peu graves ou non urgents, ou lorsque la guerre est terminée, des contestations de ce genre appartiennent exclusivement à la procédure arbitrale.

VII. Le tribunal arbitral prononce *ex bono et aequo* sur les dommages et intérêts que l'Etat neutre doit, par suite de sa responsabilité, payer à l'Etat lésé, soit pour lui-même, soit pour ses ressortissants.

[2] Moore, *Digest of International Arbitrations*, 589.

such cases good foundation for an award of compensation or computation of damages between nations and should upon such principles be wholly excluded from the consideration of the tribunal in making its award, even if there were no disagreement between the two governments as to the competency of the tribunal to decide thereon." This declaration disposed of the difficulty.[3]

The result of this commission was an award of $15,500,000 in favor of the United States.

By Article XXII of the Treaty of Washington of 1871, it was said to be "asserted by the Government of Her Britannic Majesty that the privileges accorded to the citizens of the United States under Article XVIII of this treaty are of greater value than those accorded by Articles XIX and XXI of this treaty to the subjects of Her Britannic Majesty, and this assertion is not admitted by the Government of the United States, it is further agreed that Commissioners shall be appointed to determine . . . . the amount of any compensation which, in their opinion, ought to be paid : . . . in return for the privileges so accorded to citizens of the United States." Under this one commissioner was appointed by either party and the third named by the representative at London of the Emperor of Austria. These commissioners met at Halifax. The result of their labors was an award against the United States of $5,500,000. This award was protested by the United States as unjust and because not signed by the American commissioner and therefore simply the act of a majority of the commissioners. After some correspondence, however, the award was accepted and paid.

The next important arbitration of a general nature between the two countries was that of the Behring's Sea Seal Fisheries. The gravamen of the dispute related to the control of the United States over seals outside of territorial waters. This was referred to a commission of seven, two chosen by each party and one each by France, Italy, and the King of Sweden and Norway. The questions submitted to the commission by a convention of February 29, 1892, were the following:

1. What exclusive jurisdiction in the sea now known as the Behring's Sea, and what exclusive rights in the seal fisheries therein, did Russia assert and exercise prior and up to the time of the cession of Alaska to the United States?

2. How far were these claims of jurisdiction as to the seal fisheries recognized and conceded by Great Britain?

3. Was the body of water now known as the Behring's Sea included in the phrase "Pacific Ocean," as used in the Treaty of 1825 between Great Britain and

[3] Moore, *ibid.*, 646.

Russia; and what rights, if any, in the Behring's Sea were held and exclusively exercised by Russia after said Treaty?

4. Did not all the rights of Russia as to jurisdiction, and as to the seal fisheries in Behring's Sea east of the water boundary, in the Treaty between the United States and Russia of the 30th March, 1867, pass unimpaired to the United States under that Treaty?

5. Has the United States any right, and if so, what right of protection of property in the fur-seals frequenting the islands of the United States in Behring's Sea when such seals are found outside the ordinary three-mile limit?

An unusual feature of this commission was that "if the determination of the foregoing questions as to the exclusive jurisdiction of the United States shall leave the subject in such position that the concurrence of Great Britain is necessary to the establishment of regulations for the proper protection and preservation of the fur-seal in, or habitually resorting to, the Behring's Sea," the arbitrators were then to determine "what concurrent regulations outside the jurisdictional limits of the respective governments are necessary, and over what waters" they should extend.

In a general way the decision was against the extreme claims of the United States, but left the subject in such a position that the concurrence of Great Britain was necessary for the establishment of regulations which were thereupon made a part of the award. In addition to the foregoing a majority of the commission joined in recommendations as to stipulations and measures to be enacted by the two powers.

An arbitral decision of an exceptional nature was that between Germany, Great Britain, and the United States. This amounted to a division of the fourteen islands of Samoa, which by the Final Act of the Berlin Conference of June 14, 1889, were declared to be an independent and neutral territory. Difficulties arising over the succession after the death of King Malietoa, a civil war resulted in 1899. The three parties named formed what was called a Samoan Joint High Commission, and this commission divided up the islands among the three countries.

A further question arose as to compensation for losses sustained at Samoa by subjects of the three powers because of unwarranted military action between January 1, 1899, and the arrival of the Joint Commission in Samoa. These claims by convention of November 7, 1899, by the three countries were referred to the King of Sweden and Norway as arbitrator, who was to decide "in conformity with the principles of international law or considerations of equity," and his award determined in favor of Germany in the sum of about $250,000.

144. North Atlantic Fisheries Arbitration.—By special agreement signed between the two countries on January 27, 1909, there was submitted to arbitration at The Hague questions as to the fisheries arising under Article I of the treaty signed October 20, 1818. This submission came under the general treaty of arbitration between the United States and Great Britain of April 4, 1908. The arbitral court consisted of one American, one Englishman, and one each from Austria, the Netherlands, and the Argentine Republic. There were seven distinct questions submitted to the tribunal for answers, as to which five received a response favorable to the United States and on the remaining two there was a partial success. The tribunal was given power to recommend for the consideration of the parties rules and procedure under which all future questions concerning the exercise of the fisheries liberties might be determined in accordance with the principles laid down in the award, with a proviso that "if the high contracting parties shall not adopt the rules and method of procedure so recommended, or if they shall not, subsequently to the delivery of the award, agree upon such rules and methods, then any differences which may arise in the future between the high contracting parties relating to the interpretation of the Treaty of 1818 or to the effect and application of the award of the tribunal shall be referred informally to the Permanent Court at The Hague for decision" under the summary procedure of the Hague Convention of 1907.

CHAPTER XIX

ARBITRATIONS BETWEEN THE UNITED STATES AND MEXICO

145. The first Mexican arbitration.—Continuing the historical treatment of arbitrations between the United States and its nearest neighbors, it is to be remembered that next after Great Britain, with which nation arbitrations have been most frequent because of proximity along a long boundary line and innumerable business relations, the Mexican arbitrations naturally come next in importance and for like reasons.

The first arbitration between the two countries occurred under the Treaty of April 11, 1839, taking the place of conventions unratified by Mexico of September 10, 1838. This treaty provided for two commissioners on the part of each of the two countries and in the event of differences a reference to an arbitrator who should be appointed by the King of Prussia. A large number of claims were passed upon by this commission, many being finally determined by the fifth arbitrator, who, however, never gave any reasons for his conclusions to the parties in interest, but reported them to the authority naming him. The aggregate amount of claims allowed by agreement of the commissioners or by award of the umpire was $2,025,111.69, though at the conclusion of the labors of the commission a number of claims remained unsettled. For the disposition of these and any other claims of citizens of either country or its government against the other, a new convention was provided for under date of January 30, 1843. Internal disturbances in Mexico and the Mexican War prevented this convention from functioning.

146. Commission under Treaty of Guadalupe Hidalgo.—By the Treaty of Peace of Guadalupe Hidalgo, the United States appointed a board of commissioners to pass upon the validity of outstanding claims against Mexico, the awards of which to an amount not exceeding three and one-quarter million dollars were to be paid by the United States. The commission so appointed, however, was purely a domestic tribunal, although guided by the law of nations.

The treaty to which we refer, concluded Feb. 2, 1848, was notable in that by its Article 21, still in force, it provided that

If unhappily any disagreement should hereafter arise between the governments of the two republics, whether with respect to the interpretation of any stipulation in this treaty, or with respect to any other particular concerning the political or

203

commercial relations of the two nations, the said Governments, in the name of those nations, do promise to each other that they will endeavor, in the most sincere and earnest manner, to settle the differences so arising, and to preserve the state of peace and friendship in which the two countries are now placing themselves, using, for this end, mutual representations and pacific negotiations. And if, by these means, they should not be enabled to come to an agreement, a resort shall not, on this account, be had to reprisals, aggression, or hostility of any kind, by the one republic against the other, until the government of that which deems itself aggrieved shall have maturely considered, in the spirit of peace and good neighborship, whether it would not be better that such difference should be settled by the arbitration of commissioners appointed on each side, or by that of a friendly nation. And should such course be proposed by either party, it shall be acceded to by the other, unless deemed by it altogether incompatible with the nature of the difference, or the circumstances of the case.

147. Convention of 1868.—A large number of claims arising on the part of the citizens of the two countries against the government of the other, a claims convention was entered into on July 4, 1868, providing for the reference to two commissioners, one named by either party and a third commissioner to act as umpire in any case or cases on which they might differ in opinion. By this convention decisions were to be made impartially and "according to public law, justice, and equity." Dr. Lieber was the first umpire selected and he, dying, was succeeded by Sir Edward Thornton. The decisions of this commission and its umpires were of a high degree of importance, dealing largely with many phases involving the responsibility of the respective governments for the acts of their officials and citizens. The proceedings of the commissioners were to have been ended within two years and six months from the date of their first meeting, but this proved to be impracticable. The time was extended by several protocols, and the labors of the commission concluded January 31, 1876. The largest award given by the commission was that in the case of the Pious Fund of the Californias for $904,070.99, representing twenty-one years' interest on the value of one-half of the property taken, or $43,050.99 per annum. This award was treated by Mexico for many years as settling the claim in total and rendering any fresh claim "forever inadmissible."

148. Claims of Oberlander and Messenger.—Following the order of time for the moment, we refer to the fact that a protocol was signed March 2, 1897, referring to the Minister of the Argentine Republic settlement of the claims of Oberlander and Messenger, American citizens, for injuries alleged to have been done them. These claims were decided adversely to the United States.

149. Pious Fund of the Californias.—The contention of Mexico as to its non-liability for any further claim growing out of the Pious Fund of the Californias, to which contention we have already alluded, was continually rejected by the Secretaries of State of the United States, with the result that under date of May 22, 1902, a protocol was entered into conferring upon a new tribunal to be created under the provisions of the Hague Peace Convention the right to determine

1. If said claim, as a consequence of the former decision, is within the governing principles of *res judicata,* and

2. If not, whether the same be just; and to render such judgment and award as may be meet and proper under all the circumstances of the case.

The controversy of which we speak was notable in that it constituted the first case to be passed upon by the Hague Permanent Court of Arbitration, opening that court after it had been ignored for three years following the signature of the Hague Peace Convention.

The agreement we are now discussing offers a peculiarity not presented by any prior international tribunal, and one of essentially great importance. It was particularly directed by the protocol that, while the tribunal should consist of four arbitrators, two named by each of the high contracting parties and an umpire to be selected in accordance with the provisions of the Hague Convention, "none of those so named shall be a native or citizen of the parties hereto." As a result, a tribunal of the highest possible character and one entirely disinterested from the standpoint of nationality was chosen.

The award was in favor of the United States in every respect save as to the medium of payment, which was directed to be made in money "having legal currency in Mexico," meaning silver, and in the sum of $1,420,682.67, being the total of thirty-three annual instalments. The award, also strictly within the terms of reference, declared Mexico to be obliged to pay each succeeding year the amount found to be due annually by Sir Edward Thornton, that is to say, $43,050.99.

150. The Chamizal case.—On June 24, 1910, a convention was signed for the arbitration of the titles of the two governments to what was known as the Chamizal Tract. This was referred to a commission consisting of the members of the National Boundary Commission, which had been established under a convention of 1889, which commission was enlarged by the addition, "for the purposes of the consideration and decision of the" difference, of a third commissioner who was to be a

Canadian jurist. The award was against the United States, but was protested on the ground of excess of power, and the matter still remains unsettled.

151. Pending arbitrations.—Two arbitration conventions have been recently signed by the United States and Mexico, the first dated September 8, 1923. By this all claims (except those arising from acts incident to the recent revolutions) against Mexico of citizens of the United States and all claims against the United States by citizens of Mexico since the signing of the convention of July 4, 1868, and which have remained unsettled, as well as any other like claims filed by either government within a year from the date of the first meeting of the commission (with a period of extension) are submitted to a commission of three members, who are bound to decide "in accordance with the principles of international law, justice, and equity." This commission consists of one member appointed by each of the governments and a third selected by mutual agreement. By the provisions of the treaty, no claim may be disallowed or rejected by the application of the general principle of international law that legal remedies must be exhausted as a condition precedent.

An unusual provision of this convention is:

In any case the Commission may decide that international law, justice, and equity require that a property or right be restored to the claimant in addition to the amount awarded in any such case for all loss or damage sustained prior to the restitution. In any case where the Commission so decides the restitution of the property or right shall be made by the government affected after such decision has been made, as herein below provided. The Commission, however, shall at the same time determine the value of the property or right decreed to be restored and the government affected may elect to pay the amount so fixed after the decision is made rather than to restore the property or right to the claimant.

In the event the government affected should elect to pay the amount fixed as the value of the property or right decreed to be restored, it is agreed that notice thereof will be filed with the Commission within thirty days after the decision and that the amount fixed as the value of the property or right shall be paid immediately. Upon failure so to pay the amount the property or right shall be restored immediately.

About the same time, and on September 10, there was created a special claims convention between the two countries to settle and adjust claims arising from losses or damages suffered by American citizens within the period from November 20, 1910, to May 31, 1920. This commission was constituted in the same manner provided under the immediately preceding convention, but was to decide "in accordance with the principles of justice and equity." As in the preceding convention, no claim was to be rejected on the principle that legal remedies must be first exhausted.

This convention offers certain peculiarities to which attention must be drawn. A vexed question before international tribunals is as to the extent to which the claim of the individual stockholder for loss merges in the general right of recovery or want of right of the corporation in which he is interested, this arising largely out of the divorce citizenship of the corporation and the stockholder. Under the conventions we are now considering, however, "losses or damages suffered by any corporation, association, or partnership in which citizens of the United States have or have had a substantial and bona fide interest" may be presented, provided "an allotment to the American claimant by the" company and so forth, of his proportion of the loss or damage is presented by the claimant to the commission.

An apparent attempt was also made to get away from the usual non-liability of governments for acts of an unsuccessful revolution by directing the commission to examine and decide claims arising within the period named due to the following forces:

1. By forces of a government *de jure* or *de facto*.

2. By revolutionary forces as a result of the triumph of whose cause governments *de facto* or *de jure* have been established, or by revolutionary forces opposed to them.

3. By forces arising from the disjunction of the forces mentioned in the next preceding paragraph up to the time when the government *de jure* established itself as a result of a particular revolution.

4. By federal forces that were disbanded, and

5. By mutinies or mobs, or insurrectionary forces other than those referred to under subdivisions (2), (3), and (4) above, or by bandits, provided in any case it be established that the appropriate authorities omitted to take reasonable measures to suppress insurrectionists, mobs, or bandits, or treated them with lenity or were at fault in other particulars.

These commissions are now functioning.[1]

[1] 1928.

CHAPTER XX

ARBITRATIONS BETWEEN THE UNITED STATES AND COUNTRIES OTHER THAN GREAT BRITAIN AND MEXICO

152. Austria and Hungary.—By agreement with these powers[1] dated November 26, 1924, there were referred to a single commissioner to be named by agreement of the countries concerned claims of American citizens against Austria and Hungary arising since July 31, 1914, in respect of damages to or seizure of property, rights, and interests, including any company or association in which they are interested, within territory of defendant nations as it existed on August 1, 1914; other claims for injuries to person or property since July 31, 1914, as a consequence of the war; debts to American citizens by the defendant governments or nationals.

153. Brazil.—The first case of actual international arbitration between the United States and countries other than immediate neighbors was with Brazil in 1842, arising from the seizure of the American schooner, *John S. Bryan*. By agreement between the two countries[2] commissioners were appointed who gave an award October 15, 1842, directing twenty-six contos of reis to be paid by Brazil. This was not paid until May 20, 1846, when it was made without interest.

By a subsequent convention[3] dated January 27, 1849, the Government of Brazil placed at the disposal of the United States the sum of five hundred thirty thousand milreis to cover all claims the United States might have on behalf of its citizens against Brazil, leaving it to the United States to make the distribution.

By protocol[4] dated March 14, 1870, between officials of Brazil and the United States there was submitted to the arbitrament of Sir Edward Thornton, the claim of the United States against Brazil, arising out of the loss of the steamer *Canada*. One of the questions referred was whether the United States, having once presented the claim, was barred by lapse of time incident to the negligent prosecution of the case. The further questions were whether the vessel was lost and the voyage ended by the illegal interference of Brazilian officials, and the

---

1 U. S. Statutes-at-Large, Vol. 44, p. 2213, Treaty Series No. 730.
2 Moore, *History and Digest of International Arbitrations*, 4613.
3 Malloy's *Treaties*, etc., 145.
4 Moore, 4687.

amount of damages. The arbitrator decided the question of prescription for the United States, delay in prosecuting claim once presented not amounting to waiver, and refused to consider a compromise at one time offered, giving an award for $100,740.04.

By protocol[5] dated September 6, 1902, between the United States and Brazil, there was referred to the arbitrament of the Swedish-Norwegian Minister at Washington claim for damages for the firing upon and detention of the vessel *James A. Simpson*. This claim after being presented to the Minister was withdrawn from his consideration for want of evidence.

154. Chile.—A convention was entered into between the United States and Chile[6], November 10, 1858, to settle claims of American citizens as owners of silver taken by order of the commandant of the Chilean squadron. By this convention the King of Belgium was created arbitrator. It was particularly agreed that the defense of prescription should be excluded from consideration. The result was an award of $42,400 in favor of the United States.

On December 6, 1873, a protocol[7] was concluded for the submission to arbitration between the United States and Chile of the claim for the seizure of the whaling vessels, *Franklin* and *Good Return*. This case, however, was not arbitrated because of an agreement of settlement.

On August 7, 1892, a claims convention[8] was entered into between the United States and Chile for the adjustment of claims of either country against the government of the other growing out of acts committed by civil or military authorities. These were referred to a commission of three, one to be selected by either party and the third by mutual agreement. They were required to decide "according to public law, justice, and equity," and any two could make the award. Under this convention awards aggregating $240,564.35 were made in favor of the United States. By further convention[9] of May 24, 1897, the convention of August 7, 1892, was revived and further time allowed for the conclusion of its duties. The second commission awarded $28,062.29 in favor of citizens of the United States and $3,000 in favor of Chile.

On December 1, 1909, a protocol[10] was entered into between the United States and Chile for the reference to arbitration of a long-standing demand upon Chile known as the "Alsop Claim." By its terms the King of England was authorized to determine as an *amiable*

5 Malloy, 152.   6 Malloy, 183.   7 Moore, 1468.
8 Malloy, 185.   9 *Ibid.*, 190.   10 *Ibid.*, 2508.

compositeur the amount which might equitably be due the claimants. The award,[11] dated July 5, 1911, involving a number of questions of international law and, deciding as a matter of law but not as a matter of compromise, granted the sum of 2,275,375 bolivianos in favor of the United States.

155. China.—In 1884 an informal agreement[12] was suggested by the American Minister at Peking to the Chinese authorities for the arbitration of the Ashmore claim for dispossession of certain fisheries. The dispute was referred to the British and Netherlands Consuls at Swatow, who awarded $4,600 as damages.

On September 7, 1901, a protocol was executed[13] between China and a number of powers, including the United States, providing among other matters for payment of indemnities for Boxer outrages. A commission was appointed to determine amounts properly payable in damages to Americans, and the balance over this and governmental expenses was later returned to China.

156. Colombia and New Granada.—On September 10, 1857, a claims convention was entered into between the United States and New Granada,[14] the predecessor of Colombia, providing for the arbitration of all claims presented prior to September 1, 1859, either to the Department of State at Washington or to the American Minister at Bogotá, especially for damages caused by riot at Panama on April 15, 1856, for which New Granada acknowledged liability arising out of its privilege and obligation to preserve peace and good order along the transit route. These claims were referred to a board of two commissioners, one appointed by either country, who were to decide according to justice and equity, and with power to name an umpire. This commission, which did not entirely complete its work, awarded $496,235.47. The uncompleted claims were the subject of a further convention of February 10, 1864. Similar provisions were made as to the appointment of commissioners and umpire. The work of this commission resulted in awards amounting to $88,267.68.

On August 17, 1874, an agreement of arbitration[15] was entered into between the American Minister at Bogotá, acting on behalf of the United States, and the Colombian Government, providing for the adjustment of claims arising from the taking of the steamer *Montijo*

---

[11] *American Journal of International Law,* V, 1079.
[12] Moore, 1858.
[13] *American Journal of International Law,* Supplement I, p. 338.
[14] Malloy, *op. cit.,* 319.   [15] Moore, 1425.

by revolutionists of the State of Panama. Under this, two arbitrators were appointed, one on either side, and an umpire agreed upon, all of whom were to decide "according to public law and treaties in force between the two countries and these present stipulations." The umpire decided in favor of the United States and rendered an award for $33,401.

157. Costa Rica.—On July 2, 1860, a claims convention was entered into between the United States and Costa Rica[16] for the settlement of American claims up to the date of the convention. A board of commissioners was provided for, one to be appointed by either party, with power in them to name an umpire to decide any cases concerning which they might disagree or upon any points of difference arising during the proceedings. The commissioners were authorized to decide "according to the principles of justice and of equity and to the stipulations of treaty." No claim of any American citizen proved to have been a belligerent during the occupation of Nicaragua by the troops of Costa Rica and no exercise of authority by the latter within the territory of the former, were to be considered. This commission resulted in an award of $25,704.14 against Costa Rica.

158. Denmark.—By an agreement concluded December 6, 1888, the United States and the Kingdom of Denmark agreed to refer to arbitration[17] a claim against Denmark for indemnity for the seizure and detention by the authorities of the Island of St. Thomas of two vessels belonging to the claimant, refusal of ordinary right to land cargo to make repairs, and injuries from the firing of a shot. This claim was referred to the British Minister at Athens. The arbitrator rejected the claim.

159. Dominican Republic.—By agreement[18] in 1898 between the two governments, an American engineer was appointed to value the Ozama River bridge and determine the amount to be paid therefor. He awarded the American claimant $74,411.17 with interest.

In January 1903 the Dominican Government and J. Sala & Company agreed to refer to arbitration[19] of the Assistant Solicitor of the State Department and the Bolivian Minister at Washington its claim for supplies furnished the President of Santo Domingo. The result was an award of $215,000.

[16] Malloy, 346.
[17] Ibid., 387.
[18] Moore's Digest of International Law, VI, 729.
[19] Darby, 904.

By the terms of a protocol[20] dated January 31, 1903, there was referred to a board of arbitration consisting of two Americans and one Dominican the arrangement of the terms upon which an indemnity should be paid to the San Domingo Improvement Company and its allied companies. The award secured payment upon certain customs revenues and turned the custom houses over to a financial agent to be appointed by the United States.

160. Ecuador.—On November 25, 1862,[21] the United States and Ecuador agreed upon a claims convention to adjust the claims of either country against the other. By its terms, there were referred to a board of two commissioners, one named by either country, who were to decide "according to justice and in compliance with the provisions of this convention, all claims that should be submitted to them," and with power to name an umpire to decide any case as to which they disagreed or any point of difference arising in the proceedings. The result of this commission was a group of awards in favor of the United States in the sum of $94,799.56.

By convention entered into on February 28, 1893,[22] between the United States and Ecuador, there was referred to arbitration the claim of one Santos, born in Ecuador but naturalized in the United States, for injuries to person and property. This was referred to the British Minister at Quito as arbitrator. He was authorized to pass upon a question of forfeiture of citizenship under the Treaty of Naturalization between the two countries, and in case of nonforfeiture whether the claimant had been guilty of such acts of unfriendliness and hostility to the government as would deprive him of protection as a neutral. If the case were decided in the claimant's favor, the arbitrator was to award just and equitable damages. The award was in favor of the United States and for $40,000. This award, however, merely carried out an agreement reached between the countries before the arbitrator had completed his examination of the evidence.[23]

161. France.—By a convention dated January 15, 1882,[24] extended July 19, 1882,[25] and February 8, 1883,[26] there were referred to arbitration claims against France for acts of French officials against Americans during the late French-Mexican War or Franco-German War or insurrection of the Commune and claims of French citizens against the United States growing out of the Civil War. The commission was of three persons, one each named by the two countries and a third by the

---

[20] Malloy, 414.   [21] *Ibid.*, 432.   [22] *Ibid.*, 438.   [23] Moore, *Digest*, 1591.
[24] Malloy, *op. cit.*, 535.   [25] *Ibid.*, 539.   [26] *Ibid.*, 540.

Emperor of Brazil. The commission awarded $625,566.35 against the United States and 13,659.14 francs against France.

162. Germany.—By agreement dated August 10, 1922,[27] a commission was created to pass upon claims of American citizens against Germany arising since July 31, 1914, in respect of damages to or seizure of property rights and interests, including any company or association in which they were interested within German country as it existed on August 1, 1914; other claims for injuries to person or property since July 31, 1914, as a consequence of the war; debts to American citizens by the German Government or German nationals. This consisted of one commissioner named by each and umpire to be agreed upon. This commission is still functioning.

163. Guatemala.—By protocol dated February 23, 1900,[28] with a supplementary one of May 10, 1900,[29] there were referred to arbitration by the United States and Guatemala cross claims between Guatemala and Robert H. May, the British Minister to the Central American republics being made the arbitrator. An award was given in favor of May for the sum of $143,750.73.

164. Hayti.—On May 28, 1884,[30] a protocol was entered into between the United States and Hayti for the determination of the claims of Pelletier and Lazare for indemnity for acts against person and property alleged to have been done by Haytian authorities. Reference was had to an ex-justice of the Supreme Court of the United States, and the case was to be decided "according to the rules of international law existing at the time of the transaction complained of." He rendered an award in favor of Pelletier for $57,250, and in favor of Lazare for $117,500. Further consideration by the Secretary of State demonstrated to him the fact that the awards were mistaken and unjust, and they were accordingly set aside.

By verbal agreement between the American Minister at Port-au-Prince and the Haytian Minister for Foreign Affairs, on January 25, 1885, the claims[34] of citizens of the United States for damages sustained during a riot at Port-au-Prince were referred to a mixed commission of two Haytians and two Americans. This commission agreed upon all claims but two, awarding $5,700. The two claims upon which they did not agree were settled between the two governments, $9,000 being paid.

By protocol dated May 24, 1888,[32] the governments of Hayti and

27 *Ibid.*, 2601.   28 *Ibid.*, 871.   29 *Ibid.*, 873.   30 *Ibid.*, 932.
31 Moore, *Digest*, 860.   32 Malloy, *op. cit.*, 935.

the United States referred to the decision of a person to be agreed upon by the representatives of the two countries the claim of Van Bokkelen for wrongful imprisonment. The referee (an American) rendered an award in favor of the claimant for $60,000.

By protocol entered into between Hayti and the United States dated October 18, 1899,[33] the claim of John Metzger & Company, American citizens, for seizure and sale of goods for non-payment of license taxes, failure to furnish them an adequate supply of water for the operation of a mill, and liability of Hayti because of sale of lumber by claimants to a relief committee on the occasion of devastation by fire at Jacmel, was referred to arbitration to determine the questions of liability and amount of indemnity, if any, justly due. This protocol was followed by a supplementary one of June 30, 1900,[34] with reference to the submission of evidence. Under these protocols, the arbitrator gave judgment for $23,000.

By protocol between Hayti and the United States dated October 3, 1919,[35] all foreign claims against Hayti were referred to a claims commission of three members, one named by the Secretary of State for Finance of Hayti, one by the Secretary of State of the United States, and a third a citizen of neither nation nominated by the Financial Adviser, the three so nominated to be appointed by the government of Hayti. This commission had jurisdiction over all pecuniary claims against Hayti except for certain bond issues and certain interest upon some railway bonds. This commission did not, however, consider itself as international in character, although created to pass expressly upon claims of foreigners.

165. Netherlands.—By an arbitral agreement[36] dated January 23, 1925, there was referred to The Hague the question of sovereignty over the Island of Palmas or Miangas. This was to be decided "in accordance with the principles of international law and any applicable treaty provisions." Reference was had to an arbitration of the Permanent Court of Arbitration at The Hague. A decision was reached adverse to the United States.

166. Nicaragua.—By protocol[37] dated March 22, 1900, the two governments referred to the arbitration of General E. P. Alexander the claims of Orr and Laubenheimer for seizure and detention of the launches, *Buena Ventura* and *Alerta,* and of the Post-Glover Electric

---

[33] Malloy, *op. cit.,* 936.   [34] *Ibid.,* 938.   [35] *Ibid.,* 2678.
[36] *American Journal of International Law,* XIX, Supplement, 108.
[37] Molloy, *op. cit.,* 1290.

Company for seizure of its property. An award was given to the first-named claimants of $6,963, and of $1,402.04 to the last-named claimant.

A decree of the Nicaraguan Constitutional Assembly dated May 17, 1911, created a Mixed Claims Commission consisting of two Americans and one Nicaraguan who passed *inter alia* upon many American claims against Nicaragua.

167. Norway.—By an agreement[38] dated June 30, 1921, there were referred to The Hague by the United States and Norway claims of Norwegian subjects against the United States arising out of certain requisitions by the United States Shipping Board Emergency Fleet Corporation, with relation to which the two governments were unable to reach an agreement. The arbitral tribunal, to be formed under the provisions of the Hague Peace Convention of 1907, was to consist of one arbitrator each to be named by the heads of the two governments with a third to be selected by mutual agreement, or, in the event of failure of agreement, by the President of the Swiss Confederation. The claims were to be decided "in accordance with the principles of law and equity." A claim, however, which was also to be considered, on the part of certain American citizens and which might be awarded out of any sum granted a Norwegian claim, was to be decided in accordance with the same principles. The result of the arbitration at The Hague was a judgment against the United States in the sum of about twelve million dollars.

168. Panama.—By agreement American claims against Panama growing out of a riot were referred to a single arbitrator.[39] The highest award was $9,000 for death, with other awards of lesser amounts.

169. Paraguay.—A claims convention between the United States and Paraguay, dated February 4, 1859, was entered into for the purpose of settling the claims of the United States and Paraguay Navigation Company, composed of American citizens, against Paraguay.[40] This commission consisted of two commissioners, with a third to be appointed in case of disagreement. The commissioners, however, united in rejecting the claim.

170. Peru.—By a convention of December 20, 1862, between the United States and Peru, claims of American citizens arising out of the capture and confiscation by Peru of the ships, *Lizzie Thompson*

---

38 *American Journal of International Law*, XVI, Supplement, 16.
39 *Foreign Relations for 1915*, 1193, and *Foreign Relations for 1916*, 918.
40 Malloy, *op. cit.*, 1364.

and *Georgiana,* belonging to American citizens, were referred to the arbitrament of the King of Belgium who was named as "arbiter, umpire, and friendly arbitrator."[41] The King of Belgium declined to act, perceiving that the arbitration would be "of a very delicate nature by reason of the exceptional circumstances" of the case and complicated questions of law and fact, difficult to decide at a distance without having a perfect knowledge of local legislation not easy to obtain. He further intimated that he had looked into the case and felt that he would have been constrained to decide against the United States. The claims were therefore abandoned by the United States Government.[42]

On January 12, 1863, a general claims convention was entered into between Peru and the United States. This covered the claims of the citizens of each country against the other. The convention provided for the appointment of a mixed commission of four members, two named by the government of the United States and two by Peru, who should have power to name a fifth. They were authorized to decide "according to the principles of justice and equity, the principles of international law and treaty stipulations" all claims submitted to them.[43] As the result of the action of this commission the awards against the United States aggregated $25,300, and those against Peru, $57,196.23.

A further claims commission[44] was signed between the two countries on December 4, 1868, covering mutual claims presented to either government since the sitting of the former commission and yet unsettled, as well as other claims to be presented within two months of the first meeting of the commissioners. This convention provided for one commissioner named by each party, who were to exercise their powers "according to justice and equity." They were also authorized to name a "third person of some third" nation to act as umpire. Under this convention, the awards against the United States were $57,040 and against Peru, $194,417.62.

By protocol dated May 17, 1908, the two countries referred to the arbitrament of the Chief Justice of the Supreme Court of Canada the claim of Victor H. MacCord.[45] In this case the Peruvian Government agreed as an act of deference to the United States to exclude from the arbitration the discussion of its liability or irresponsibility, and the only question to be determined was the amount of pecuniary indemnity to be paid to MacCord. Under this protocol, an award was given in favor of the United States for $40,000.

---

[41] Malloy, *op. cit.,* 1406.   [42] Moore, *Digest of Arbitrations,* 1611.
[43] *Ibid.,* 1408.   [44] *Ibid.,* 1411.   [45] *Ibid.,* 1443.

By protocol dated May 21, 1921, Peru and the United States referred to arbitration the claim of the heirs and assigns of John Célestin Landreau arising out of a decree of the government of Peru providing for payment of awards to his brother for the discovery of guano deposits and out of contracts between John Téophile and John Célestin Landreau.[46] This commission was composed of three members, consisting of one Peruvian and one American, the third finally agreed upon being Lord Finlay of England. The result of this arbitration was a decision in favor of the United States for $125,000.

171. **Portugal.**—By claims convention concluded February 26, 1851, between the United States and Portugal, there was referred to the President of the French Republic the decision of the vexed question between the two countries which had even threatened war arising out of the destruction of the American privateer brig, *General Armstrong*, destroyed by British vessels in the harbor of the Island of Fayal.[47] The President, Louis Napoleon, decided against the contentions of the United States.

By protocol between the United States and Great Britain on the one hand and Portugal on the other, dated June 13, 1891, there was referred to arbitration the task of fixing the amount of the indemnity due by Portugal to the claimants of the other two countries on account of the rescission of the concession of the Lourenço Marques Railroad and of the taking possession of that railroad by the Portuguese Government.[48] By the terms of the protocol the Swiss Federal Council selected three lawyers among those of the greatest distinction to constitute an arbitral tribunal. The amount of the indemnity awarded was to be paid to the governments, who were charged to make distribution of it to the claimants. The ground of the complaint was seizure of a concession granted to an American citizen and the annulment of a charter formed under this concession. By the award, Portugal was directed to pay and did pay 15,314,000 francs (Swiss) in addition to 28,000 pounds paid on account in 1890, and with interest.

172. **Russia.**—On August 26, 1900, the United States and Russia referred to arbitration, claims arising against Russia because of the seizure of several American schooners by Russian cruisers on a charge of having been illegally engaged in fur-seal fishery. This was by agreement sent to Mr. T. M. C. Asser of The Hague, who was to follow "the general principles of international law and the spirit of international agreements applicable to the subject . . . . at the moment

---

[46] Malloy, *op. cit.*, 2797.   [47] *Ibid.*, 1458.   [48] *Ibid.*, 1460.

when the seizures" took place.[49] The result was the granting of awards in favor of the United States aggregating $114,670. This award, although given at The Hague, was not held under the provisions of the Hague Peace Convention of 1899.

173. Salvador.—An arbitration[50] was agreed to on May 4, 1864, between Salvador and the United States with reference to the claim of Henry Savage for the value of gunpowder imported by him into Salvador, the decree forbidding sale of which was claimed to be *ex post facto* and in violation of the Constitution of Salvador as well as of the treaty existing between the two countries. This was referred to two arbitrators, who were empowered to choose an umpire. They adjudicated in favor of Mr. Savage for $4,497.50, with certain deductions and with interest until paid.

Under a protocol[51] dated December 19, 1901, the United States and Salvador referred to arbitration the claims of the Salvador Commercial Company and other citizens of the United States, stockholders in the corporation styled El Triunfo Company, Ltd., who had not acquired stock from citizens of Salvador or other non-citizens of the United States since the date of the filing of the memorial of the Salvador Commercial Company. The essential point in this case was as to whether the Republic of Salvador had power without judicial proceedings to declare a franchise forfeited. The arbitrators, presided over by the Chief Justice of the Dominion of Canada, were individually named in the protocol. The award was to be compensatory, but not to include speculative or imaginary damages. The tribunal also had power to pass upon the question of costs and attorney's fees. Under this the arbitrators allowed $537,178.64 with attorney's fees and costs.

174. Siam.—A mixed commission of investigation,[52] afterward changed into a board of arbitration, was appointed in 1897, which determined the liability of Siam for an assault made by Siamese soldiers upon the United States Vice-Consul in Siam in 1896. An award was rendered in favor of the United States, which award was peculiar and entirely unusual in its character. It provided for the degradation of certain Siamese officials, condemned the government of Siam to express its official regrets, and stipulated that publication of copies of the decision be made in the official *Gazette*.

By agreement between the United States and Siam,[53] the claim of

---

49 Malloy, *op. cit.*, 1532.   50 Moore, *Digest*, 1857.
51 Malloy, *op. cit.*, 1568.   52 Moore, *op. cit.*, 1862.   53 *Ibid.*, 1899.

the heirs of the estate of Cheek, an American citizen, against the government for illegal seizure and sale of property in 1889 was referred to the arbitrament of the Chief Justice of the British Supreme Court for China and Japan. The offense was said to have taken place in violation of the treaty between the two governments. An award was given for 706,721 ticals, or about $200,000.

173. Spain. After Great Britain and Mexico, the most numerous arbitrations between the United States and other nations were had with Spain. The first of these was pursuant to the Treaty of October 27, 1795, which provided for the appointment of two commissioners who could agree upon a third or, if they failed to so agree, one was to be chosen by lot. They were to decide the claims arising from losses sustained by the citizens of the United States in consequence of vessels and cargo taken by the subjects of Spain during the then late war between France and Spain.[54] This resulted in awards in favor of the United States to the amount of $325,440.07½.

The second commission was authorized by a convention between the two countries dated August 11, 1802, but was not finally ratified by Spain until July 9, 1818, and by that time other claims existed.[55] The convention was annulled by a subsequent treaty dated February 22, 1819. Under this, each nation reciprocally renounced all claims for damages, and the United States agreed to cause satisfaction to be made for injuries, if any, which should be established to have been suffered by Spanish officers and individual Spanish claimants by the then recent operations of the American army in Florida. The treaty created a domestic tribunal of the United States to pass upon such claims to an amount not exceeding five millions of dollars. The commission allowed claims to an amount in excess of this, which amount was scaled down to the sum named.[56]

By another treaty concluded February 17, 1834, an adjustment was made between the two countries of further claims arising on behalf of citizens of the United States against Spain.[57] Awards were to be made by a domestic tribunal pursuant to this agreement amounting to $549,850.28, upon which perpetual payment of interest was to be made at the rate of five per cent per annum.

In 1870, by an exchange of notes, the two governments agreed to refer to a commission consisting of one representative of either nation with power in them to select an umpire, the claim arising from the

[54] Malloy, *op. cit.*, 1640.   [55] *Ibid.*, 1650.
[56] *Ibid.*, 1651.   [57] *Ibid.*, 1659.

seizure of the steamer *Col. Lloyd Aspinwall.* The decision of the umpire awarded $19,702 to the claimant.[58]

In 1871, by an exchange of notes between the two countries,[59] there were referred to arbitration of representatives of each country and, in case of disagreement, of an umpire, the claims of citizens of the United States for wrongs and injuries against their persons and property, or against the persons and property of citizens of whom the heirs were the legal representatives, by the authorities of Spain in the Island of Cuba or within its maritime jurisdiction since the commencement of the insurrection in Cuba. These were to hear them and decide "according to public law, and the treaties in force between the two countries, and these present stipulations." The disallowance of a claim by a Spanish tribunal was not to bar it except in case of a Spanish-born subject who failed to claim American naturalization before the court. Under this commission there was allowed the sum of $1,293,450.55.

In 1885, by exchange of notes, Spain and the United States agreed upon arbitration by the Italian Minister at Madrid of a dispute arising out of the seizure of the American ship *Masonic* at Manila.[60] An award was given in the sum of $51,674.07.

Under Article 7 of the Treaty of Peace of Paris of December 10, 1898, the United States agreed to adjudicate and settle the claims of its citizens against Spain which had arisen since the beginning of the "late insurrection in Cuba and prior to the exchange of ratifications of the present treaty, including all claims for indemnity for the cost of the war." Under this provision, the Spanish Treaty Claims Commission was formed in the United States, which passed on such claims under the rules of international law.

176. Venezuela.—By convention between Venezuela and the United States, dated April 25, 1866, all claims on behalf of American citizens upon Venezuela which had been presented to the government or to its legation in Caracas were submitted to a mixed commission consisting of two members, one appointed by either government, with authority to choose an umpire to decide any case concerning which they might disagree or upon any point of difference which might arise in the proceedings.[61] These commissioners were to decide according to justice and in compliance with the provisions of the convention, and their decisions were to be "conformable to justice even though such decisions amount to an absolute denial or illegal pretensions." The proceedings

---

[58] Moore, *op. cit.,* 1013.   [59] Malloy, *op. cit.,* 1661.

[60] Moore, *op. cit.,* 1060

[61] Malloy, *op. cit.,* 1856.

of this convention resulted in awards aggregating $1,253,310.30 against Venezuela. The integrity of the conduct of the commission was attacked by Venezuela, and its career forms the blackest spot in the history of arbitrations. A result of the protest of Venezuela was the formation of a new commission under a convention[62] of December 5, 1885, later extended by conventions[63] of October 5, 1888. This commission was one of the ablest up to that time, and as finally determined upon consisted of one Venezuelan and two Americans. Their duties were similar to those of the prior commission, but required them to re-examine the claims before submitted, hearing additional evidence if presented. The aggregate awards against Venezuela under the new commission were $980,572.60, in place of the much larger total allowed by the first commission.

On January 19, 1892, the United States and Venezuela agreed to refer to arbitration the claim of the Venezuela Steam Transportation Company arising out of the alleged wrongful seizure, detention, and employment in war of several steamers of the Company, the Company itself being an American citizen, and for the imprisonment of the officers of these steamers. The arbitrators were to be named by the convention, one by each party and a third who should be a citizen of neither. They were to decide the claims "in accordance with justice and equity and the principles of international law." Under this commission an award was made allowing $141,800 to the United States and $300 in favor of Venezuela.[64]

During the years 1901 and 1902 there was a constant demand on the part of Germany and England, in which Italy joined, upon Venezuela for the settlement or reference to arbitration of the claims of these countries for their respective nationals. This was met by a denial on the part of Venezuela of her liability, grounded, doubtless in a large measure, upon the fact that the titular government under General Cipriano Castro was engaged in a constant struggle against other claimants or revolutionists. The result was a so-called "pacific" blockade of a portion of the coast of Venezuela. We are told by Thayer[65] that President Roosevelt informed the German Ambassador that, unless Germany consented to arbitrate (Venezuela by this time having expressed a desire to arbitrate), the American squadron under Admiral Dewey would be given orders by noon ten days later to proceed to the Venezuelan coast and prevent any taking possession of Venezuelan

62 Malloy, op. cit., 1858.   63 Ibid., 1866.
64 Ibid., 1868.   65 Life and Letters of John Hay, 285-89.

territory. The Ambassador protested that his Imperial Master, having refused to arbitrate, could not change his mind. After a week had passed by the Ambassador called on the President, saying nothing of the Venezuelan matter, and when the President asked him about it said he had received nothing from his government. Thereupon he was informed that Admiral Dewey would be instructed to sail a day earlier than the day he, the President, had originally mentioned. The Ambassador protested, but was informed that if the Emperor would agree to arbitrate the United States would praise him for his action and treat it as taken on Germany's initiative, otherwise within forty-eight hours there must be an offer or Dewey would sail with the orders indicated. Within thirty-six hours, the President was informed a dispatch had come from Berlin saying the Kaiser would arbitrate.

Whether Mr. Thayer is right or not, the fact is that shortly after that time the three European nations mentioned all agreed to arbitrate, and, Venezuela expressing a desire to settle similarly all claims against her on the part of nations which had taken no part in the blockade, this arbitration assumed two phases.

The first phase was that of a reference to the Hague Tribunal of the question whether payment of the custom house receipts, which were agreed to be allotted to settle any findings against Venezuela, should be made preferentially to the three blockading powers or pro rata to all the powers, whether taking part in the blockade or not. As to this portion of the dispute, Mr. Thayer falls into an error in his statement in saying that "Venezuela's claims went to The Hague for arbitrament." In fact the only interest Venezuela possessed in the matter referred to The Hague was entirely a sentimental one, as the amount ultimately to be paid by her was not in the slightest degree affected. Of the results of this arbitration we shall speak elsewhere (§ 227).

The second portion of the dispute related to the determination of the amounts to be paid by Venezuela to the three blockading powers, and to seven nations which had taken no part in the blockade, these being the United States, Belgium, France, the Netherlands, Spain, Mexico, and Sweden-Norway.

Before being willing to arbitrate at all, in the end Great Britain insisted absolutely upon the payment in cash or its equivalent by Venezuela of 5,500 pounds sterling because of alleged seizure and plundering of British vessels and outrages on their crews, and maltreatment and false imprisonment of British subjects. Not to be behind in the reception of money, the Italian Government without any ostensible reason, but as the protocol termed it in "satisfaction of the point of honor," demanded a similar amount of money. Germany was more exacting, and required the payment, in cash or what it regarded as its equivalent, of the sum of about $350,000, being the full amount of German demands for damages from the Venezuelan civil wars of 1898 to 1900. As to the merits of this demand no absolute conclusion can be drawn. We may, however, form some idea of its probable justice from the fact that claims of an identical nature with those of which we speak were passed upon by the German-Venezuelan Commission then created, and its allowances were but twenty-seven per cent of the aggregate amount claimed. Applying the same rule it would seem fair to conclude that Venezuela paid not far from $250,000 not due from her in order to buy her peace.

The protocols which were entered into by the ten countries of which we have spoken were alike in their general character, laying aside the question of primary exactions of which we have spoken. In each case there was to be appointed a commission consisting of one national of Venezuela and one of the other parties to the protocol. The umpires were not chosen by any general rule, but those who passed upon the claims of England, Germany, Italy, and the Netherlands were named by the President of the United States. The umpires of the Belgian, American, and French Commissions were named by the Queen of the Netherlands. The umpires of the Mexican and Swedish Commissions were named by the King of Spain, and the umpire of the Spanish Commission by the President of Mexico.

The claims under the several protocols were to be decided "according to justice and the provisions of this convention," and upon a "basis of absolute equity, without regard to objections of a technical nature, or of the provisions of local legislation."

A large number of questions of international law arose before these different commissions, which sat almost entirely at Caracas during the summer of 1903. There were considered by them among other matters of importance the subjects of the right of governments to expel foreigners, how far prescription entered into international affairs, responsibility of governments for the acts of their agents and for the actions of revolutionary bodies, measure of damages in cases of injury or death, circumstances under which and extent to which interest is allowable internationally, liability before an international tribunal for bonds, conflict of laws particularly with relation to questions of citizenship and including citizenship of a corporation, what was or was not receivable as evidence, liability of government for breach of contract or concession, jurisdiction of international tribunals, what constituted objections of a technical nature, meaning of the term "equity," et cetera.

As tending to make one slow to accept the statement of claimants as to losses to which they have been subjected by reason of the wrongful acts of government of which they complain, we may refer to several striking illustrations given by the proceedings of these various arbitrations. In round numbers, the American claimants demanded $15,550,-000, but were awarded $436,450.70, or not far from three per cent of their claims. The German awards amounted to about twenty-seven per cent of the sums demanded. The English fared better, receiving sixty-three per cent of the amount asked for, but the reason for this was to be found in the fact that the English Government declined to present any but claims which it considered to be of a good character, whereas some of the other governments presented everything to the commissions as an international clearing-house.

Under date of February 13, 1909, Venezuela and the United States agreed to refer to arbitration[66] at The Hague the claims of the Orinoco Steamship Company, and the Orinoco Corporation. The Crichfield claim is also referred to in the protocol. This was, however, settled between the two countries without going to arbitration, and the same was the case with regard to the claim of the Orinoco Corporation. The claim of the Orinoco Steamship Company had been presented to the board of arbitration at Caracas, but the decision of the umpire with regard to it was alleged to have been void. The arbitrators at The Hague, named from among the members of the Hague Court, one by either party, and the third selected by the two, were authorized to decide "in accordance with justice and equity." It was particularly provided that "no member of said court who is a citizen of the United States of America or of the United States of Venezuela shall form part of said arbitral tribunal, and no member of said court (the Permanent Court of Arbitration) can appear as counsel for either nation before said tribunal." The court decided some of the contentions in favor of the United States and some in favor of Venezuela, giving an aggregate award in favor of the United States in the sum of $46,867.42.

177. General observations.—We have spent considerable time in noting the various arbitrations to which the United States has been a party. We have done this because the United States has been foremost,

66 Malloy, *op. cit.*, 1881.

until at least a very recent period, in its advocacy of the peaceful settlement of international disputes through some sort of judicial procedure,
and because the examples given will serve to illustrate the wide scope
of subjects decided through arbitration, or some like form of judicial or
quasi-judicial procedure, and relieve us from giving attention to any
except the most important of the arbitrations affecting other countries.

Analysis of the instances so far furnished will indicate that, while
the United States in its arbitrations has illustrated some advance in the
application of a true theory of arbitration, yet in certain particulars
this country as others has not learned and, one may be tempted to say,
has not particularly desired to learn, the lessons experience should have
taught.

One of the salient respects in which progress has been made has
been in the selection of an umpire. Some of the earlier arbitrations, as
we have seen, selected the umpire by lot, a haphazard method likely to
breed injustice and consequent dissatisfaction. This method does not
appear to have been resorted to in any of the American arbitrations
cited since that between the United States and England under the convention of 1854. In certain other important particulars, however, assured and settled progress has not been made. Mixed tribunals are still
selected, one person representing either country. Furthermore, when
selected, as a rule the commissioner so named is paid by the country
naming him. With this method of selection and payment for services,
the arbitrator so named is almost of necessity compelled to be the
particular representative of his country rather than a judge. Twice,
however, before The Hague a different method has been pursued. In
this regard the case of the Pious Fund of the Californias represents
the highest degree of advancement yet obtained, four persons being
selected in the first instance, two by Mexico and two by the United
States, and they without interference or suggestion from the parties
selected the fifth, who presided over their deliberations. The result was
a tribunal of unsurpassed excellence and of absolute impartiality. A
like procedure was followed in the Orinoco case, where, however, there
was but one judge named by either party. In this instance old ideas were
not entirely departed from, because the man selected by the United
States was from the Republic of Cuba, a country in its foreign affairs
under the supervision of the United States.

It is, of course, to be noted that in the matter of the Geneva Tribunal
three of the five members of the court were from neutral countries,
England and the United States being represented on the tribunal each

by one. This case may be considered as paying deference to the very common idea that the sovereign power of the contestants should find representation on the court, an idea which finds an illustration even in the Permanent Court of International Justice. The theory is that the representatives of the parties can speak with authority within the bosom of the court with regard to the law and contentions of their governments, an idea which would not be tolerated because of manifest evils within the bosom of a national court.

The arbitrations in which the United States has been concerned and which we have briefly recited, illustrate perhaps every variety of question likely to receive attention before arbitral tribunals and demonstrate that there is no class of questions which may not properly be made the subject of judicial concession. Before the first one of importance of them all, that under Article 7 of the Jay Treaty, there were questions of the right of neutrals and of prize law, as well as of the fundamental right of such a tribunal to pass upon its own jurisdiction. Before many arbitral tribunals there have arisen and been determined disputes as to the interpretation of treaties. Questions of so-called "honor," as in the Geneva award, proved to have no value in themselves, but the damages were to be extinguished by the payment of money. Many tribunals have passed upon international laws (so-called) of war as well as of peace. Concessions and contracts and disputes as to their violation or annulment have been settled. Matters of sovereignty over territories have received adjudication.

The term "vital interests" has not been employed in any of the arbitrations as indicating a referable or non-referable matter, the simple fact being that these words have no meaning except as they are used as an excuse for the non-reference of some things which are of importance to someone unnamed or to people possessing undue influence with the government.

No question of national independence has arisen or been referred to arbitration. This has naturally been the case since the signature to a protocol of arbitration is postulated upon the independence of the parties submitting thereto. In this respect the position of a national citizen is exactly parallel to that of independent nations. The rights of citizens are equal. Submitting themselves perforce, it may be granted, to the decision of judicial tribunals, their independence is threatened only because of their violation of a regularly enacted criminal statute, a condition which has no parallel as between nations.

CHAPTER XXI

ARBITRATIONS BETWEEN OTHER NATIONS

178. General considerations. We will now take up the subject of arbitrations with which nations foreign to the United States have been concerned. In so doing, it will be our purpose to touch upon only the more important disputes, reserving for separate chapters cases which have been referred to the Permanent Court of Arbitration at The Hague or the Hague Permanent Court of International Justice, and also to the various mixed tribunals between European countries formed consequent upon the conclusion of the World War or to the Central-American Court of Justice.

179. Allied Powers and the Netherlands.—A dispute of historical interest arose respecting the inheritance of the Duchy of Bouillon. By Article 4 of the Treaty between Great Britain, Austria, Prussia, Russia, and the Netherlands, signed May 31, 1815, it was referred to an arbitral tribunal[1] of five members, one chosen by each of the claimants and one each by Austria, Prussia, and Sardinia. The award was in favor of the Prince de Rohan. Much of the interest in this tribunal is because of the fact that it was the second instance of arbitration with regard to the inheritance, the first occurring in the seventeenth century.

180. France and Mexico.—A dispute arising between these countries because of personal injuries and capture of ships during a recent war, all questions were referred to the arbitration[2] of Queen Victoria under a convention of March 9, 1839, who held that claims of both sides were invalid because of the state of hostilities between them.

181. Great Britain and the Two Sicilies.—It was claimed[3] in 1840 that certain English houses suffered considerable loss through the establishment of a monopoly for the extraction and sale of sulphur by a decree of the King of Naples, dated July 9, 1838. A joint commission was appointed consisting of two selected by each government and one by France, which gave an award for about one-third of the amount claimed.

182. France and Great Britain.—An arbitration frequently referred to is that involving the Portendick claims, so-called, for injuries sustained by British merchants in consequence of the absence of notification of the blockade of the Portendick coast of Morocco by France in

---

[1] Darby, *International Tribunals*, 4th edition, 773.
[2] *Ibid.*, 777.   [3] *Ibid.*, 779.

the war of 1834–35 against the Moors.[4] This was referred, November 14, 1842, to the King of Prussia as arbitrator, who gave an award in favor of Great Britain, but who referred the individual claims to commissioners, one of either party, and an umpire to be appointed by the King of Prussia. This commission awarded about five per cent of the amount claimed. The award of the King and the proceedings of this commission tended to clarify the laws of blockade.

183. Great Britain and Greece.—A case which nearly led to war between these two countries was that arising out of the claim of Don Pacifico, who was claimed to be a British subject and who charged that his house had been sacked by a mob in the city of Athens and papers destroyed.[5] A blockade was entered upon, but the case finally was referred to arbitration through the good offices of the French Government. The amount claimed was 21,295 pounds sterling, and the award gave Pacifico 150 pounds. It is at least doubtful whether any award whatever should have been given in this case, which nearly brought two countries to war.

184. Great Britain and Portugal.—In 1856 Lord Palmerston supported vigorously, even to the point of intimidation, the claims of Mr. and Mrs. Croft against Portugal, the British Government lending a ready ear to the falsehoods of its nationals. In the end, however, the dispute was referred[6] to the Senate of Hamburg and found to be without justification. In 1861, shortly after the foregoing affair, a further dispute arose between the two countries relative to the claims of Yuille, Shortridge & Company, and reference was again had to the Hamburg Senate.[7] This claim, as well as the preceding one, involved the administration of justice in Portugal. In this case, however, there was an award of some 20,000 pounds in favor of the claimants as against about 51,000 pounds sterling sought by Great Britain.

185. France and Great Britain against Uruguay.—For the purpose of determining claims for damages inflicted upon French and English subjects during the war which came to an end in 1853, a convention[8] was entered into June 23, 1857, referring them to a "mixed commission having the character of a Judge-arbitrator." This was composed of two appointed by Uruguay and one by each of the others,

---

[4] *Recueil des arbitrages*, I, 512.

[5] *Ibid.*, I, 581.

[6] February 7, 1858; cf. *Recueil des arbitrages*, II, 1.

[7] October 21, 1861; cf. *Recueil des arbitrages*, II, 78.

[8] La Fontaine, *Pasicrisie internationale, Histoire documentaire des arbitrages internationaux*, 115.

an umpire if necessary to be selected by lot from a list of eight to be chosen the same way as the arbitrators themselves. Awards aggregating four million piasters were reached.

186. **Great Britain and Nicaragua.**—An arbitration[9] of somewhat unusual character in its determinations was agreed upon January 28, 1860, between these countries to settle the claims of British subjects in connection with concessions of land in the territory of the Mosquito Indians. This consisted of one representative of each power, with power to name a third person as arbitrator or umpire, or, failing to agree, to name two persons from whom one should be chosen by lot to act as such in any particular case. Their labors were concluded by issuing a notice calling on all parties to come forward within six months and receive their grants as confirmed by the commission.

187. **Muscat and Zanzibar.**—The two sons of Synd Saced disputing as to their rival claims to Zanzibar, the difference involving independence, by their several engagements, dated September 21, 1859, and October 3, 1860, agreed[10] to refer to the Viceroy of India, then Lord Canning, the division between them, this with a view to averting war. An examination was made by the political resident at Aden. By the terms of the award, which was based upon this report, the Sultan Seyid-Medjid was recognized as the sovereign of Zanzibar and the African possessions of his deceased father, but he was required to pay certain subsidies to the sovereign of Muscat. This arbitration was not spontaneous but imposed upon the claimants, and may be regarded as a mediation rather than a pure arbitration.

188. **Great Britain and Brazil.**—In 1861 and 1862 the relations between these countries were exceedingly strained, arising out of acts of pillage committed upon the persons of the dead sailors of the British ship, *Prince of Wales*. A monetary indemnity was demanded by England, for which, however, it declared itself ready to accept arbitration. The English officers on the spot, however, were peremptory in their demands, refusing to wait until the Brazilian Cabinet could communicate with its minister in London. As a result, however, of the differences between the two countries a number of Brazilian vessels were seized by the English squadron. In the end[11] an agreement was reached between the two countries, reprisals were abandoned, and under an exchange of notes the differences were referred to the King· of

---

[9] Darby, 787.
[10] *Recueil des arbitrages*, II, 55.
[11] June 18, 1863; *Recueil des arbitrages*, II, 230.

Belgium, who decided that in the application of Brazilian laws to the English officers there was neither premeditated offense nor offense toward the British navy. The affair illustrates out of what trivial incidents war may grow.

189. Brazil and Great Britain.—By a simple exchange of notes between Brazil and Great Britain, on April 22, 1873, there was sent to arbitration[12] the claim of Count Dundonald for services and advances. This claim was referred to the United States and Italian Ministers at Rio de Janeiro and resulted in an award, diminishing largely the claim, but still allowing 38,675 pounds sterling.

190. China and Japan.—In 1874 a claim arose on the part of Japan against China for the murder of Japanese subjects by Chinese in the Island of Formosa. The cabinets of Great Britain and the United States induced these countries, which were about to go to war, to refer the claim to arbitration. It was decided by the British Minister at Peking, who awarded 100,000 taels to be paid by China.

191. Colombia and Costa Rica.—These countries, with Panama succeeding to the claims of Colombia, have repeatedly had arbitrations of a territorial character. Their disputes date back to the Treaty of Confederation between Colombia and the Central American Republic, dated March 15, 1825. The first attempt at arbitration[13] was signed in 1880, and sent the question of limits to the King of the Belgians, or, failing him, the King of Spain. The Belgian King declined to act and the King of Spain consented. He dying, an additional treaty on the subject was concluded in 1886 and the office of arbitrator accepted by the Queen Regent of Spain. This arbitration lapsed owing to a dispute as to matters of procedure. Later, on November 4, 1896, a new arbitration was undertaken, referring the case to the President of the French Republic. On the report of a commission appointed to examine all documents relative to the litigation, the President gave his award September 11, 1897, fixing the frontier. Costa Rica and Panama agreed, by a convention signed March 17, 1910, that, while the award just mentioned was clear to a certain point, they were not able to agree as to the interpretation to be given it with regard to the rest of the boundary line, and would submit the difference to the Chief Justice of the United States as arbitrator to determine the correct interpretation and true intention of the award. The matter being so referred to Chief Justice White, he held[14] that a part of the prior award was not within

---

[12] La Fontaine, *op. cit.,* 189.   [13] Darby, 802.

[14] *American Journal of International Law,* XIII, 913.

the matter of dispute or within the disputed territory, and therefore
that the arbitrator was without power to make it. To this extent he
treated it as nonexistent. He rejected any discretion to compromise or
adjust the differences. His award gave dissatisfaction to Panama, which
was, however, finally compelled to accept it.

192. **Chile and Great Britain.**—Claims arising on the part of
British subjects against Chile, a treaty of arbitration was entered into
March 1, 1884, and subsequently extended, under which two arbitrators
of the respective countries were appointed and the umpire named by the
Emperor of Brazil. The umpire first named, Senhor Lopez Netto, decided certain claims for bombardment and blockade against Chile, with
the result that his further continuance in office was made disagreeable
to him and he retired to Brazil, being succeeded by Senhor Lafayette
R. Pereira, who did not follow the precedents set by Senhor Netto.

193. **Colombia and Italy.**—A case which has received much attention in connection with international disputes is that of Cerruti &
Company,[15] whose property was confiscated, while Cerruti took refuge
on an Italian ship. During the long history of this case many important
events happened at which we can only glance. In the first instance a
question of his nationality and all other claims on his behalf or of other
Italian subjects were referred to the Spanish Government as "mediator."
The "award of mediation" was in favor of Italy, declaring that Cerruti
and Italians befriending him had not infringed the laws of neutrality
and that he was entitled to restoration of his property and damages.
The protocol under which this conclusion was reached stipulated that
"should it result from the said mediation that Colombia must pay indemnities," an amount should be fixed by an arbitral judgment through a
mixed commission consisting of representatives of the two countries and
a representative of Spain at Bogotá. Nothing, however, came of this
reference. The next step following a long disagreeable correspondence
was the reference by convention signed August 18, 1894, of the Cerruti
claims to President Cleveland as arbitrator. He awarded 60,000 pounds
sterling to Cerruti, which was paid. This decision has been the subject
of severe criticism. To begin with, no reasons were stated for the conclusions reached. In addition the arbitrator directed payment of the
claims of all creditors of Cerruti. In this respect the President was
regarded as having exceeded the terms of reference. Later under a
protocol at Bogotá of December 29, 1898, an international commission
was constituted to pass upon the claims of the creditors, and this com-

15 *Ibid.,* VI, 964.

mission failed to agree. While these proceedings were going on Italy threatened war. The amounts payable by Colombia to the claimants against Cerruti were finally referred to arbitration by an agreement between the two countries on October 28, 1909. The arbitrators included one representative from each country and an umpire. The result of this arbitration was a further award against Colombia of about 460,000 francs.

194. Germany and Great Britain.—In April 1899 an agreement[16] was entered into between these countries referring to arbitration a dispute between the British East Africa Company and the German Company of Witu relative to rights as to the farming of customs and the administration of the island of Lamu on the east coast of Africa. Baron Lambermont, Minister of State of Belgium, was made arbitrator, rendering a decision discussing quite at length the issues involved[17] in a letter accompanying the award. The arbitrator expressed an entirely correct view with regard to his functions, saying "arbiter and not mediator, I had only to give the law and could not enter upon the field of bargaining."

195. Germany and Great Britain.—By agreement[18] these countries on July 1, 1890, referred to Señor Prida of Spain, the question of the delimitation of the southern boundary of the British territory of Walfisch Bay. His decision[19] discusses at great length the elements of international jurisdiction over territories relatively savage or unoccupied and the essentials to be shown in order to establish possession. From an international point of view the decision was one of especial importance.

196. France and Venezuela.—By convention dated February 24, 1891, these countries[20] referred to the arbitration of the Federal Council of Switzerland the claim of Fabiani. This arose for the most part out of the fact that the claimant had recovered judgments from the Venezuelan courts, but obstacles had been placed in the way of his obtaining their payment. The council found itself without jurisdiction to pass upon certain claims, but awarded 4,346,656.51 francs, something less than ten per cent of the amount claimed. The award[21] discusses at great length the meaning and application of the term "denial of justice" (*déni de justice*) as well as a number of other questions, including that of indirect damages. This award left open the matters as to which jurisdiction was declined by the Council, and the Fabiani case was again sent

---

[16] Darby, *op. cit.*, 814.   [17] Moore, 4940.   [18] Darby, 815.
[19] Hertslet, *Commercial Treaties*, XXVI, 215.
[20] Darby, 817.   [21] Moore, 4878.

to arbitration before the French–Venezuelan Mixed Claims Commission created by a protocol between the two countries, dated February 19, 1902, consisting of one representative of each country, who chose as a third an American umpire. The umpire decided the case against the claims of Fabiani.[22] This final award in favor of the defendant nation was the subject of criticism.[23]

197. Chile, France, and Peru.—During the war between Chile and Peru, by decree of February 9, 1882, Chile directed the sale of a million tons of guano from deposits situated in Peruvian provinces conquered by her. The decree provided that the money resultant from the sale should be equally divided between the Chilean Government and the Peruvian bondholders. Its Article 14 directed the appointment of a board of arbitrators to liquidate the claims of these creditors, and, if not named within a limited period by agreement with the creditors, Chile would appoint them directly. The half designed for Peruvian creditors meanwhile was to be placed in the Bank of England, the treaty of peace[24] confirming the decree of February 9. The arbitrators not being appointed either by agreement or by Chile, and the stipulations for arbitration being ignored in a subsequent protocol, Chile and Peru were in disagreement as to the effect of the omission. Meanwhile France pressed the payment of claims connected with the matter. Finally by protocol dated July 23, 1892, France and Chile referred the matter to the arbitration of the President of the Swiss Federal Tribunal, or of that body in its entirety. The Peruvian Government disputed their competency to settle the matter without its intervention, and in June 1893 the contending parties addressed to Switzerland a request for arbitration. An award was given in favor of the claimants and against Peru. This arbitration is of particular interest because of the large number of questions involved, as well as because of the amount of money represented. Many matters of procedure and of jurisdiction were passed upon, and questions of international law reviewed involving discussions as to the attributes of sovereignty, citizenship of corporations, distribution of costs of arbitration, the effect of military occupation on the property of the state, et cetera.

198. Great Britain and Portugal. A dispute arose between these countries as to the frontiers of Manicaland, which resulted in a treaty[25] dated June 11, 1891, under which Count Vigliani was appointed arbi-

---

[22] Ralston, *Report of French-Venezuelan Mixed Claims Commission of* 1902, p. 81.
[23] *American Journal of International Law*, I, 389.
[24] Darby, 819.   [25] Moore, 4985.

trator. His decision was partly in favor of each of them. The award discusses in great detail the geographical features of the situation, and from this point of view particularly is useful.

199. Argentine Republic and Chile.—Because of its political aspects this arbitration is important. For many years there had existed a difference with regard to the common boundary of the two countries. By treaty of peace concluded as far back as August 30, 1855, there was a general agreement[26] to submit the decision to the arbitration of a friendly power. Numerous difficulties and futile attempts at arrangement occurred, preventing prompt carrying out of this agreement. At last by a convention dated April 17, 1896, the dispute was referred to a commission, with a request that Queen Victoria act as final arbitrator. A British tribunal was appointed to act for the Queen, and the result was an award which was accepted by both, and a delimitation commission appointed to indicate the frontier on its lines.

200. Great Britain and the Netherlands.—Under a convention[27] between the two governments dated May 16, 1895, there was referred to M. de Martens, of Russia, the claim of Mr. Carpenter the master, and the crew and owners of the whaling ship *Costa Rica Packet*. These arose out of the arrest and detention of Carpenter on a charge of theft. The award was in favor of the master, crew, and owners in amounts much less than claimed, and has been greatly criticized as a compromise on the theory that no award should have been given for the claimants.

201. Great Britain and Venezuela.—A very severe dispute arose between Great Britain and Venezuela with reference to the boundary between Venezuela and British Guiana.[28] To assuage this dispute, the United States repeatedly tendered its good offers to procure an amicable settlement by arbitration. These offers were continually rejected by Great Britain. Finally the United States itself appointed a commission to examine and report on the facts in the case. The relations even between the United States and England grew strained. Finally, however, an arbitral tribunal was agreed upon by convention between Great Britain and the United States, dated November 12, 1896, to determine the boundary line. This consisted of four members, two appointed by each country and the fifth to be agreed upon. By the treaty definite rules with regard to what should constitute adverse holding or prescription were laid down, although the arbitrators were authorized to "recognize and give effect to rights and claims resting on any other ground whatever valid according to international law, and on any principles of interna-

---

[26] Darby, 826.   [27] Moore, V, 4948.   [28] Darby, 828; Moore, 5017.

tional law which the arbitrators may deem to be applicable to the case, and which are not in contravention of" the rules laid down, which related to exclusive political control as well as actual settlement as constituting adverse holding or prescription. If the territory of one party should be found "by the tribunal to have been at the date of this treaty in the occupation of the subjects or citizens of the other party, such effect shall be given to such occupation as reason, justice, the principles of international law, and the equities of the case shall, in the opinion of the tribunal, require." The tribunal reached an award satisfactory to all parties, including Venezuela, which was not represented on a tribunal which undertook to pass upon its rights. A mixed commission was appointed to mark the boundary on the spot.

202. Greece and Turkey.—An unusual agreement tantamount to an agreement to arbitrate was contained in Article 9 of the Preliminary , Treaty of Peace terminating war between these powers, dated September 18, 1897. The agreement was that any difference in the course of negotiations should be submitted to the arbitration of the representatives of the great powers at Constantinople, whose decisions should be compulsory as to both governments.[29] This arbitration could be exercised either by the representatives themselves collectively, or by persons especially chosen by the parties interested, directly or through the intermediation of special delegates, with power to choose an additional arbitrator in the event of an equal division of votes. The Article referred to was confirmed by Article 15 of the definitive treaty of December 4, 1897. Greece demanded recourse to the arbitration thus provided. The arbitral decision formulated the consular convention binding on the two interested parties. It therefore assumed a legislative rather than a judicial character.

203. Belgium and Great Britain.—An arbitration of interest because of the prominence of the person involved[30] was that between Belgium and Great Britain under convention dated March 19, 1898, to determine damages, if any, to be awarded for the arrest and confinement under alleged rigorous circumstances and consequent expulsion from Belgium of Ben Tillet. The arbitrator failed to find the complaints justified and under all the circumstances sustained the expulsion.

204. France and Great Britain.—Several painful incidents occurring between these countries were made the subject of arbitration[31] by

---

29 Darby, 831.
30 La Fontaine, 583; *Journal du droit international privé*, XXVI, 203.
31 Darby, 900.

convention dated April 3, 1901. In 1893 a British force at Waima, West
Africa, was attacked by a French force and a number of members of
the Sierra Leone police killed. Some years before a French vessel,
Sergent Malamine, had been seized and sunk by the British. There were,
therefore, counter claims. Baron Lambermont was chosen as arbitrator
and awarded 9,000 pounds sterling to Great Britain in the Waima case,
and 6,500 pounds to France for the loss of the vessel.

205. Austria and Hungary.—Differences between these two countries relative to the possession of certain territories around Lake Meer-
auge, lying between Galicia and Hungary, were in 1897 referred to a tribunal[32] consisting of one representative of each country and a Swiss
umpire. The award was for the most part in favor of Galicia. It deserves attention because of its exposition of international law as relating
to the determination of boundary lines.

206. France and Venezuela.—By protocol[33] dated February 19,
1902, these countries referred to arbitration claims which had been presented for damages received from Venezuela through the revolutionary
events of 1892. These claims were referred to commissioners appointed
one by each party, and they agreed upon an American umpire. The
results of its labors were awards of 3,346,439.05 francs, against 40,663,-
783.50 francs demanded.

207. Peru and Bolivia.—By protocol between these countries dated
December 30, 1902, there were referred to the government of the Argentine Republic important questions of boundaries. This government gave
its decision,[34] July 9, 1909. The award in a general way was in favor
of Peru and has been the subject of severe animadversions, it being
widely believed that the arbitrator exceeded the bounds of the reference
in deciding equitably and without power the question referred to it.

208. France and Switzerland.—By an exchange of notes of November 18, 1910, and July 13, 1911, France and Switzerland referred
to arbitration,[35] the umpire of which was Lord Reay of England, a
question as to the interpretation of a provision of the French tariff
regulations, determining whether it was in conflict with a treaty between the two countries. The decision was in favor of Switzerland,
but made no award for tariff duties collected by France prior to its

---

[32] *Revue de droit international et de législation comparée,* Second Series, VIII,
196.

[33] Ralston, *Report of French-Venezuelan Mixed Claims Commission of 1902,* 1.

[34] *Revue générale de droit international public,* 1910, XVII, 231.

[35] *American Journal of International Law,* 1912, p. 995.

date. For this course, the commission gave as a good and sufficient reason the fact that the tribunal had received no precise information regarding the importation and that it was difficult to decide under these circumstances any indirect damages and loss of profit to which Switzerland might have been subjected. Having given this all-sufficient reason, the tribunal added that "moreover, friendly and cordial relations existing between the contesting parties make it desirable not to deduce rigorously all the juridical consequences that might result from the considerations above developed." No such consideration has anything whatsoever to do with the determination of such questions of law and fact as were submitted to the tribunal.

209. Great Britain and Costa Rica.—By an agreement between these countries, ratifications of which were exchanged on March 7, 1923, there were referred to the arbitration of Chief Justice William H. Taft claims against Costa Rica, of which certain British corporations were the owners. The fundamental question was as to the right of the Costa Rican Government to assume to declare void the acts of a prior administration, which it was claimed by England was a government *de facto*. The award of the arbitrator[36] discusses the powers and attributes of *de facto* governments, considering that their validity rests in the actual fact of exercising powers of government with the apparent consent of the general public rather than resting upon the circumstance of recognition or non-recognition by foreign governments. The decision was in a general way in favor of Costa Rica, although as to the claim of one of the parties said to have been injured it recognized the idea of subrogation and directed that "as a condition of the award against the bank, as to the whole 998,000 colones claimed by it, Costa Rica should transfer and assign the mortgage to the bank for its benefit, together with any interest which may have been meantime collected thereon." The other claim was rejected as being based upon a concession granted in violation of the constitution of Costa Rica.

210. Conventions controlling river traffic.—There has been a series of conventions between governments intended to regulate the conditions under which traffic should be carried on upon rivers, particularly those forming natural boundaries which are necessarily useful to two or more nations.[37] We need not do more than refer to these, as they shed little light upon any question relating to international arbitration. Thus by "Regulations for the Free Navigation of Rivers" settled March 1815 and forming Annex 16 to the Vienna Congress Treaty of June 9,

[36] *Ibid.*, 1924, p. 147.   [37] Darby, 84.

1815, embodied in that treaty as Articles 108 to 116, powers "whose states are separated or traversed by the same navigable river engaged to regulate by common consent all that regards its navigation." Under treaty, commissioners were named the basis of whose proceedings was that the navigation of such rivers "along their whole course . . . . from the point where each of them becomes navigable to its mouth shall be entirely free, and shall not, in respect to commerce, be prohibited to anyone," subject to police regulations. A number of other treaties were had supplementing or amending the treaty referred to.

In the "Regulations for the Free Navigation of Rivers" above referred to, freedom was extended also to the Neckar, Mayne, Meuse, Scheldt, and other rivers.

211. Congress of Paris of 1856 and disputes affected by it.— Certain occurrences in this Congress affecting arbitration should not pass unnoticed. At the instigation of the London Peace Society, or at any rate simultaneously with its application to him, Lord Clarendon proposed to the Congress an article which was put in this shape:

> If there should arise, between the Sublime Porte and one or more of the other signing Powers, any misunderstanding which might endanger the maintenance of their relations, the Sublime Porte and each of such Powers, before having recourse to the use of force, shall afford the other contracting parties the opportunity of preventing such an extremity by means of their mediation.[38]

While on the face of it this amounts merely to a declaration in favor of mediation, yet it has been interpreted as calling for arbitration, this being the interpretation given it by Mr. Gladstone and Lord Derby, although the plenipotentiaries "agreed that the desire expressed by the Congress did not trammel in any respect full appreciation of questions touching its dignity which no Power could abandon."[39]

It was the opinion of de Roquefort[40] that this work was not sterile. To its existence he attributed peaceful settlement of disputes between Neufchatel and Luxembourg and Prussia, while it also served to settle difficulties between Greece and Turkey.

212. Delimitation commissions.—From time to time a large number of delimitation commissions have been appointed for the purpose of marking boundaries between the foreign countries. Sometimes such commissions have been appointed consequent upon the findings of an arbitral tribunal which has settled the general principles controlling the

---

[38] Darby, 299.
[39] De Laveleye, *Des causes actuelles de guerre en Europe*, 269.
[40] *De la solution juridique des conflits internationaux*, 143.

fixation of a boundary line and sometimes through the direct initiation of the states concerned. However appointed, their constitution and procedure offers little of interest to the student of international arbitration and for our purposes may be ignored.

213. National commissions.—It frequently happens, in connection with the payment of money by one nation to another for damages to which the nationals of the second nation have been subjected, that a lump sum is paid estimated to be sufficient to cover the amount of such damages. The complaining nation is then left to determine the amount to be awarded to its individual citizens. This determination is largely arrived at through reference to a domestic commission. Although the commission so appointed is domestic rather than international, nevertheless such a tribunal is properly controlled in its findings by the principles of international law. The basis of its determination always must be the amount which the offending nation would have been obliged to pay under the rules of international law if the complainants had been brought before an international tribunal. Illustrations of this sort of tribunal are afforded by the two Alabama Treaty Claims Commissions and the Spanish Treaty Claims Commission.

CHAPTER XXII

CENTRAL AMERICAN COURT OF JUSTICE

214. The Court and its formation.—In 1906 numerous differences leading to warlike situations arose between the Central American countries.[1] President Roosevelt of the United States and President Diaz of Mexico interposed their good offices with the result that Guatemala, San Salvador, and Honduras, with the moral sanction of Costa Rica and Nicaragua, entered into an agreement re-establishing peace and providing for the reference of future differences to arbitration by the presidents of the intervening nations. This agreement was entered into on board the American cruiser, *Marblehead,* on the open sea near Corinto. The following year a conference was had in the city of Washington in which representatives of five nations took part, and this led to treaties covering a number of points, the most important for our purposes being the Convention for the establishment of the Central American Court of Justice, which was signed under date of December 20, 1907.

By this the several countries agreed to maintain a permanent tribunal to which they

bound themselves to submit all controversies which may arise among them, of whatsoever nature and no matter what their origin may be, in case the respective Departments of Foreign Affairs should not have been able to reach an understanding.

A further article provided that

this court shall also take cognizance of the questions which individuals of one Central American country may raise against any of the other contracting governments, because of the violation of treaties or conventions, and other cases of an international character; no matter whether their own government supports said claim or not; and provided that the remedies which the laws of the respective countries provide against such violation shall have been exhausted or that denial of justice shall have been shown.

By an amended protocol it also had "jurisdiction over cases arising between any of the contracting governments and individuals, when by common accord they are submitted to it." The court could in addition take cognizance of international questions which by special agreement any one of the Central American governments and a foreign government might determine to submit.

---

[1] For a succinct account of the occurrences, reference may be had to an article by Dr. James Brown Scott, "The Central American Peace Conference of 1907," *American Journal of International Law*, II, 121.

The seat of the court was fixed at Cartago, Costa Rica, with privilege of temporary transfer.

The court consisted of five justices, one appointed by each republic, and qualified for the exercise of high judicial offices because of character and ability. Vacancies were filled by substitute justices named at the same time and manner as the regular justices. The attendance of five justices was necessary to make a quorum. These judges were appointed by the legislative power of each republic and paid out of the treasury of the court, and the expenses were met by equal contribution from the several governments. The judges were appointed for five years, with vacancies to be filled in like manner as the original appointment until the conclusion of the term of the retiring justice. The judges were also granted diplomatic immunity, and the holding of the office was held incompatible with the exercise by the justice of his profession. The same provision extended to substitute judges, engaged in the actual performance of their duties.

The court was given power by its rules of procedure to meet allegations of personal interest.

The Convention contained a number of provisions relative to questions of procedure, and declared that the court was competent to determine its jurisdiction, "interpreting the treaty and conventions germane to the matter in dispute, and applying the principles of international law." Every decision called for the concurrence of at least three justices and was to be in writing with a statement of reasons. Full power was given to formulate rules of procedure.

Another article of the treaty anticipated something in the nature of injunctive relief, for it provided that

from the moment in which any suit is instituted against any one or more governments up to that in which a final decision has been pronounced, the court may at the solicitation of any one of the parties fix the situation in which the contending parties must remain, to the end that the difficulty shall not be aggravated and that things shall be conserved *in statu quo* pending a final decision.

The matter of sanctions was covered by an article saying

the interested parties solemnly bind themselves to submit to said judgments, and all agree to lend all moral support that may be necessary in order that they may be properly fulfilled, thereby constituting a real and positive guaranty of respect for this Convention and for the Central American Court of Justice.

The Convention was to remain in effect irrevocably for ten years from the last ratification.[2]

2 *American Journal of International Law*, Supplement II, 231.

The rules of procedure[3] contained extensive provisions, one subject covered at length being that of challenges. Under Article XIII of the Convention they were evidently anticipated upon "allegations of personal interest," although not "because of the interest which the Republics to which they owe their appointment may have in any case or question."

Shortly after the ratification of the Convention, the court organized and began its operations, passing upon a number of contests between Central American countries and of individuals against some of them. The decisions will be referred to hereafter. These were gathered into five volumes known as the *Anales de la Corte de Justicia Centro-Americana.*

The most important of its final cases was that of Salvador against Nicaragua, in which, incidentally, privileges granted the United States were involved and the decision was displeasing to the American State Department. Undoubtedly because of this fact, and also because the end of the ten-year period found the world in a state of general warfare, the treaty was allowed to expire without renewal in 1917, and this most interesting attempt at securing international justice through a court came to an untimely end.

Without question in many respects the Convention creating the Central American Court of Justice represented an advance in judicial procedure beyond even that later attained by the Permanent Court of International Justice. Its jurisdiction, for example, was clear cut and most extensive.

On February 7, 1923, the representatives of the Central American countries came together again for the purpose of establishing an International Central American Tribunal, again acting upon the invitation of the United States. Some of the salient points of the Convention then signed we shall proceed to mention. The new court's jurisdiction was extended to "all controversies or questions which now exist between" the contracting parties

or which may hereafter arise, whatever their nature or origin, in the event that they have failed to reach an understanding through diplomatic channels, or have not accepted some other form of arbitration, or have not agreed to submit said questions or controversies to the decision of another tribunal. Nevertheless, the questions or controversies which affect the sovereign and independent existence of any of the signatory Republics cannot be the object of arbitration or complaint.

It was agreed that the decision was to be final, irrevocable, without

[3] *American Journal of International Law,* VIII, 194.

appeal, and binding if rendered within the prescribed period. It may only be null and void and any one of the parties interested in the controversy may refuse to comply with it when (a) the tribunal shall not have been organized in strict accordance with the Convention, or when (b) in summoning the parties or in the presentation of evidence the provisions of the Convention or prescribed rules of procedure have not been observed.

Its sentence was to be null and void and open to revision (a manifest contradiction in terms, since that which is null and void cannot be revised into life) when any of the arbitrators had a material interest or may have appeared in any capacity before any tribunal or commission of inquiry or acted as counsel or agent.

Revision was permitted on the ground of discovery of a new fact calculated to exercise a decisive influence upon the award and unknown to the tribunal and party demanding revision at the time the discussion was closed.

The operative provisions of the Convention looked to the formation of a permanent list of thirty jurists from whom in each case a choice was to be made. This list was to be completed by each contracting party naming six, four of whom should be nationals and the other two chosen one each from a list submitted by the Government of the United States and by the government of some Latin-American country outside of Central America which might be asked by any of the contracting powers to submit to it another list of five jurists of its nationality.

The term of service of those finally named was five years, with a right to finish any pending case. A court was to be called into being out of the panel so named whenever a Central American nation desiring to have recourse to the tribunal should advise the opposing party of its purpose, to the end that within sixty days thereafter they should sign a protocol setting out the subject of the dispute. Then each party to the controversy selected an arbitrator from the permanent list of jurists, but not originally named by it, and a third arbitrator should be selected by common accord, or, if the governments failed, by the arbitrators already appointed, or, they failing, by lot, the third arbitrator to be of different nationality from either of the other two. Each of the parties had the right to challenge not more than two of the persons who might be designated by lot as third arbitrator.

The *status quo* in the event of the filing of a complaint was to be preserved until the final award was pronounced, and to this end the tribunal had power to make any investigation.

The tribunal was competent to decide international questions which any of the Central American governments and the government of a foreign nation might agree to submit to it by special convention.

The Convention was to continue in force until January 1, 1934, and thereafter for one year after denunciation by any party. No case has yet been heard under the provisions of this Convention.

215. Decisions of the Central American Court of Justice.— The first case before the court of 1907 was that of Honduras against Salvador and Guatemala.[4] This arose out of the fact that the defendants were charged by Honduras with responsibility for a revolutionary movement in Honduras. Some preliminary questions relating to the inadmissibility of the complaint entered by the representative of Guatemala, under an allegation that it was filed without negotiations for an agreement by the respective Foreign Offices having been exhausted, and was not accompanied by evidence when originally notified to the opposing party, were quickly overruled. The court thereafter by a majority vote acquitted the defendants of the charges brought against them.

Shortly thereafter one Díaz, a Nicaraguan, brought suit against Guatemala for alleged wrongful arrest, but the court held that under international law as well as under the Convention the plaintiff had no footing, not having exhausted his remedies within the nation at the hands of whose alleged agents he had suffered. Other cases of complaints of individuals were brought before the court and failed, among them that of Núñez,[5] the question being "Can the Government of Costa Rica deny asylum or expel the Nicaraguan citizen, Alejandro Bermúdez y Núñez, political immigrant, by reason of his having formed part of the armed expedition had against Nicaragua?" The court voted "Yes."

A case of interest was one brought asking the court to declare null and void the election in Costa Rica by the Constitutional Congress of Alfredo Gonzáles Flores as premier. The court very properly refused to consider the complaint, it not being international in character.

The two cases to which we shall now refer were the last of importance in the court and the dissatisfaction surrounding them had much to do as we have before stated with the fact that the operations of the court ceased. The first of these was that of Costa Rica against Nicaragua, in which Costa Rica contended[6] that the Bryan-Chamorro

---

[4] *American Journal of International Law*, Supplement III, 729.

[5] *Law and Procedure of International Tribunals*, 291.

[6] See decision, *American Journal of International Law*, XI, 181.

Treaty violated its rights in that thereby Nicaragua approved of the opening of an inter-oceanic canal through Nicaraguan territory in violation of existing treaties and of the award of President Cleveland.

The court declared itself competent, notwithstanding the contest related to contractual interests of a nation not subject to its jurisdiction, and held that the Bryan-Chamorro Treaty violated the rights of Costa Rica. The court did not, however, undertake to nullify the treaty because the Government of the United States was not subject to its jurisdiction.

The second case of those we are now referring to was that of Salvador against Nicaragua[7] and related to rights of co-ownership claimed by Salvador in the Gulf of Fonseca. The court decided in favor of its own competency, and by a vote of four to one held that the Government of Nicaragua had, in granting the concessions contained in the Bryan-Chamorro Treaty for the establishment of a naval base, violated the right of co-ownership possessed by Salvador in the Gulf of Fonseca. It declined to enjoin the Government of Nicaragua from fulfilling the treaty on the ground that the United States was not subject to the jurisdiction of the court, yet held that Nicaragua, by availing itself of measures possible under the authority of international law, was under obligation to re-establish the former status.

Nicaragua never complied with these decisions, contending the court had no jurisdiction to render them.

[7] *Ibid.*, XI, 674.

CHAPTER XXIII

MIXED ARBITRAL TRIBUNALS FOLLOWING THE WORLD WAR

216. Their formation.—The treaty of Versailles, dated June 28, 1919, provided for the institution of Mixed Arbitral Tribunals, and its provisions served as a model for a number of like tribunals created under subsequent treaties.

By the provisions of its Article 296 there were established clearing offices to settle various classes of debts due to or from the nationals of Germany and of the opposing contracting parties, including interest where payable and capital sums which had become payable before and during the war to nationals of the contracting powers in respect of securities of an opposing power, the payment of which had not been suspended during the war. The same section in its Annex provided that all disputes which the clearing offices were unable to settle between themselves could either be referred to arbitration or to the mixed tribunal provided thereafter.

Paragraph 18 of the Annex to Article 296 provides for the appointment of an agent on either side, responsible for presentation to the Mixed Arbitral Tribunal of cases conducted on behalf of its clearing office. The decisions of the tribunal, by Paragraph 24, were to be regarded as final and conclusive and binding upon the respective nationals.

A number of sections are devoted to a description of the rights and claims of the parties in interest.

Recovery being provided in the treaty for losses due to "exceptional war measures," Paragraph 3 of the Annex to Article 297 defines the expression as including

measures of all kinds, legislative, administrative, judicial, or others, that have been taken or will be taken hereafter with regard to enemy property, and which have had or will have the effect of removing from the proprietors the power of disposition over their property, though without affecting the ownership, such as measures of supervision, of compulsory administration, and of sequestration; or measures which have had or will have as an object the seizure of, the use of, or the interference with enemy assets, for whatsoever motive, under whatsoever form or in whatsoever place.

By Article 299 contracts concluded by the enemies were regarded as having been dissolved as from the time when any two of the parties became enemies, except as to any debt or other pecuniary obligation arising out of any act done or money paid thereunder; and subject to exceptions in the treaty, while all periods of prescription were, by Article 300 of the treaty, declared to have been suspended for the duration of the war.

Clauses in a contract referring differences to arbitration could not defeat jurisdiction of the tribunal.

For the purpose of enforcing all of the provisions of the treaty relative to the relations between the respective nationals and the opposing governments, including many questions of possible conflict over insurance and a great variety of other contracts, there were created by Article 304 Mixed Arbitral Tribunals between each of the Allied and Associated Powers, on the one hand, and Germany on the other. Each tribunal was to consist of three members, one to be named by either of the governments concerned, and the president to be chosen by mutual agreement between the governments.

These tribunals were authorized to decide on questions within their competence under Sections III, IV, V, and VII of the treaty. Their jurisdiction extended to deciding any case between German nationals and nationals of Allied and Associated Powers which might be brought by the national or Allied or Associated Power if not prohibited by the laws of his country.

If the number of cases justified it, additional members could be appointed and each Mixed Arbitral Tribunal could sit in divisions.

Each government was to pay the remuneration of its member of a tribunal and of its agent, the remuneration of the president to be determined by special agreement.

The Annex to Article 304 provided a number of rules of procedure to govern the tribunal, but nevertheless permitted the tribunal to adopt other rules.

The provisions we have briefly indicated were in substance followed in the treaty of peace between the Allied and Associated Powers and Austria, signed at St. Germain September 10, 1919. They were also followed in a treaty of peace between the same parties and Hungary, signed at Trianon June 4, 1920; also between the principal Allied and Associated Powers and Bulgaria, signed at Neuilly November 27, 1919, and with Turkey, signed at Sèvres, August 10, 1920. In a less extended way a Mixed Arbitral Tribunal was also provided for in the treaty of peace of Lausanne between the British Empire, France, Italy, Japan, Greece, Roumania, and the Serb-Croat-Slovene State, on the one hand, and Turkey, on the other. Article 95 of the last-named treaty provided that "the Mixed Arbitral Tribunals shall be guided by justice, equity, and good faith."

We include these tribunals as coming properly within the purview of our subject-matter, although it is to be noted that for the most part the questions brought before all of them related to disputes between the nationals of the respective countries and only in a small degree to claims directly against the nation. The most of the cases, therefore, dealt with by the tribunals involved private law only, offering little of international importance.

When describing arbitrations to which the United States has been a party we referred to the arbitrations between the United States on the one hand, and Germany and Austria on the other, succeeding the World War. Their jurisdiction was by no means as extensive as those of the Mixed Arbitral Tribunals we are now discussing, and were of a purely international character.

217. Operations of the Mixed Arbitral Tribunals.—The tribunals we are describing commenced their operations very quickly upon the ratification of the Treaty of Versailles, at least so far as the principal powers were concerned, the first to operate being the Franco-German Commission whose first decision was under date of July 21, 1920. The reports of all the commissions are contained in the *Recueil des décisions des tribunaux arbitraux mixtes institués par les traités de paix,* of which five volumes have so far been issued.

As is evident from what already has been said, the work of the commissions, aside from questions of interpretation and application of the treaties, has been in small degree with relation to questions of international law. Undoubtedly the most important and vexed questions discussed before them were with regard to the meaning of exceptional war measures. We note with interest in addition that Germany, having recognized responsibility for the war and its consequences, was not allowed to avail itself of the defense of *force majeure* due to the war, and relied upon by Germany to excuse the non-execution of a contract of transportation.

An interesting proposition arose before the American arbitrator under the treaty of St. Germain, Mr. Walker D. Hines, as to whether seizures of enemy-owned boats on the Danube were "regulated by the international law pertaining to naval warfare, and therefore ought to be upheld." Mr. Hines held that "international law as applied to warfare is a body of limitations, and is not a body of grants of power," and rejected the idea of Roumania.[1]

Matters of citizenship were also under consideration, and perhaps

---

[1] *American Journal of International Law,* XVI, 376, 385.

no decision of the commissions has been more criticized than that which declared that the people of Alsace-Lorraine were possessed of a sort of indigenous status distinct from French or German nationality up to the time of their reintegration into the French nation.[2]

[2] Severe criticisms of the work of the commissioners are contained in an article by Dr. Karl Strupp entitled "The Competence of the Mixed Arbitral Courts of the Treaty of Versailles," *American Journal of International Law*, XVII, 661. We are inclined to think that the serious trouble with these commissions has arisen from the fact that they were one-man commissions, although ostensibly composed of three, with all the evils attendant upon such a situation, and sitting at a time when passions inflamed by the war had not begun to subside and when it was difficult for even the most impartial man not to be influenced by his surroundings prejudicially, particularly toward Germany. Nevertheless, some of the commissions under the guidance of cool-headed umpires have met with a fair degree of success from the standpoint of impartial justice.

PART IV

HAGUE PEACE CONFERENCES AND THEIR
RESULTS

CHAPTER XXIV

HISTORY OF HAGUE CONFERENCES

218. The original call.—On August 12, 1898, without preliminary notice, Count Mouravieff, Russian Foreign Minister, at his weekly reception at St. Petersburg handed the diplomatic representatives a note reciting the importance of "ensuring to all peoples the benefits of a real and lasting peace, and above all of limiting the progressive development of existing armaments." After describing the evil effects of the then present conditions the Foreign Minister stated that the Russian Czar had commanded him to propose to the governments having accredited representatives at the Russian Court the holding of a conference to consider the problem.[1]

The circular mentioned met with great favor among the nations, and in consequence on January 11, 1899 (new style), Count Mouravieff presented a second circular to the diplomatic representatives at St. Petersburg suggesting that in the opinion of the Russian Government it would be possible forthwith to proceed to a preliminary exchange of ideas, with the object of (1) limiting armaments, and (2) discussing prevention of armed conflicts by pacific means. He summarized subjects for discussion and his eighth proposition looked to

Acceptance, in principle, of the use of good offices, mediation, and voluntary arbitration, in cases where they are available, with the purpose of preventing armed conflicts between nations; understanding in relation to their mode of application and establishment of a uniform practice in employing them.

Count Mouravieff thought the conference should not sit at the capital of one of the great powers where were centered political interests which might impede its work.

About a month later Count Mouravieff informed the diplomatic representatives that the Netherlands Government informed him, pursuant to inquiry from him, that it assented to a meeting at The Hague.

Not included in the invitation were the Pope, the South African and the Latin-American Republics, except Mexico.

On April 7, 1899, the Netherlands Government extended a formal

---

[1] For this and other following recited documents reference may be had *inter alia* to *Actes et documents relatifs au programme de la conférence de la paix*, The Hague 1899; Holls, *The Peace Conference at The Hague*; Scott, *The Hague Peace Conferences of 1899 and 1907*; Scott, *Instructions to the American Delegates to the Hague Peace Conferences and Their Official Reports*; Moore, *International Law Digest*, VII, 80.

invitation to the selected powers to meet in conference at The Hague to discuss the matters suggested by Count Mouravieff, with the qualification as outlined by him that "everything which refers to the political relations of states, or the order of things established by treaties" should be excluded from the deliberations.

The foregoing sketch discloses the antecedents of the first Hague Conference in so far as they are shown in published documents. Something remains to be added touching its interior history, for which addition we are largely indebted to the recently published German Archives entitled *Die grosse politik der europäischen Kabinette,* Vol. XV.

It seems that the attention of the Czar, who was peace-loving, was called by Finance Minister Witte to the then recent book of Bloch. The consequence was that the Czar called Bloch in and became very much interested in his work. Thereupon, in 1898, he directed that somebody should prepare a memoir upon the subject of disarmament. Such work was given to Mr. Basily, who had taken part in a peace congress at Pest in 1895. Basily was directed by his superior, Hartwig, to work up a report in favor of a congress for general disarmament and the establishment of a permanent tribunal of arbitration. With his subsequent report the Czar was in agreement, but, Russia having theretofore rejected the ideas of the Pest Peace Congress, a report was prepared not mentioning the tribunal of arbitration and discussing only disarmament. With this the Czar agreed, but many of his assistants raised numerous objections. Basily, however, revived the subject, with the result that the note of August 12 was sent.

It is noteworthy that Witte considered that the note covering disarmament and peace was "only verbiage."[2] From his standpoint he had favored the idea as a ruse to get Austria to stay her hand and discuss disarmament in lieu of investing in an improved gun. Later he told the German Ambassador that the Continental Powers were in danger from England because of its sea power, and that with it England would easily control the world. He remarked: "If the conference can do something against this I shall be very glad."

France was shocked officially by the note, but its Prime Minister thought that some concessions in arbitration might be made to avoid a fiasco. There still being danger of French opposition, Bloch went to Paris and brought the French officials into a more favorable attitude.

The instructions to the German delegates to the conference were to the effect that no first-class power could submit to obligatory arbitra-

---

[2] Dillon, *The Eclipse of Russia,* 274.

tion; that it was doubtful whether Russia would submit great political questions to such an Areopagus, and that Russia wanted to use it against England; that arbitration through interested judges, and in which all great powers were interested, was nothing but intervention; that courts of arbitration would result in bringing up the interests of different countries, forming groups for war, and taking advantage of the weaker group; that the state, the larger it is, regards itself as an end in itself and not as a means for higher things; that it has no other interests than taking care of its own interest; that such are regarded by the great Powers—not maintenance of peace but taking advantage of enemies and competitors.

The Kaiser was indignant at the Czar and in a private letter wrote:

Could we, for instance, figure to ourselves a monarch, holding personal command of his army, dissolving his regiments sacred with a hundred years of history, and relegating their glorious colors to the walls of armories and museums, and handing over his towns to anarchists and democracy?

But the letter ends by saying that the Czar will be praised by the world, and Germany will give the proposal attention.

When the Russian proposal reached Austria, its foreign minister laughed in a benevolent way, and the Emperor, Franz Joseph, was very unfavorable. Turkey feared that the Russian project meant a new move on the Balkans. Lord Salisbury was skeptical.

The Pope desired his representatives to attend the conference, but Italy objected, and Germany feared for the rupture of the Triple Alliance, as Austria was dependent upon the clericals. Germany, therefore, advised Holland not to invite the Pope, who during all the conference wanted admission.

Holland asked Germany about inviting the Transvaal; but the German representatives indicated that Germany had nothing to do with that and Holland should ask England, which, apparently, Holland did. The Transvaal was not invited.

219. First Hague Peace Conference.—As a result of the preliminaries we have briefly sketched, the first Hague Conference met on May 18, 1899, with M. de Staal, Ambassador of Russia, as its President. The work of the Conference was divided among three committees, the third, covering the matter of arbitration, being in all respects the most important, effective, and lasting, and in this the leading parts were taken by America, England, and Russia.

The American delegates, headed by Hon. Andrew D. White, were instructed by Secretary Hay to propose a plan for an international tribunal outlined by him, and to use their influence to procure the adoption of its substance or resolutions to the same purpose.

Sir Julian Pauncefote of England also offered a plan, many features of which entered into the final draft, as was also the case with another scheme presented by the Russians. The last contained the first suggestion of International Commissions of Inquiry, at least under this name. It is a curious fact of history that Russia and England were the first to take advantage of this admirable suggestion.

At one moment[3] it appeared likely that the whole scheme of arbitration might fail because of the opposition of the German Emperor, as derogatory to his sovereignty, to any plan for a regular tribunal. The upshot was that Mr. White, acting as Minister to Berlin, as he then was, wrote a long letter to the German Foreign Minister[4] summarizing the situation and the arguments, and dispatched it to Berlin by the hands of Mr. Holls.[5] German opposition soon sensibly diminished for reasons we shall see, though Germany always opposed anything obligatory.

The German Archives furnish us some information in regard to Mr. Holls' visit. The Kaiser wrote to Secretary of State Bülow on June 19, 1899, with reference to this: "Since the Englishmen are at present behaving in such a peculiar way at The Hague, I am particularly interested to have good relations with the Americans." Mr. Holls was received by representatives of the Foreign Office, who said that

Mr. Holls gave reasons why the United States so decidedly wants an arbitration tribunal and we said why we were against it. Mr. Holls' reasons were that the United States, on account of internal politics, had to return from The Hague with concrete results, and as such the United States could only consider a tribunal for arbitration. The Irish element of the population had at one time prevented ratification of the arbitration treaty with England; the question now was to bring the German element of the United States into the foreground. For this purpose it would be well if the United States, together with Germany and England, achieved the establishment of an arbitration tribunal. For, although public opinion was very cool in the United States toward The Hague in the beginning, at present, since the permanent arbitration tribunal had come up, public opinion was very much warmed up.

Holls said that Germany, by not joining, would prevent the tribunal from being established. He followed this with a contradictory statement: "Since the four powers (England, United States, Russia, and

---

[3] *Autobiography of Andrew D. White*, II, 293.   [4] *Ibid.*, II, 309.

[5] The writer recalls, as a possible check upon the accuracy of Mr. Holls' reports about the Conference, that in 1903 Secretary of State John Hay, bitterly denouncing Mr. Holls to him, said that whatever Andrew D. White or Seth Low or himself proposed Holls claimed credit for.

France) favored the tribunal it would be established anyhow even if Germany or the Triple Alliance remain outside."

The German Foreign Office asked its ambassador at St. Petersburg which would be the lesser of two evils, acceptance or rejection, and he responded in favor of arbitration, apparently to preserve amicable relations with Russia. The Kaiser, therefore, accepted arbitration to save the Russian situation, but declared that he would not bind himself by conventions. This feeling, doubtless, more than anything said by Holls or the strong appeal of Ambassador White, saved the situation and brought about the reluctant consent of Germany to the convention finally adopted.

At the conclusion of the Conference several resolutions were adopted calling upon the governments for further study as to regulation of artillery and limitation of armed forces and war budgets, and referring to a future conference the questions of rights and duties of neutrals, immunity of private property at sea during war, and bombardment of ports, cities, or villages by a naval force.

220. Second Hague Peace Conference.—The preliminary steps looking toward the calling of the second Conference, which finally met three years later, were taken in 1904. In that year the Interparliamentary Union meeting in St. Louis called upon President Roosevelt to request the several governments to send delegates to an international conference to consider subjects referred to a later conference by the first, the negotiation of arbitration treaties, and establishment of periodic international congresses to discuss international questions.[6]

Pursuant to the suggestion so made, Secretary Hay directed our diplomatic representatives to take up the matter with foreign governments in such a manner as to form an "overture for a second Conference to complete the postponed work of the first Conference." This was received with general favor, though with a suggestion from Russia as to the impracticability of present (1904) action on its part. On September 13, 1905, Russia, thinking a favorable moment had arrived, suggested the calling of a second Conference as soon as favorable responses from other states could be secured.

On April 12, 1906, Russia, acting upon the suggestion of President Roosevelt, called the second Conference, emphasizing the necessity of certain improvements in the Convention relating to the pacific settlement of international disputes and in the *modus operandi* of international commissions of inquiry, and these topics were first on its program

---

6 Scott, *Instructions to the American Delegates*, etc., 60.

for the Conference. As with the first, this was not to deal with political relations of the states or conditions established by treaties. All powers agreed to the program, the United States reserving the right to submit the limitation of armaments and limitations on use of force for collection of ordinary public contractual debts. In the instructions to the American delegation it was directed not to present the question of the limitation of armaments, but to promote it if proposed by any European power and to urge the abolition of use of force for collection of contract debts until arbitration, if demanded by alleged debtor, which should fix time and manner of payment and security. The delegation was also to urge formation of a permanent court.

Forty-four nations were represented at the Hague Conference which assembled June 15, 1907. With its work we are concerned only as far as it affects our topic.

The Convention of 1899, with reference to Pacific Settlement of International Disputes, was enlarged from 61 to 97 articles, without making fundamental or even considerable changes except as we note elsewhere. An addition providing for summary procedure was proposed by France and embodied in it. Procedure affecting international courts of inquiry was made more complete and specific. Power was given the Hague Court on application to frame a *compromis*.

A new Convention covering the matter of arbitration for collection of contract debts was formulated as desired by America and adopted.

While a Convention for the creation of an International Prize Court was adopted, the Convention never went into effect, because of opposition on the part of Great Britain.[7]

In its final Act the Conference declared as "unanimously admitted" "the principles of compulsory arbitration," and that "certain disputes, in particular those relating to the interpretation and application of the provisions of International Agreements, may be submitted to compulsory arbitration without any restriction."[8]

The Conference further called the attention of the Signatory Powers to the advisability of adopting a draft convention, which it submitted, for the creation of a Judicial Arbitration Court, and of bringing it into force as soon as an agreement was reached respecting the selection of the judges and the constitution of the Court. Upon many points this draft[9] furnished an excellent basis for subsequent work in connection with the formation of the Permanent Court of International Justice.

---

[7] James Brown Scott, *American Journal of International Law*, VIII, 274.
[8] Malloy's *Treaties, etc.*, 2378.   [9] *Ibid.*, 2380.

CHAPTER XXV

THE HAGUE PEACE CONVENTIONS
OF 1899 AND 1907

221. Preliminary.—The Hague Peace Conference of 1899 resulted in the taking of an important further step in the line of arbitrations between nations. Before 1899, while there had been numerous instances of references to arbitration, such a thing as an all-around agreement to arbitrate between a considerable number of nations, with certain partial exceptions in South America, was unknown. The Convention of 1899, signed by twenty-six states, declared that

with the object of facilitating an immediate recourse to arbitration for international differences, which it has not been possible to settle by diplomacy, the Signatory Powers undertake to organize a permanent Court of Arbitration, accessible at all times and operating, unless otherwise stipulated by the parties, in accordance with the Rules of Procedure inserted in the present Convention.

Practically the same language was employed in the Convention of 1907. The differences between the two conventions, the later one having been signed by forty-four nations, are not great, except in arrangement and such alterations as were necessary because of the fact that the first related to a court to be established and the second to what may be styled "a going concern." We might add that some changes were based upon developments arising in connection with the four cases which between the periods named had been referred to The Hague. The term, "Delegates," as representing a nation, referred to in the first, is dropped in the second convention. The language of the second Convention is imperative as forbidding members of the Permanent Court from acting as agents, counsel, or advocates, except on behalf of the power which appointed them members of the court. The reason for this prohibition is to be found in the fact that M. Beernaert of Belgium, a member of the Permanent Court, acted as counsel for Mexico in the Pious Fund case, while Renault, another member of the Permanent Court, acting on behalf of his own nation, France, was challenged in the Venezuela Preferential case. By the earlier Convention it was left to the tribunal to decide what languages should be employed before it, but by the later one the tribunal was given power to act only if the question was not settled by the *compromis*.

We should note further, however, that the earlier Convention provided without limitation that in default of other agreement each party resorting to the Court should name two arbitrators without limitation as to citizenship, who would choose a fifth, while the later Convention provided that under like conditions each could name only one national or one chosen from among those selected by it as members of the Permanent Court.

222. Appointment and privileges of judges under the Hague Peace Conventions.—The Permanent Court of Arbitration, while given such a title, is in point of fact neither permanent nor a court. It is merely a panel of possible arbitrators who may, to the number usually of three or five, be called together to act in any given instance. It is a court only in the sense that it adjudicates upon questions of fact and law, and settles differences. It is not a court in that it meets to the limited extent spoken of only when a difference arises and some of its members are selected, and that, far from being named in advance of the dispute and from people foreign to the parties in interest, it is, except as to its presiding officer, selected by those not so much concerned in the establishment of justice as in their success in the particular controversy. It is not permanent for reasons already given, and also because of it not necessarily having any fixed place of meeting, and because of its members being named for a limited period, six years.

The panel of possible arbitrators is created through the selection, by any nation which may choose to act, of not to exceed four persons at the most, "of known competency in questions of international law, of the highest moral reputation, and disposed to accept the duties of arbitrator." The names of these persons form a list notified to all the powers joining in the convention, who are also notified of any alterations. Unless called on to act in a particular case, the appointments are purely honorific.

The parties may select as arbitrators of a given dispute whomever they may choose from the list. In default of an agreement in a *compromis*

each party appoints two arbitrators, of whom one only can be its national or chosen from the persons selected by it as members of the Permanent Court. These arbitrators together choose an umpire.

In the Pious Fund case it was expressly provided by the protocol that no national should sit on the Board of Arbitration, and the same course was pursued in the Muscat and the Venezuelan Preferential cases. The members of the tribunal in the exercise of their duties and out of their own country enjoy diplomatic privileges and immunities.

223. Administration of court.—All arrangements with reference to the office of the Permanent Court, which is presided over by its registrar, and all questions of administration with regard to the operations of the court and control of general expenditures are in the charge of the Permanent Administrative Council, composed of the diplomatic representatives of the contracting powers accredited to The Hague and of the Netherlands Minister for Foreign Affairs as its president.

224. Procedure.—Many of the important points relative to procedure before the Permanent Court of Arbitration are considered under other headings. Several, however, should be further elucidated.

The powers resorting to arbitration sign a *compromis,* defining the subject of dispute, the time allowed for appointing arbitrators, the order and time in which their respective cases, counter-cases, or, if necessary, replies, shall be communicated to each other, including all papers and documents called for. This communication may be made either directly or through the intermediation of the International Bureau, and the time may be extended by mutual agreement between the parties or by the tribunal when necessary for reaching a just decision. The *compromis* may also define if need be the manner of appointing arbitrators and any special powers to be given them, the place of meeting, the language to be used or authorized, and generally speaking all the conditions on which the parties have agreed. The Permanent Court is declared competent to settle the *compromis* if the parties have agreed to have recourse to it for the purpose, at least in certain cases. No such recourse, however, has ever been had.

The procedure before the Permanent Court comprises the pleadings and oral discussion. The nature of the pleadings is fixed by the *compromis,* and except under special circumstances the tribunal does not meet until the pleadings are closed. The discussions are under the control of the president and only public if so desired by the tribunal with the assent of the parties. They are recorded in minutes drawn up by the secretary, appointed by the president, and after the close of the pleadings the tribunal is entitled to refuse discussion of all new papers or documents without the mutual consent of the parties. The tribunal can require from the agents of parties production of all papers and demand necessary explanations, while the agents and counsel of the parties may present orally all arguments that they deem expedient, and are entitled to raise objections and points.

Quite in accordance with the powers generally understood to pertain to commissions at the present day, the tribunal is authorized to declare its competence in interpreting the *compromis* as well as the other treaties which may be invoked, and to apply the principles of law. It may also issue rules of procedure and govern the time and order of argument and arrange formalities for dealing with the evidence. A tribunal may also arrange for service of notices in the territory of a third contracting party to the convention. Decisions are considered in private and proceedings are secret relating thereto, all questions being decided by a majority of the members of the tribunal. As heretofore stated, the award must give the reasons on which it is based. It is read at a public sitting, agent and counsel being present or duly summoned to attend. It settles the dispute definitely and without appeal, while any dispute as to its interpretation and execution shall in the absence of an agreement to the contrary be submitted to the tribunal which pronounced it.

225. Revision of award.—Revision may be provided for in the *compromis,* but only on the ground of the discovery of some new fact calculated to exercise some decisive influence upon the award and unknown to the tribunal and to the party which demanded the revision at the time the discussion was closed. Revision, however, can only be instituted by a decision of the tribunal recording the existence of the new fact, recognizing in it the character described, and declaring the demand admissible therefor. The period in which the demand for revision must be made is fixed by the *compromis.*

The award binds only the parties in dispute, but where a question arises of the interpretation of the convention to which powers other than those in dispute are parties they shall inform all the signatory powers in good time, who shall be entitled to intervene, and if they intervene the interpretation becomes equally binding on them.

Each party pays its own expenses and an equal share of the expenses of the tribunal.

We discuss Commissions of Inquiry in chapter xxvii.

CHAPTER XXVI

CASES BEFORE THE HAGUE PERMANENT COURT OF ARBITRATION

226. United States and Mexico.—For the first three years after the formation of the Hague Permanent Court of International Arbitration, no nation referred any cause to it for determination and there existed a belief among the statesmen of Europe that this promising attempt at securing international justice through judicial processes was to be a failure and that the Court would die of inanition. However, such was not to be the case. The time came when under date of December 16, 1901, the American Minister in Mexico wrote to the Secretary of State that

Mr. Mariscal [the Mexican Minister of Foreign Affairs] suggested that the question could be submitted either to the Hague Tribunal or to a tribunal created by the International Conference of American States now in session at this capital should one be created; and I suggested that in case neither should be acceptable to both parties, the two governments might agree upon a special board or tribunal for the purpose, to which he assented. In view of the nonexistence of the second tribunal referred to, we finally agreed to leave the selection of the tribunal open to further consideration.

In response to this, under date of January 23, 1902, Secretary Hay wrote to Mr. Clayton, the American Minister in Mexico

You will say to Mr. Mariscal that the Government of the United States would be pleased to have the case submitted to arbitration under Article XXXII of the Hague Convention.

Mr. Clayton so informed Mr. Mariscal shortly after and, not hearing from him promptly, the State Department further instructed the American Minister to press the determination of the case at The Hague, stating that

the President feels that it would especially redound to the credit of the United States and of Mexico if the two North American republics might be the first states to submit to the Hague Tribunal for determination by it of an international controversy.

Then followed negotiations to bring about the signing of the protocol of submission.

We have been thus explicit in stating the course of negotiations because the statement has frequently been made that the Hague Court was opened through the initiation of President Roosevelt. In point of fact the first suggestion came from Mr. Mariscal, and it is doubtful if the President even knew of the use of his name by the State Department until after the event.

We have heretofore, in the chapter entitled "Arbitrations between the United States and Mexico," referred to the Pious Fund of the Californias. Some observations remain to be added. The original claims arose briefly out of the following state of facts: During the seventeenth and eighteenth centuries a number of pious Catholics, by contribution, devise, and otherwise, gave large sums of money for the purpose of conversion of the Indians of Upper and Lower California to Christianity and the establishment of Missions. As the result of these contributions, the celebrated California Missions were created. During its early career the Fund was in charge of the Jesuits, later when they were banished, the Missions of Lower California were turned over to the Dominicans and those of Upper California to the Franciscans. In 1832 the Government undertook the management of the Pious Fund, later passing the property to the administration of a Bishop of the Catholic Church. In 1842 the Government seized the entire property, at the same time charging itself with the payment for the benefit of the Fund of six per cent per annum. Except for a very trivial amount no payment was ever made, and at the time of the formation of the Mexican-American Mixed Claims Commission under the Treaty of 1868, twenty-two annual instalments were due. An award was made, as we have heretofore stated, in favor of the Bishops of California, and, as further stated, the questions referred to The Hague were: In the first instance, whether the prior award was *res judicata* so that subsequent annual instalments should be paid by virtue of it; or, if not, whether the claim was just and what award should be made. The main question to be determined by the tribunal was therefore the very important one of the extent to which the awards of a tribunal of arbitration are to be treated as *res judicata* of their subject-matter.

By the terms of the protocol signed May 22, 1902, two members of the Hague Court, not nationals of either party, were to be named on each side, and these were to name the fifth member of the Court as the president. The United States named Sir Edward Fry of England and de Martens of Russia; and Mexico, Mr. T. M. C. Asser and Jonkheer A. F. de Savornin-Lohman, both of Holland; and these unitedly chose Professor Matzen of Denmark as president. The proceedings were conducted for the most part in English, although some of the speeches were made in French and the protocols of the proceedings were in French. The award sustained the contentions of the United States except as to the medium of payment, granting $1,420,-682.67, Mexican money, with the annual payment of $43,050.99 by Mexico on account of the Pious Fund.

227. **Germany, England, and Italy against Venezuela.**—We have elsewhere referred to the events leading up to the signing of protocols between Venezuela, on the one hand, and ten different powers, on the other, relative to the settlement of the claims of their respective nationals against Venezuela. The protocols providing for this submission of the claims of Great Britain, Germany, and Italy directed that for their settlement there should be set aside by the Venezuelan Government, commencing March 1, 1903, thirty per cent of the customs revenues of La Guaira and Puerto Cabello, the two principal ports of entry of Venezuela. It was also provided that

any question as to the distribution of the customs revenues so to be assigned, and as to the rights of Italy, Great Britain, and Germany to a separate settlement of their claims, shall be determined, in default of arrangement, by the tribunal at The Hague, to which any other power interested may appeal.

The protocols of the other parties, after providing for the payment indicated of customs revenues, directed that

the payments thus set aside shall be divided and distributed in conformity with the decision of the Hague tribunal.

By separate protocols with Great Britain, Germany, and Italy, which were known as the "Blockading Powers," and dated May 7, 1903, it was provided that

the question as to whether or not Great Britain, Germany, and Italy are entitled to preferential or separate treatment in the payment of their claims against Venezuela shall be submitted for final decision to the Tribunal at The Hague. Venezuela having agreed to set aside thirty per cent of the customs revenues of La Guaira and Puerto Cabello for the payment of the claims of all nations against Venezuela, the Tribunal at The Hague shall decide how the said revenues shall be divided between the Blockading Powers, on the one hand, and the other Creditor Powers on the other hand, and its decision shall be final.

If preferential or separate treatment is not given to the Blockading Powers, the Tribunal shall decide how the said revenues shall be distributed among all the Creditor Powers, and the parties hereto agree that the Tribunal, in that case, shall consider, in connection with the payment of the claims out of the thirty per cent, any preference of pledges of revenue enjoyed by any of the Creditor Powers, and shall accordingly decide the question of distribution so that no power shall obtain preferential treatment, and its decision shall be final.

The protocols further provided that the Emperor of Russia be invited to name from among the members of the Permanent Court at The Hague three arbitrators to constitute the tribunal to determine and settle the questions submitted to it, none of whom should be a subject or citizen of Venezuela or of any of the other powers concerned.

The proceedings were directed to be carried on in English, but arguments might, with the permission of the tribunal, be made in any other language.

Pursuant to the authorization given him, the Emperor of Russia named as arbitrators N. V. Mouravieff and Mr. de Martens of Russia, and Professor H. Lammasch of Austria.

Before the tribunal appeared representatives of Belgium, France, Germany, Great Britain, Italy, the Netherlands, Spain, Sweden and Norway, the United States, Mexico, and Venezuela, thus including all the nations in any wise concerned in the distribution of the fund to be created in Venezuela. Venezuela and the United States were represented by the same counsel.

Notwithstanding the fact that the protocols with the Blockading Powers particularly provided that proceedings should be carried on in the English language with permission for the making of arguments, if granted by the tribunal, in any other language, the tribunal decided that

1. The protocols, the decisions, and the sentences of the Tribunal of Arbitration shall be drawn up in English and in French, both having the same authoritative and judicial value;

2. The written and printed memoranda shall be drawn up in the English language and may be accompanied by a translation in the language of the Power by which they are filed;

3. The oral discussion before the Tribunal shall take place in English or in French.

Being asked for an explanation of this decision, the tribunal declared

1. In accordance with Article 4 of the Protocol of the 7th of May, 1903, that the English language is recognized as the official language of the proceeding, but in accordance with the exact meaning of the said Article arguments may be presented in another language only with the permission of the Tribunal;

2. That the Tribunal, by the decision just pronounced, has admitted, within the limits indicated by this decision, the French language as subsidiary, since it is familiar to the Members of the Tribunal and to the majority of the Representatives of the Parties.

The question as to whether the countries should be arranged as parties plaintiff or defendant was raised before the tribunal, which, however, determined that the several nations should be heard alphabetically through their delegates according to their names in English; and that all the delegates of the several parties could take part in the first pleadings, the replies, however, to be limited to one from each party. It was thus declared by the president that "there was no first or last but that every party had equal rights."

The final award of the commission was rendered on February 22, 1904. It considered that "the Blockading Powers, in admitting the adhesion to the stipulations of the protocols of February 13, 1903, of the other Powers which had claims against Venezuela, could evidently not have the intention of renouncing either their acquired rights or their actual privileged position"; and that the Government of Venezuela as to the Blockading Powers recognized "in principle the justice of the claims but failed to make such recognition as to the claims of other powers." Further the award found that the Government of Venezuela "until the end of January, 1903, in no way protested against the pretensions of the Blockading Powers to insist on special securities for the settlement of their claims" and during the diplomatic negotiations made a formal distinction between "the Allied Powers" and "the neutral or pacific Powers." The award further found that the neutral powers "did not protest" against the pretensions of the Blockading Powers to a preferential treatment "either at the moment of the cessation of the war against Venezuela or immediately after the signature of the protocols of February 13th, 1903." It was further insisted in the award that it appeared "from the negotiations which resulted in the signature of the protocols of February 13 and May 7, 1903, that the German and British Governments constantly insisted on their being given guaranties for 'a sufficient and punctual discharge of the obligations'." This reservation, as the award terms it, was accepted by the plenipotentiary of the Government of Venezuela without the least protest, that government engaging "with respect to the allied powers alone to offer special guaranties for the accomplishment of its engagements." It was further held that the words "all claims" used by the representative of the Government of Venezuela in conference with the representatives of the allied powers could only mean the claims of these latter. The court further argued that "the neutral powers, having taken no part in the warlike operations against Venezuela, could in some respects profit by the circumstances created by those operations, but without acquiring any new rights."

The tribunal therefore decided that the Blockading Powers had a right to preferential treatment for the payment of their claims against Venezuela and the right to preference in their payment by means of the thirty per cent of the receipts of the two Venezuelan ports we have named. The decision further directed that each party should bear its own costs and an equal share of the costs of the tribunal. The court undertook to charge the Government of the United States with seeing to the execution of the clause with regard to costs within a term of three months. This responsibility the United States declined to assume, and the attempt to make it responsible for such a duty was plainly beyond the power of the tribunal.

Except one be completely educated in an atmosphere of war and a devotee of the rights of war, it is difficult to sustain a decision which recognizes that by the exercise of force one may gain a legitimate advantage over those who resort to the ways of peace.

228. Great Britain, France, and Germany against Japan.—The third case to go to The Hague was between the nations we have named and is commonly known as the "House Tax Case." The question between the parties was "whether or not the provisions of the treaties and other engagements" existing between the several plaintiff countries and Japan "exempt only land held under leases in perpetuity granted by or on behalf of the Japanese Government," or land and buildings of whatever "description constructed or which may hereafter be constructed on such land, from any imposts, taxes, charges, contributions, or conditions whatsoever, other than those expressly stipulated in leases" in which the parties were concerned. The protocol provided for the appointment of a tribunal of three members who were members of the Permanent Court of Arbitration; each party to name one arbitrator and the two to choose an umpire.

Under the provisions of the protocol, a tribunal was formed consisting of M. Louis Renault, Mr. Itchiro Motono of Japan, and Mr. Gregers Gram of Norway, as umpire. The essence of the question was whether, the land embraced within certain concessions having been relieved from Government tax, the buildings upon the land were to be considered as going with it and under the leases to be likewise relieved.

The language of the tribunal was French; however, when a request was made that German should be recognized, followed by a demand for the equal recognition of Japanese, the decision was adjourned. The award, after arguing at some length the questions involved, decided that

the provisions of the treaties and other engagements mentioned in the protocols of arbitration exempt not only the land held under perpetual lease granted by the Japanese Government or in its name but they exempt the lands and buildings of every nature constructed or which could be constructed upon these lands from all imposts, taxes, charges, contributions, or conditions whatsoever other than those expressly stipulated in the leases in question.

This decision was made by the majority, and the Japanese member of the tribunal, in signing, stated his "absolute dissent" with the majority of the tribunal so far as concerned the reasons of the *"dispositif"* of the award.

229. France and Great Britain.—A *compromis* was entered into between these countries October 13, 1904, having reference to a declaration between them dated March 10, 1862, "to engage reciprocally to respect" the independence of the Sultan of Muscat. This *compromis* recited that

difficulties as to the scope of that Declaration have arisen in relation to the issue, by the French Republic, to certain subjects of His Highness the Sultan of Muscat of papers authorizing them to fly the French flag, and also as to the nature of the privileges and immunities claimed by subjects of His Highness who are owners or masters of dhows and in possession of such papers or are members of the crew of such dhows and their families, except as to the manner in which such privileges and immunities affect the jurisdiction of His Highness the Sultan over his said subjects.

The agreement provided for the nomination on each side of one arbitrator who should choose an umpire, or, in default of agreement within one month, the choice of umpire should be entrusted to the King of Italy. It was provided further that the arbitrators and the umpire should not be subjects or citizens of either of the parties and should be chosen from among the members of the Hague Tribunal. The time fixed for the delivery of the cases on each side, which was limited by the compromise to three months after the date of agreement, was subsequently extended by understanding between them. It was agreed that both English and French could be used concurrently in the debates, but the tribunal decided the language should be French, the minutes, however, to be accompanied by an official English translation.

The tribunal consisted of Dr. Lammasch, as umpire, and Chief Justice Fuller of the United States as arbitrator, chosen by the British Government, and Dr. A. F. de Savornin-Lohman of the Netherlands, named by France.

By the terms of submission either party was to submit a written case and, within three months after its delivery, a counter-case. The French Government submitted in addition supplementary conclusions, to which the English representative objected, but they were admitted by the court with the right to the representatives of the English Government to present an answer at a later date.

The tribunal decided that before January 2, 1892, France had the right to authorize ships belonging to the subjects of the Sultan to float the French flag, subject only to her own laws and administrative rules; that those who before 1892 had been authorized by France to float the French flag preserved this authorization as long as France renewed it to the grantee; that after January 2, 1892, France did not have any right to authorize boats to float the French flag except on the condition that their owners or fitters-out established that they had been considered by France as her protégés before 1863. The tribunal further declared that the dhows of Muscat which were thus authorized to float the French flag had in the territorial waters of Muscat the right to inviolability by the French-Muscat Treaty of November 17, 1844; that the authorization to float the French flag could not be transmitted or transferred to any other person or dhow, even if belonging to the same owner; that the subjects of the Sultan of Muscat who are proprietors or masters of dhows authorized to float the French flag, or who are members of the crews of such dhows, or who belong to their families, do not enjoy in consequence of this fact any right of extraterritoriality which could exempt them from the sovereignty, especially from the jurisdiction, of His Highness the Sultan of Muscat.

This decision, while not in itself important, is interesting as offering a solution of a question not often submitted to arbitration.

230. France and Germany.—Serious difficulties arose between these governments relative to occurrences at Casablanca on September 25, 1908, involving, as was claimed, the dignity and honor of both countries, and more immediately questions of invasion of military discipline, claimed by France to have occurred on the part of the German consulate, and interference with consular authority on the part of the French military authorities as against Germany. These were referred to The Hague by the two governments under a protocol of November 10, 1908, and an agreement to arbitrate dated November 24, 1908. The board of arbitration consisted of one representative from the Hague Court of the nationality of each of the countries in dispute and another member of the Court named by each country, who themselves chose an umpire. Those named to sit upon the tribunal were Sir Edward Fry of England, M. Renault of France, Dr. Guido Fusinato of Italy, and Dr. Kriege of Germany, with Dr. de Hammarskjöld of Sweden as umpire.

The work of this commission, as shown by its award, was highly diplomatic in its nature and in scarcely any sense to be called judicial. The award gently chides the excess of zeal shown by the agents of the two countries in the affair. It concludes that it was erroneous for the Secretary of the Imperial German Consulate at Casablanca to attempt to have embarked on a German steamship deserters from the French Foreign Legion who were not of German nationality, but that the German Consul and other officers of the consulate were not responsible in this regard, although in signing these safe conducts presented to him the Consul committed an unintentional error; that the error of law committed by the officers of the Consulate in granting protection to the deserters of German nationality could not be imputed against them either as an intentional or unintentional error; that it was wrong for the French military authorities not to respect as far as possible the actual protection granted to these deserters in the name of the German Consulate, but that, leaving out of consideration the duty to respect consular protection, the circumstances did not warrant on the part of French soldiers either the threat made with a revolver or the prolongation of the shots fired at the Moroccan soldier of the Consulate.

Having in the manner indicated satisfied the *amour propre* of the two countries, the arbitration may be regarded as highly satisfactory.

231. Norway and Sweden.—By convention dated March 14, 1908, Norway and Sweden referred to arbitration at The Hague certain boundary questions of interest. The arbitrators consisted of Mr. F. V. N. Beichmann, President of the Court of Appeals of Trondhjem, Dr. de Hammarskjöld of Sweden, and Dr. J. A. Loeff of the Netherlands, the last named as umpire. The award which was given at The Hague October 23, 1909, discusses various questions of the law of nations with relation particularly to maritime boundary. It finds that in conformity to this law, maritime territory is an essential appurtenance of land territory; that a number of circumstances support a demarcation which would assign the islands in dispute to Sweden, one of the principal ones being that lobster fishing in the shoals of Grisbadarna had been carried on for a longer time, to a greater extent, and by a much larger number of the subjects of Sweden than those of Norway; that Sweden had at considerable expense placed beacons, measured the sea, and installed a light boat, whereas Norway was much less solicitous. The court applied as a settled principle of the law of nations the thesis that a state of things which actually exists and has existed for a long time should be changed as little as possible.

232. Great Britain and the United States.—A long-pending dispute between Great Britain and the United States relating to fisheries on the North Atlantic Coast of the United States and British possessions was, by agreement between the two countries, dated January 27, 1909, referred to arbitration at The Hague.[1] By this agreement differences which had arisen as to the scope and meaning of Article 1 of the Convention signed at London on October 20, 1818, between the two countries were to be settled. These difficulties were embodied in seven questions, and in connection with the first of them, relative to the power of British control of the situation by means of municipal laws and regulations, the contentions of the United States were stated.

The agreement provided that any question arising in the arbitration concerning the reasonableness of any regulation, or otherwise requiring an examination of the practical effect of any provisions in relation to the conditions surrounding the exercise of the liberty of fishery enjoyed by the inhabitants of the United States or requiring expert information about the fisheries themselves, could be referred to a commission of three expert specialists, one designated by each of the parties, and the third a non-national designated by the tribunal. This commission as appointed was required to report conclusions to the tribunal, and, if incorporated in the award, they were to be accepted as a part of it.

The tribunal was also given power to recommend for the consideration of the parties rules and procedure under which future questions should be determined in accordance with principles laid down in the award. If not adopted, the parties to the agreement were to refer, in the absence of rules and methods, any future difference relating to the interpretation of the Treaty of 1818, or to the effect and application of the award, to the Permanent Court at The Hague for decision by summary procedure provided for in chapter IV of the Hague Convention of October 18, 1907.

It was further provided that the tribunal of arbitration should be chosen from the general list of members of the Permanent Court in accordance with the Convention of 1907, which as far as applicable, excepting Articles 53 and 54, should control the proceedings under the submission.

The cases of the two governments were to be delivered in the same period of seven months after exchange of notes, making the agreement binding; and a further period of four months was provided for like delivery of a printed counter-case, each with the accompanying evidence.

[1] Malloy, *op. cit.,* 835.

A proviso was added to the effect that these directions should not prevent either party from relying at the hearing upon documentary or other evidence becoming open or available too late to be submitted within the period fixed, subject, however, to such conditions as the tribunal might impose, and granting the other party a reasonable opportunity to offer additional evidence in rebuttal.

Another provision looked to the furnishing of certified copies of originals referred to by either party. English was the language prescribed.

The final article of the agreement gave either party the right to demand a revision of the award, application to be made within five days after its promulgation, and to be heard within ten days thereafter. This, however, could be based only upon "the discovery of some new fact or circumstance calculated to exercise a decisive influence upon the award and which was unknown to the Tribunal and to the party demanding the revision at the time the discussion was closed, or upon the ground that the said award did not fully and sufficiently, within the meaning of this Agreement, determine any question or questions submitted."

This agreement was modified as to Question Five, submitted by resolution of the Senate, consented to by England, excluding from determination any question that the Bay of Fundy considered as a whole or the Gut of Canso should be considered in the measurement of three marine miles from the coasts, et cetera, referred to in the articles of the agreement.

The tribunal of arbitration so directed to be organized consisted of Dr. Lammasch, as president, Judge George Gray, named by the United States, Sir Charles Fitzpatrick, Chief Justice of Canada, Dr. A. F. de Savornin-Lohman of the Netherlands, and Sr. Luis Maria Drago of the Argentine Republic.

The award of the tribunal[2] in answering the first question considered that the right to regulate the liberties conferred by the Treaty of 1818 was an attribute of sovereignty, and as such must be held to reside in the territorial sovereign, unless the contrary be provided; that, as one of the essential elements of sovereignty is that it is to be exercised within territorial limits, and that, failing proof to the contrary, the territory is co-terminous with the sovereignty, it followed that the burden of the assertion involved in the contention of the United States (viz., that the right to regulate does not reside independently in Great Britain, the territorial sovereign) must fall on the United States.

[2] *American Journal of International Law*, IV, 948.

It held further that there was no necessary connection between the duration of a grant and its essential status in its relation to local regulation; that a servitude in international law predicates an express grant of a sovereign right, whereas the Treaty of 1818 granted only a liberty to fish, which is not a sovereign but purely an economic right, to the inhabitants of another state; that, even if these liberties of fishery constitute international servitude, the servitude would derogate from the sovereignty of the servient state only in so far as the exercise of the rights of sovereignty by the servient state would be contrary to the exercise of the servitude right by the dominant state; that the fact that Great Britain rarely exercised the right of regulation in the period immediately succeeding 1818 was to be explained by various circumstances and was not evidence of the nonexistence of the right; that the recognition of a concurrent right of consent in the United States would affect the independence of Great Britain and create a co-dominion; that if the consent of the United States were requisite for the fishery a general veto would be accorded them, the full exercise of which would be socially subversive and would lead to the consequence of an unregulatable fishery; that a line which would limit the exercise of sovereignty of a state within the limits of its own territory can be drawn only on the ground of express stipulation and not by implication from stipulations concerning a different subject-matter; that the right to make reasonable regulations, not inconsistent with the obligations of the treaty, which was all that was claimed by Great Britain for a fishery which both parties admit requires regulation for its preservation, is not a restriction of or an invasion of the liberty granted to the inhabitants of the United States; that to hold that the United States, the grantee of the fishing right, had a voice in the preparation of fishery legislation involved the recognition of a right in that country to participate in the internal legislation of Great Britain and her colonies, and to that extent would reduce these countries to a state of dependence.

The tribunal therefore decided that the right to regulate the liberty to take fish, in the form of municipal laws, et cetera, was inherent in the sovereignty of Great Britain, limited by the fact that such regulations must be bona fide and not in violation of the treaty; that regulations appropriate or necessary for the protection and preservation of such fisheries, or desirable or necessary on grounds of public order and morals, and equitable and fair between local and American fishermen, were not inconsistent with good faith and were reasonable and not in violation of treaty.

The tribunal in this same connection made sundry suggestions as to the procedure to govern fishing liberties, and provided for the appointment of the special commission referred to in the agreement.

In answering the second question the tribunal declared that the liberty to take fish was an economic right attributed to the inhabitants of the United States without any mention of nationality and included the right to employ servants without referring to their nationality or inhabitancy; that as an economic liberty it referred not only to the individuals doing the manual act of fishing but also to those for whose profit the fish were taken.

As to the third question, relating to whether inhabitants of the United States could be subjected to the requirements of entry or report at custom houses or the payment of light, harbor, or other dues or any similar requirement, the tribunal found that the requirement of reporting if proper conveniences and an opportunity were provided was not unreasonable or inappropriate; that light and harbor dues, if not imposed on Newfoundland fishermen, should not be imposed on American fishermen exercising the liberty granted by the treaty; that inhabitants of the United States exercising the liberty of fishing should not be subjected to the commercial formalities of report, entry, and clearance at a custom house, or light, harbor, or other dues not imposed upon Newfoundland fishermen.

In answering the fourth question, the tribunal refused to recognize the necessity of payment of light, harbor, or other dues, or of reporting in order to enable American fishermen to enter bays and harbors for shelter, repairs, wood, and water.

The fifth question involved the point from which must be measured the "three marine miles of any of the coasts, bays, creeks, or harbors" referred to in the article under discussion. The majority of the tribunal held that the three-mile rule should not be strictly and systematically applied to bays. It called attention to the fact that in various treaties Great Britain had adopted the rule that only bays of ten miles in width should be considered as those wherein fishing was reserved to nationals, and therefore recommended that "in every bay not hereinafter specifically provided for the limitation of exclusion shall be drawn three miles seaward from a straight line across the bay at the part nearest the entrance at the first point where the width does not exceed ten miles."

The sixth question related to the right of fishery on the part of the inhabitants of the United States over certain portions of the southern coast of Newfoundland. The tribunal held that, considering that evidence seemed to show that the intention of the parties to the Treaty of 1818, as indicated by the records of the negotiations and by the subsequent attitude of the government, was to admit the United States to such fishery, it was incumbent on Great Britain to produce satisfactory proof that the United States were not so entitled under the treaty.

In answering the seventh question, the tribunal held that the inhabitants of the United States whose vessels were enjoying the liberties referred to in Article I of the Treaty of 1818 could not at the same time and during the same voyage exercise their treaty rights and enjoy their commercial privileges, because treaty rights and commercial privileges were submitted to different rules, regulations, and restraints.

In the foregoing award all members of the court joined, although Sr. Drago expressed his dissent from the considerations and enacting part of the award as to the fifth question, touching the matter of bays.

The foregoing arbitration is notable in that it served to settle disputes about one hundred years old and as well shed light upon important questions of international law.

233. United States and Venezuela.—We have referred to the dissatisfaction of the United States under the award rendered in the American-Venezuelan Commission by the umpire in the case of the Orinoco Steamship Company. It was at all times contended by the United States that the award contained elements of invalidity as being in excess of jurisdiction. Cipriano Castro, president of Venezuela from the time of the award until 1909, declined to recognize the American contentions, but he being absent from Venezuela and displaced by the vice-president, General Gomez, the latter came to an agreement on February 13, 1909, for the reference of this and other claims (the remaining claims being settled, however, between the parties) to The Hague. As to this claim the arbitral tribunal was to decide whether the decision of the umpire, in view of all the circumstances and under the principles of international law, was not void, and whether it must be considered so conclusive as to preclude an examination of the case on its merits. If the arbitral tribunal should decide that the decision was not final, then it was to hear, examine, and determine the case and render its decision on the merits.

The protocol provided that no citizens of either party should form part of the arbitral tribunal, and no member of the court could appear as counsel for either nation before the tribunal. The award was to be made in accordance with justice and equity and in the presentation of the case French, English, and Spanish could be used.

The court, which met in September 1910, consisted of Dr. Lammasch of Austria as president, and M. Beernaert of Belgium and Sr. de Quesada of Cuba as the remaining judges.

The award[3] recited that the plaintiff had alleged excessive exercise of jurisdiction and numerous errors in law and fact equivalent to essential error, but that as, when an arbitral award embraced several independent claims and consequently several decisions, the nullity of one was without influence on any of the others, more especially when as in the present case the integrity and good faith of the arbitrators were not questioned, it was necessary to pronounce separately on each of the points at issue. As to the largest item involved in the dispute, amounting to $1,209,701.04, the tribunal held that the appreciation of the facts and the interpretation of the documents were within the competence of the umpire, and his decision was not subject to revision by the tribunal, whose duty was not to say if the case had been well or ill judged but whether the award was to be annulled. The fact that the umpire had not been content to base his award on his interpretation of the contracts, which of itself should be deemed sufficient, but had invoked other subsidiary reasons of a rather more technical character, was held not to vitiate the decision.

The award further declared that "excessive exercise of power may consist, not only in deciding a question not submitted to the arbitrators, but also in misinterpreting the express provisions of the agreement in respect to the way in which they are to reach their decisions, notably with regard to the legislation or the principles of law to be applied." So ruling, the tribunal held that, as to one claim of $19,200, the motives for rejection constituted an insufficient justification and such as would have been incompatible and unreconcilable with the arbitration which had been instituted. It further held, and in so doing created a precedent for the action taken in the Landreau case, that "the omission to notify previously the cession of a debt constitutes but a failure to observe a prescription of local legislation, although a similar prescription also exists in other legislations," and "cannot be considered as required by absolute equity, at least when the debtor actually possesses knowledge of the cession and has paid neither the assignor nor the assignee." Other portions of the umpire's decision were regarded as based on "a consideration of facts and on an interpretation of legal principles which are subject neither to re-examination nor to revision by this tribunal, the decisions awarded on these points not being void."

[3] *American Journal of International Law,* V, 230.

As the result of the opinion, the tribunal allowed items aggregating $46,867.42, with an additional sum of $7,000 for counsel fees and expenses of litigation.

234. France and Great Britain.—By agreement dated October 25, 1910, these countries agreed to refer to The Hague the questions of law and fact raised by the arrest and restoration to the mail steamer, *Morea,* at Marseilles of the Indian, Savarkar, who had escaped from that vessel, on board of which he was in custody, and on the other hand the demand of France that he be restored to it.

The tribunal provided for by the protocol was to consist of five arbitrators from among the members of the Permanent Court at The Hague. Each of the parties, however, was to have the right to choose as arbitrator one of its nationals. Either French or English was to be employed by the tribunal. The decisions were to be drawn up in the two languages.

The court so provided for consisted of M. Beernaert of Belgium as president, Earl Desart of England, Professor Renault of France, Mr. Gram of Norway, and Dr. de Savornin-Lohman of the Netherlands.

The facts surrounding the dispute were substantially as follows: The Chief of Police in London informed the Directeur de la Sureté Générale at Paris that Savarkar would be sent to India on charges of abetting murder and would be on board the ship, *Morea,* stopping at Marseilles. A few days later the prefect at Marseilles was notified that revolutionary Hindus then on the Continent might seek this occasion to facilitate the escape of Savarkar, and he was asked to take the necessary steps to avoid such an attempt; that upon the arrival of the *Morea,* Savarkar did succeed in escaping and swimming to the shore and started to run; that he was arrested by the French gendarmes and brought back to the ship; that the arresting officer was absolutely ignorant with whom he was dealing, believing that the individual who was pursued by public clamor was a man of the crew who had perhaps committed some offense on board; that all the circumstances showed that the persons on board charged with watching Savarkar believed they could count on the assistance of the French police agents; that it was manifest from the statement made that this was not a case where there had been recourse to fraudulent maneuvers or acts of violence to secure possession of a refugee upon foreign territory, and that in the facts of the arrest, delivery, and conduct of Savarkar in India, there was nothing to offend the sovereignty of France; that the act of the brigadier not having been disavowed before the departure of the *Morea* from Marseilles, the British agents could naturally believe that the police officer had acted in conformity with his instructions or that his conduct had been approved.

The court concluded that, even admitting that an irregularity had been committed by the arrest and the return of Savarkar to the British agents, there was not in international law any rule by virtue of which the power which has, under the conditions indicated, a prisoner under its control was bound to restore him on account of a fault committed by the foreign agent who has delivered him up. The tribunal, therefore, decided that Great Britain was not required to restore Savarkar to the Government of France.

The foregoing case is probably of as little practical importance internationally in itself as any of all those submitted to The Hague. Its claimed merit was that it served to allay feeling which had been somewhat excited at the time.

235. **Italy and Peru.**—A claim which appeared in different phases before international tribunals at various times was that of the Italian citizens, Carlos and Raphael Canevaro. Its last appearance was due to a protocol between Italy and Peru, dated April 25, 1910. In this shape it required a determination as to whether a certain sum should be paid in cash or under the provision of a Peruvian law governing the internal debt, and further, whether the whole claim could be demanded, and if Raphael Canevaro had a right to be considered as an Italian claimant.

The case went to a court of three judges consisting of Dr. Renault of France, Dr. Fusinato of Italy, and Dr. Calderon of Peru.

In the award the tribunal first considered the question of the nationality of Raphael Canevaro, who, it declared, was according to Peruvian legislation a Peruvian and according to Italian legislation Italian, as being born of an Italian father; that in fact this Canevaro had, as a Peruvian citizen, been a candidate for the Senate where were admitted only Peruvian citizens, and he had also accepted the functions of Consul-General of the Netherlands after having solicited the authorization of the Peruvian Government. In view of these circumstances, the tribunal considered that the Government of Peru was right in regarding him as a Peruvian citizen and denying him the quality of Italian claimant. As to the citizenship of the firm to which the bonds claimed upon were delivered, it found that the commercial house owning them had preserved the old name but was composed of members, all of whom were found to be Peruvian and, for this reason as well as because of its location, the firm itself was Peruvian. The court discussed at some length the origin of the claim. It found that the original claim had passed into the hands of three Italians, of whom Raphael was one, and that their rights were not greater than that of the original owner.

The award was in favor of the claimants for two-thirds (excluding Raphael) of one amount claimed in bonds of the interior debt and 9,388 pounds 17 shillings and one pence sterling.

236. Russia and Turkey.—An arbitral agreement between Russia and Turkey dated July 22, 1910, recited that a disagreement had arisen between the two countries under the provisions of Article 5 of a treaty between Russia and Turkey, dated January 27, 1879, as to questions of law arising from the dates on which the Turkish Government made certain payments and as to responsibility to Russian claimants for interest because of delay in prompt settlement. It was resolved to end the controversy by submitting the question to arbitration. Each party was authorized to name two arbitrators, and the four to choose an umpire. More specifically the questions submitted to arbitration were

I. Whether or not the Imperial Ottoman Government must pay the Russian claimants interest-damages by reason of the dates on which the said government made payment of the indemnities determined in pursuance of Article 5 of the Treaty of January 27 (February 8, 1879) as well as of the Protocol of the same date?

II. In case the first question is decided in the affirmative, what would be the amount of these interest-damages?

The tribunal consisted of Dr. Lardy of Switzerland, Baron Von Taube and Doctor Mandelstam of Russia, Herante Abro Bey and Ahmed Réchid Bey of Turkey.

In the course of the proceedings, the tribunal decided that but one speaker should be heard on either side in replying and in rebuttal.

The opinion of the tribunal deals largely with the nature of a demand for interest. Upon this point the conclusion was that

the general principle of the responsibility of states implies a special responsibility in the matter of delay in the payment of a money-debt unless the existence of a contrary international custom is proven.[4]

It further found that

it would not be possible for the tribunal to declare this responsibility inapplicable in the matter of money-debts without extending this inapplicability to all the other categories of responsibility.

Nevertheless, the tribunal, "basing its conclusion upon the statements of law and fact" which it recited, was

[4] *American Journal of International Law*, VII, 178.

of the opinion that in principle the Imperial Ottoman Government was liable to moratory indemnities to the Imperial Russian Government from December 31, 1890 (January 12, 1891), the date of the receipt of the explicit and regular demand for payment, but that, in fact, the benefit to the Imperial Russian Government of this legal demand having ceased as a result of the subsequent relinquishment by its embassy at Constantinople, the Imperial Ottoman Government is not held liable to pay interest-damages by reason of the dates on which the payment of the indemnities was made.

As a consequence, the tribunal decided the first question submitted in the negative, which settled the case.

237. France and Italy.—The twelfth and thirteenth cases submitted to The Hague were between these two countries, and arose out of the arrest of the French steamers, *Manouba* and *Carthage.* These were referred by joint notes entered into between the French Ambassador and the Italian Minister of Foreign Affairs, and while on the docket of the Hague Court the *Manouba* is given the earlier number, it is mentioned second in the note[5] which was signed January 26, 1912. This note provides, as to the *Carthage,* that the questions arising from its capture and temporary arrest should be referred to The Hague under the Franco-Italian Arbitration Convention of December 23, 1903, renewed December 24, 1908.

As to the seizure of the *Manouba* and the Ottoman passengers on board ship, claimed to have been taken by virtue of the rights which the Italian Government declared it possessed according to the general principles of international law and Article 47 of the Declaration of London of 1909, the circumstances and consequences of such action were likewise to be submitted, and the Ottoman passengers seized to be delivered to the French Consul at Cagliari, who was to see that they were taken back to the place from which they sailed, this under the responsibility of the French Government. France was to take necessary measures to prevent Ottoman passengers, not belonging to the "Red Crescent" but to fighting forces, from sailing from a French port to Tunis or to the scene of military operations.

In deciding the *Carthage* case, the questions submitted were

1. Were the Italian naval authorities right in proceeding as they did to the capture and the temporary seizure of the French mail steamer *Carthage?*

2. What pecuniary or other consequences should result from the solution given to the preceding question?

The court consisted of Dr. Fusinato of Italy, Dr. Hammarskjöld of

[5] *American Journal of International Law,* VII, Supplement, 176.

Sweden, Dr. Kriege of Germany, Professor Renault of France and Baron de Taube of Russia, who designated Dr. Hammarskjöld as president.

The tribunal decided that the Italian naval authorities were wrong in detaining the *Carthage* and should pay to the French Government the sum of 160,000 francs for losses and damages experienced from the capture and seizure of the *Carthage* by the individuals interested in the ship.

The same arbitrators determined claims arising out of the *Manouba* affair.

The specific propositions referred to The Hague in this case were as follows:

1. Were the Italian naval authorities in a general way, or under the special circumstances under which the operation was carried on, right in proceeding as they did to the capture and temporary seizure of the French mail steamer *Manouba*, as well as to the arrest of twenty-nine Ottoman passengers who were found embarked upon it?

2. What consequences pecuniary or otherwise should result from the determination of the preceding question?

The award of the tribunal concluded that the Italian naval authorities were, in a general way, or under the circumstances under which the operation was accomplished, right in proceeding as they did to the capture of the *Manouba* and its conduct to Cagliari; that once captured and conducted to Cagliari, the Italian naval authorities were right in so far as the seizure did not extend beyond the limits of a temporary or conditional sequestration having for its end to compel the captain of the *Manouba* to turn over the twenty-nine Ottoman passengers found embarked in it, and that the *Manouba*, once captured, taken to Cagliari and seized, the naval authorities were under the circumstances right in proceeding as they did to the arrest of the passengers; that as to the second question presented by the agreement, the Italian Government should, within three months, turn over to the French Government the sum of 4,000 francs, which, less the costs of watching the *Manouba* due to the Italian Government, constituted the amount of losses and damages experienced because of the capture and conduct of the *Manouba* to Cagliari by the individuals interested in the vessel and its voyage.

238. France and Italy.—While by *compromis* of November 8, 1912, the two governments agreed to refer a dispute over the seizure of the *Tavignano* to The Hague, the subject-matter was afterward settled through reference to a commission of inquiry. (See below, § 247.)

239. Portugal and the Netherlands.—By an arbitral convention entered into between Portugal and the Netherlands, dated April 3, 1918, the two countries determined to settle by submission to a single arbitrator to be chosen from the members of the Permanent Court of Arbitration a dispute relative to the boundary between Dutch and Portuguese possessions in the Island of Timor.[6] The decision was to be made on the basis of facts furnished and according to treaties and the general principles of international law and was to be in French.

A decision was rendered by Mr. Charles Edward Lardy of Switzerland[7] and involved the consideration of questions touching the interpretation of treaties as bearing particularly upon boundaries.

240. Great Britain, Spain, and France, and Portugal.—By *compromis* entered into July 31, 1913, between France, Great Britain, and Spain on the one hand and Portugal on the other, there was referred to arbitration at The Hague a dispute relative to claims for religious properties. By its express terms the arbitrators were named as Hon. Elihu Root of the United States, Dr. de Savornin-Lohman of the Netherlands, and Dr. Charles Edward Lardy of Switzerland, and the claims were to be decided according to the applicable conventional law and, in its default, according to the general principles of justice and equity. The language of the tribunal was named as French. The claims were to be examined successively and in alphabetical order according to the individuals interested, with power in the claimant governments to present a single claim for the various ones owned by an interested party.

The hearings of the commission were much delayed on account of the World War and it did not meet until September, 1920.

The decisions of this commission related almost entirely to questions of fact of little general moment arising out of the seizure of religious properties. The only questions to be noted were minor ones relating to matters of citizenship.

241. France and Peru.—A protocol was entered into between these countries[8] on February 2, 1914. A claim made on behalf of the French creditors who had been represented in 1910 in negotiations between the two countries by the Banque de Paris et des Pays-Bas, in order that the tribunal at The Hague should decide whether the claims were well founded, and if so the amount. It was, however, provided that no award should be demanded greater than twenty-five million francs. Under

---

[6] *American Journal of International Law*, 1915, Supplement, 107.

[7] *Ibid.*, 1915, 240.

[8] *Ibid.*, 1914, Supplement, 240.

the provisions of the protocol each country was to appoint an arbitrator, and an umpire was to be chosen in accordance with the Hague Convention of 1907. Certain other claims contemplated by the Peruvian Law of Authorization of December 31, 1912, and brought to the knowledge of the Peruvian Government within four months were also submitted.

The tribunal did not meet until October 3, 1921, and was composed of M. Frederic Ostertag, president of the Swiss Federal Tribunal, as umpire; M. Louis Sarrut, president of the Court of Cassation of Paris; and Sr. Frederico Elguera of Peru.

The award of the tribunal[9] rejected certain claims, and allowed others including twenty-five million francs which were to be apportioned by the several claimants in proportion to the sums due them which were found by the award. The only matters of general importance adjudged by the tribunal were that

it is of slight importance that a Peruvian law of October 25, 1886, declared "all the internal acts of the government performed by Nicholas de Pierola null" since this law cannot be applied to foreigners, who treated in good faith,

and further as had been many times decided by arbitral tribunals that interest could not be capitalized except as resulting

from a stipulation or similar circumstances of fact, making clear the consent of the debtor to assume such onerous obligation; whereas the consent of the government of Peru has not been given.

242. United States and Norway.—There arose out of the World War many claims on behalf of Norwegian citizens and corporations against the United States from the seizure by the United States of contracts for the construction of vessels and vessels under completion in this country. It was agreed on July 30, 1921, that all such claims should be referred to arbitration at The Hague, and to a board to consist of one arbitrator appointed by either country, and the third to be selected by mutual agreement or in the want of such an agreement within a limited time to be named by the President of the Swiss Confederation. The tribunal was authorized to decide these claims in accordance with the principles of law and equity and determine what sum, if any, should be paid in settlement of each claim. A possible counter claim on behalf of certain American citizens arising out of one of the transactions was also to be passed upon.

By the protocol, the language was to be English.

[9] *American Journal of International Law*, 1922, 480.

The tribunal consisted of Dr. James Vallotton of Switzerland, Hon. Chandler P. Anderson of the United States, and Mr. Benjamin Vogt of Norway.

Extended arguments were had, and the award[10] dealt with a number of questions of international importance. There was considered at some length the meaning of the term "law and equity" in international application and also the extent to which the municipal law of the United States could be applied. The bearing of the statutes of the United States upon international law received examination. The extent to which the power of eminent domain may be exercised as to the property of foreign citizens was discussed. Compound interest was refused. A succession of awards aggregating about twelve million dollars was made in favor of Norway with an offset against one of the claims allowed to be retained by the United States because of amounts due certain American citizens.

The arbitrator named by the United States did not concur in the award and declined to be present when it was announced, contending that the majority of the commission had disregarded the terms of submission and exceeded the authority conferred upon the tribunal, and the American agent, Mr. Dennis, in open court reserved all the rights of the United States "arising out of the plain and manifest departure of the award from the terms of submission and from the 'essential error,' to use the language of the authorities, by which it is invalidated."

Against this award, Secretary of State Hughes warmly protested in a note to the Norwegian Minister at Washington,[11] at the same time forwarding him a draft in payment. He took the position that the tribunal had failed to apply uniformly the idea of due process of law, and against this the United States protested and denied any obligation hereafter to be bound. He also criticized the award as failing to give a satisfactory explanation of the manner in which the tribunal arrived at the amounts awarded, and not revealing the rates of interest allowed, or the period of time for which it was calculated, or amounts awarded as principal and as interest.

243. United States and the Netherlands.—By an agreement between the United States and the Netherlands dated January 3, 1925, there was referred to a single arbitrator from the Permanent Court of Arbitration at The Hague, the determination of the question whether or not the Island of Palmas or Miangas in its entirety formed part of terri-

[10] *American Journal of International Law,* 1923, 362.
[11] *Ibid.,* 1923, 287.

tory belonging to the United States or to the Netherlands.[12] The parties were at liberty to use the English or Netherlands language or the native language of the arbitrator. The award was to be accompanied by the statement of the grounds upon which it was based.

Reference was had to Dr. Max Huber of the Permanent Court of International Justice, who, on April 4, 1928, held that the island "forms in its entirety a part of Netherlands territory."[13]

[12] *American Journal of International Law,* 1925, Supplement, 108.
[13] *Ibid.,* XXII, 867.

CHAPTER XXVII

INTERNATIONAL COMMISSIONS OF INQUIRY

244. General observations.—The customary use of the term "International Commissions of Inquiry" seems to date from the first Hague Conference of 1899. Before this time the thing itself had but a rudimentary existence. Its nearest approximations were furnished by some territorial commissions and possibly arbitrations in special phases. It will be noted, however, that territorial commissions have usually had relation to a more or less fixed situation whereas commissions of inquiry concern themselves for the most part with the existence or character of a fact and it may be an examination into the law arising as a result of the fact. From another point of view the older commissions, in so far as they might be called commissions, determined some long antecedent state of affairs, whereas the modern commission relates itself to something of immediate and pressing importance.

A suggestion of a territorial commission of inquiry, by way of illustration, was contained in the proposed treaty between the United States and England dated January 11, 1897, and originally submitted by President Cleveland and afterward by President McKinley, but so amended as to lead to its abandonment. By its provisions[1] under Article 6 a controversy involving the determination of territorial claims was to be submitted to a tribunal of six members, three judges of the Supreme Court or Justices of Circuit Courts and three judges of the British Supreme Court of Judicature or members of the judicial committee of the Privy Council, whose award by a majority of not less than five should be final, and if of a lesser number could be final unless either power protested it as erroneous, in which case it was to have no validity.

It is worthy of at least passing remark that so many centuries of warlike disputes should have passed by before the statesmen of the world were able to discover that it was better to resort to a committee of investigation to uncover the grounds of conflict before rather than after their bloody disputes.[2]

245. The First Hague Conference.—The Russian draft with ref-

---

[1] *Arbitration and the United States*, 511.

[2] It is the contention of André Le Ray (*Les commissions internationales d'enquête au XX⁰ siècle*, 18) that, reviewing history, international commissions of inquiry were not created but only perfected at The Hague in 1899. His supposed precedents are not convincing, as near an approach as any being afforded by the Pacifico case between England and Greece in 1850.

erence to arbitration contained the outlines of a convention covering
International Courts of Inquiry, and we may note that Article 15 of the
Russian project was the foundation of Article 11, as finally adopted by
the Conference, and Article 16 of the same project became Article 12
of the Convention.

M. de Martens of Russia, who probably is entitled to more credit
than any other one man for the institution of International Commissions of Inquiry, in his speech before the Conference, pointed out that
such commissions afforded a safety-valve (*soupape de sûreté*) and that

the object of commissions of inquiry is the same as that of arbitration, good offices,
and mediation, namely: to point out all the means of appeasing conflicts arising
among nations and to prevent war.[3]

The proposition did not pass without some preliminary demur from
Roumania, Greece, and Servia, who were not contented until there
was inserted the qualifying clause "affecting neither honor nor vital
interests." It required in addition the assurance of M. Bourgeois that
if the members of the committee

had believed that the propositions which were adopted contained anything whatever in impairment of the sovereignty or the dignity of any Power, great or small,
they would not have received the vote of a single member.

The provisions of the First Hague Convention with reference to
the subject we are discussing are embraced in six articles. These commence by recommending that

in differences of an international nature involving neither honor nor vital interest,
and arising from a difference of opinion on points of fact, the signatory powers
recommend that the parties who have not been able to come to an agreement by
means of diplomacy should, as far as circumstances allow, institute an international
commission of inquiry, to facilitate a solution of these differences by elucidating
the facts by means of an impartial and conscientious investigation.

This provision has been criticized by Bokanowski[4] as being in the
first place merely a recommendation, and further because of the qualification with regard to honor and vital interests. These qualifications,
however, were necessary, as we have seen, in order to secure the
adoption of the provision in any shape. A further criticism is made
because of the use of the language, "as far as circumstances allow."
But doubtless this language is justified for the reason above given. As
we shall find, notwithstanding these criticisms, the proposition under
discussion has proved extremely useful.

[3] Holls, *The Peace Conference at The Hague*, 206.
[4] *Les commissions internationales d'enquête*, 46.

Further articles of the Convention provide the manner of its institution as being by a special agreement, specifying the facts, powers of commissioners, procedure, hearing of both sides, and also that the procedure to be observed, if not provided for especially, shall be fixed by the commission. The commissions are, unless otherwise stipulated, to be formed as are commissions of arbitration, and are to be supplied with all means and facilities necessary to arrive at a complete acquaintance with and correct understanding of the facts, although there is the apparently unnecessary qualification that the powers in dispute agree to supply these only "as fully as they may think possible." The commission's report is to be signed by all its members, but the report is limited to a statement of the facts and has not the character of an arbitral award. The powers in controversy have perfect freedom as to the effect to be given it.

Based upon experience in the Dogger Bank case, to be hereafter referred to, and in part upon greater thought given the matter, the Hague Conference of 1907 enlarged the half-dozen articles covering the subject into twenty-eight articles, going much into detail, particularly as to procedure, and giving greater powers to the commission not necessary now to be elaborated.

246. Later international commissions of inquiry.—The example given by the Hague Conference of 1899, and the practical application of the conference in the Dogger Bank case, increased the world interest in the general subject-matter. One of the first evidences of this was contained in the proposed treaties between the United States, on the one hand, and France and Great Britain, on the other. These treaties, which were negotiated during the summer of 1911, provided that the respective parties should institute as occasion arose, and as therein provided, a joint high commission of inquiry

to which, upon the request of either party, shall be referred for impartial and conscientious investigation any controversy between the parties within the scope of Article I [This article referred to differences not possible to adjust by diplomacy relating to international matters under a claim of right made by one against the other under treaty or otherwise and justiciable by reason of being susceptible of decision by the application of the principles of law or equity] before such controversy has been submitted to arbitration, and also any other controversy hereafter arising between them, even if they are not agreed that it falls within the scope of Article I.

This commission was to consist of three nationals on each side and was to be conducted as far as applicable and not inconsistent therewith according to the Hague Convention of 1907.

The treaty further provided that, in cases where the parties disagreed as to whether or not the difference was subject to arbitration thereunder, the question should be submitted to the joint high commission.

Such changes in the treaty were made by the Senate as led to its final failure.[5]

An interesting form of International Joint Commission is furnished by the treaty[6] between the United States and Great Britain of 1909. Under this treaty was created a body of six, three representing each side, to have jurisdiction over waterways between the two countries, and there were also referred to it for investigation and report differences involving rights, obligations, and interests of either in relation to the other and inhabitants of the other along the common frontier. This commission has operated with great success and unanimity.

The general subject-matter was taken up in a new form by Secretary of State William J. Bryan early in 1913. It will be noted that up to this time all propositions for commissions of inquiry contemplated their institution after difficulties arose. Mr. Bryan's proposition contemplated the formation of a commission in advance of the existence of any difficulties. To this commission, diplomacy failing, there were to be submitted for investigation and report all disputes between the respective countries. In a general way the plan adopted contemplated the choice of one member from each country by its government, one by each government from some third country, and the fifth to be chosen by common agreement. The international commission, however, had the right to act upon its own initiative, and in such case was to notify both governments and request their co-operation. The report of the international commission on any matter was to be completed within one year, unless the time was extended by mutual agreement by the parties. The parties to the treaty reserved the right to act independently as soon as the report of the commission should have been submitted, but were not to declare war or begin hostilities during investigation and report. Treaties of this description were entered into and ratifications exchanged with twenty-one countries. In seven other cases, although advised and consented to by the Senate, they were not ratified by the other party, and as to two nations the Senate has never acted upon the treaty.

The treaty with France[7] and that with Sweden[8] give to the commission, the first by consent of a majority, the second by the action of

---

[5] *Arbitration and the United States,* World Peace Foundation Pamphlets, Vol. IX, Nos. 6–7, 434.

[6] Malloy, *op. cit.,* 2607.   [7] *Ibid.,* 2587.   [8] *Ibid.,* 2855.

its president, the right to offer their services to the powers. Each gives the commission power to indicate as soon as possible what measures should be taken to preserve the rights of each party pending the delivery of the report of the commission. This, of course, would afford something in the nature of injunctive relief.

The idea of a commission of inquiry has received recognition in the Covenant of the League of Nations, Article 15 of which provides that any dispute likely to lead to a rupture which is not submitted to arbitration or settlement in accordance with Article 13 is to be submitted to the Council. This endeavors to effect a settlement of the dispute, and if successful a statement is made to the public in such terms as the Council deems appropriate. If not settled the Council publishes the facts of the dispute and its recommendations. The settlement of the dispute between Greece and Bulgaria, leading these nations rapidly to war, illustrates the workings of this section.

The treaty signed at Washington between the United States and the Central American Republics referred to above is to much the same effect[9] and provides for the appointment of commissions of inquiry to determine questions of fact relative to

failure to comply with the provisions of any of the treaties or conventions existing between them and which affect neither the sovereign and independent existence of any of the signatory republics, nor their honor or vital interests.

A further extension of the plan for International Commissions of Inquiry was given by what is known as the "Gondra Convention," which was adopted by the delegates to the Fifth Pan-American Conference held at Santiago[10] in 1923.

This provided that all controversies between two or more of the parties which it was impossible to settle through diplomatic channels or arbitration should be investigated by a commission composed of five members, all nationals of American States, each government appointing two, only one of whom should be a national of its own country and the fifth to be appointed by agreement and act as president. He could not, however, be a citizen of a nation represented on the commission. A right of challenge was given to the elected member, when a substitute could be appointed by mutual consent, or, failing that, be designated by the president of an uninterested American republic. Provisions were made for his selection in the event of further disagreement.

---

[9] *American Journal of International Law*, XVII, Supplement, 108.

[10] *Report of the Delegates of the United States of America*, Government Printing Office, 1924, 110.

The controversies so to be determined had to be submitted under the circumstances named whenever a government interested applied for the convocation of the commission. This application had to be made to one of two permanent commissions, established at Washington and at Montevideo, composed of the three American diplomatic agents longest accredited to those capitals, the government requesting the convocation at the same time appointing its representatives and the other party likewise as soon as notified.

The commission had power to establish its rules of procedure, but was recommended to follow a treaty signed in Washington in February 1923, between the United States and the Central American republics. The parties were obliged to furnish the antecedents and data necessary for the investigation, and the commission was to report within one year, with a possible extension of six months under agreement.

The findings of the commission were considered as reports upon the dispute, but without the value or force of judicial decisions or arbitral awards. After the report was submitted six months more time was allowed for renewed negotiations, and only upon their failure were the parties to enjoy entire liberty of action to proceed as their interests might dictate.

The treaty was to remain in force indefinitely, but subject to denunciation after a year's notice.

The treaty of which we speak has been ratified by Brazil, Chile, Cuba, Guatemala, Haiti, Panama, Paraguay, United States, Uruguay, and Venezuela, while Bolivia, Mexico, Peru, and Salvador have adhered to it, but not yet ratified it. The remaining countries have signed and will probably ratify in the near future.

The Locarno Peace Treaties between Germany on the one part and Belgium, France, Poland, and Czechoslovakia on the other provide for the formation of permanent conciliation commissions, a large part of whose duties rest in acting as Commissions of Inquiry although possessing the name indicated. These commissions are composed each of five members, one named by Germany and the others by the remaining parties, respectively, and three commissioners from among the nationals of third powers all of different nationalities, the president of the commission being appointed by mutual agreement of the governments. The commissioners are appointed for three years.

Article 2 of the several treaties provides that before resort to arbitration or the Permanent Court of International Justice the dispute may be referred to the commission with a view to amicable settlement. The commission commences to function through a request addressed to the president by the two parties in agreement or in the absence of such agreement by one or other of the parties. Provision is made for the several governments to replace their commissioners by persons possessing special competence.

The task of the commission is to elucidate questions in dispute, collect with that object all necessary information by means of inquiry or otherwise, and endeavor to bring about an agreement. After examining the case, it may inform the parties of the terms of settlement deemed suitable and lay down a period within which they are to make their decision. At the conclusion of its labors the commission draws up a report stating that an agreement has been effected, and if need be its terms, or that it has been impossible to effect a settlement.

As to inquiries, the commission acts in accordance with the provisions of the Hague Peace Convention of 1907 covering International Commissions of Inquiry.

The proceedings of the commission are not public except with the consent of the parties, and it is the duty of the governments to facilitate their labors with all relevant documents and assist in the summoning and hearing of witnesses and visiting localities in question. The parties before the commission are represented by agents and counsel.

The commissioners are paid equally by the two governments.

If no amicable agreement is reached before the commission, the dispute is submitted either to the Permanent Court of International Justice or to an arbitral tribunal.

All questions in difference as to which the governments have failed to reach an amicable solution, and the settlement of which cannot be obtained by a judicial decision, and for which no procedure has been laid down by other conventions, are submitted to the commission, which has to propose to the parties an acceptable solution, and in any case present a report.

It is noteworthy that the conciliation commission, or, if the latter has not been notified, the arbitral tribunal or the Permanent Court of International Justice, acting under Article 41 of its Statutes, shall lay down as speedily as possible any provisional measures to be adopted, and the duty of the Council is to insure that suitable provisional measures are taken. Meanwhile the two governments undertake to accept such measures, abstain from anything likely to have repercussion prejudicial to conclusions in any manner reached, and to abstain from any sort of aggravating action. In this way we have a sort of interlocutory injunction.

247. Cases referred to international commissions of inquiry.—
The first and most noted case of this description was that relating to
the firing of a man-of-war of the Russian squadron upon English
fishing boats in the North Sea, and generally known as the "Hull" or
"Dogger Bank" incident. On the morning of October 9, 1904, the
Russian admiral with his squadron, while passing a fleet of English
fishing vessels, believed his ship about to be attacked by a torpedo boat
and directed fire, with the result that some men were killed and
wounded, a boat sunk, and others injured. The Russian and English
Governments signed a protocol referring to a commission of inquiry
examination into the facts. This was composed of British, Russian,
French, and American naval officers, one representing each country,
and a fifth, who was an Austrian, chosen by the four. A protocol provided some of the details of procedure and adopted a number of rules
to control the commission.

The commission found the facts of the case, and the matter was
later adjusted by the payment of money by Russia to England covering
the loss and injury inflicted.[11]

Subsequent resorts to international commissions of inquiry occurred
with reference to the arrest of the *Tavignano* and the firing of shots
on the *Camouna* and *Gaulois,* French vessels, by Italian men-of-war.
By convention of May 20, 1912, the commission was instructed to
inquire as to the precise geographic locality where the arrest of the
first-named vessel was had, and also where to place the pursuit of the
others; to describe precisely the hydrography, configuration, and nature
of the coast and neighboring banks, distance between them of different
points which any commissioner thought it well to determine, and the
distance of the points to those where the events under examination took
place, and report the result of these investigations. Three commissioners
were named, one French, one Italian, and one English, the last as
president. French was the language and all proceedings were had under
provisions of the Hague Convention. The evidence included log books,
protests of officers, letters, and depositions. As a result of this examination, by agreement of May 2, 1913, Italy agreed to pay and France
to accept five thousand francs to indemnify individual losses.

The fourth and last commission under this provision of the Hague
Peace Convention was that investigating the loss of the Netherlands
steamer, *Tubantia.* The commission[12] under the terms of the convention

---

11 *Law and Procedure of International Tribunals,* 433.
12 *American Journal of International Law,* XVI, 485.

dated March 30, 1921, consisted of representatives of the navies of the Netherlands, Denmark, Sweden, and Germany, presided over by a former member of the Swiss Federal Council. After considering the pleadings and facts adduced, including the testimony of experts, it decided against Germany, and held that the *Tubantia* had been sunk March 16, 1916, by a torpedo discharged by a German submarine, leaving undecided the question whether this act was made knowingly or as the result of an error of the commandant of the submarine.

PART V

THE PERMANENT COURT OF INTERNATIONAL
JUSTICE

CHAPTER XXVIII

PERMANENT COURT OF INTERNATIONAL JUSTICE: ITS ORIGIN

248. Antecedent Steps.—In some ways the present Permanent Court of International Justice sums up the larger part of all prior work for peaceful international settlement. The best labor of writers, idealists, legislators, statesmen, students of international law, finds its present fruition, if not the fruit it will finally be, in this body. Its roots go back deep in the centuries. While it is the natural outcome of the gradual growth in civilization, and not to be attributed largely to the suggestion of any one man or set of men, even those immediately connected with its formation, it is interesting to note, as illustrating the recurrence of fundamental ideas, that the plan of an international tribunal was suggested[1] by the Frenchman Pierre Dubois in 1305. Nevertheless, we attach importance necessarily to the steps immediately antecedent to the formation. Then it is that the brain moves quicker and the pulse beats faster.

We have noted the fact that shortly before the conclusion of the World War the Scandinavian nations and Holland had busied themselves with preparation of schemes for world peace, including plans for a world court. The situation found recognition in an address by President Wilson at Mount Vernon on July 4, 1918, in which he called for the creation of a political organization which would assure use of the combined force of free nations to prevent aggression and guarantee peace and justice through a final and conclusive tribunal of opinion to which all would submit and which would sanction international agreements not obtainable amicably by the interested nation. The expression was vague, and it seems probable the President thought less of judicial methods than of other portions of the later League plan. This will become manifest in considering his drafts of a League.

The Phillimore Report of March 20, 1918, to the British Cabinet regarding the organization of a League of Nations[2] was submitted to President Wilson. This plan recognized arbitration as the most effective and equitable way of settling disputes as to treaty interpretation, questions of international law, or existence of any fact constituting breach of an international obligation, and of determining measures of

---

[1] Hudson, *The Permanent Court of International Justice*, 1.
[2] Ray Stannard Baker, *Woodrow Wilson and World Settlement*, III, 67.

reparation. If not so settled, application might be made to a conference of the allied States. Other suggestions finally forming in substance part of the Covenant of the League were made, but no provision was made for a court.

In July 1918 Colonel E. M. House, to whom the President had referred the British plan, returned it to the President with comments[3] and his own draft. His Article 10 provided for an international court of not more than fifteen members, with large powers.[4] The judges were to be chosen by the delegates of the contracting powers.

President Wilson's first draft of the Covenant[5] contemplated in its Article V reference to arbitration of all disputes of whatever nature not settled by diplomacy, and provided for the selection of a board of arbitrators. Its Article IX speaks of submission of a dispute to judicial decision or arbitration, but how judicial decision was to be secured was unexplained.

President Wilson's second draft of the Covenant distributed January 10, 1919, again speaks of arbitration,[6] with no provision for a court, but provides for an appeal from a board of arbitrators to the Body of Delegates of the contracting powers, three-fourths of whom could set aside the arbitral decision if unanimous, and two-thirds if not unanimous. If arbitration proved impracticable, the Executive Council could take the matter under consideration. Again (Article IX) reference was made to "judicial decision," but none was provided.

President Wilson's third draft[7] closely followed the second in the respects of which we speak. This was not completed to his satisfaction, and he accepted the subsequent Hurst-Miller draft for discussion. The plan of General Jan Smuts[8] submitted December 16, 1918, contemplated arbitration generally for international disputes and, when impracticable, application to the Council.

There was submitted to the President on January 20, 1919, by Lord Cecil, a British draft Covenant.[9] This contemplated reference, pending creation of a permanent court of international justice, to a court agreed on by the parties or stipulated in a convention between them, and if the dispute were not so submitted it should be open to either to demand reference to the League. This had power to submit the dispute to a court, but its action had no effect unless confirmed by the Conference or Council.

3 Baker, *op. cit.*, III, 79.   4 *Ibid.*, III, 83.
5 *Ibid.*, III, 88.   6 *Ibid.*, III, 100.   7 *Ibid.*, III, 117.
8 *Ibid.*, III, 94.   9 Baker, *op. cit.*, III, 130.

At the first meeting of the League of Nations Commission on February 3, 1919, there was submitted to it an official French plan.[10] This contemplated the organization of an international tribunal to which, when amicable settlement proved impossible, matters should be referred, if the question at issue was open to a legal decision. In case of violation of law the court had to order necessary reparation and was provided with sanctions. In fact a large part of the plan was devoted to an elaboration of sanctions.

The working draft of the League of Nations Covenant used as a basis of discussion before the League of Nations Commission and introduced in it on February 3, 1919, was prepared by Sir C. J. B. Hurst of England and David Hunter Miller of the United States.[11] This forbade resort to armed force in the event of dispute without submitting the questions and matters at issue, either to arbitration, or to inquiry by the Executive Council, and until three months after award at arbitration or recommendation by the Executive Council. The Council was charged with the duty of formulating plans for the establishment of a Permanent Court of International Justice to hear and determine any matter which the parties might recognize as suitable for "arbitration" (making no distinction between it and judicial settlement).

The result of these preliminary essays—plus the final labors of the representatives of the Allied Powers—was the Covenant of the League of Nations as finally signed. The material articles of the Covenant so far as we are concerned are 13 and 14, reading as follows:

ARTICLE 13.—The Members of the League agree that whenever any dispute shall arise between them which they recognize to be suitable for submission to arbitration and which cannot be satisfactorily settled by diplomacy, they will submit the whole subject-matter to arbitration.

Disputes as to the interpretation of a treaty, as to any question of international law, as to the existence of any fact which if established would constitute a breach of any international obligation, or as to the extent and nature of the reparation to be made for any such breach, are declared to be among those which are generally suitable for submission to arbitration.

For the consideration of any such dispute the court of arbitration to which the case is referred shall be the court agreed on by the parties to the dispute or stipulated in any convention existing between them.

The Members of the League agree that they will carry out in full good faith

10 *Ibid.*, III, 152.
11 *Ibid.*, III, 144.

any award that may be rendered, and that they will not resort to war against a Member of the League which complies therewith. In the event of any failure to carry out such an award, the Council shall propose what steps should be taken to give effect thereto.

ARTICLE 14.—The Council shall formulate and submit to the Members of the League for adoption plans for the establishment of a Permanent Court of International Justice. The Court shall be competent to hear and determine any dispute of an international character which the parties thereto submit to it. The Court may also give an advisory opinion upon any dispute or question referred to it by the Council or by the Assembly.

Article 15 relates to disputes likely to lead to a rupture and not submitted to arbitration, and which the members of the League agree to submit to the Council.

249. Statute of the Court.—It will be noted that by Article 14 it was the duty of the Council of the League to submit to the Members for adoption plans for the establishment of a Permanent Court of International Justice. The Council meeting at London on February 12, 1920, adopted the plan of appointing an Advisory Committee of Jurists to prepare the scheme, and in a preliminary way made a list of persons to serve on the Committee, most of whom afterward served.[12]

The list named includes five representatives of the great and five of the smaller powers. Their labors began at The Hague on June 16, and ended July 24, 1920.

The most difficult question to decide was that of the manner of selection of judges. The Hague Peace Conference of 1907 had proved unequal to the task of answering it in preparing its draft of a Permanent Court and solution was now difficult. However, as Dr. James Brown Scott says:

[12] M. M. Mineichiro Adatci, Envoy Extraordinary and Minister Plenipotentiary of Japan at Brussels; Rafael Altamira, Senator and Professor of Law at the University of Madrid; Clovis Bevilaqua, legal adviser to the Ministry of Foreign Affairs of Brazil, represented at first by Raoul Fernandes, former Brazilian delegate to the Paris Conference, who later was appointed a member of the Committee because M. Bevilaqua was unable to be present; Baron Descamps, Senator and Belgian Minister of State; Francis Hagerup, Envoy Extraordinary and Minister Plenipotentiary of Norway at Stockholm; Albert de Lapradelle, Professor of Law at the University of Paris; Dr. Loder, member of the Supreme Court of the Netherlands; Lord Phillimore, member of the Privy Council of England; Arturo Ricci-Busatti, Minister Plenipotentiary of Italy and legal adviser to the Ministry of Foreign Affairs of Italy; Elihu Root, former Secretary of State of the United States of America. Dr. James Brown Scott was present at the meetings of the Committee as legal adviser to Mr. Root. The Secretary General of the League of Nations appointed Commander Anzilotti, Under-Secretary General of the League, as Secretary General of the Committee, with M. Ake Hammarskjöld, Secretary of Legation and a member of the Permanent Secretariat of the League, to replace him when he could not be present.

Mr. Root took a leaf out of Madison's Debates in the Federal Convention of 1787, supplemented by his experience as Senator from the State of New York; and the Permanent Court of International Justice was made. He proposed the election of the judges by the separate and concurrent action of the Assembly (where the smaller states predominate in numbers if not in influence) and the Council (where the larger states predominate both in numbers and in influence), and a conference committee of three from both to propose a compromise acceptable to the Assembly and the Council when they happen to differ as they did on the first election of the judges in 1921.[13]

This great question being settled, the remaining numerous points to be resolved offered little difficulty, and the Statute as formulated by the Committee of Jurists was submitted to the League.[14]

When the Draft was presented to the League sundry more or less important changes were made in it. For instance, three paragraphs giving a large jurisdiction over advisory opinions was stricken out, as well as one allowing cases to be brought by any complaining party when it had been impossible to settle a dispute by diplomatic means and no agreement had been made to choose another jurisdiction. In their place the League went back to the Covenant and provided that "The jurisdiction of the Court is defined by Articles 12, 13, and 14 of the Covenant." The Draft-Scheme had provided that "the official language of the Court shall be French," but the Statute as finally adopted included English also as official and allowed parties to select either, and if both were used the Court determined which was authoritative. At the request of the parties, the Court could authorize another language.

The League also gave the parties power to agree that the Court should decide a case *ex aequo et bono*.

Other changes of relatively minor importance were made.

On December 16, 1920, the Protocol containing the Statute was ready for signature. When the next Assembly met, twenty-eight States having deposited their ratifications, the Statute went into effect. From the fourteenth to the eighteenth of September, 1921, the Council and Assembly elected the judges of the first World Court, who were chosen under the procedure devised by Mr. Root. On February 15, 1922, the Court was installed and inaugurated at The Hague.

[13] Scott, *Sovereign States and Suits*, 223.

[14] For the Draft-Scheme for the Institution of the Permanent Court of International Justice as presented by the Advisory Committee of Jurists, see Scott, *Sovereign States and Suits*, 310.

CHAPTER XXIX

JURISDICTION OF THE PERMANENT COURT OF INTERNATIONAL JUSTICE

250. Foundations of jurisdiction.—The provision for the formation of a court and the jurisdiction to be entertained by it is to be found in Article 14 of the Covenant of the League of Nations, which reads as follows:

> The Council shall formulate and submit to the Members of the League for adoption plans for the establishment of a Permanent Court of International Justice. The Court shall be competent to hear and determine any dispute of an international character which the parties thereto submit to it. The Court may also give an advisory opinion upon any dispute or question referred to it by the Council or by the Assembly.

Before reaching this point the Covenant had already provided for the reference to arbitration or to inquiry by the Council of any matter likely to lead to rupture, and that whenever any dispute should arise between the members of the League which they recognized to be suitable for submission to arbitration and which could not be satisfactorily settled by diplomacy they would submit the whole subject-matter to arbitration. By declaration of a general character the Covenant said (Article 13) that

> disputes as to the interpretation of a treaty, as to any question of international law, as to the existence of any fact which if established would constitute a breach of any international obligation, or as to the extent and nature of the reparation to be made for any such breach, are declared to be among those which are generally suitable for submission to arbitration.

It will be readily recognized that the matters just indicated are quite as susceptible of being referred to a court of justice as to arbitration and this we shall later find was the view entertained by the League when its members very generally subscribed to the Statute formally creating the Court.

It will be noted that by Article 14 of the Covenant, the duty of formulating and submitting to the members of the League plans for the establishment of a Permanent Court of International Justice rested upon the Council. Pursuant to this obligation the Council asked a commission of ten eminent lawyers to prepare the form of the Statute—virtually the constitution—for a new international court.

We have already sufficiently discussed the steps taken from a historical point of view, and have now only to repeat that a Statute was formed pursuant to the action of the Assembly based upon the report of the ten jurists referred to, which with modifications speedily became effective. By this Statute the broad general jurisdiction of the Court extended to all cases which the parties might refer to it and all matters specially provided for in treaties and conventions in force.

Article 36 of the Statute further provides that

the Members of the League of Nations and the States mentioned in the Annex to the Covenant may, either when signing or ratifying the protocol to which the present Statute is adjoined, or at a later moment, declare that they recognize as compulsory, *ipso facto* and without special agreement in relation to any other Member or State accepting the same obligation, the jurisdiction of the Court in all or any of the classes of legal disputes concerning:

a) The interpretation of a Treaty.

b) Any question of International Law.

c) The ascertainment of any fact which, if established, would constitute a breach of an international obligation.

d) The nature or extent of the reparation to be made for the breach of an international obligation.

The declaration referred to above may be made unconditionally or on condition of reciprocity on the part of several or certain Members or States, or for a certain time.

In the event of a dispute as to whether the Court has jurisdiction, the matter shall be settled by the decision of the Court.

It will be noted that the Covenant does not undertake to describe the nature of the disputes suitable for settlement by arbitration except in the most general terms, referring this question apparently to members of the League and to their recognition of the fact or as each individual case shall arise. The only limitation upon this is contained in Article 13 and this is expanded and in a degree defined in Article 36 of the Statute. Although the jurisdiction is stated in such general terms and may be a sort of tacit limitation as to whether the dispute in question is as the Statute says one of a class of "legal disputes," it will be noted that not every class of legal dispute is to go to the court for decision but only those relating to the clauses (*a*), (*b*), (*c*), (*d*). True it is that it would be rather difficult to discover any kind of legal dispute not coming under one of these heads, but no all-inclusive language is used.

A suggestion is made by Señor Bustamante that the word "legal" finds its French equivalent in the word "*juridique*" and that

the intention in using this phrase was to refer to judicial or justiciable questions rather than to juridical problems; the framers of the Statute characterized these legal questions by the fact that it would be possible to arrive at a solution for them by applying principles of law.[1]

It is practicably impossible to define the word "legal" so that without doubt in all imaginable cases there may exist no difficulty about classifying them. It would seem, however, that as good a touchstone as any may be found in the nature of the remedy sought to be obtained. Thus we can understand that if an amount in damages be required and the complaint is of such nature as to be a subject of resolution by an award of damages, the dispute is juridical or legal, as you will. If the treaty is to be interpreted and directions are to be given for its enforcement, the same remark holds good. When, however, it is desired that a defendant nation be required to apologize for an assumed insult or fire a salute of guns, we have no difficulty in saying that the dispute complained of, tested by the relief sought, is not legal in its nature. One might well be tempted to add that, incapable of admeasurement in a court, it is not properly a ground of complaint to be settled legally or by means of war.

Referring again to Section 36 of the Statute we find that within the scope of the jurisdiction of the Court fixed by it, this jurisdiction may be recognized "as compulsory, *ipso facto* and without special agreement, in relation to any other Member or State accepting the same obligation."

Pursuant to this provision a large number of the states signing the protocol have accepted this as compulsory, sometimes for a limited period of years ranging from five to ten years, and usually on condition of reciprocity. In those cases where the acceptance has not been absolute, nevertheless an appeal may be made to the Court under special agreements.

Before leaving this subject we call particular attention to the concluding sentence of Article 36: "In the event of a dispute as to whether the Court has jurisdiction, the matter shall be settled by the decision of the Court." We may imagine a case where two nations on equal conditions of reciprocity have agreed to refer their disputes under Section 36, but where, nevertheless, although this obligation was compulsory, one of the states denies that the dispute is of a nature capable of reference. This question becomes jurisdictional immediately and as such is passed upon by the Court.

It will be noted that as bearing upon the decision of the Court and in a certain sense as affecting its jurisdiction, under Article 38 of the Statute,

[1] *The World Court*, 204.

"The Court shall apply

"1. International conventions, whether general or particular, establishing rules expressly recognized by the contesting States;

"2. International custom, as evidence of a general practice accepted as law;

"3. The general principles of law recognized by civilized nations;

"4. Subject to the provisions of Article 59 [limiting the binding force of the decision of the court to the parties and in respect of that particular case], judicial decisions and the teachings of the most highly qualified publicists of the various nations, as subsidiary means for the determination of rules of law."

This provision, however, does not prejudice the power of the Court "to decide a case *ex aequo et bono* if the parties agree thereto."

The exact meaning of the expression *ex aequo et bono* has yet to be determined by the Court.

251. Parties before the Court.—The parties before the Court are in all events nations. It is not possible for the citizens of one country to invoke the aid of the Court as against the government of another country. This was permissible before the Central American Court of Justice if an international question were involved, and did not work well. However, indirectly the wrongs of private individuals receive the attention of the Court when their interests have once taken on a diplomatic character and the foreign office of their government seeks reparation from the opposing government. Thus in the case of Mavrommatis the Court said:

It is true that the dispute was at first between a private person and a State— i.e., between M. Mavrommatis and Great Britain. Subsequently the Greek Government took up the case. The dispute then entered upon a new phase; it entered the domain of international law and became a dispute between two states. Henceforward, therefore, it is a dispute which may or may not fall under the jurisdiction of the Permanent Court of International Justice.

The nations which are recognized as having a right to any relief indicated by the League of Nations are by Article 1 of the Covenant the original members of the League and also such of other states named in the Annex as accept without reservation the Covenant. In addition any fully self-governing state, dominion, or colony not named in the Annex may become a member of the League if its admission is agreed to by two-thirds of the Assembly. Furthermore, by Article 17 of the Covenant, in the event of a dispute between a member of the League and a state not a member or between states not members of the League, the state or states of such description shall be invited to accept the obligations of membership in the League for the purposes of such dispute under such conditions as the Council may deem just.

We may add to the foregoing paragraph that, by resolution of the Council of May 17, 1922, the Court is open to any nation not a member of the League or named in the Annex to the Covenant which deposits an acceptance of its jurisdiction with the Registrar in accordance with the Covenant and Statute and Rules of the Court. This may be either general (accepting jurisdiction of all or particular classes of disputes) or particular (as to a particular dispute which has already risen).

252. Sanctions.—The decisions of the Permanent Court are not without a sanction, for, while Article 13 of the Covenant provides that the members of the League, finding a dispute suitable for submission to arbitration or judicial settlement and that it cannot be satisfactorily settled by diplomacy, will submit the whole subject-matter to arbitration or judicial settlement, the members of the League by the same Article "agree that they will carry out in full good faith any award or decision that may be rendered, and that they will not resort to war against a Member of the League which complies therewith. In the event of any failure to carry out such an award, the Council shall propose what steps should be taken to give effect thereto."

The language of the section referred to was doubtless with intention left vague, and the extent to which sanctions may be carried is undetermined. It remains the fact that the great and ever working sanction for the decisions of the Permanent Court of International Justice lies in their appeal to the public opinion of the world.

CHAPTER XXX

WORKINGS OF THE PERMANENT COURT OF INTERNATIONAL JUSTICE

253. Inception of the Court.—We have followed the development of the theory of international tribunals to the last great step which has been taken so far in the world. In another portion of this work we describe the history of international tribunals to their present state of development. In the consideration of the theory we have found it necessary to anticipate at many points the principles of the Permanent Court of International Justice. It now becomes necessary to give a more complete exposition of its workings.

The controlling law relating to the formation and operation of the Court is contained in its Statute, formed pursuant to Article 14 of the Covenant of the League of Nations, which forms a protocol signed separately by the nations adhering to it. It is, therefore, not a part of the League of Nations, although functioning as a judicial body parallel with the League, and although its expenses are provided for by the League. It has authority to render advisory opinions, as we shall see, at the request of the Council or Assembly of the League. It was for reasons above indicated that not the League but representatives of the nations signing the protocol for its establishment determined whether and how far it was possible to accept the signature of the United States to the Protocol.

254. Selection of judges.—The first point to arrest our attention is the matter of the selection of the judges. Having already given sufficient attention to the history by which the result was reached, we find by the Statute that it was not the intention of its framers to displace the Conventions of The Hague of 1899 and 1907 or to render unnecessary special tribunals of arbitration, "to which states are always at liberty to submit their disputes for settlement," but to create

a body of independent judges, elected regardless of their nationality from among persons of high moral character, who possess the qualifications required in their respective countries for appointment to the highest judicial office, or are jurisconsults of recognized competence in international law.

The qualifications mentioned are varied in the different countries, and, as we shall see, however nominated, the final say as to their qualifications rests with the Council and Assembly of the League. Certain precautions, however, which have only the strength of recommendations, are indulged in. Each national group making the nomination is recommended "to consult its Highest Court of Justice, its Legal Faculties and Schools of Law, and its National Academies and national sections of International Academies devoted to the study of Law." The nominations for judgeships are made, subject to the foregoing provisions, by the national groups in The Hague Court of Arbitration. These groups by the provisions of The Hague Conventions may not exceed four in number, and each such group is allowed to nominate not more than two of their own nationals nor more than two of other nationalities, and in no case may name more than double the number of seats to be filled. If there be any member of the League of Nations not represented in the Permanent Court of Arbitration of The Hague, national groups may be appointed by the governments to draw up lists of candidates.

The Court itself consists at the present time of fifteen members, eleven being full judges and four deputy judges, although this number may be hereafter increased by the Assembly upon the proposal of the Council to a total of fifteen judges and six deputy judges.

At least three months before the date of any election, the Secretary General of the League of Nations invites members of the Court of Arbitration belonging to the states mentioned in the Annex to the Covenant or of the states which join the League subsequently, and of the governmentally selected persons already spoken of, to nominate within a given time by national groups persons in a position to accept the duties of a member of the Court.

The names of the nominees so provided for are submitted to both the Council (in which the larger nations have greater influence) and to the Assembly (in which the smaller nations are in the majority). These two bodies acting separately and simultaneously proceed to vote upon the nominations brought before them. If they unite in the selection of one or more men, dependent upon the number of judges to be elected or vacancies filled, those receiving the majority are elected, the judges first and then the deputy judges.

Not more than one national shall be selected from the same member of the League, and if more are selected by the votes of the Assembly and Council the eldest only shall be considered as chosen.

If seats remain to be filled by such joint action after the first election, a second or a third meeting may take place, and if after the third meeting one or more seats still remain unfilled, a joint conference is provided for between six members, three appointed by the Assembly and three by the Council, for the purpose of choosing one name for each seat still vacant, and this is submitted to the Assembly and Council for their respective acceptance. If the conference unanimously agrees upon any person to fill the required position he may be included in its list even though not included in the list of nominations. If a joint conference is satisfied that it will not be successful in procuring an election, the already chosen members of the Court shall within a period fixed by the Council proceed to fill the vacant seats from among the candidates who have obtained votes either in the Assembly or in the Council, and in the event of an equality of votes among the judges the eldest judge shall have the casting vote.

Again the Statute makes certain recommendations to the electors, who are asked to bear in mind that

not only should all the persons appointed as members of the Court possess the qualifications required, but the whole body also should represent the main forms of civilization and the principal legal systems of the world.

It is not to be believed, however, that a failure on the part of the electors to follow strictly the recommendations would in anywise affect the validity of the election.

It is notable that under such provisions John Bassett Moore of the United States, a country outside the League and outside the protocol, was chosen as one of the judges, and, on his resignation, Judge Charles E. Hughes was chosen as his successor.

The members of the court are elected for nine years and may be re-elected, continuing, however, to discharge their duties until their places have been filled, and although replaced shall finish any case on which they may have begun.

Vacancies are filled in the manner indicated, but a judge so elected holds the appointment only for the remainder of his predecessor's term.

Deputy judges may be called upon to fill any vacancies reducing the number of judges below eleven, the list of deputy judges to be so called upon to be prepared by the Court with regard first to priority of election and second to age.

255. Restrictions upon judges.—The ordinary members of the Court may not exercise any political or administrative function. This provision is not applied to deputy judges except when performing their duties on the Court, and any doubt on this point is settled by the decision of the Court.

No member of the Court can act as agent, counsel, or advocate in any case of an international nature, although this provision only applies to deputy judges as regarding cases in which they are called upon to exercise their functions on the Court. Nor may any member participate in the decision of any case in which he has previously taken an active part as agent, counsel, or advocate for one of the contesting parties or as a member of a national or international court or a commission of inquiry or in any other capacity, while any doubt on this point is settled by the decision of the Court. These provisions limiting the power of judges to act before the Court were undoubtedly provoked by occurrences before the Hague Court of Arbitration, where members of the court on several occasions undertook to act for a contestant. It is, of course, to be borne in mind that agents or counsel when so acting did not violate any obligation as judges, although undoubtedly the nations employing them believed that their prestige would be of assistance before the tribunal.

256. Privileges and disabilities of judges.—Once appointed, no power of removal exists in either Council or Assembly. A member can be dismissed only when in the unanimous opinion of the other members he has ceased to fulfill the required conditions. This language seems ambiguous, but will probably be practically interpreted to mean that any person violating the provisions of his oath of office would be held by his associates to have failed to meet the necessary conditions.

The judges enjoy political privileges and immunities, and are paid annually an amount determined by the Assembly of the League on the proposal of the Council, and this amount may not be diminished during the period of appointment. On retiring they receive pensions.

257. Oath of judges.—A judge on entering upon his duties makes a solemn declaration under the rules and pursuant to the Statute that he will exercise all his "powers and duties as a judge honorably and faithfully, impartially and conscientiously." It is made the duty of the Court to elect a President and a Vice-President for three years, and these may be re-elected.

258. Disqualification of judges.—There is no provision for the direct challenge of any member of the court, but nevertheless Article 24 of the Statute provides that

if, for some special reason, a member of the Court considers that he should not take part in the decision of a particular case, he shall so inform the President. If the President considers that for some special reason one of the members of the Court should not sit in a particular case, he shall give him notice accordingly. If in any such case the member of the Court and the President disagree the matter shall be settled by the decision of the Court.

259. Quorum of Court.—The Statute contemplates that the full Court shall sit, but if eleven judges are not available even after there has been a call upon deputy judges, a quorum of nine judges shall suffice to constitute the Court. None of the nine, however, shall be a national of one of the countries in dispute, who may be called in under the following circumstances. While judges of the nationality of each contesting party retain their right to sit in a case before the Court, yet

if the Court includes upon the Bench a judge of the nationality of one of the parties only, the other party may select from among the deputy judges a judge of its nationality, if there be one. If there should not be one, the party may choose a judge, preferably from among those persons who have been nominated as candidates as provided [elsewhere in the statute]. If the Court includes upon the Bench no judge of the nationality of the contesting parties, each of these may proceed to select or choose a judge as [above provided for]. Should there be several parties in the same interest, they shall, for the purpose of the preceding provisions, be reckoned as one party only. Any doubt upon this point is settled by the decision of the Court.

260. National representation by judges.—These provisions with regard to the representation of nationals upon the Court indicate that procedure in the highest court of the world has not yet reached the point of perfection. It still retains some of the defects which have disfigured many arbitral proceedings. These defects are somewhat attenuated, however, by the fact that while in the case of arbitration the opposing nations have been represented by a single judge on each hand and there has been an umpire or at the most, as in the case of the Geneva Tribunal, three representatives of disinterested powers, in the Court of International Justice there are likely to be ten in no wise concerned in the merits of the controversy, as against two judges probably pulling in different directions.

It has happened that several of the nations in the history of this Court have deemed it necessary to be represented by their nationals. These nations have included Germany, Poland, and Greece, and, on an advisory question, Roumania. The nominees of the countries named have run true to form in standing out for the positions of their particular nations, following innumerable arbitral precedents. To the contrary, permanent judges have had enough independence of character to disregard their nations' contentions.

In this respect the World Court has fallen short, except as indicated, of the judicial position of the United States Supreme Court. This is evident when we consider that when Illinois and Missouri or Kansas and Colorado have found it necessary to bring their differences before the Supreme Court of the United States, no state has ever been in any wise concerned as to whether or not it found one of its own citizens on the bench.

261. Initiation of proceedings before the Court.—Under Article 40 of the Statute, cases are brought before the Court either by notification of a special agreement or by written application addressed to the Registrar. "In either case the subject of the dispute and the contesting parties must be indicated." This application is forthwith communicated by the Registrar to all concerned, who shall also notify the members of the League of Nations through the Secretary-General. The Court has the power to indicate (Article 41), if it considers that circumstances so require, any provisional measures which ought to be taken to preserve the respective rights of either party; and, pending the final decision, notice of the measures suggested shall forthwith be given to the parties and the Council.

262. Agents and counsel.—Agents represent the parties before the Court and may be assisted by counsel or advocates.

263. Written procedure.—This consists of the communication to the judges and parties of cases, counter-cases, and, if necessary, replies, and papers and documents in support. The rules fix the nature of the documents to be submitted, and, as we have before stated, what cases and counter-cases shall contain.

264. Language of Court.—The official languages of the Court are French and English. If the parties agree the case shall be conducted in French, the judgment shall be delivered accordingly, the same rule prevailing as to English. In the absence of an agreement each party uses the language it prefers, the decision to be in French and English and the Court at the same time determining which shall be considered as authoritative.

265. Oral proceedings.—The rules determine the manner in which the oral proceeding shall take place, subject to the control of the Court in each particular case. At the opening of the oral proceedings each party informs the Court and the other parties of the evidence to be produced, with data as to witnesses to be heard. The Court may, however, call for the production of any other evidence on points of fact in regard to which the parties are not in agreement. Other provisions with regard to taking testimony need not now be elaborated. All decisions are made by a majority of the judges present at the hearing, and in the event of equality of votes, the President or his deputy shall give the casting vote.

266. The judgment.—By the rules the judgment contains

1. The date on which it is pronounced; 2. The names of the judges participating; 3. The names and style of the parties; 4. The names of the agents of the parties; 5. The conclusions of the parties; 6. The matters of fact; 7. The reasons in point of law; 8. The operative provisions of the judgment; 9. The decision, if any, referred to in Article 64 of the Statute; 10. The number of the judges constituting the majority contemplated in Article 55 of the Statute.

The article mentioned has reference to the question of costs and provides that "unless otherwise decided by the Court, each party shall bear its own costs."

The Statute and rules, wisely as we think, give to dissenting judges the power to deliver a separate opinion if they so desire, or simply state their dissent.

Ample provisions of the rules (Appendix D) cover applications for the re-hearing, revision, and construing of judgments.

CHAPTER XXXI

SPECIAL TRIBUNALS OF THE PERMANENT COURT OF INTERNATIONAL JUSTICE

267. Labor cases.—An important special jurisdiction of the Court relates to control over cases originating under the labor provisions of the Treaty of Versailles in Part XIII. This subject is covered by Article 26 of the Statute providing that the Court shall appoint every three years a special chamber of five judges having the diverse qualifications required for membership in the Court itself. Two supplementary or deputy judges may also be selected for the purpose of replacing a judge who finds it impossible to sit. The judges are assisted by four technical assessors sitting with them but without the right to vote and selected with a view of insuring a just representation of all competing interests. If there is a national of one only of the parties sitting as a judge in the special chamber referred to above, the President will invite one of the other judges to retire in favor of the judge chosen by the other party, which selects from among deputy judges a judge of its own nationality if there be one, and if not it may choose one preferably from among the persons nominated as candidates for the judgeship.

The technical assessors are chosen for each particular case in accordance with rules of procedure laid down by the Court. These are drawn from a list of persons, two nominated by each member of the League and an equivalent number nominated by the governing body of the Labor Office, which latter names as to one-half of the whole body representatives of the workers and as to one-half representatives of employers from the list referred to in Article 412 of the Treaty of Versailles and corresponding articles of the other treaties of peace. The International Labor Office is at liberty to furnish the Court with all relevant information and for this purpose the Director is to receive copies of all written proceedings.

268. Transit and communication cases.—Cases referring to transit and communications particularly mentioned in Part XII of the Treaty of Versailles and the corresponding parts of other peace treaties are referred to a special chamber of five judges appointed every three years and as far as possible meeting diverse requirements of candidates for judgeships of the Court. As in the case of labor questions two judges are selected to replace one who finds it impossible to sit. If the parties so demand, the Court will sit as a full bench, and, when desired by

316

the parties, the judges will be assisted by four technical assessors sitting with them without the right to vote. As in other cases if there be a national of one only of the parties sitting as a judge in the chamber above referred to, the President will invite one of the other judges to retire in favor of a judge chosen by the other party in accordance with the practice we have outlined.

The technical assessors in each case are selected in accordance with rules of procedure under Article 30 from a list of "Assessors for Transit and Communication cases" composed of two persons nominated by each member of the League of Nations.

In connection with the special jurisdictions of which we have spoken, the rules (Articles 14, 15, and 16) are to be considered, and by their provisions the members of the chambers are appointed at a meeting of the full Court by a majority of votes, and the substitutes in the same manner. The election takes place at the end of the ordinary session of the Court, and the period of appointment commences January 1 of the following year, except that after a new election the election takes place at the beginning of the following session. The presidents of the chambers are appointed at the sitting of the full Court although the President of the Court shall *ex officio* preside over any chamber of which he may be elected a member and similarly the Vice-President, provided the President is not also a member.

The special chambers above described may not sit with more than five judges, and the composition of the chamber for summary procedure may not be altered except by the replacement of a member who may be unable to sit.

As stated by Article 29 of the Statute the Court shall form annually to secure the speedy dispatch of business a chamber composed of three judges who at the request of the contesting parties may hear and determine cases by summary procedure. When such a case arises and the documents instituting proceedings in a case which by virtue of an agreement between the parties is to be dealt with by summary procedure, are received by the Registrar, the President convenes as soon as possible the chamber of which we have been speaking. Before it the proceedings are opened by the presentation of a case by each party, the cases then being communicated by the Registrar to the members of the Court and to the opposing party. These cases contain reference to all evidence the parties may desire to produce, and, if inadequate, the chamber may, in the absence of a contrary agreement between the parties, institute oral proceedings and fix a date for their commencement. At the hearing the chamber will call upon the parties to supply oral explanations and may sanction the production of any evidence mentioned in the cases. It may also hear experts or witnesses whose names are mentioned in the case. The judgment of the chamber is the judgment of the Court and is read at a public sitting.

269. The Registrar of the Court.—The Statute provides for the appointment of a Registrar, who is chosen for a term of seven years, commencing on January 1 of the year following that in which the election takes place. He may be re-elected. His office is at the Peace Palace at The Hague, and he is required to live within ten kilometers of it.

It is the duty of the Registrar to take care of the archives, to receive and transmit all documents required to be filed with or forwarded by him, to attend the Court and be the channel of all communications to and from it, and to draft the minutes of all meetings.

CHAPTER XXXII

DECISIONS OF THE PERMANENT COURT OF INTERNATIONAL JUSTICE

270. General observations.—In reviewing the various judgments of the Permanent Court of International Justice, we shall for the sake of brevity rely largely upon the summaries prepared by Professor Manley O. Hudson and contained in the *World Peace Foundation Pamphlets,* Vol. IX, No. 2, (1926); *The American Bar Association Journal,* Vol. XII, No. 1 (1926), p. 34, and Vol. XIV, No. 3 (1928), p. 163, coupled with references to the text of the opinions themselves.

271. Steamship *Wimbledon*.—The decision (No. 1) in this case may be summarized as follows:

> Article 380 of the Treaty of Versailles of June 28, 1919, forbids Germany's applying to the Kiel Canal a neutrality order which would close the canal to a British vessel under French charter carrying munitions to Danzig for transshipment to Poland during a war between Poland and Russia.

This case was inaugurated upon the application of the governments of Great Britain, France, Italy, and Japan because the German authorities had refused to allow the British steamship, *Wimbledon,* chartered by a French company, free access to the Kiel Canal, for the reason that it was bound for Danzig with military supplies destined for the Polish Government while a state of war existed between Poland and Russia, and the German regulations with regard to neutrality prohibited the transit of war material through German territory to these countries. Poland asked leave to intervene on the ground that the refusal constituted a violation of the rights and material advantages guaranteed to Poland by the Versailles Treaty. Poland did not ask for any special damages, and the court found it unnecessary to consider whether its intervention was justified by an interest of a legal nature. Holding, however, that the interpretation of certain clauses of the Treaty of Versailles was involved and that the Polish Republic was one of the parties to the Treaty, the Court accepted the intervention.

The Court held that the canal had ceased to be an internal and national navigable waterway and had become international, subject only to the condition that the vessels passing through it must belong to nations at peace with Germany. The Court drew a distinction between this canal and the other internal navigable waterways of the German Empire. It further held that a restrictive interpretation maintaining rights of sovereignty would be contrary to the terms of the treaty, destroying what had been clearly granted.

The Court therefore concluded that Germany had wrongfully refused passage to the *Wimbledon* and was responsible for the loss occasioned thereby. Judgment was given against Germany for 149,749.35 francs with interest, payment to be made within three months.

Dissenting opinions were filed by three of the judges, including the special German judge upon the Court.

272. Mavrommatis Palestine concession.—This may be summarized as follows (Judgment No. 2):

Under the Mandate for Palestine, the Court has jurisdiction of a case brought by Greece against Great Britain notwithstanding the latter's objection.

This case, which subsequently appeared again before the Court, was first decided on a jurisdictional question.

The dispute first arose between a Greek citizen and Great Britain. The Greek Government subsequently taking up the case, the Court held that it thereupon assumed a new phase and entered the domain of international law, becoming a dispute between two states; that once a state presented a case on behalf of one of its subjects before an international tribunal, in the eyes of the latter the state became sole claimant; further that the difference became one which could not be settled by diplomatic negotiation when one of the national parties gave what was regarded by the Court as a definitively negative reply. The Court held, in addition, that the dispute had to be decided on the basis of provisions of the Mandate and was therefore as to certain phases of it within the category of disputes for which the Mandatory had accepted the jurisdiction of the Court.

To this opinion there were five dissents.

273. Reparation clause in Treaty of Neuilly.—The decision (Judgment No. 3) in this case may be summarized as follows:

The Treaty of Neuilly was held to authorize certain classes of claims against Bulgaria for damage both as regards property and as regards persons.

This case was decided by three judges sitting in the Chamber of Summary Procedure. It was held that under the Treaty of Neuilly claims were authorized in respect of acts committed even outside Bulgarian territory as constituted before October 11, 1915, and in respect of damages incurred by claimants not only as regarded their property, rights, and interests, but also as regarded their persons. It is to be noted, as a matter of interest, that the Court declared that

The claims in respect of property et cetera arise out of exceptional war measures and therefore are governed by the laws of war, whilst the claims in respect of "acts committed" refer to events which must have taken place before the interested Power entered the war, so that the law governing peace and neutrality is applicable as concerns them.

274. Interpretation of preceding decision.—The Greek Government requested an interpretation (Judgment No. 4) of the decision last referred to, based upon Article 60 of the Statute of the Court which provides that while a judgment is final and without appeal,

In the event of a dispute as to the meaning or scope of the judgment, the Court shall construe it upon the request of any party.

This request came before the same Chamber of Summary Procedure. This body, considering the character of the Greek request, concluded that it

envisages a matter other than the determination of the basis and extent of the obligations referred to in the clause in question.

The Court, therefore, holding that it had no power to go beyond the limits of the judgment interpreted, refused the request.

275. Mavrommatis Jerusalem concessions.—The judgment (No. 5) in this case may be summarized as follows:

The British Government as mandatory had bound itself to respect certain concessions in Palestine, and, while a grant of new concessions may not have been in conformity with its obligations, no loss resulted and hence no liability for indemnity is imposed.

It appeared incidentally in the course of this case that, while the beneficial claimant was a Greek subject, nevertheless in the concessions under consideration he was described as a Turkish subject, which fact it was argued, although not invalidating the concessions, might deprive him of the right to benefit under the protocol under which claim was made. The Court, however, was of the opinion that it would be contrary to the spirit and intention of such instrument to withhold its benefits because another nationality was, in error, set down in the concessionary contract. The real nationality was held to be Greek.

The Court gave judgment to the effect that the concessions granted to Mavrommatis were valid; that the existence for a certain space of time on the part of an English concessionary of a right to require the annulment of the concessions of Mavrommatis was not in conformity with the international obligations accepted by the Mandatory for Palestine; that no loss to Mavrommatis having been proven resulting from this circumstance, the Greek Government's claim for an indemnity should be dismissed. One of the judges dissented from some features of the decision.

276. German interests in Polish Upper Silesia.—This decision (Judgment No. 6) is summarized as follows:

> Under the German-Polish convention, the Court has jurisdiction to determine the legality of certain expropriations made by Poland in spite of the latter's objections.

This case was initiated by the German Government against Poland, and charged that the Polish Government had expropriated certain industrial property at Chorzow in violation of Article 8 of the Geneva Convention. The Polish Government asked the Court to declare that it had no jurisdiction or, in the alternative, that the German application could not be entertained. These contentions were disapproved by the Court, which further refused to let its jurisdiction await the decision of pending cases by the Mixed Arbitral Tribunal. A suggestion that it should do so might be treated as a plea of *litispendence,* but would fail because the courts were not co-ordinate and the litigations not identical. It found, therefore, no reason why jurisdiction should not be entertained, and the case reserved for judgment on the merits. The Polish representative on the Court alone dissented, although another judge made special observations with regard to one of the points in controversy.

277. Again as to German interests in Polish Upper Silesia.— We summarize the decision (Judgment No. 7) in this case as follows:

> Certain Polish laws affecting German nationals or companies controlled by them, and the attitude of the Polish Government as to other named German properties, and notice of intention to liquidate certain other estates were not in accordance with provisions of the Geneva Convention, while as to one property the German contention no longer had any object and as to several more the application had to be dismissed.

In this case application was made for relief for its nationals by the German Government against certain laws and operations of the Polish Government prejudicial to them. The history of this case was briefly indicated in Judgment No. 6 to which the Court refers. The Court held that the only measures prohibited by the Geneva Convention were those generally accepted international law would not sanction with respect to foreigners, excepting expropriation for reasons of public utility, judicial liquidation, and similar measures. The position of Poland with reference to the Treaty of Versailles was largely discussed.

One member of the Court, while agreeing in the conclusions arrived at, submitted personal observations and the Polish national judge delivered a separate opinion.

278. Denunciation of Chinese-Belgian Treaty of 1865.—This was a unilateral application made by Belgium asking judgment (No. 8) to the effect that the Government of the Chinese Republic was not entitled unilaterally to denounce the Treaty of November 2, 1865, and to indicate, pending judgment, any provisional measures to be taken for the preservation of rights which might subsequently be recognized as belonging to Belgium or her nationals. In addition, the Court was asked to give notice of the present application to the Chinese Government in accordance with the Statute of the Court. The Court in a preliminary order held that the two powers had recognized as compulsory the Court's jurisdiction, and provisionally, pending final decision, directed that the protection which was internationally due to the Belgian legation and consulates and to Belgian nationals' property and ships included the right of any Belgian losing his passport or committing any offense against the law to be conducted in safety to the nearest Belgian consulate; that Belgian missionaries should be effectively protected; that any Belgian offending against a Chinese or against the law should be arrested only through a consul and not subjected, as regarded the execution of any penalty involving personal violence or duress, to any except the legal action of Belgian law; that there should be no sequestration or seizure except in accordance with principles of international law and no destruction other than accidental; that any legal proceedings involving Belgians before Chinese authorities should be heard under modern codes of law, with right of appeal, et cetera.

Belgium and China coming to an agreement before the appearance of China in the Permanent Court relative to the points mentioned, the order was suspended by the Court. The time for the filing of pleadings having been fixed by the President of the Court, subsequently under an agreement between the parties this time was further modified and extended by its order.

279. Factory at Chorzow.—This (Judgment No. 9) was a suit brought by Germany against Poland concerning the reparation claimed by Germany to be due to some of its citizens by virtue of the attitude adopted by the Polish Government toward German companies when it took possession of the nitrate factory situated at Chorzow, which attitude the Court by Judgment No. 7 had declared not to be in conformity with the articles of the convention concluded at Geneva between Germany and Poland. Poland filed a plea asking that the Court should, without entering into the merits, declare it had no jurisdiction. Later and on intermediate pleadings, Poland asked the Court to hold either that it had no jurisdiction or that the application could not be entertained until the German-Polish Mixed Arbitral Tribunal had given judgment. The Court, as we have seen, decided against Poland, as it did later when the Polish Government sought to have Germany non-suited. Some subsequent negotiations occurred between the countries relative to a settlement, but they resulted in nothing and appeal was taken to the Court.

Poland now contended that the Geneva Convention, giving the Court jurisdiction over differences of opinion resulting from the interpretation and application of articles of the treaty, did not contemplate differences in regard to reparations claimed for violation of its articles. The Court considered it to be a principle of international law that the breach of an engagement involved an obligation to make reparation in an adequate form, and, being the indispensable complement of a failure to apply a convention, this need not be stated in the convention itself. "Differences relating to reparations, which may be due by reason of failure to apply a convention, are consequently differences relating to its application." The Court added that to say

The *clause compromissoire,* while confessedly providing for the submission of questions of right and obligation, must now be restrictively interpreted as excluding pecuniary reparation, would be contrary to the fundamental conceptions by which the movement in favor of general arbitration has been characterized.

The Court then reviewed again *in extenso* the reasons why its jurisdiction should be maintained and, dismissing the jurisdictional plea, reserved the suit for judgment on the merits.

280. The affair of the *Lotus*.—Judgment No. 10 concerned a collision which occurred on the high seas on August 2, 1926, between the French steamship *Lotus* and the Turkish steamship *Boz-Kourt.* Upon the arrival of the French ship at Stamboul, because of the fact that the *Boz-Kourt* sank, involving the death of eight Turkish nationals, Turkey instituted criminal proceedings in pursuance of Turkish laws against Lieutenant Demons, officer of the watch on board the *Lotus.* The lieutenant objected that the Turkish courts had no jurisdiction, but he was overruled, and the criminal court sentenced him to eighty days imprisonment and a fine, the commander of the Turkish vessel being likewise sentenced. An appeal was taken which operated to suspend the execution of the sentence.

The Governments of France and Turkey, after complaint made by the French Government, signed a special agreement submitting to the Permanent Court the question whether or not Turkey in proceeding in pursuance of Turkish law against Demons had acted in conflict with the principles of international law and contrary to Article 15 of the Convention of Lausanne of July 24, 1923, respecting conditions of residence and business and jurisdiction.

The Court held that Turkey had not so acted and that there was no occasion therefore to give judgment upon the further proposition before the Court as to what reparation should be made.

In this case the votes of the Court were equally divided—six to six —and the case was decided by the casting vote of the President. Separate opinions were filed by the dissenting judges.

The prevailing opinion held that

according to the special agreement, therefore, it is not a question of stating principles which would permit Turkey to take criminal proceedings, but of formulating the principles, if any, which might have been violated by such proceedings.

It was also held that, failing the existence of a permissive rule to the contrary, a state may not exercise its power in any form in the territory of another state. But it did not follow that international law prohibited it from exercising jurisdiction in its own territory in respect of any case which relates to acts which have taken place abroad, and in which it cannot rely on some permissive rule of international law; that all or nearly all systems of law extend their action to offenses committed outside the territory of the state which adopts them, even though they do so in ways which vary from state to state.

281. Mavrommatis concessions at Jerusalem.—The Mavrommatis concessions in Palestine came for the third time (Judgment No. 11) before the Court on a claim against Great Britain as the Mandatory for having delayed approval of plans deposited by Mavrommatis, thereby preventing execution of the concessionary contracts, and thus and through hostilities displayed, rendering it materially and normally impossible for him to obtain the financing of his concessions. The Greek Government on behalf of Mavrommatis claimed an award of £217,000. The British Government disputed the jurisdiction of the Court, contending, in opposition to one of the Greek positions to the effect that the British Government had not complied with Judgment No. 5, that there was no provision giving the Court jurisdiction to decide whether one of its judgments had or had not been complied with. Great Britain also contended that the Court's jurisdiction extended only to dealing with a breach of its international obligations in so far as such breach resulted from the manner in which the Palestine administration had exercised its full power over the subject-matter, claiming that there had been no exercise of the power and that mere delay was not to be regarded as an exercise. It was contended that jurisdiction did not relate to the contracts between Mavrommatis and the Turkish authorities in 1914, as they had been expressly annulled by those concluded between him and the Palestine administration. After discussing at length the character of an exercise of the full power to provide for public control, the Court by seven votes to four upheld the objection to jurisdiction. Three dissenting opinions were filed.

282. Interpretation of Judgments 7 and 8 relating to the Chorzow factory.—In this case (Judgment No. 11—Series A, No. 13), the German Government requested an interpretation of the decisions referred to, and the Court by a vote of eight votes to three decided that in the first judgment the Court did not reserve to the Polish Government the right of asking for a declaration that the entry in the land register of the German company as owners of the Chorzow factory was null and void, but that the Court meant to recognize with binding effect its right of ownership under municipal law.

In the course of the opinion the Court held that, in order that a difference of opinion should become the subject of a request for an interpretation, it must relate to those points in the judgment which have been decided with binding force.

The German Government, before this case was decided, applied to the Court for provisional means of interim protection, which the Court treated as designed to obtain an interim judgment in favor of a part of the claim in the main Chorzow case, and refused. This application is designated as No. 12, Series A.

283. Denunciation of treaty between China and Belgium.—This amounted simply to an application for an extension of time to both parties for the filing of pleadings and calls for no extended consideration (Judgment No. 14).

A later application for a further extension being made by Belgium, and China interposing no objection, the Court granted it, fixing the dates for the filing of further pleadings (Judgment No. 16).

284. Rights of minorities in Upper Silesia.—In this case (Judgment No. 15) between Germany and Poland the Court declared that certain articles of the German-Polish Convention concerning Upper

Silesia bestowed upon every national the right freely to declare according to his conscience and upon his personal responsibility that he does or does not belong to a racial, linguistic, or religious minority, and to declare what is the language of the pupil or child for whose education he is legally responsible; but that these declarations, while they must be true, do not constitute an unrestricted right to choose the language in which instruction is to be imparted or the corresponding school; and that the questions involved in them are subject to no verification, dispute, pressure, or hindrance whatsoever on the part of the authorities. The Court declined to give judgment on so much of the applicant's submission as related to any measure singling out the minority schools to their detriment as incompatible with equal treatment guaranteed by the Convention.

A question of jurisdiction having been raised by Poland, the Court held that:

There seems to be no doubt that the consent of a state to the submission of a dispute to the Court may not only result from an express declaration, but may also be inferred from acts conclusively establishing it,

and this the Court found to be the case in the present instance.

This case was decided by a vote of eight to four, with three dissenting opinions filed.

285. Chorzow Factory.—This case again came before the Court and was disposed of in its Judgment No. 17. The Court reviewed the previous occasions in which the case had been considered and in the course of its opinion held that the reparation due by one state to another was not changed in character by reason of the fact that it took the form of an indemnity for the calculation of which the damages suffered by private persons was taken as the measure. The fundamental questions the Court held were: (1) the existence of the obligation to make reparation; (2) the existence of the damage which must serve as a basis for the calculation of the amount of indemnity; (3) the extent of damage. The first point was held settled by the prior judgments and was to be treated as *res judicata*.

In considering whether the damage afforded ground for reparation the Court held that in estimating the loss caused by an unlawful act only the value of property rights and interest affected for which compensation was claimed to the owner or the damage done to him must be taken into account. In arguing this, the Court considered it different from a case where dispossession had been preceded by judgment given by a competent tribunal, which the Court found was not the case. It declined to limit compensation to the value of the undertaking at the moment of dispossession plus interest to the date of payment, but held that reparation must as far as possible wipe out all the consequences of the illegal act and re-establish the situation that would in all probability have existed if the act had not been committed.

The Court considered itself faced with the task of determining what sum must be awarded to the German Government in order to enable it to place the dispossessed companies as far as possible in the economic situation in which they would probably have been if the seizure had not taken place, and held that the data furnished were insufficient.

Incidentally the Court treated a proposition advanced by Poland, although in form a counter-claim, in reality merely an objection to the German claim, and further declined to take into consideration admissions or proposals looking toward a settlement which had been made during the direct negotiations contemplating agreement.

In the conclusion the Court by a vote of nine to three decided that the Polish Government was under an obligation to pay as reparation a compensation corresponding to damages sustained, and declined to recognize the judgment of a local tribunal, it not controlling internationally. It declined to recognize any obligation to enforce stipulations as to non-exportation of the products of factory to particular countries. The fixing of the amount of compensation was left to future judgment after receiving reports of experts to be appointed.

By separate judgment the court directed these experts to consist of three to be appointed by the president of the Court, who should work together with assessors appointed one by each of the parties. The experts were to consider the value of the undertaking at the time taken; what would have been the financial results if operations had been continued to the date of judgment from the time of taking and had been in the hands of the companies; and what would have been the value at the date of the judgment of the whole undertaking had it remained in the hands of the original German holders to the date of the judgment.

Lord Finlay, who dissented in part from the judgment, considered that the value should be of the property as of the date of its taking, without estimating later possibilities. Dissenting opinions were also filed by two other judges and observations by another.

CHAPTER XXXIII

ADVISORY JURISDICTION OF THE PERMA-NENT COURT OF INTERNATIONAL JUSTICE

286. National precedents for an advisory jurisdiction.—Recent years have brought about a development in the administration of justice internationally through courts much resembling the development which has taken place over a much greater period of time in the field of national law. One of the most striking features of this development is the advisory jurisdiction of the Court of International Justice provided for in the first instance by Article 14 of the Versailles Treaty. By the terms of this treaty in its French version the Court will give (*donnera*) and in the English version "may give an advisory opinion on any dispute or question referred to it by the Council or by the Assembly." While there may exist a difference of opinion as to which text is authoritative, nevertheless in practical operation full effect has been given to the French version and the Court has never questioned its duty to give, when the legal situation permitted, an opinion upon its being asked. The origin of this peculiar jurisdiction may be found in the power entertained by the English Crown of calling upon judges for their opinions. Following the English precedent upon this point, many states of the United States have authorized either the executive or the houses of the legislature jointly or separately to call upon the highest courts of the state for an opinion. This practice found itself first illustrated in the state of Massachusetts, and its example has been followed in New Hampshire, Maine, Rhode Island, Florida, Colorado, Delaware, Mississippi, Oklahoma, Alabama, and South Dakota, as well as, for a time, Missouri. To these jurisdictions may be added those of the Dominion of Canada and several Canadian provinces.

287. Interpretation of the Versailles Treaty.—Under the language of the Treaty of Versailles any question may be referred by the Council or Assembly to the Court for its opinion. The language is broad, but, broad as it is, has not been interpreted as including any political question in the sense of a question involving policies to be pursued. In this respect, the Court of International Justice has so far in its career resembled the courts of the states enjoying a similar provision. There is no instance of record among the states of the Union of a reference to a court to determine a question as to the policy to be followed. Very often references have related to the matter of the right and power of the legislature to take a given course, but not to the matter of the advantage or disadvantage to result from the taking of such a course.

It has been urged with regard to the broad language of the treaty allowing the reference of any question to the Court that this includes of necessity political questions, although no political question in the sense of a matter of policy making has been referred to the Court. We may, therefore, glance for a moment to discover the real meaning of the term. Says Professor Ellingwood:

> What are "political questions?" The meaning of the phrase is decidedly elusive. It may have reference to the identity of the person or organization who deals with the question, or it may relate to the nature of the subject-matter involved, or it may mean merely that the question is one of "policy," wisdom, or expediency.[1]

If, therefore, the meaning of the word has in practice both within the United States, and as far as exemplified in the many cases of opinions asked at The Hague, been construed to mean matters of interpretation of laws or treaties as the case may be and never to include instruction as to the policy to be pursued, we may believe that, as far as the Court is affected, its limitations have been determined by practice and are not likely to be exceeded. This is the more true when we bear in mind the fact that even the most important governmental institutions are jealous of their prerogatives and powers. We may thus believe that in the future as in the past the Assembly and Council of the League will not surrender their powers to another body.

It will be borne in mind that the advisory powers given the Court are exactly what the name implies, the power of giving advice and not an order or direction as is the case in the granting of a judgment. This advice, however, may exercise the most important influence upon the parties seeking it, and this has been true when, for instance, the question was referred to the Court as to whether matters of citizenship in French possessions offered a national or international question and the opinion of the Court was expressed that while ordinarily citizenship was a national matter in this instance the whole opinion was so bound up with the interpretation of a treaty as to render it international. France and England at once acted upon the opinion of the Court and came to a satisfactory arrangement.

It is further to be remembered that although the French version of the provision of the Versailles Treaty be accepted, yet there are

---

[1] "The Advisory Function of the World Court," *American Bar Association Journal*, February 1916, 102.

limitations upon the power of the Court to give opinions, limitations which are not set down in any treaty. Thus, for instance, when it was found that Russia was interested in the treaty question with Finland with regard to which an opinion was asked and Russia declined to be heard before the Court, the Court recognized its want of jurisdiction because of the want of power to give an opinion in anywise controlling as to Russia.[1a]

The provisions covering the advisory jurisdiction of the Court, except for Article 14 of the Versailles Treaty, are contained in Articles 71–74 of the Rules of the Court and in themselves are of a skeletal nature. Article 72 amplifies the treaty by providing that "questions upon which the advisory opinion of the Court is asked shall be laid before the Court by means of a written request, signed either by the President of the Assembly or the President of the Council of the League of Nations, or by the Secretary-General of the League under instructions from the Assembly or the Council. The request shall contain an exact statement of the question upon which an opinion is required, and shall be accompanied by all documents likely to throw light upon the question." It will be noted that no very formal procedure is outlined in any matters relating to advisory jurisdiction.

Following is this provision of Article 73:

> The Registrar shall forthwith give notice of the request for an advisory opinion to the members of the Court, to the members of the League of Nations, through the Secretary-General of the League, and to any State entitled to appear before the Court.

Provision is also made for notification to any member of the League or state admitted to appear before the Court or any international organization likely to be able to furnish information, and these are allowed to comment on the statement of others.

Everything connected with presentation of a question for an advisory opinion is properly given as great publicity, as to the hearings and in every other respect, as is granted to any ordinary judicial proceeding. In other words, advice is asked in the open and an opinion is rendered in the open with the most complete consideration of everything pre-

---

[1a] It is the view of Dr. Hammarskjöld (*International Conciliation,* September, 1927, 374) that "if it had been a question of a contested case, the Court would have had no jurisdiction to deal with it unless both parties had accepted its jurisdiction as compulsory. It could not, therefore, through the roundabout way of a request for an advisory opinion, assume jurisdiction over the case at the demand of one of the parties only, in the absence of an agreement establishing compulsory jurisdiction."

sented by any party conceiving itself in interest and appearing orally or by way of written communication. It will be noted that the Court seeks light as to all advisory questions from sources outside of parties to the Annex to the Covenant which are most likely to be able to give light, such as Institutes and Associations of International Law. In this respect the practice much resembles that existing in certain states of the Union where there is a similar institution, and not alone the Attorney-General of the state but any lawyer may appear and present his views as a friend of the Court.

The advisory opinions of the Court, like those in regular judicial proceedings, are rendered in open court instead of being treated as between attorney and client. They thus reach the public with the utmost celerity, which is proper in matters where after all the real parties in interest are the people who are represented by the government. These opinions are also promptly printed and published in a special collection, for which the Registrar is responsible.

288. Advisory opinion as precedent.—It was the opinion of John Bassett Moore that the giving of advisory opinions "obviously is not a judicial function."[2] This has also been the view of Professor Thayer[3] and Judge Cardozo.[4] If it be a judicial function to pass upon questions of law, we may doubt the entire accuracy of the view so expressed. We may rather believe that, however presented to the Court, whether in an anticipatory way as in the case of advisory opinions or for final judgment as ordinarily presented to a court, the utterances are judicial in that, whether directing a final judgment or not, they point out the law in the most solemn manner. A function which has been exercised by the courts for a hundred years in England and for lesser periods in a number of states of the Union can hardly be called non-judicial. Particularly is this true as all parties in interest are given the opportunity to present themselves before the Court and to advocate their varied views. We may agree with Professor Manley Hudson that "it is difficult to see why advisory opinions of the international courts cannot in themselves be contributions to international law, and the opinions rendered to date would seem to have made very substantial contributions."[5] Perhaps the original view of Judge Moore was expressed without his having in mind the course later pursued by the Court to

[2] *Columbia Law Review*, XXII, 507.

[3] *Harvard Law Review*, VII, 129–53.

[4] 224 New York 13, 16.

[5] *Permanent Court of International Justice*, 158. Professor Hudson further discusses advisory opinions in the *American Journal of International Law*, XXII, 790–93.

the effect that the rules adopted "assimilate the process as far as possible to a judicial proceeding, and exclude any supposition that advisory opinions may be rendered in a diplomatic sense and without publicity." It is, of course, nevertheless true that an advisory opinion, as its title implies, lacks the absolute character of finality. When, therefore, a concrete case is presented, the view of the Court may be modified by circumstances not theretofore developed or by views at first insufficiently stressed. As bearing on the ideas just expressed the Court has declared that "being a court of justice [it] cannot even in giving advisory opinions depart from the essential rules governing their activities as a court."

CHAPTER XXXIV

ADVISORY OPINIONS OF THE PERMANENT COURT OF INTERNATIONAL JUSTICE

289. General observations.—In considering the work of the Permanent Court of International Justice, it is worthy of note that the advisory opinions have been about as numerous as those given in regularly contested suits. It is not within the scope of this book to go very much into detail as to the points decided in the several cases before the Permanent Court, and in the summary we now give we shall rely largely upon the reviews of the conclusions of the Court which have been published from time to time by Professor Manley O. Hudson.[1]

290. Nomination of delegates to the International Labor Conference.—The opinion (Advisory Opinion No. 1) of the Court is summarized by Professor Hudson as follows:

A member of the International Labor Organization is not bound to consult the largest employers' or workers' organization, in selecting its delegates to the International Labor Conference, where other organizations consulted total more members.

The effect of this opinion was to confirm the action of the Netherlands in selecting labor delegates who held the combined nomination of organizations representing the larger number of workers, although a single other organization might be more numerous than any one of those making up the majority of workers.

291. International regulation of conditions of labor of persons employed in agriculture.—In this case the Court advised (Advisory Opinion No. 2) that

The competence of the International Labor Organization does extend to international regulation of the conditions of labor of persons employed in agriculture.

It held that

Every argument used for the exclusion of agriculture might with equal force be used for the exclusion of navigation and fisheries.

Two of the judges dissented.

292. Agricultural production and the International Labor Or-

[1] *World Peace Foundation Pamphlet,* Vol. IX, No. 2, 1926; "The Work of the Permanent Court of International Justice," *American Bar Association Journal* (January 1926) XII, 34; and (March 1928) XIV, 163.

ganization.—In this case the Court advised in substance (Advisory Opinion No. 3) that:

> The competence of the International Labor Organization extends to agricultural production only in so far as conditions of labor are concerned.

293. Nationality decrees in Tunis and Morocco.—The opinion (No. 4) in this case is summarized as follows:

> The British-French dispute over nationality decrees in Tunis and Morocco is not by international law solely a matter of domestic jurisdiction within paragraph 8 of Article 15 of the Covenant, though nationality questions in general fall within a state's domestic jurisdiction.

Some expressions of the court in connection with this decision are of importance. For instance, it was said that

> the question whether a certain matter is or is not solely within the jurisdiction of a State is an essentially relative question; it depends upon the development of international relations. Thus, in the present state of international law, questions of nationality are, in the opinion of the Court, in principle within this reserved domain.

In this case questions of treaty construction arose, nevertheless, and the Court observed that it would be "necessary to have recourse to international law in order to decide what the value of an agreement of this kind may be as regards third States, and that the question consequently ceases to be one which, by international law, is solely within the domestic jurisdiction of a State, as that jurisdiction is defined" by the Court.

Later the Court added: "It is clearly not possible to make any pronouncement upon this point [as to the lapsing of a treaty] without recourse to the principles of international law concerning the duration of the validity of treaties. It follows, therefore, that in this respect also the question does not, by international law, fall solely within the domestic jurisdiction of a State, as that jurisdiction is defined" by the Court.

294. Dispute between Finland and Russia.—This opinion (No. 5) is summarized as follows:

> When an advisory opinion on the legal effect of treaty provisions would involve a prejudging of a dispute with reference to the execution of such treaty provisions, the Court will not give such an advisory opinion unless both parties submit to the Court's jurisdiction.

The Council of the League of Nations asked the opinion of the Court on the following question: "Do Articles 10 and 11 of the Treaty of Peace between Finland and Russia, signed at Dorpat on October 14,

1920, and the annexed Declaration of the Russian Delegation regarding the autonomy of Eastern Carelia, constitute engagements of an international character which place Russia under an obligation to Finland as to the carrying out of the provisions contained therein?"

In this case the Court declined to give an opinion in view of the fact that Russia was outside the League of Nations and the assumption of jurisdiction would violate a fundamental principle of international law, that of the independence of states, and Russia refused to submit to the jurisdiction of the Court. As a subsidiary reason, the Court found it inexpedient to attempt to deal with the question before it because, Russia refusing to take part, it would be doubtful whether "there would be available to the Court materials sufficient to enable it to arrive at any judicial conclusion upon the question of fact; What did the parties agree to?"

The Court thought that the circumstance that it was not requested to decide a dispute but merely to give an advisory opinion did not essentially modify this consideration, since answering the question would be substantially equivalent to deciding the dispute between the parties.

Four judges dissented, being unable to share the views of the majority as to the impossibility of giving an advisory opinion.

295. Protection of German settlers in Poland.—This opinion (No. 6) is summarized as follows:

Poland's international obligations under the Minorities Treaty of June 28, 1919, involve the protection of German colonists sent into German Poland before the war, requiring Poland to respect contracts and leases made by the German Government with these colonists; and the position taken by Poland after the war was not in conformity with its international obligations.

In the course of its opinion the Court said:

The main object of the Minorities Treaty is to assure respect for the rights of Minorities and to prevent discrimination against them by any act whatsoever of the Polish state. It does not matter whether the rights the infraction of which is alleged are derived from a legislative, judicial, or administrative act, or from an international engagement. If the Council ceased to be competent whenever the subject before it involved the interpretation of such an international engagement, the Minorities Treaty would to a great extent be deprived of value.

A large part of the discussion in the opinion of the Court relates to the question of land titles in Poland and what constitutes property therein, an attempt having been made to take away property for the benefit of a colonization scheme. With regard to this the Court declared:

The fact that there was a political purpose behind the colonization scheme cannot affect the private rights acquired under the law, and indeed it is self-evident that no scheme of colonization of this nature could possibly succeed unless the settlers had security in the property for which they had paid in money and in kind.

296. Acquisition of Polish nationality by German settlers.—In this case the Court advised in substance (Advisory Opinion No. 7) that:

Under the Treaty for the Protection of Minorities in Poland, the Council of the League of Nations is competent to deal with questions as to acquisition of Polish nationality by German settlers, and Article 4 of the Treaty makes habitual residence of parents at the date of birth of settlers concerned, but not at any later date, a condition of acquiring nationality.

Although the questions in this case dealt with possible citizenship of Germanic minorities in Polish territory and Germany was therefore only indirectly concerned, the Court sent notice to Germany and, among others, heard oral arguments on its behalf.

The Polish Government decided to treat certain persons, former German nationals, as not having acquired Polish nationality and as continuing to possess German nationality because their parents were not habitually resident in the territory both on the date of birth of the person concerned and on the date when the Minorities Treaty came into effect. Poland contended in the Council of the League that its jurisdiction was limited to questions concerning minorities consisting of Polish nationals. The Court held the opinion, however, that the matter was within the competence of the League, and further held that the Polish Government had improperly required that parents of the persons in question should be living in the territory on January 10, 1920, as well as on the date of birth of their children.

The matter was subsequently the subject of negotiations between Poland and Germany and finally submitted to arbitration and the award of the arbitrator accepted.

297. The Jaworzina Boundary Question.—This opinion (No. 8) is summarized as follows:

A decision by the Conference of Ambassadors with reference to the boundary between Poland and Czechoslovakia, accepted by both States, was definitive and the question was not reopened by later negotiations.

The question was as to whether delimitation of the frontier between Poland and Czechoslovakia in the region known as the Spisz district (Jaworzina) was open or was to be considered as settled by a Conference of Ambassadors at Paris on July 28, 1920, which decision had been accepted by both Poland and Czechoslovakia. The Court was unanimous in finding that the decision was to be treated as definitive, having not only been "fulfilled by the decision of the conferences but the decision itself was put into execution."

A question arose as to the effect of later interpretations of the decision by the Conference of Ambassadors, but the Court refused to admit that the Conference could change the clear effect of a decision by later interpretation.

298. The Monastery of St. Naoum and the Albanian frontier. —This decision is summarized as follows (Advisory Opinion No. 9):

By a decision of the Conference of Ambassadors of December 6, 1922, the Principal Allied Powers exhausted the mission contemplated by a resolution of the Assembly of the League of Nations of October 2, 1921, with respect to the frontier between Albania and the Kingdom of the Serbs, Croats, and Slovenes at the Monastery of Saint Naoum.

In this case the Council of the League of Nations asked an opinion as to whether the Principal Allied Powers, by a decision of the Conference of Ambassadors of December 6, 1922, exhausted as to the frontier question the mission as recognized between interested parties contemplated by a resolution of the Assembly of the League of Nations of October 2, 1921, and the Court decided as indicated.

The decision of the Council of Ambassadors having been also attacked on the ground that it had been reached on erroneous information and without regard to certain essential facts, the Court found this was not the case, without committing itself to the possibility of any action if the facts had turned out to be otherwise, but also failed to find that any new facts had been brought to light not known to the Conference at the time of its decision.

299. Exchange of Greek and Turkish populations.—The opinion (No. 10) in this case is summarized as follows:

To be considered as "established' in Constantinople under the terms of the convention of Lausanne of January 30, 1923, and therefore not included in the exchange of populations between Greece and Turkey, Greek inhabitants must reside within certain boundaries of the Prefecture of the City of Constantinople, and must have arrived prior to October 30, 1918, with an intention to reside there for an extended period.

The opinion largely relates to matters of special treaty construction and calls for no extended discussion.

We simply note the fact that it was the opinion of the Court that it would not necessarily follow by reason of the situation contemplated in the convention under discussion that there must be an implied reference to national legislation. It was considered that it could well be that the convention contemplated a mere situation of fact sufficiently defined by the convention itself without any reference to national legislation.

300. Polish postal service in the free city of Danzig.—The decision in this case is summarized as follows (Advisory Opinion No. 11):

> The Polish Government is entitled under treaties in force to maintain a postal service in the Port of Danzig, not restricted to a single office, which may be open to the public use.

It would seem as if the questions in this case were too trifling ever to have been brought to an international court and should have been settled between the parties in controversy by a little mutual consideration. Nevertheless, in the course of its opinion the Court lays down one or two propositions of importance in connection with the construction of treaties. "The rules," the Court says, "as to a strict or liberal construction of treaty stipulations can be applied only in cases where ordinary methods of interpretation have failed. It is a cardinal principle of interpretation that words must be interpreted in the sense which they would normally have in their context, unless such interpretation would lead to something unreasonable or absurd."

301. Nature of the Council's action as to frontier between Turkey and Iraq.—This decision may be summarized as follows (Advisory Opinion No. 12):

> The reference of a dispute as contained in Article 3 of the Treaty of Lausanne empowers the Council to give a binding decision for which the votes of all members of the Council except the parties to the dispute are required.

One of the questions submitted for an opinion was as to the character of the decision to be taken by the Council in virtue of Article 3, Paragraph 2 of the Treaty of Lausanne, whether an arbitral award, a recommendation, or simply a mediation. The Court, however, treated it simply as a decision.

302. Competence of the International Labor Organization to regulate incidentally the personal work of the employer.—The Court expressed the opinion (No. 13) in this case that:

> It is within the competence of the International Labor Organization to draw up and to propose labor legislation which, in order to protect certain classes of workers, also regulates incidentally the same work when performed by the employer himself.

This opinion of the Court was an answer to the direct question asked by the Council of the League, which was brought forth by the fact that the International Labor Conference had passed a draft convention extending the prohibition of night work in bakeries to proprietors as well as workers. The Court considered that the passing upon such a question obviously involved the exercise of judgment by the proper authorities on the circumstances of each case as it arose, but the Court did not intend to indicate the limits of any discretionary power which the International Labor Organization might possess in regard to the making of incidental regulations.

303. Jurisdiction of the European Commission of Danube between Galatz and Braila.—The opinion (No. 14) of the Court may be summarized as follows:

The European Commission of the Danube has the same powers over that part of the Danube from Galatz to Braila, including the port of Braila, as over lower portions, and its powers over the whole of the maritime Danube are divided from those of the Roumanian authorities by criteria of navigation and the obligation to ensure freedom of navigation and equal treatment of all flags.

The decision of the Court, relating as it did to the control of a river, does not from the standpoint of facts involved offer large interest to the general reader. The decision of the Court was unanimous save for a single dissent, although two judges of the majority, as well as the dissenter, filed separate opinions.

304. Jurisdiction of the courts of Danzig.—The Court advised in this opinion (No. 15) that:

The decision of the High Commissioner of the League of Nations at Danzig as to jurisdiction of the Danzig courts given as the result of requests made by the Danzig Government, in so far as his decision does not comply with these requests, is not legally well founded.

In this case the Government of Danzig appealed to the Council of the League of Nations from a decision of the High Commissioner and the Council requested the opinion of the Court. The decision of the Court was unanimous.

305. Interpretation of the Greco-Turkish Agreement of December 1, 1926.—The question before the Court in this case (No. 16) as finally framed by it upon documents produced, was as follows:

1. Is it for the Mixed Commission for the Exchange of Greek and Turkish Populations to decide whether the conditions laid down by Article IV of the Final Protocol annexed to the agreement concluded at Athens on December 1, 1926, between the Greek and Turkish Governments, for the submission of the questions

contemplated by that article to the arbitration of the President of the Greco-Turkish Mixed Arbitral Tribunal at Constantinople, are or are not fulfilled? or is it for the arbitrator contemplated by that article to decide this?

2. The conditions laid down by the said Article IV having been fulfilled, to whom does the right of referring a question to the arbitrator contemplated by the Article belong?

As neither of the nations in interest was represented on the Court, they were offered the opportunity to appoint such judges, but waived their right.

The Court considered that within the Mixed Commissions for Exchange of Populations, its members, neutral, Greek, or Turkish, are to vote as members and not by nationalities; that it being clear that as a general rule any body possessing jurisdictional powers has the right in the first place to determine the extent of its jurisdiction, such a question must be settled by the Commission itself; that the right of reference by it to another tribunal belongs only to the Commission as a matter of determining the extent of its own competence and deciding whether the conditions making reference possible are fulfilled; that the Mixed Commission possesses two clearly differentiated jurisdictions, one to decide whether conditions required for the reference to the arbitrator of a question of principle of some importance are or are not fulfilled, the other to give judgment on this question of principle on its merits, once it is established that the required conditions are fulfilled. It is further held that reference to the arbitrator of questions of principle of some importance is not confined to the case where there is a difference of opinion among the members of the Commission, but may be made when all are in agreement. This is not properly an appeal to an arbitrator, since there are not two parties but a commission of individual members.

The questions submitted were therefore decided in favor of the Mixed Commission for the Exchange of the Populations.

APPENDIX AND BIBLIOGRAPHY

APPENDIX A

LIST OF ARBITRAL AND OTHER JUDICIAL TRIBUNALS FUNCTIONING BETWEEN NATIONS FROM 1794

November 19, 1794. Great Britain and United States of America, St. Croix River Boundary. (Darby, *International Tribunals*, 769.)

November 19, 1794. Great Britain and United States, Recovery of Debts. (Darby, 769.)

November 19, 1794. Great Britain and United States, Maritime Seizures and the Rights of Neutrals. (Darby, 770.)

October 27, 1795. Spain and United States, Maritime Captures. (Darby, 770.)

January 26, 1797. Austria, Prussia and Russia, Liquidations. (Darby, 771.)

January 26, 1797. Austria, Prussia and Russia, Polish Debts. (Darby, 771.)

August 11, 1802. Spain and United States, Mutual Claims. (Darby, 771.)

May 30, 1814. Allied Powers and France, Pecuniary Claims. (Darby, 773.)

May 30, 1814. France and Russia, Mutual Pecuniary Claims. (Darby, 771.)

December 24, 1814. Great Britain and United States, Northeastern Boundary Question. (Darby, 772.)

December 24, 1814. Great Britain and United States, Northern Boundary of the United States. (Darby, 772.)

December 24, 1814. Great Britain and United States, Questions of Territory. (Darby, 772.)

December 24, 1814, and September 29, 1827. Great Britain and United States, Northeastern Boundary Question. (Darby, 772.)

March 24, 1815. Allied States and German Princes, Charges on Navigation of the Rhine. (*Recueil des arbitrages*, I, 218.)

May 18, 1815. Prussia, etc., and Saxony, Territorial Arrangements. (Darby, 773.)

May 31, 1815. Allied Powers and the Netherlands, Personal Claims. (Darby, 773–74.)

May 31, 1815. Nassau and Prussia, Cession of Territory. (Darby, 774.)

July 18, 1815. Tessin and Uri, Tolls in the Levantine Valley. (*Recueil des arbitrages*, I, 269.)

November 20, 1815. Allied Powers and France, Pecuniary Claims. (Darby, 774.)

November 20, 1815. France and Great Britain, Private Pecuniary Claims. (Darby, 774.)

November 20, 1815. France and the Netherlands, Arrears of Interest. (Darby, 775.)

October 20, 1818. Great Britain and United States, Obligation as to Slaves. (Darby, 775.)

July 12, 1822. Great Britain and United States, Amount of Indemnity. (Darby, 775.)

March 12, 1823. Great Britain and Spain, Mutual Claims. (Darby, 776.)

May 5, 1829. Brazil and Great Britain, Maritime Captures. (Darby, 776.)

July 19, 1830. Buenos Aires (Argentina) and Great Britain, Acts of War. (Darby, 776.)

August 5, 1830. Schaumburg-Lippe and Lippe-Detmold, Leasings of Schieder, Blomberg, and Lipperode. (*Recueil des arbitrages*, I, 401.)

November 15, 1831. Belgium and Holland, Dissolution of Union. (Darby, 777.)

February 17, 1934. Spain and United States, Adjustment of Claims. (Malloy, *Treaties, Conventions, etc.*, 1659.)

1835. Persia, Question of Inheritance. (Darby, 777.)

June 26, 1838. Afghanistan and Lahore, Rights of Sovereignty. (Darby, 777.)

March 9, 1839. France and Mexico, Acts of War. (Darby, 777.)

April 11, 1839. Mexico and United States, Personal Indemnities. (Darby, 778.)

October 28, 1840. Argentina and France, Personal Indemnities. (Darby, 778.)

November 17, 1840. Great Britain and the Two Sicilies, Sulphur Monopoly. (Darby, 779.)

August 26, 1842. Great Britain and Portugal, Military Service. (Darby, 778–79.)

October 15, 1842. Brazil and United States, Maritime Capture. (Darby, 779.)

November 14, 1842. France and Great Britain, Portendick Claims and Individual Claims in 1834. (Darby, 779.)

1843. Great Britain and Hanover, Ownership of Crown Jewels. (Darby, 780.)

1845. Austria and Sardinia, Salt Trade. (Darby, 780.)

May 31, 1847. Persia and Turkey, Frontier Questions. (Darby, 780.)

July 18, 1850. Great Britain and Greece, Loss of Documents (Pacífico case). (Darby, 781.)

February 15, 1851. France and Spain, Maritime Seizures. (Darby, 781.)

February 26, 1851. Portugal and United States, Duty of Neutrals (Brig *Armstrong* case). (Darby, 781.)

April 17, 1851 (date of award). Canada and New Brunswick, An Inter-Provincial Arbitration. (Darby, 781.)

February 8, 1853. Great Britain and United States, Reciprocal Claims. (Darby, 782.)

March 16, 1853. Ecuador and Peru, Maritime Seizure. (Darby, 782.)

June 5, 1854. Great Britain and United States, Reserved Fisheries Question. (Darby, 782; Malloy, *Treaties, Conventions, etc.*, 668.)

July 9, 1855. Great Britain and Portugal, Personal Claim. (Darby, 783.)

June 23, 1857. France and Great Britain, and Uruguay, Acts of War. (Darby, 783.)

August 5, 1857. Holland and Venezuela, Territorial Dispute (Island of Aves). (Darby, 783.)

September 10, 1857. New Granada and United States, Personal Claims. (Darby, 783.)

June 2, 1858. Brazil and Great Britain, Mutual Claims. (Darby, 784.)

July 30, 1858. Moldavia and Wallachia, Dedicated Convents. (Darby, 784.)

August 21, 1858. Argentina and France, Great Britain, and Sardinia, Results of Civil War. (Darby, 784.)

November 10, 1858. Chile and United States, *Macedonian* Case. (Darby, 785.)

February 4, 1859. Paraguay and United States, Commercial Claims. (Darby, 785.)

April 30, 1859. Great Britain and Guatemala, Boundary Questions. (Darby, 785.)

November 28, 1859. Great Britain and Honduras, Claims and Concessions. (Darby, 786.)

January 28, 1860. Great Britain and Nicaragua, Claims and Concessions. (Darby, 786.)

July 2, 1860. Costa Rica and United States, Pecuniary Claims. (Darby, 786.)

October 3, 1860. Muscat and Zanzibar, Rival Claims. (Darby, 786; *Recueil des arbitrages*, II, 55.)

March 8, 1861. Great Britain and Portugal, Personal Claims. (Darby, 787.)

November 25, 1862. Ecuador and United States, Mutual Claims. (Darby, 787.)

December 20, 1862. Peru and United States, Maritime Captures. (Darby, 787.)

January 5, 1863. Brazil and Great Britain, Arbitrary Arrest. (Darby, 787.)

January 12, 1863. Peru and United States, Mutual Claims. (Darby, 788.)

July 1, 1863. Great Britain and United States, Companies' Claims. (Darby, 788.)

July, 1863. Great Britain and Peru, Arbitrary Arrest. (Darby, 788–89.)

February 10, 1864. Colombia and United States, Panama Riot and Other Claims. (Darby, 789.)

May 4, 1864. Salvador and United States, Government Monopoly. (Darby, 789.)

July 15, 1864 and January 18, 1865. Argentine Republic and Great Britain, Results of Blockade. (Darby, 789.)

April 21, 1864. Egypt and Suez Canal Company, Concession Claims. (Darby, 789.)

April 25, 1866. United States and Venezuela, Claims by Citizens of the United States against the Government of Venezuela. (Darby, 790.)

June 26, 1866. Great Britain and Mexico, Personal Claims. (Darby, 790.)

August 22, 1866. Bavaria and Prussia, Claim to Art Treasures. (Darby, 791.)

March 4, 1868. Great Britain and Spain, The *"Mermaid"* Difficulty. (Darby, 791.)

July 4, 1868 (with supplemental protocols). Mexico and United States, Mutual Claims. (Darby, 791.)

September 21, 1868. Great Britain and Venezuela, Particular Claims. (Darby, 792.)

December 4, 1868. Peru and United States, Mutual Claims. (Darby, 792.)

January 13, 1869. Great Britain and Portugal, Disputed Territory (Bulama case). (Darby, 792–93.)

February 12, 1869. Great Britain and Orange Free State, Claims and Compensation. (Darby, 793.)

October 30, 1869. Orange Free State and Transvaal, Frontier Dispute. (Darby, 793.)

December 30, 1869. Italy and Turkey, Case of *Principe di Carignano*. (*Recueil des arbitrages*, II, 618.)

March 14, 1870. Brazil and United States, Loss of Ship. (Darby, 793.)

May 25, June 16, 1870. Spain and United States, Detention of Ship. (Darby, 793.)

September 4, 1871, and August 19, 1872 (dates of award). Kelat and Persia, Boundary Dispute. (Darby, 794; *Recueil des arbitrages*, II, vii *note*.)

February 12, 1871. Spain and United States, Events of Cuban Insurrection. (Darby, 794.)

March 1, 1871. Barolong, Batlapins, Griquas, and Transvaal, Boundary Rights. (Darby, 796.)

May 8, 1871. Great Britain and United States, *Alabama* Claims. (Darby, 794–95.)

May 8, 1871. Great Britain and United States, Civil War Claims. (Darby, 795.)

May 8, 1871. Great Britain and United States, Fishery Rights. (Darby, 795.)

May 8, 1871. Great Britain and United States, San Juan Water Boundary. (Darby, 796.)

August 16, 1871. Brazil and Sweden and Norway, Damage to Ship. (Darby, 797.)

September 27, 1871, and March 2, 1874. Chile and Peru, Common Expenses. (Darby, 797.)

January 9, 1872. Brazil and Paraguay, Damages during War. (Darby, 797.)

August 19, 1872. Afghanistan and Persia, Seistan Boundary. (Darby, 793–94.)

September 25, 1872. Great Britain and Portugal, Disputed Territory. (Darby, 797.)

December 5, 1872, and August 6, 1874. Bolivia and Chile, Mining Operations. (Darby, 798.)

December 14, 1872. Colombia and Great Britain, Pecuniary Claims. (Darby, 798.)

January 30, 1873, and April 22, 1873. Brazil and Great Britain, Naval Services. (Darby, 798.)

June 19 and 25, 1873. Japan and Peru, Detention of Ship. (Darby, 798.)

July 23, 1873. France and Great Britain, Customs Duties. (Darby, 799.)

December 6, 1873. Chile and United States, Seizure of Ships. (Darby, 799.)

December 31, 1873. Italy and Switzerland, Frontier Question. (Darby, 799.)

August 17, 1874. Colombia and United States, Seizure and Detention of Ship. (Darby, 799.)

1874 (award, October 31, 1874). China and Japan, Personal Indemnities. (Darby, 800.)

1875. Chile and Great Britain, Loss of a Ship. (Darby, 800.)

February 3, 1876. Argentine Republic and Paraguay, The El Chaco Boundary. (Darby, 800.)

July 13, 1878. Greece and Turkey, Question of Territory. (Darby, 802.)

August 3, 1878 (date of award). Great Britain: Canada and Ontario, Boundary of the Province of Ontario. (Darby, 800.)

1878 (date of award, August 3, 1878). Canada and Ontario, Boundary of the Province of Ontario. (Darby, 800.)

1879 (award dated July 2, 1881). Great Britain and Nicaragua, Sovereignty over the Mosquito Indians. (Darby, 801.)

October 15, 1879. France and Nicaragua, Case of *Phare*. (Darby, 801.)

January 15, 1880. France and United States, Mutual Claims. (Darby, 801.)

December 18, 1880. Honduras and Salvador, Boundary Question. (Darby, 802.)

December 25, 1880, December 26 and January 20, 1886 (lapsed), and November 4, 1896. Colombia and Costa Rica, Boundary Question. (Darby, 802.)

March 26, 1881., Holland and San Domingo, Confiscation of Ship and Imprisonment. (Darby, 803.)

August 3, 1881. Great Britain and the South African Republic, Mutual Claims for Losses Sustained in the Late War. (Darby, 803.)

1881. Basutoland and Cape Colony, Tribal Revolt. (Darby, 804.)

September 14, 1881. Colombia and Venezuela, Boundary Question. (Darby, 804.)

January 15, 1882 (extended July 19, 1882, and February 8, 1883). France and the United States, Mutual Claims. (Malloy, *Treaties, Conventions, etc.*, 535, 539, and 540.)

November 2, 1882. Chile and France, Damages in War. (Darby, 804.)

December 7, 1882. Chile and Italy, Similar Claims. (Darby, 804–5.)

January 4, 1883. Chile and Great Britain, Similar Claims. (Darby, 805.)

January 13, 1883. Egypt and Foreign Powers, Damages Resulting from Riots, etc. (Darby, 805.)

1884 (award May 24, 1884).   China and United States, Ashmore Fishery Claim. (Darby, 905.)

February 27, 1884.   Great Britain and South African Republic, Southwestern Boundary of South African Republic. (Darby, 806.)

April 4, 1884, and May 30, 1885.   Bolivia and Chile, Confiscations of Property and Goods. (Darby, 806.)

May 28, 1884.   Hayti and United States, Personal Claims. (Darby, 806.)

June 19 and 21, 1884.   Germany and Great Britain, Land Concessions. (Darby, 807.)

June 28, 1884.   Colombia and Ecuador, Private Claims. (Darby, 807.)

August 23, 1884.   Chile and Germany, Damages in War. (Darby, 807.)

August 30, 1884.   Belgium and Chile, Similar Claims. (Darby, 807.)

September 22, 1884, and March 6 and 8, 1886.   Germany and Great Britain, Territorial Claims. (Darby, 808.)

January 25, 1885.   Hayti and United States, Civil Disturbances. (Darby, 808.)

February 28, 1885.   Spain and United States, Maritime Capture. (Darby, 808.)

July 11, 1885.   Austria-Hungary and Chile, Losses in War. (Darby, 809.)

September, 1885.   Germany and Spain, Disputed Territory. (Darby, 809.)

September 10, 1885.   Great Britain and Russia, Northwest Boundary. (Darby, 809.)

November 11, 1885.   Great Britain and Liberia, Boundary Question. (Darby, 801.)

December 5, 1885.   United States and Venezuela, Claims by Citizens of the United States against the Government of Venezuela. (Darby, 790.)

December 5, 1885, and October 5, 1888.   Venezuela and the United States, Review Commission. (Malloy, *Treaties, Conventions, etc.*, 1858 and 1866.)

January 19, 1886.   Chile and Switzerland, Losses in War. (Darby, 809–10.)

May 24, 1886, August 18, 1894, December 29, 1898 (three arbitrations).   Colombia and Italy, Cerruti Claim. (Darby, 810.)

1886 (award August 25, 1886).   Bakwena and Bamangwato, Ownership of Wells. (Darby, 811.)

September 28, 1886.   Honduras and Salvador, Boundary Question. (Darby, 812.)

October 25, 1886.   Bulgaria and Servia, Disputed Territory. (Darby, 811.)

December 24, 1886.   Costa Rica and Nicaragua, Boundary Question. (Darby, 811.)

April, 1887.   Great Britain and Spain, Marine Collision. (Darby, 812.)

August 1, 1887, and December 15, 1894.   Colombia, Ecuador, and Peru, Disputed Territory. (Darby, 812.)

January 26, 1888.   Guatemala and Mexico, Mutual Claims. (Darby, 813.)

April 9, 1888.   Morocco and United States, Illegal Arrest. (Darby, 813.)

May 24, 1888.   Hayti and United States, Arbitrary Arrest. (Darby, 813.)

November 9, 1888.   Afghanistan and Persia, Hashtadan Boundary Dispute. (Darby, 808.)

November 29, 1888, and April 28, 1890.   France and Holland, Boundary Dispute. (Darby, 813.)

December 6, 1888.   Denmark and United States, Seizure and Detention of Ships. (Darby, 814.)

1889.   United States and Siam, Check Claim. (Moore, *International Arbitrations,* 1899.)

January 10, 1889.   Costa Rica and Nicaragua, Inter-Oceanic Canal. (Darby, 814.)

April, 1889 (award, August 17, 1889).   Germany and Great Britain, Disputed Territory. (Darby, 814.)

September 7, 1889. Argentine Republic and Brazil, The Misiones Territory. (Darby, 814.)

February 7, 1890. Congo and Portugal, Frontier Disputes. (Darby, 815.)

March 17, 1890. China and Great Britain, Reserved Questions. (Darby, 815.)

June 5, 1890. Italy and Persia, Customs Dispute. (Darby, 815.)

July 1, 1890. Germany and Great Britain, Boundary of Walfisch Bay. (Darby, 815.)

August 5, 1890. France and Great Britain, Boundary Settlement. (Darby, 816.)

August 5, 1890. France and Great Britain, Niger and Gold Coast Boundaries. (Darby, 815.)

August 13, 1890. Great Britain and United States, and Portugal, Railway Concession. (Darby, 816.)

1890. Great Britain and Hayti, Various Claims. (Darby, 816.)

1890. France and Hayti, Similar Claims. (Darby, 817.)

February 24, 1891. France and Venezuela, Denial of Justice. (Darby, 817.)

March 11, 1891. France and Great Britain, Fishery Dispute. (Darby, 817.)

June 11, 1891. Great Britain and Portugal, Differences in East Africa. (Darby, 817.)

June 13, 1891. United States and Great Britain vs. Portugal, Loss of Concession. (Malloy, *Treaties, Conventions, etc.,* 1458.)

September 1, 1891. Italy and Portugal, Action of Port Authorities. (Darby, 818.)

January 19, 1892. United States and Venezuela, Seizure of Ships. (Darby, 818.)

February 29, 1892. Great Britain and United States, The Behring Sea Seal Fisheries. (Darby, 819.)

June 11, 1892. France and Great Britain, Greffülhe Concessions. (Darby, 819.)

July 23, 1892. Chile, France, and Peru, Distribution of Proceeds of Sale of Guano. (Darby, 819.)

August 7, 1892, May 24, 1897. Chile and United States, Mutual Claims. (Darby, 820.)

February 28, 1893. Ecuador and United States, Alleged Illegal Arrest. (Darby, 820–821.)

1893. Afghanistan, Great Britain, and Russia, Boundary Differences. (Darby, 821.)

September 26, 1893. Chile and Great Britain, Results of Civil War. (Darby, 821.)

March 21, 1894. Great Britain and South African Republic, Question of Immigration. (Darby, 821.)

October 7, 1894. Honduras and Nicaragua, Boundary Dispute. (Darby, 822.)

October 19, 1894. Chile and France, Injuries in Civil War. (Darby, 822.)

January 7, 1895. Great Britain and Portugal, Boundary Dispute. (Darby, 822.)

March 1, 1895. Guatemala and Honduras, Frontier Delimitation. (Darby, 822.)

April 1, 1895. Guatemala and Mexico, Military Occupation. (Darby, 823.)

May 16, 1895. Great Britain and Holland, Illegal Arrest. (Darby, 823.)

July 3, 1895. Hayti and San Domingo, Frontier Delimitation. (Darby, 823.)

July 6, 1895. Chile and Sweden and Norway, Results of Civil War. (Darby, 824.)

August 26, 1895. Bolivia and Peru, Salute to flag. (Darby, 824.)

November 1, 1895. Great Britain and Nicaragua, Injury to Property and Goods. (Darby, 824.)

1895. Germany and Hayti, Various Claims. (Darby, 824.)

December 3, 1895. Brazil and Italy, Personal Claims. (Darby, 825.)

January 15, 1896. France and Great Britain, The Niger Convention. (Darby, 825.)

February 8, 1896. Great Britain and United States, Claims under Fur Seal Arbitration. (Darby, 825–26.)

February 12, 1896. Brazil and Italy, Military Requisitions. (Darby, 826.)

March 27, 1896. Costa Rica and Nicaragua, Boundary Questions. (Darby, 826.)

April 17, 1896. Argentine Republic and Chile, Frontier Difficulties. (Darby, 826–27.)

July 2, 1896. Great Britain and Siam, Personal Claims. (Darby, 827.)

July 8, 1896. Great Britain and United States, Fur Seal Claims and Interference with British Sealing Fisheries. (Malloy, *Treaties, Conventions, etc.,* 766.)

July 31, 1896. Colombia and Great Britain, Breach of Contract. (Darby, 827–28.)

February 2, 1897. Great Britain and Venezuela, Territorial Contest. (Darby, 828.)

March 2, 1897. Mexico and United States, Personal Injuries. (Darby, 828.)

April 5, 1897. Chile and Peru, Damages in War. (Darby, 805.)

April 10, 1897. Brazil and France, Boundary Dispute. (Darby, 829.)

July 3, 1897. Chile and France, Personal Claims. (Darby, 829.)

1897. Chile and France, Failure of Contract. (Darby, 829.)

1897. France and Germany, Boundary Question. (Darby, 830.)

1897. Germany and Great Britain, Personal Losses. (Darby, 830.)

1897. Lippe-Detmold and Schaumburg-Lippe, Question of Inheritance. (Darby, 830.)

July 6, 1897. Siam and United States, Personal Injuries. (Darby, 831.)

September 18, 1897. Greece and Turkey, Consular Convention. (Darby, 831.)

September 20, 1897 (date of award). Siam and United States, Military Assault. (Darby, 831.)

1898. Dominican Republic and the United States, Ozama River Bridge. (Moore, *Digest of International Law,* VI, 729.)

March 18, 1898. Guatemala and Italy, Withdrawal of Employment. (Darby, 832.)

March 19, 1898. Belgium and Great Britain, Personal Injuries. (Darby, 832.)

March 28, 1898, and June 21, 1899. Ecuador and Italy, Arbitrary Expulsion. (Darby, 832.)

April 16, 1898. Chile and Peru, Form of Plebiscite. (Darby, 834.)

April 26, 1898. Costa Rica and the Republic of Central America, Mutual Complaints and Claims. (Darby, 832.)

May 17, 1898. Peru and United States, Personal Injuries. (Darby, 832–33.)

May 20, 1898. Great Britain and United States, Outstanding Questions. (Darby, 833.)

November 2, 1898. Argentine Republic, Bolivia, and Chile, Boundary Dispute. (Darby, 834.)

December, 1898, and July 20, 1917. Colombia and Venezuela, Boundaries. (*American Journal of International Law,* XVI, 428.)

March 20, 1899. Great Britain and Honduras, Detention of Ship. (Darby, 834.)

October 18, 1899, and June 30, 1900. Hayti and United States, Seizure and Sale of Goods. (Darby, 835; Malloy, 936.)

November 2, 1899. Great Britain and Russia, Title to Property. (Darby, 835.)

November 7, 1899. Germany and Great Britain and United States, Military Operations. (Darby, 835.)

November 7, 1899. Germany, Great Britain, and United States, Samoan Difficulty. (Darby, 835.)

November 25, 1899. Italy and Peru, Losses in Civil War. (Darby, 836.)

December 10, 1899. China and Great Britain, Sinking of Ship. (Darby, 836.)

1900 (award September 4, 1900). Germany and Great Britain, Seizure of Ships. (Darby, 836.)

February 23, 1900, and May 10, 1900. Guatemala and United States, Mutual Claims. (Darby, 837; Malloy, 871 and 873.)

March 22, 1900. Nicaragua and United States, Alleged Illegal Seizures. (Darby, 837.)

May 31, 1900. Bolivia and Chile, Losses during Civil War. (Darby, 837.)

August 26, 1900. Russia and United States, Seizure of Ships. (Darby, 837; Malloy, 1532.)

November 22, 1900. Italy and Peru, Interpretation of Treaty. (Darby, 838.)

April 3, 1901. France and Great Britain, Waima and *Sergent Malamine* Incidents. (Darby, 900.)

April 16, 1901. Great Britain and Italy, Boundary and Other Differences. (Darby, 906.)

September 7, 1901. China and Great Britain, Customs Differences. (Darby, 907.)

September 7, 1901. United States and China, Boxer Claims. (*American Journal of International Law,* Supplement I, 388.)

November 6, 1901. Brazil and Great Britain, Guiana Boundary. (Darby, 900.)

December, 1901. Great Britain and Nicaragua, Company Concessions. (Darby, 901.)

December 19, 1901. Salvador and United States, Company Claims. (Darby, 901.)

1902. Afghanistan and Persia, Boundary Differences. (Darby, 907.)

February 19, 1902. France and Venezuela, Indemnity for Losses, under Insurrection of 1892. (*Report of French-Venezuelan Mixed Claims Commission of 1902,* p. 1.)

April 29, 1902. Great Britain and Russia, Seizure of Property. (Darby, 902.)

April, 1902. Guatemala and Italy, Claims of Italian Subjects. (Darby, 903.)

May 22, 1902. Mexico and United States, Pious Fund of the Californias. (Darby, 901.)

June, 1902. Austria and Hungary, Territorial Claims. (Darby, 902.)

August 28, 1902. France, Germany, and Great Britain versus Japan, Leases Held in Perpetuity. (Darby, 902.)

September 6, 1902. United States and Brazil, Firing upon American Vessel. (Malloy, 152.)

December, 1902. France and Guatemala, Personal Claim. (Darby, 903.)

December, 1902. Russia and Turkey, Russian Claims for Interest. (Darby, 907.)

1903. Afghanistan and Great Britain, Tribal Quarrels. (Darby, 908.)

January, 1903. Austria-Hungary and Turkey, Non-Execution of Contracts. (Darby, 904.)

January, 1903. Dominican Republic and United States, Claim of J. Sala & Co. (Darby, 904.)

January, 1903. San Domingo and United States, Company Claims. (Darby, 905.) 905.)

January 2, 1903. Bolivia and Peru, Question of Boundary. (Darby, 904.)

January 24, 1903. Great Britain and United States, Alaska Boundary. (Darby, 908.)

January 31, 1903. San Domingo and United States, Liquidation of Debt. (Darby, 904.)

February, 1903. Turkey and the United Powers, Ottoman Public Debt. (Darby, 905.)

February 13, 1903, and May 7, 1903. Germany, Great Britain, and Italy versus Venezuela, Preferential Claims. (Darby, 905.)

February 13, 1903. Germany and Venezuela, Pecuniary Claims. (Ralston, *Venezuelan Arbitrations of 1903*, 511.)

February 13, 1903. Italy and Venezuela, Pecuniary Claims. (Ralston, *Venezuelan Arbitrations of 1903*, 643.)

February 17, 1903. United States and Venezuela, Pecuniary Claims. (Ralston, *Venezuelan Arbitrations of 1903*, p. 1.)

February 26, 1903. Mexico and Venezuela, Pecuniary Claims. (Ralston, *Venezuelan Arbitrations of 1903*, 875.)

February 27, 1903. France and Venezuela, Pecuniary Claims. (Ralston, *Venezuelan Arbitrations of 1903*, 483.)

February 28, 1903. Netherlands and Venezuela, Pecuniary Claims. (Ralston, *Venezuelan Arbitrations of 1903*, 89.)

March 7, 1903. Belgium and Venezuela, Pecuniary Claims. (Ralston, *Venezuelan Arbitrations of 1903*, 261.)

March 10, 1903. Sweden and Norway and Venezuela, Pecuniary Claims. (Ralston, *Venezuelan Arbitrations of 1903*, 945.)

April 2, 1903. Spain and Venezuela, Pecuniary Claims. (Ralston, *Venezuelan Arbitrations of 1903*, 917.)

May 7, 1903. Great Britain and Venezuela, Pecuniary Claims. (Ralston, Venezuelan Arbitrations of 1903, 294.)

August 12, 1903. Great Britain and Portugal, The Barotzeland Boundary. (Darby, 904.)

1904. Colombia and Peru, Boundary Question. (Darby, 906.)

1904. Colombia and Ecuador, Boundaries. (*Revue générale de droit international*, XIX, 256.)

1904. Nicaragua and Honduras, Boundaries. (*Revue générale de droit international*, XIX, 256.)

1904. Hayti and France, Personal Claim. (*Revue générale de. droit international*, XIX, 256.)

1904. France and Great Britain, Alleged Misuse of the French Flag in Muscat. (Darby, 906.)

March, 1904. Ecuador and Peru, Question of Boundary. (Darby, 906.)

October 13, 1904. France and Great Britain, Muscat Case. (*American Journal of International Law*, II, 921.)

1906. Brazil and Netherlands, Demarcation of Limits. (*Revue générale de droit international*, XIX, 256.)

March 14, 1908. Norway and Sweden, Maritime Frontier. (*American Journal of International Law,* IV, 226.)

May 17, 1908. Peru and United States, Individual Claim. (Malloy, 1443.)

November 10, 1908. Germany and France, Casablanca Case. (*American Journal of International Law,* III, 755.)

January 27, 1909. Great Britain and United States, North Atlantic Fisheries. (Malloy, 835.)

January 30, 1909. Great Britain and Germany, Walfisch Bay. (*American Journal of International Law,* Supplement III, 306.)

February 13, 1909. Venezuela and United States, Orinoco Shipping Company. (Malloy, 1881.)

December 1, 1909. United States and Chile, Alsop Claim. (Malloy, 2508.)

April 25, 1910. Italy and Peru, Canevaro Case. (*American Journal of International Law,* Supplement VI, 212.)

June 24, 1910. Mexico and United States, Chamizal Tract. (Malloy, 2729.)

July 22 and August 4, 1910. Russia and Turkey, Claim for Interest. (*American Journal of International Law,* VII, 178.)

August 18, 1910. Great Britain and United States, Pecuniary Claims. (Malloy, 2619.)

October 25, 1910. France and Great Britain, Savarkar Case. (*American Journal of International Law,* Supplement V, 37.)

May 9, 1911 (date of ratification exchange). Mexico and France, Clipperton Island. (*International Law Association Report for 1912.*)

March 6, 1912. France and Italy, *Carthage* Case. (*American Journal of International Law,* VII, 623.)

March 6, 1912. France and Italy, *Manouba* Case. (*American Journal of International Law,* VII, 629.)

November 8, 1912. France and Italy, *Tavignano* and other cases. (*Protocols of Hague Permanent Court of Arbitration.*)

April 3, 1913. Netherlands and Portugal, Island of Timor. (*American Journal of International Law,* Supplement IX, 107.)

July 31, 1913. Spain, France and Great Britain, and Portugal, Seizure of Religious Property. (*American Journal of International Law,* VIII, Supplement, 165.)

February 2, 1914. France and Peru, French Claims.

November 27, 1915. Panama and United States, Riot Claims. (*Foreign Relations for 1915,* 1183.)

June 28, 1919. Allied and Associated Powers and Germany (Versailles), International and Individual Claims. (*The Treaties of Peace, 1919–1923,* Carnegie Endowment for International Peace, 3.)

September 10, 1919. Allied and Associated Powers and Austria (St. Germain-en-Laye), International and Individual Claims. (*The Treaties of Peace, 1919–1923,* Carnegie Endowment for International Peace, 267.)

October 3, 1919. Hayti and United States, All Foreign Claims. (Malloy, 2678.)

November 27, 1919. Allied and Associated Powers and Bulgaria (Neuilly), International and Individual Claims. (*The Treaties of Peace, 1919–1923,* Carnegie Endowment for International Peace, 653.)

June 4, 1920. Allied and Associated Powers and Hungary (Trianon), International and Individual Claims. (*The Treaties of Peace, 1919–1923,* Carnegie Endowment for International Peace, 461.)

August 10, 1920. Allied and Associated Powers and Turkey (Sèvres), International and Individual Claims. (*The Treaties of Peace, 1919–1923,* Carnegie Endowment for International Peace, 789.)

May 21, 1921. Peru and United States, Landreau Claim. (Malloy, 2797.)

June 30, 1921. United States and Norway, Claims for Taking of Ships. (*American Journal of International Law,* Supplement XVI, 16.)

July 23, 1921. Belgium, France, Great Britain, Greece, Italy, Rumania, Serb-Croat-Slovene State, and Czechoslovakia, Danube Commission. (*American Journal of International Law,* XVII, 13.)

August 27, 1921. Great Britain and Peru, Mineral Properties. (*American Journal of International Law,* XVI, Supplement, 137.)

July 20, 1922. Peru and Chile, Tacna-Arica Dispute. (*American Journal of International Law,* Vol. XVII, Supplement, 11.)

August 10, 1922. Germany and United States, American Claims. (Malloy, 2601.)

January 30, 1923. Greece and Turkey, Exchange of Greek and Turkish Populations and Property Interests. (*The Treaties of Peace, 1919–1923,* Carnegie Endowment for International Peace, 1036.)

July 24, 1923. British Empire, France, Italy, Japan, Greece, Rumania and the Serb-Croat-Slovene State and Turkey (Lausanne), Individual and International Claims. (*The Treaties of Peace, 1919–1923,* Carnegie Endowment for International Peace, 959.)

September 8, 1923. United States and Mexico, General Mutual Claims. (U.S. Treaty Series, 678.)

September 10, 1923. Mexico and United States, Claims Arising out of Revolutions. (U.S. Treaty Series, 676.)

August 9, 1924. Reparation Commission and German Government, Disputes as to Reparations. (*American Journal of International Law,* XIX, Supplement, 24.)

November 22, 1924. France, Great Britain, Italy, Japan, Belgium, Serb-Croat-Slovene State, Interpretation of Treaty. (*American Journal of International Law,* XIX, Supplement, 111.)

November 26, 1924. Austria and Hungary, Claims of American Citizens. (*U.S. Statutes at Large,* Vol. 44, 2213.)

January 14, 1925. Belgium, France, Great Britain, United States, Italy, Japan, Brazil, Greece, Poland, Portugal, Rumania, Serb-Croat-Slovene State and Czechoslovakia, Distribution of Dawes Annuity. (*American Journal of International Law,* XIX, Supplement, 63.)

January 23, 1925. United States and Netherlands, Sovereignty over Palmas. (*American Journal of International Law,* Supplement XIX, 108.)

November 19, 1926. Great Britain and Mexico, Revolutionary acts. (*American Journal of International Law,* XXIII, Supplement 13.)

NOTE.—The foregoing list is believed to be approximately correct, but omissions are possible, and differences of opinion may exist as to classification in some cases as between mediation and arbitration.

APPENDIX B

CONVENTION FOR THE PACIFIC SETTLEMENT OF INTERNATIONAL DISPUTES[1]

PART I. THE MAINTENANCE OF GENERAL PEACE

ARTICLE 1. With a view to obviating, as far as possible, recourse to force in the relations between states, the contracting powers agree to use their best efforts to insure the pacific settlement of international differences.

PART II. GOOD OFFICES AND MEDIATION

ART. 2. In case of serious disagreement or dispute, before an appeal to arms, the contracting powers agree to have recourse, as far as circumstances allow, to the good offices or mediation of one or more friendly powers.

ART. 3. Independently of this recourse, the contracting powers deem it expedient and desirable that one or more powers, strangers to the dispute, should, on their own initiative and as far as circumstances may allow, offer their good offices or mediation to the states at variance.

Powers strangers to the dispute have the right to offer good offices or mediation even during the course of hostilities.

The exercise of this right can never be regarded by either of the parties in dispute as an unfriendly act.

ART. 4. The part of the mediator consists in reconciling the opposing claims and appeasing the feelings of resentment which may have arisen between the states at variance.

ART. 5. The functions of the mediator are at an end when once it is declared, either by one of the parties to the dispute or by the mediator himself, that the means of reconciliation proposed by him are not accepted.

ART. 6. Good offices and mediation undertaken either at the request of the parties in dispute or on the initiative of powers strangers to the dispute have exclusively the character of advice, and never have binding force.

ART. 7. The acceptance of mediation cannot, unless there be an agreement to the contrary, have the effect of interrupting, delaying, or hindering mobilization or other measures of preparation for war.

If it takes place after the commencement of hostilities, the military operations in progress are not interrupted in the absence of an agreement to the contrary.

ART. 8. The contracting powers are agreed in recommending the application, when circumstances allow, of special mediation in the following form:

In case of a serious difference endangering peace, the states at variance choose respectively a power, to which they intrust the mission of entering into direct communication with the power chosen on the other side, with the object of preventing the rupture of pacific relations.

[1] Concluded October 18, 1907.

For the period of this mandate, the term of which, unless otherwise stipulated, cannot exceed thirty days, the states in dispute cease from all direct communication on the subject of the dispute, which is regarded as referred exclusively to the mediating powers, which must use their best efforts to settle it.

In case of a definite rupture of pacific relations, these powers are charged with the joint task of taking advantage of any opportunity to restore peace.

PART III. INTERNATIONAL COMMISSIONS OF INQUIRY

ART. 9. In disputes of an international nature involving neither honor nor vital interests, and arising from a difference of opinion on points of fact, the contracting powers deem it expedient and desirable that the parties who have not been able to come to an agreement by means of diplomacy, should, as far as circumstances allow, institute an international commission of inquiry, to facilitate a solution of these disputes by elucidating the facts by means of an impartial and conscientious investigation.

ART. 10. International commissions of inquiry are constituted by special agreement between the parties in dispute.

The inquiry convention defines the facts to be examined; it determines the mode and time in which the commission is to be formed and the extent of the powers of the commissioners.

It also determines, if there is need, where the commission is to sit, and whether it may remove to another place, the language the commission shall use and the languages the use of which shall be authorized before it, as well as the date on which each party must deposit its statement of facts, and, generally speaking, all the conditions upon which the parties have agreed.

If the parties consider it necessary to appoint assessors, the convention of inquiry shall determine the mode of their selection and the extent of their powers.

ART. 11. If the inquiry convention has not determined where the commission is to sit, it will sit at The Hague.

The place of meeting, once fixed, cannot be altered by the commission except with the assent of the parties.

If the inquiry convention has not determined what languages are to be employed, the question shall be decided by the commission.

ART. 12. Unless an undertaking is made to the contrary, commissions of inquiry shall be formed in the manner determined by Articles 45 and 57 of the present convention.

ART. 13. Should one of the commissioners or one of the assessors, should there be any, either die, or resign, or be unable for any reason whatever to discharge his functions, the same procedure is followed for filling the vacancy as was followed for appointing him.

ART. 14. The parties are entitled to appoint special agents to attend the commission of inquiry, whose duty it is to represent them and to act as intermediaries between them and the commission.

They are further authorized to engage counsel or advocates, appointed by themselves, to state their case and uphold their interests before the commission.

ART. 15. The international bureau of the Permanent Court of Arbitration acts as registry for the commissions which sit at The Hague, and shall place its offices and staff at the disposal of the contracting powers for the use of the commission of inquiry.

ART. 16. If the commission meets elsewhere than at The Hague, it appoints a secretary general, whose office serves as registry.

It is the function of the registry, under the control of the president, to make the necessary arrangements for the sittings of the commission, the preparation of the minutes, and, while the inquiry lasts, for the charge of the archives, which shall subsequently be transferred to the international bureau at The Hague.

ART. 17. In order to facilitate the constitution and working of commissions of inquiry, the contracting powers recommend the following rules, which shall be applicable to the inquiry procedure in so far as the parties do not adopt other rules.

ART. 18. The commission shall settle the details of the procedure not covered by the special inquiry convention or the present convention, and shall arrange all the formalities required for dealing with the evidence.

ART. 19. On the inquiry both sides must be heard.

At the dates fixed, each party communicates to the commission and to the other party the statements of facts, if any, and, in all cases, the instruments, papers, and documents which it considers useful for ascertaining the truth, as well as the list of witnesses and experts whose evidence it wishes to be heard.

ART. 20. The commission is entitled, with the assent of the powers, to move temporarily to any place where it considers it may be useful to have recourse to this means of inquiry or to send one or more of its members. Permission must be obtained from the state on whose territory it is proposed to hold the inquiry.

ART. 21. Every investigation, and every examination of a locality, must be made in the presence of the agents and counsel of the parties or after they have been duly summoned.

ART. 22. The commission is entitled to ask from either party for such explanations and information as it considers necessary.

ART. 23. The parties undertake to supply the commission of inquiry, as fully as they may think possible, with all means and facilities necessary to enable it to become completely acquainted with, and to accurately understand, the facts in question.

They undertake to make use of the means at their disposal, under their municipal law, to insure the appearance of the witnesses or experts who are in their territory and have been summoned before the commission.

If the witnesses or experts are unable to appear before the commission, the parties will arrange for their evidence to be taken before the qualified officials of their own country.

ART. 24. For all notices to be served by the commission in the territory of a third contracting power, the commission shall apply direct to the government of the said power. The same rule applies in the case of steps being taken on the spot to procure evidence.

The requests for this purpose are to be executed so far as the means at the disposal of the power applied to under its municipal law allow. They cannot be rejected unless the power in question considers they are calculated to impair its sovereign rights or its safety.

The commission will equally be always entitled to act through the power on whose territory it sits.

ART. 25. The witnesses and experts are summoned on the request of the parties or by the commission of its own motion, and, in every case, through the government of the state in whose territory they are.

The witnesses are heard in succession and separately, in the presence of the agents and counsel, and in the order fixed by the commission.

ART. 26. The examination of witnesses is conducted by the president.

The members of the commission may, however, put to each witness questions which they consider likely to throw light on and complete his evidence, or get information on any point concerning the witness within the limits of what is necessary in order to get at the truth.

The agents and counsel of the parties may not interrupt the witness when he is making his statement, nor put any direct question to him, but they may ask the president to put such additional questions to the witness as they think expedient.

ART. 27. The witness must give his evidence without being allowed to read any written draft. He may, however, be permitted by the president to consult notes or documents if the nature of the facts referred to necessitates their employment.

ART. 28. A minute of the evidence of the witness is drawn up forthwith and read to the witness. The latter may make such alterations and additions as he thinks necessary, which will be recorded at the end of his statement.

When the whole of his statement has been read to the witness, he is asked to sign it.

ART. 29. The agents are authorized, in the course of or at the close of the inquiry, to present in writing to the commission and to the other party such statements, requisitions, or summaries of the facts as they consider useful for ascertaining the truth.

ART. 30. The commission considers its decisions in private and the proceedings are secret.

All questions are decided by a majority of the members of the commission.

If a member declines to vote, the fact must be recorded in the minutes.

ART. 31. The sittings of the commission are not public, nor the minutes and documents connected with the inquiry published except in virtue of a decision of the commission taken with the consent of the parties.

ART. 32. After the parties have presented all the explanations and evidence, and the witnesses have all been heard, the president declares the inquiry terminated, and the commission adjourns to deliberate and to draw up its report.

ART. 33. The report is signed by all the members of the commission.

If one of the members refuses to sign, the fact is mentioned; but the validity of the report is not affected.

ART. 34. The report of the commission is read at a public sitting, the agents and counsel of the parties being present or duly summoned.

A copy of the report is given to each party.

ART. 35. The report of the commission is limited to a statement of facts, and has in no way the character of an award. It leaves to the parties entire freedom as to the effect to be given to the statement.

ART. 36. Each party pays its own expenses and an equal share of the expenses incurred by the commission.

PART IV. INTERNATIONAL ARBITRATION

CHAPTER I. THE SYSTEM OF ARBITRATION

ART. 37. International arbitration has for its object the settlement of disputes between states by judges of their own choice and on the basis of respect for law.

Recourse to arbitration implies an engagement to submit in good faith to the award.

ART. 38. In questions of a legal nature, and especially in the interpretation or application of international conventions, arbitration is recognized by the contracting powers as the most effective, and, at the same time, the most equitable, means of settling disputes which diplomacy has failed to settle.

Consequently, it would be desirable that, in disputes about the above-mentioned questions, the contracting powers should, if the case arose, have recourse to arbitration, in so far as circumstances permit.

ART. 39. The arbitration convention is concluded for questions already existing or for questions which may arise eventually.

It may embrace any dispute or only disputes of a certain category.

ART. 40. Independently of general or private treaties expressly stipulating recourse to arbitration as obligatory on the contracting powers, the said powers reserve to themselves the right of concluding new agreements, general or particular, with a view to extending compulsory arbitration to all cases which they may consider it possible to submit to it.

CHAPTER II. THE PERMANENT COURT OF ARBITRATION

ART. 41. With the object of facilitating an immediate recourse to arbitration for international differences which it has not been possible to settle by diplomacy, the contracting powers undertake to maintain the Permanent Court of Arbitration, as established by the First Peace Conference, accessible at all times, and operating, unless otherwise stipulated by the parties, in accordance with the rules of procedure inserted in the present convention.

ART. 42. The Permanent Court is competent for all arbitration cases, unless the parties agree to institute a special tribunal.

ART. 43. The Permanent Court sits at The Hague.

An international bureau serves as registry for the court. It is the channel for communications relative to the meetings of the court; it has charge of the archives and conducts all the administrative business.

The contracting powers undertake to communicate to the bureau, as soon as possible, a certified copy of any conditions of arbitration arrived at between them, and of any award concerning them delivered by a special tribunal.

They likewise undertake to communicate to the bureau the laws, regulations, and documents eventually showing the execution of the awards given by the court.

ART. 44. Each contracting power selects four persons at the most, of known competency in questions of international law, of the highest moral reputation, and disposed to accept the duties of arbitrator.

The persons thus selected are inscribed, as members of the court, in a list which shall be notified to all the contracting powers by the bureau.

Any alteration in the list of arbitrators is brought by the bureau to the knowledge of the contracting powers.

Two or more powers may agree on the selection in common of one or more members.

The same person can be selected by different powers.

The members of the court are appointed for a term of six years. These appointments are renewable.

Should a member of the court die or resign, the same procedure is followed for filling the vacancy as was followed for appointing him. In this case the appointment is made for a fresh period of six years.

ART. 45. When the contracting powers wish to have recourse to the Permanent Court for the settlement of a difference which has arisen between them, the arbitrators called upon to form the tribunal with jurisdiction to decide this difference must be chosen from the general list of members of the court.

Failing the direct agreement of the parties on the composition of the arbitration tribunal, the following course shall be pursued:

Each party appoints two arbitrators, of whom one only can be its national or chosen from among the persons selected by it as members of the Permanent Court. These arbitrators together choose an umpire.

If the votes are equally divided, the choice of the umpire is intrusted to a third power, selected by the parties by common accord.

If an agreement is not arrived at on this subject, each party selects a different power, and the choice of the umpire is made in concert by the powers thus selected.

If, within two months' time, these two powers cannot come to an agreement, each of them presents two candidates taken from the list of members of the Permanent Court, exclusive of the members selected by the parties and not being nationals of either of them. Drawing lots determines which of the candidates thus presented shall be umpire.

ART. 46. The tribunal being thus composed, the parties notify to the bureau their determination to have recourse to the court, the text of their *Compromis*,[1] and the names of the arbitrators.

---

[1] The foundation agreement in an international arbitration defining the point at issue and arranging the procedure to be followed; sometimes used as equivalent to protocol. See Article 52 [Ralston].

The bureau communicates without delay to each arbitrator the *Compromis* and the names of the other members of the tribunal.

The tribunal assembles at the date fixed by the parties. The bureau makes the necessary arrangements for the meeting.

The members of the tribunal, in the exercise of their duties and out of their own country, enjoy diplomatic privileges and immunities.

ART. 47. The bureau is authorized to place its offices and staff at the disposal of the contracting powers for the use of any special board of arbitration.

The jurisdiction of the Permanent Court may, within the conditions laid down in the regulations, be extended to disputes between noncontracting powers or between contracting powers and noncontracting powers, if the parties are agreed on recourse to this tribunal.

ART. 48. The contracting powers consider it their duty, if a serious dispute threatens to break out between two or more of them, to remind these latter that the Permanent Court is open to them.

Consequently, they declare that the fact of reminding the parties at variance of the provisions of the present convention, and the advice given to them, in the highest interests of peace, to have recourse to the Permanent Court, can only be regarded as friendly actions.

In case of dispute between two powers, one of them can always address to the international bureau a note containing a declaration that it would be ready to submit the dispute to arbitration.

The bureau must at once inform the other power of the declaration.

ART. 49. The permanent administrative council, composed of the diplomatic representatives of the contracting powers accredited to The Hague and of the Netherland Minister for Foreign Affairs, who will act as president, is charged with the direction and control of the international bureau.

The council settles its rules of procedure and all other necessary regulations.

It decides all questions of administration which may arise with regard to the operations of the court.

It has entire control over the appointment, suspension, or dismissal of the officials and employés of the bureau.

It fixes the payments and salaries, and controls the general expenditure.

At meetings duly summoned the presence of nine members is sufficient to render valid the discussions of the council. The decisions are taken by a majority of votes.

The council communicates to the contracting powers without delay the regulations adopted by it. It furnishes them with an annual report on the labors of the court, the working of the administration, and the expenditure. The report likewise contains a résumé of what is important in the documents communicated to the bureau by the powers in virtue of Article 43, paragraphs 3 and 4.

ART. 50. The expenses of the bureau shall be borne by the contracting powers in the proportion fixed for the international bureau of the Universal Postal Union.

The expenses to be charged to the adhering powers shall be reckoned from the date on which their adhesion comes into force.

Chapter III. Arbitration Procedure

Art. 51. With a view to encouraging the development of arbitration the contracting powers have agreed on the following rules, which are applicable to arbitration procedure, unless other rules have been agreed on by the parties.

Art. 52. The powers which have recourse to arbitration sign a *Compromis,* in which the subject of the dispute is clearly defined, the time allowed for appointing arbitrators, the form, order, and time in which the communication referred to in Article 63 must be made, and the amount of the sum which each party must deposit in advance to defray the expenses.

The *Compromis* likewise defines, if there is occasion, the manner of appointing arbitrators, any special powers which may eventually belong to the tribunal, where it shall meet, the language it shall use, and the languages the employment of which shall be authorized before it, and, generally speaking, all the conditions on which the parties are agreed.

Art. 53. The Permanent Court is competent to settle the *Compromis,* if the parties are agreed to have recourse to it for the purpose.

It is similarly competent, even if the request is only made by one of the parties, when all attempts to reach an understanding through the diplomatic channel have failed, in the case of:

1. A dispute covered by a general treaty of arbitration concluded or renewed after the present convention has come into force, and providing for a *Compromis* in all disputes and not either explicitly or implicitly excluding the settlement of the *Compromis* from the competence of the court. Recourse cannot, however, be had to the court if the other party declares that in its opinion the dispute does not belong to the category of disputes which can be submitted to compulsory arbitration, unless the treaty of arbitration confers upon the arbitration tribunal the power of deciding this preliminary question.

2. A dispute arising from contract debts claimed from one power by another power as due to its nationals, and for the settlement of which the offer of arbitration has been accepted. This arrangement is not applicable if acceptance is subject to the condition that the *Compromis* should be settled in some other way.

Art. 54. In the cases contemplated in the preceding article, the *Compromis* shall be settled by a commission consisting of five members selected in the manner arranged for in Article 45, paragraphs 3 to 6.

The fifth member is president of the commission *ex officio.*

Art. 55. The duties of arbitrator may be conferred on one arbitrator alone or on several arbitrators selected by the parties as they please, or chosen by them from the members of the Permanent Court of Arbitration established by the present convention.

Failing the constitution of the tribunal by direct agreement between the parties, the course referred to in Article 45, paragraphs 3 to 6, is followed.

Art. 56. When a sovereign or the chief of a state is chosen as arbitrator, the arbitration procedure is settled by him.

Art. 57. The umpire is president of the tribunal *ex officio.*

When the tribunal does not include an umpire, it appoints its own president.

Art. 58. When the *Compromis* is settled by a commission, as contemplated in Article 54, and in the absence of an agreement to the contrary, the commission itself shall form the arbitration tribunal.

Art. 59. Should one of the arbitrators either die, retire, or be unable for any reason whatever to discharge his functions, the same procedure is followed for filling the vacancy as was followed for appointing him.

Art. 60. The tribunal sits at The Hague, unless some other place is selected by the parties.

The tribunal can only sit in the territory of a third power with the latter's consent.

The place of meeting once fixed cannot be altered by the tribunal, except with the consent of the parties.

Art. 61. If the question as to what languages are to be used has not been settled by the *Compromis*, it shall be decided by the tribunal.

Art. 62. The parties are entitled to appoint special agents to attend the tribunal to act as intermediaries between themselves and the tribunal.

They are further authorized to retain, for the defense of their rights and interests before the tribunal, counsel or advocates appointed by themselves for this purpose.

The members of the Permanent Court may not act as agents, counsel, or advocates except on behalf of the power which appointed them members of the court.

Art. 63. As a general rule, arbitration procedure comprises two distinct phases: pleadings and oral discussions.

The pleadings consist in the communication, by the respective agents to the members of the tribunal and the opposite party, of cases, counter-cases, and, if necessary, of replies; the parties annex thereto all papers and documents called for in the case. This communication shall be made either directly or through the intermediary of the international bureau, in the order and within the time fixed by the *Compromis*.

The time fixed by the *Compromis* may be extended by mutual agreement by the parties, or by the tribunal when the latter considers it necessary for the purpose of reaching a just decision.

The discussions consist in the oral development, before the tribunal, of the arguments of the parties.

Art. 64. A certified copy of every document produced by one party must be communicated to the other party.

Art. 65. Unless special circumstances arise, the tribunal does not meet until the pleadings are closed.

Art. 66. The discussions are under the control of the president.

They are only public if it be so decided by the tribunal, with the assent of the parties.

They are recorded in minutes drawn up by the secretaries appointed by the president. These minutes are signed by the president and by one of the secretaries, and alone have an authentic character.

ART. 67. After the close of the pleadings, the tribunal is entitled to refuse discussion of all new papers or documents which one of the parties may wish to submit to it without the consent of the other party.

ART. 68. The tribunal is free to take into consideration new papers or documents to which its attention may be drawn by the agents or counsel of the parties.

In this case, the tribunal has the right to require the production of these papers or documents, but is obliged to make them known to the opposite party.

ART. 69. The tribunal can, besides, require from the agents of the parties the production of all papers, and can demand all necessary explanations. In case of refusal the tribunal takes note of it.

ART. 70. The agents and the counsel of the parties are authorized to present orally to the tribunal all the arguments they may consider expedient in defense of their case.

ART. 71. They are entitled to raise objections and points. The decisions of the tribunal on these points are final and cannot form the subject of any subsequent discussion.

ART. 72. The members of the tribunal are entitled to put questions to the agents and counsel of the parties, and to ask them for explanations on doubtful points.

Neither the questions put, nor the remarks made by members of the tribunal in the course of the discussions, can be regarded as an expression of opinion by the tribunal in general or by its members in particular.

ART. 73. The tribunal is authorized to declare its competence in interpreting the *Compromis,* as well as the other treaties which may be invoked, and in applying the principles of law.

ART. 74. The tribunal is entitled to issue rules of procedure for the conduct of the case, to decide the forms, order, and time in which each party must conclude its arguments, and to arrange all the formalities required for dealing with the evidence.

ART. 75. The parties undertake to supply the tribunal, as fully as they consider possible, with all the information required for deciding the case.

ART. 76. For all notices which the tribunal has to serve in the territory of a third contracting power, the tribunal shall apply direct to the government of that power. The same rule applies in the case of steps being taken to procure evidence on the spot.

The requests for this purpose are to be executed as far as the means at the disposal of the power applied to under its municipal law allow. They cannot be rejected unless the power in question considers them calculated to impair its own sovereign rights or its safety.

The court will equally be always entitled to act through the power on whose territory it sits.

ART. 77. When the agents and counsel of the parties have submitted all the explanations and evidence in support of their case the president shall declare the discussion closed.

ART. 78. The tribunal considers its decisions in private and the proceedings remain secret.

All questions are decided by a majority of the members of the tribunal.

ART. 79. The award must give the reasons on which it is based. It contains the names of the arbitrators; it is signed by the president and registrar or by the secretary acting as registrar.

ART. 80. The award is read out in public sitting, the agents and counsel of the parties being present or duly summoned to attend.

ART. 81. The award, duly pronounced and notified to the agents of the parties, settles the dispute definitively and without appeal.

ART. 82. Any dispute arising between the parties as to the interpretation and execution of the award shall, in the absence of an agreement to the contrary, be submitted to the tribunal which pronounced it.

ART. 83. The parties can reserve in the *Compromis* the right to demand the revision of the award.

In this case and unless there be an agreement to the contrary, the demand must be addressed to the tribunal which pronounced the award. It can only be made on the ground of the discovery of some new fact calculated to exercise a decisive influence upon the award and which was unknown to the tribunal and to the party which demanded the revision at the time the discussion was closed.

Proceedings for revision can only be instituted by a decision of the tribunal expressly recording the existence of the new fact, recognizing in it the character described in the preceding paragraph, and declaring the demand admissible on this ground.

The *Compromis* fixes the period within which the demand for revision must be made.

ART. 84. The award is not binding except on the parties in dispute.

When it concerns the interpretation of a convention to which powers other than those in dispute are parties, they shall inform all the signatory powers in good time. Each of these powers is entitled to intervene in the case. If one or more avail themselves of this right, the interpretation contained in the award is equally binding on them.

ART. 85. Each party pays its own expenses and an equal share of the expenses of the tribunal.

CHAPTER IV. ARBITRATION BY SUMMARY PROCEDURE

ART. 86. With a view to facilitating the working of the system of arbitration in disputes admitting of a summary procedure, the contracting powers adopt the following rules, which shall be observed in the absence of other arrangements and subject to the reservation that the provisions of Chapter III apply so far as may be.

ART. 87. Each of the parties in dispute appoints an arbitrator. The two arbitrators thus selected choose an umpire. If they do not agree on this point, each of them proposes two candidates taken from the general list of the members of the Permanent Court exclusive of the members appointed by either of the parties and not being nationals of either of them; which of the candidates thus proposed shall be the umpire is determined by lot.

The umpire presides over the tribunal, which gives its decisions by a majority of votes.

ART. 88. In the absence of any previous agreement the tribunal, as soon as it is formed, settles the time within which the two parties must submit their respective cases to it.

ART. 89. Each party is represented before the tribunal by an agent, who serves as intermediary between the tribunal and the government who appointed him.

ART. 90. The proceedings are conducted exclusively in writing. Each party, however, is entitled to ask that witnesses and experts should be called. The tribunal has, for its part, the right to demand oral explanations from the agents of the two parties, as well as from the experts and witnesses whose appearance in court it may consider useful.

PART V. FINAL PROVISIONS

ART. 91. The present convention, duly ratified, shall replace, as between the contracting powers, the Convention for the Pacific Settlement of International Disputes of the 29th July, 1899.

ART. 92. The present convention shall be ratified as soon as possible.

The ratifications shall be deposited at The Hague.

The first deposit of ratifications shall be recorded in a *procès-verbal* signed by the representatives of the powers which take part therein and by the Netherland Minister for Foreign Affairs.

The subsequent deposits of ratifications shall be made by means of a written notification, addressed to the Netherland government and accompanied by the instrument of ratification.

A duly certified copy of the *procès-verbal* relative to the first deposit of ratifications, of the notifications mentioned in the preceding paragraph, and of the instruments of ratification, shall be immediately sent by the Netherland government, through the diplomatic channel, to the powers invited to the Second Peace Conference, as well as to those powers which have adhered to the convention. In the cases contemplated in the preceding paragraph, the said government shall at the same time inform the powers of the date on which it received the notification.

ART. 93. Non-signatory powers which have been invited to the Second Peace Conference may adhere to the present convention.

The power which desires to adhere notifies its intention in writing to the Netherland government, forwarding to it the act of adhesion, which shall be deposited in the archives of the said government.

This government shall immediately forward to all the other powers invited to the Second Peace Conference a duly certified copy of the notification as well as of the act of adhesion, mentioning the date on which it received the notification.

ART. 94. The conditions on which the powers which have not been invited to the Second Peace Conference may adhere to the present convention shall form the subject of a subsequent agreement between the contracting powers.

ART. 95. The present convention shall take effect, in the case of the powers which were not a party to the first deposit of ratifications, sixty days after the date of the *procès-verbal* of this deposit, and, in the case of the powers which ratify subsequently or which adhere, sixty days after the notification of their ratification or of their adhesion has been received by the Netherland government.

ART. 96. In the event of one of the contracting parties wishing to denounce the present convention, the denunciation shall be notified in writing to the Netherland government, which shall immediately communicate a duly certified copy of the notification to all the other powers informing them of the date on which it was received.

The denunciation shall only have effect in regard to the notifying power, and one year after the notification has reached the Netherland government.

ART. 97. A register kept by the Netherland Minister for Foreign Affairs shall give the date of the deposit of ratifications effected in virtue of Article 92, paragraphs 3 and 4, as well as the date on which the notifications of adhesion (Article 93, paragraph 2) or of denunciation (Article 96, paragraph 1) have been received.

Each contracting power is entitled to have access to this register and to be supplied with duly certified extracts from it.

In faith whereof the plenipotentiaries have appended their signatures to the present convention.

Done at The Hague, the 18th October, 1907, in a single copy, which shall remain deposited in the archives of the Netherland government, and duly certified copies of which shall be sent, through the diplomatic channel, to the contracting powers.

[*Here follow signatures.*]

APPENDIX C

STATUTE OF THE PERMANENT COURT OF INTERNATIONAL JUSTICE

PROVIDED FOR BY ARTICLE 14 OF THE COVENANT OF THE LEAGUE OF NATIONS

ARTICLE 1. A Permanent Court of International Justice is hereby established in accordance with Article 14 of the Covenant of the League of Nations. This Court shall be in addition to the Court of Arbitration organized by the Conventions of The Hague of 1899 and 1907, and to the special Tribunals of Arbitration to which States are always at liberty to submit their disputes for settlement.

CHAPTER I. ORGANIZATION OF THE COURT

ART. 2. The Permanent Court of International Justice shall be composed of a body of independent judges, elected regardless of their nationality from among persons of high moral character, who possess the qualifications required in their respective countries for appointment to the highest judicial offices, or are jurisconsults of recognized competence in international law.

ART. 3. The Court shall consist of fifteen members: eleven judges and four deputy-judges. The number of judges and deputy-judges may hereafter be increased by the Assembly, upon the proposal of the Council of the League of Nations, to a total of fifteen judges and six deputy-judges.

ART. 4. The members of the Court shall be elected by the Assembly and by the Council from a list of persons nominated by the national groups in the Court of Arbitration, in accordance with the following provisions.

In the case of Members of the League of Nations not represented in the Permanent Court of Arbitration, the list of candidates shall be drawn up by national groups appointed for this purpose by their Governments under the same conditions as those prescribed for members of the Permanent Court of Arbitration by Article 44 of the Convention of The Hague of 1907 for the pacific settlement of international disputes.

ART. 5. At least three months before the date of the election, the Secretary-General of the League of Nations shall address a written request to the Members of the Court of Arbitration belonging to the States mentioned in the Annex to the Covenant or to the States which join the League subsequently, and to the persons appointed under paragraph 2 of Article 4, inviting them to undertake, within a given time, by national groups, the nomination of persons in a position to accept the duties of a member of the Court.

No group may nominate more than four persons, not more than two of whom shall be of their own nationality. In no case must the number of candidates nominated be more than double the number of seats to be filled.

ART. 6. Before making these nominations, each national group is recommended to consult its Highest Court of Justice, its Legal Faculties and Schools of Law, and its National Academies and national sections of International Academies devoted to the study of Law.

ART. 7. The Secretary-General of the League of Nations shall prepare a list in alphabetical order of all the persons thus nominated. Save as provided in Article 12, paragraph 2, these shall be the only persons eligible for appointment.

The Secretary-General shall submit this list to the Assembly and to the Council.

ART. 8. The Assembly and the Council shall proceed independently of one another to elect, firstly the judges, then the deputy-judges.

ART. 9. At every election, the electors shall bear in mind that not only should all the persons appointed as members of the Court possess the qualifications required, but the whole body also should represent the main forms of civilization and the principal legal systems of the world.

ART. 10. Those candidates who obtain an absolute majority of votes in the Assembly and in the Council shall be considered as elected.

In the event of more than one national of the same Member of the League being elected by the votes of both the Assembly and the Council, the eldest of these only shall be considered as elected.

ART. 11. If, after the first meeting held for the purpose of the election, one or more seats remain to be filled, a second and, if necessary, a third meeting shall take place.

ART. 12. If, after the third meeting, one or more seats still remain unfilled, a joint conference consisting of six members, three appointed by the Assembly and three by the Council, may be formed, at any time, at the request of either the Assembly or the Council, for the purpose of choosing one name for each seat still vacant, to submit to the Assembly and the Council for their respective acceptance.

If the Conference is unanimously agreed upon any person who fulfils the required conditions, he may be included in its list, even though he was not included in the list of nominations referred to in Articles 4 and 5.

If the joint conference is satisfied that it will not be successful in procuring an election, those members of the Court who have already been appointed shall, within a period to be fixed by the Council, proceed to fill the vacant seats by selection from among those candidates who have obtained votes either in the Assembly or in the Council.

In the event of an equality of votes among the judges, the eldest judge shall have a casting vote.

ART. 13. The members of the Court shall be elected for nine years.

They may be re-elected.

They shall continue to discharge their duties until their places have been filled. Though replaced, they shall finish any cases which they may have begun.

ART. 14. Vacancies which may occur shall be filled by the same method as that laid down for the first election. A member of the Court elected to replace a member whose period of appointment had not expired will hold the appointment for the remainder of his predecessor's term.

ART. 15. Deputy-judges shall be called upon to sit in the order laid down in a list.

This list shall be prepared by the Court and shall have regard firstly to priority of election and secondly to age.

ART. 16. The ordinary Members of the Court may not exercise any political or administrative function. This provision does not apply to the deputy-judges except when performing their duties on the Court.

Any doubt on this point is settled by the decision of the Court.

ART. 17. No Member of the Court can act as agent, counsel or advocate in any case of an international nature. This provision only applies to the deputy-judges as regards cases in which they are called upon to exercise their functions on the Court.

No Member may participate in the decision of any case in which he has previously taken an active part, as agent, counsel or advocate for one of the contesting parties, or as a Member of a national or international Court, or of a Commission of inquiry, or in any other capacity.

Any doubt on this point is settled by the decision of the Court.

ART. 18. A member of the Court can not be dismissed unless, in the unanimous opinion of the other members, he has ceased to fulfil the required conditions.

Formal notification thereof shall be made to the Secretary-General of the League of Nations, by the Registrar.

This notification makes the place vacant.

ART. 19. The members of the Court, when engaged on the business of the Court, shall enjoy diplomatic privileges and immunities.

ART. 20. Every member of the Court shall, before taking up his duties, make a solemn declaration in open Court that he will exercise his powers impartially and conscientiously.

ART. 21. The Court shall elect its President and Vice-President for three years; they may be re-elected.

It shall appoint its Registrar.

The duties of Registrar of the Court shall not be deemed incompatible with those of Secretary-General of the Permanent Court of Arbitration.

ART. 22. The seat of the Court shall be established at The Hague.

The President and Registrar shall reside at the seat of the Court.

ART. 23. A session of the Court shall be held every year.

Unless otherwise provided by rules of Court, this session shall begin on the 15th of June, and shall continue for so long as may be deemed necessary to finish the cases on the list.

The President may summon an extraordinary session of the Court whenever necessary.

ART. 24. If, for some special reason, a member of the Court considers that he should not take part in the decision of a particular case, he shall so inform the President.

If the President considers that for some special reason one of the members of the Court should not sit on a particular case, he shall give him notice accordingly.

If in any such case the member of the Court and the President disagree, the matter shall be settled by the decision of the Court.

ART. 25. The full Court shall sit except when it is expressly provided otherwise.

If eleven judges can not be present, the number shall be made up by calling on deputy-judges to sit.

If, however, eleven judges are not available, a quorum of nine judges shall suffice to constitute the Court.

ART. 26. Labor cases, particularly cases referred to in Part XIII (Labor) of the Treaty of Versailles and the corresponding portions of the other Treaties of Peace, shall be heard and determined by the Court under the following conditions:

The Court will appoint every three years a special chamber of five judges, selected so far as possible with due regard to the provisions of Article 9. In addition, two judges shall be selected for the purpose of replacing a judge who finds it impossible to sit. If the parties so demand, cases will be heard and determined by this chamber. In the absence of any such demand, the Court will sit with the number of judges provided for in Article 25. On all occasions the judges will be assisted by four technical assessors sitting with them, but without the right to vote, and chosen with a view to insuring a just representation of the competing interests.

If there is a national of one only of the parties sitting as a judge in the chamber referred to in the preceding paragraph, the President will invite one of the other judges to retire in favor of a judge chosen by the other party in accordance with Article 31.

The technical assessors shall be chosen for each particular case in accordance with rules of procedure under Article 30 from a list of "Assessors for Labor cases" composed of two persons nominated by each Member of the League of Nations and an equivalent number nominated by the Governing Body of the Labor Office. The Governing Body will nominate, as to one half, representatives of the workers, and as to one half, representatives of employers from the list referred to in Article 412 of the Treaty of Versailles and the corresponding Articles of the other Treaties of Peace.

In Labor cases the International Labor Office shall be at liberty to furnish the Court with all relevant information, and for this purpose the Director of that Office shall receive copies of all the written proceedings.

ART. 27. Cases relating to transit and communications, particularly cases referred to in Part XII (Ports, Waterways, and Railways) of the Treaty of Versailles and the corresponding portions of the other Treaties of Peace shall be heard and determined by the Court under the following conditions:

The Court will appoint every three years a special chamber of five judges, selected so far as possible with due regard to the provisions of Article 9. In addition, two judges shall be selected for the purpose of replacing a judge who finds it impossible to sit. If the parties so demand, cases will be heard and determined by this chamber. In the absence of any such demand, the Court will sit with the number of judges provided for in Article 25. When desired by the parties or decided by the Court, the judges will be assisted by four technical assessors sitting with them, but without the right to vote.

If there is a national of one only of the parties sitting as a judge in the chamber referred to in the preceding paragraph, the President will invite one of the other judges to retire in favor of a judge chosen by the other party in accordance with Article 31.

The technical assessors shall be chosen for each particular case in accordance with rules of procedure under Article 30 from a list of "Assessors for Transit and Communications cases" composed of two persons nominated by each Member of the League of Nations.

ART. 28. The special chambers provided for in Articles 26 and 27 may, with the consent of the parties to the dispute, sit elsewhere than at The Hague.

ART. 29. With a view to the speedy dispatch of business, the Court shall form annually a chamber composed of three judges who, at the request of the contesting parties, may hear and determine cases by summary procedure.

ART. 30. The Court shall frame rules for regulating its procedure. In particular, it shall lay down rules for summary procedure.

ART. 31. Judges of the nationality of each contesting party shall retain their right to sit in the case before the Court.

If the Court includes upon the Bench a judge of the nationality of one of the parties only, the other party may select from among the deputy-judges a judge of its nationality, if there be one. If there should not be one, the party may choose a judge, preferably from among those persons who have been nominated as candidates as provided in Articles 4 and 5.

If the Court includes upon the Bench no judge of the nationality of the contesting parties, each of these may proceed to select or choose a judge as provided in the preceding paragraph.

Should there be several parties in the same interest, they shall, for the purpose of the preceding provisions, be reckoned as one party only. Any doubt upon this point is settled by the decision of the Court.

Judges selected or chosen as laid down in paragraphs 2 and 3 of this Article shall fulfil the conditions required by Articles 2, 16, 17, 20, 24 of this Statute. They shall take part in the decision on an equal footing with their colleagues.

ART. 32. The judges shall receive an annual indemnity to be determined by the Assembly of the League of Nations upon the proposal of the Council. This indemnity must not be decreased during the period of a judge's appointment.

The President shall receive a special grant for his period of office, to be fixed in the same way.

The Vice-Presidents, judges, and deputy-judges shall receive a grant for the actual performance of their duties, to be fixed in the same way.

Traveling expenses incurred in the performance of their duties shall be refunded to judges and deputy-judges who do not reside at the seat of the Court.

Grants due to judges selected or chosen as provided in Article 31 shall be determined in the same way.

The salary of the Registrar shall be decided by the Council upon the proposal of the Court.

The Assembly of the League of Nations shall lay down, on the proposal of the Council, a special regulation fixing the conditions under which retiring pensions may be given to the personnel of the Court.

ART. 33. The expenses of the Court shall be borne by the League of Nations, in such a manner as shall be decided by the Assembly upon the proposal of the Council.

CHAPTER II. COMPETENCE OF THE COURT

ART. 34. Only States or Members of the League of Nations can be parties in cases before the Court.

ART. 35. The Court shall be open to the Members of the League and also to States mentioned in the Annex to the Covenant.

The conditions under which the Court shall be open to other States shall, subject to the special provisions contained in treaties in force, be laid down by the Council, but in no case shall such provisions place the parties in a position of inequality before the Court.

When a State which is not a Member of the League of Nations is a party to a dispute, the Court will fix the amount which that party is to contribute toward the expenses of the Court.

ART. 36. The jurisdiction of the Court comprises all cases which the parties refer to it and all matters specially provided for in Treaties and Conventions in force.

The Members of the League of Nations and the States mentioned in the Annex to the Covenant may, either when signing or ratifying the protocol to which the present Statute is adjoined, or at a later moment, declare that they recognize as compulsory, *ipso facto* and without special agreement, in relation to any other Member or State accepting the same obligation, the jurisdiction of the Court in all or any of the classes of legal disputes concerning:

(a) The interpretation of a Treaty;

(b) Any question of International Law;

(c) The existence of any fact which, if established, would constitute a breach of an international obligation;

(d) The nature or extent of the reparation to be made for the breach of an international obligation.

The declaration referred to above may be made unconditionally or on condition of reciprocity on the part of several or certain Members or States, or for a certain time.

In the event of a dispute as to whether the Court has jurisdiction, the matter shall be settled by the decision of the Court.

ART. 37. When a treaty or convention in force provides for the reference of a matter to a tribunal to be instituted by the League of Nations, the Court will be such tribunal.

ART. 38. The Court shall apply:

1. International conventions, whether general or particular, establishing rules expressly recognized by the contesting States;

2. International custom, as evidence of a general practice accepted as law;

3. The general principles of law recognized by civilized nations;

4. Subject to the provisions of Article 59, judicial decisions and the teachings of the most highly qualified publicists of the various nations, as subsidiary means for the determination of rules of law.

This provision shall not prejudice the power of the Court to decide a case *ex aequo et bono,* if the parties agree thereto.

CHAPTER III. PROCEDURE

ART. 39. The official languages of the Court shall be French and English. If the parties agree that the case shall be conducted in French, the judgment will be delivered in French. If the parties agree that the case shall be conducted in English, the judgment will be delivered in English.

In the absence of an agreement as to which language shall be employed, each party may, in the pleadings, use the language which it prefers; the decision of the Court will be given in French and English. In this case the Court will at the same time determine which of the two texts shall be considered as authoritative.

The Court may, at the request of the parties, authorize a language other than French or English to be used.

ART. 40. Cases are brought before the Court, as the case may be, either by the notification of the special agreement or by a written application addressed to the Registrar. In either case the subject of the dispute and the contesting parties must be indicated.

The Registrar shall forthwith communicate the application to all concerned.

He shall also notify the Members of the League of Nations through the Secretary-General.

ART. 41. The Court shall have the power to indicate, if it considers that circumstances so require, any provisional measures which ought to be taken to reserve the respective rights of either party.

Pending the final decision, notice of the measures suggested shall forthwith be given to the parties and the Council.

ART. 42. The parties shall be represented by Agents.

They may have the assistance of Counsel or Advocates before the Court.

ART. 43. The procedure shall consist of two parts: written and oral.

The written proceedings shall consist of the communication to the judges and to the parties of cases, counter-cases, and, if necessary, replies; also all papers and documents in support.

These communications shall be made through the Registrar, in the order and within the time fixed by the Court.

A certified copy of every document produced by one party shall be communicated to the other party.

The oral proceedings shall consist of the hearing by the Court of witnesses, experts, agents, counsel, and advocates.

ART. 44. For the service of all notices upon persons other than the agents, counsel, and advocates, the Court shall apply direct to the Government of the State upon whose territory the notice has to be served.

The same provision shall apply whenever steps are to be taken to procure evidence on the spot.

Art. 45. The hearing shall be under the control of the President or, in his absence, of the Vice-President; if both are absent, the senior judge shall preside.

Art. 46. The hearing in Court shall be public, unless the Court shall decide otherwise, or unless the parties demand that the public be not admitted.

Art. 47. Minutes shall be made at each hearing, and signed by the Registrar and the President.

These minutes shall be the only authentic record.

Art. 48. The Court shall make orders for the conduct of the case, shall decide the form and time in which each party must conclude its arguments, and make all arrangements connected with the taking of evidence.

Art. 49. The Court may, even before the hearing begins, call upon the agents to produce any document or to supply any explanations. Formal note shall be taken of any refusal.

Art. 50. The Court may, at any time, intrust any individual, body, bureau, commission, or other organization that it may select, with the task of carrying out an inquiry or giving an expert opinion.

Art. 51. During the hearing any relevant questions are to be put to the witnesses and experts under the conditions laid down by the Court in the rules of procedure referred to in Article 30.

Art. 52. After the Court has received the proofs and evidence within the time specified for the purpose, it may refuse to accept any further oral or written evidence that one party may desire to present unless the other side consents.

Art. 53. Whenever one of the parties shall not appear before the Court, or shall fail to defend his case, the other party may call upon the Court to decide in favor of his claim.

The Court must, before doing so, satisfy itself, not only that it has jurisdiction in accordance with Articles 36 and 37, but also that the claim is well founded in fact and law.

Art. 54. When, subject to the control of the Court, the agents, advocates, and counsel have completed their presentation of the case, the President shall declare the hearing closed.

The Court shall withdraw to consider the judgment.

The deliberations of the Court shall take place in private and remain secret.

Art. 55. All questions shall be decided by a majority of the judges present at the hearing.

In the event of an equality of votes, the President or his deputy shall have a casting vote.

Art. 56. The judgment shall state the reasons on which it is based.

It shall contain the names of the judges who have taken part in the decision.

Art. 57. If the judgment does not represent in whole or in part the unanimous opinion of the judges, dissenting judges are entitled to deliver a separate opinion.

Art. 58. The judgment shall be signed by the President and by the Registrar. It shall be read in open Court, due notice having been given to the agents.

ART. 59. The decision of the Court has no binding force except between the parties and in respect of that particular case.

ART. 60. The judgment is final and without appeal. In the event of dispute as to the meaning or scope of the judgment, the Court shall construe it upon the request of any party.

ART. 61. An application for revision of a judgment can be made only when it is based upon the discovery of some fact of such a nature as to be a decisive factor, which fact was, when the judgment was given, unknown to the Court and also to the party claiming revision, always provided that such ignorance was not due to negligence.

The proceedings for revision will be opened by a judgment of the Court expressly recording the existence of the new fact, recognizing that it has such a character as to lay the case open to revision, and declaring the application admissible on this ground.

The Court may require previous compliance with the terms of the judgment before it admits proceedings in revision.

The application for revision must be made at latest within six months of the discovery of the new fact.

No application for revision may be made after the lapse of ten years from the date of the sentence.

ART 62. Should a State consider that it has an interest of a legal nature which may be affected by the decision in the case, it may submit a request to the Court to be permitted to intervene as a third party.

It will be for the Court to decide upon this request.

ART. 63. Whenever the construction of a convention to which States other than those concerned in the case are parties is in question, the Registrar shall notify all such States forthwith.

Every State so notified has the right to intervene in the proceedings; but if it uses this right, the construction given by the judgment will be equally binding upon it.

ART. 64. Unless otherwise decided by the Court, each party shall bear its own costs.

RULES OF THE PERMANENT COURT OF INTERNATIONAL JUSTICE[1]

CHAPTER I. THE COURT

HEADING 1. CONSTITUTION OF THE COURT

SECTION A. JUDGES AND ASSESSORS

ARTICLE 1. Subject to the provisions of Article 14 of the Statute, the term of office of judges and deputy-judges shall commence on January 1st of the year following their election.

ART. 2. Judges and deputy-judges elected at an earlier session of the Assembly and of the Council of the League of Nations shall take precedence respectively over judges and deputy-judges elected at a subsequent session. Judges and deputy-judges elected during the same session shall take precedence according to age. Judges shall take precedence over deputy-judges.

National judges chosen from outside the Court, under the terms of Article 31 of the Statute, shall take precedence after deputy-judges in order of age.

The list of deputy-judges shall be prepared in accordance with these principles.

The Vice-President shall take his seat on the right of the President. The other Members of the Court shall take their seats to the right and left of the President in the order laid down above.

Nevertheless the retiring President, whatever may be his seniority according to the preceding provisions, shall take his seat on the right of the President, the Vice-President taking in such case his seat on the left. This rule, however, shall not affect the other privileges or the powers conferred by the Statute or Rules of Court upon the Vice-President or the eldest judge.

ART. 3. Deputy-judges whose presence is necessary shall be summoned in the order laid down in the list referred to in the preceding Article, that is to say, each of them will be summoned in rotation throughout the list.

Should a deputy-judge be so far from the seat of the Court that, in the opinion of the President, a summons would not reach him in sufficient time, the deputy-judge next on the list shall be summoned; nevertheless, the judge to whom the summons should have been addressed shall be called upon, if possible, on the next occasion that the presence of a deputy-judge is required.

Should a deputy-judge be summoned to take his seat in a particular case as a national judge, under the terms of Article 31 of the Statute, such summons shall not be regarded as coming within the terms of the present Article.

ART. 4. In cases in which one or more parties are entitled to choose a judge *ad hoc* of their nationality, the full Court may sit with a number of judges exceeding the number of regular judges fixed by the Statute.

[1] Adopted July 31, 1926.

When the Court has satisfied itself, in accordance with Article 31 of the Statute, that there are several parties in the same interest and that none of them has a judge of its nationality upon the bench, the Court shall invite them, within a period to be fixed by the Court, to select by common agreement a deputy-judge of the nationality of one of the parties, should there be one; or, should there not be one, a judge chosen in accordance with the principles of the above-mentioned Article.

Should the parties have failed to notify the Court of their selection or choice when the time limit expires, they shall be regarded as having renounced the right conferred upon them by Article 31.

ART. 5. Before entering upon his duties, each member of the Court or judge summoned to complete the Court, under the terms of Article 31 of the Statute, shall make the following solemn declaration in accordance with Article 20 of the Statute:

"I solemnly declare that I will exercise all my powers and duties as a judge honourably and faithfully, impartially and conscientiously."

A special public sitting of the Court may, if necessary, be convened for this purpose.

At the public inaugural sitting held after a new election of the whole Court the required declaration shall be made first by the President, secondly by the Vice-President, and then by the remaining judges in the order laid down in Article 2.

ART. 6. For the purpose of applying Article 18 of the Statute, the President or if necessary the Vice-President, shall convene the judges and deputy-judges. The member affected shall be allowed to furnish explanations. When he has done so the question shall be discussed and a vote shall be taken, the member in question not being present. If the members present are unanimously agreed, the Registrar shall issue the notification prescribed in the above-mentioned Article.

ART. 7. The President shall take steps to obtain all information which might be helpful to the Court in selecting technical assessors in each case. With regard to the questions referred to in Article 26 of the Statute, he shall, in particular, consult the Governing Body of the International Labour Office.

The assessors shall be appointed by an absolute majority of votes, either by the Court or by the special Chamber which has to deal with the case in question.

ART. 8. Assessors shall make the following solemn declaration at the first sitting of the Court at which they are present:

"I solemnly declare that I will exercise my duties and powers as an assessor honourably and faithfully, impartially and conscientiously, and that I will scrupulously observe all the provisions of the Statute and of the Rules of Court."

SECTION B. THE PRESIDENCY

ART. 9. The election of the President and Vice-President shall take place at the end of the ordinary session immediately before the normal termination of the period of office of the retiring President and Vice-President.

After a new election of the whole Court, the election of the President and Vice-President shall take place at the commencement of the following session.

The President and Vice-President elected in these circumstances shall take up their duties on the day of their election. They shall remain in office until the end of the second year after the year of their election.

Should the President or the Vice-President cease to belong to the Court before the expiration of their normal term of office, an election shall be held for the purpose of appointing a substitute for the unexpired portion of their term of office. If necessary, an extraordinary session of the Court may be convened for this purpose.

The elections referred to in the present Article shall take place by secret ballot. The candidate obtaining an absolute majority of votes shall be declared elected.

ART. 10. The President shall direct the work and administration of the Court; he shall preside at the meetings of the full Court.

ART. 11. The Vice-President shall take the place of the President, should the latter be unable to be present, or, should he cease to hold office, until the new President has been appointed by the Court.

ART. 12. The President shall reside within a radius of ten kilometres from the Peace Palace at The Hague.

The main annual vacation of the President shall not exceed three months.

ART. 13. After a new election of the whole Court and until such time as the President and Vice-President have been elected, the judge who takes precedence according to the order laid down in Article 2, shall perform the duties of President.

The same principle shall be applied should both the President and the Vice-President be unable to be present, or should both appointments be vacant at the same time. Whenever, according to the rules in force, the functions of President should be exercised by a national of one of the parties to the suit, they shall pass, for the purposes of the case in question, in the order of seniority established by the Rules of Court, to the first judge not similarly situated.

SECTION C. THE CHAMBERS

ART. 14. The members of the Chambers constituted by virtue of Articles 26, 27, and 29 of the Statute shall be appointed at a meeting of the full Court by an absolute majority of votes, regard being had for the purposes of this selection to any preference expressed by the judges, so far as the provisions of Article 9 of the Statute permit.

The substitutes mentioned in Articles 26 and 27 of the Statute shall be appointed in the same manner. Two judges shall also be chosen to replace any member of the Chamber for summary procedure who may be unable to sit.

The election shall take place at the end of the ordinary session of the Court, and the period of appointment of the members elected shall commence on January 1st of the following year.

Nevertheless, after a new election of the whole Court the election shall take place at the beginning of the following session. The period of appointment shall commence on the date of election and shall terminate, in the case of the Chamber referred to in Article 29 of the Statute, at the end of the same year and, in the case of the Chambers referred to in Articles 26 and 27 of the Statute, at the end of the second year after the year of election.

The Presidents of the Chambers shall be appointed at a sitting of the full Court. Nevertheless, the President of the Court shall, *ex officio,* preside over any Chamber of which he may be elected a member; similarly, the Vice-President of the Court shall, *ex officio,* preside over any Chamber of which he may be elected a member, provided that the President is not also a member.

Art. 15. The special Chambers for labour cases and for communications and transit cases may not sit with a greater number than five judges.

Except as provided in the second paragraph of the preceding Article, the composition of the Chamber for Summary Procedure may not be altered.

Art. 16. Deputy-judges shall not be summoned to complete the special Chambers or the Chamber for Summary Procedure, unless sufficient judges are not available to complete the number required.

Section D. The Registry

Art. 17. The Court shall select its Registrar from amongst candidates proposed by members of the Court.

The election shall be by secret ballot and by a majority of votes. In the event of an equality of votes, the President shall have a casting vote.

The Registrar shall be elected for a term of seven years commencing on January 1st of the year following that in which the election takes place. He may be re-elected.

Should the Registrar cease to hold his office before the expiration of the term above-mentioned, an election shall be held for the purpose of appointing a successor. Each election shall be for a full term of seven years.

The Court shall appoint a Deputy-Registrar to assist the Registrar, to act as Registrar in his absence, and, in the event of his ceasing to hold the office, to perform its duties until a new Registrar shall have been appointed. The Deputy-Registrar shall be appointed in the same way as the Registrar.

Art. 18. Before taking up his duties, the Registrar shall make the following declaration at a meeting of the full Court:

"I solemnly declare that I will perform the duties conferred upon me as Registrar of the Permanent Court of International Justice in all loyalty, discretion, and good conscience."

The Deputy-Registrar shall make a similar declaration in the same conditions.

Art. 19. The Registrar and the Deputy-Registrar shall reside within a radius of ten kilometres from the Peace Palace at The Hague.

The main annual vacation of the Registrar shall not exceed two months.

Art. 20. The officials of the Registry, other than the Deputy-Registrar, shall be appointed by the Court on proposals submitted by the Registrar.

On taking up their duties, such officials shall make the following declaration before the President, the Registrar being present:

"I solemnly declare that I will perform the duties conferred upon me as official of the Permanent Court of International Justice in all loyalty, discretion, and good conscience."

ART. 21. The Regulations for the Staff of the Registry shall be adopted by the President on the proposal of the Registrar, subject to subsequent approval by the Court.

ART. 22. The Court shall determine or modify the organization of the Registry upon proposals submitted by the Registrar. On the proposal of the Registrar or Deputy-Registrar, as the case may be, the Court, or, if it is not in session, the President, shall appoint the official of the Registry who is to act as substitute for the Registrar, should both the Registrar and Deputy-Registrar be unable to be present, or should both appointments be vacant at the same time, until a successor to the Registrar has been appointed.

ART. 23. The registers kept in the archives shall be so arranged as to give particulars with regard to the following points amongst others:

1. For each case or question, all documents pertaining to it and all action taken with regard to it in chronological order; all such documents shall bear the same file number and shall be numbered consecutively within the file;

2. All decisions of the Court in chronological order, with references to the respective files;

3. All advisory opinions given by the Court in chronological order, with references to the respective files;

4. All notifications and similar communications sent out by the Court, with references to the respective files.

Indexes kept in the archives shall comprise:

1. A card index of names with necessary references;

2. A card index of subject-matter with like references.

ART. 24. The Registrar shall be the channel for all communications to and from the Court.

The Registrar shall reply to any inquiries concerning its activities, including inquiries from the Press, subject, however, to the provisions of Article 42 of the present Rules and to the observance of professional secrecy.

ART. 25. The Registrar shall insure that the date of dispatch and receipt of all communications and notifications may readily be verified. Communications and notifications sent by post shall be registered. Communications addressed to the official representatives or to the agents of the parties shall be considered as having been addressed to the parties themselves. The date of receipt shall be noted on all documents received by the Registrar, and a receipt bearing this date and the number under which the document has been registered shall be given to the sender, if a request to that effect be made.

ART. 26. The Registrar shall be responsible for the archives, the accounts and all administrative work. He shall have the custody of the seals and stamps of the Court. He, or the Deputy-Registrar, shall be present at all meetings of the full Court and either he, or the Deputy-Registrar, or an official appointed by the Registrar, with the approval of the Court, to represent him, shall be present at all sittings of the various Chambers; the Registrar shall be responsible for drawing up the minutes of the meetings.

He shall further undertake all duties which may be laid upon him by the present Rules.

The duties of the Registry shall be set forth in detail in a List of Instructions to be submitted by the Registrar to the President for his approval.

HEADING 2. WORKING OF THE COURT

ART. 27. In the year following a new election of the whole Court the ordinary annual session shall commence on the fifteenth of January.

If the day fixed for the opening of a session is regarded as a holiday at the place where the Court is sitting, the session shall be opened on the working day following.

ART. 28. The list of cases shall be prepared and kept up to date by the Registrar under the responsibility of the President. The list for each session shall contain all questions submitted to the Court for an advisory opinion and all cases in regard to which the written proceedings are concluded, in the order in which the documents submitting each question or case have been received by the Registrar. If in the course of a session, a question is submitted to the Court or the written proceedings in regard to any case are concluded, the Court shall decide whether such question or case shall be added to the list for that session.

The Registrar shall prepare and keep up to date extracts from the above list showing the cases to be dealt with by the respective Chambers.

The Registrar shall also prepare and keep a list of cases for revision.

ART. 29. During the sessions the dates and hours of sittings shall be fixed by the President.

ART. 30. If at any sitting of the full Court it is impossible to obtain the prescribed quorum, the Court shall adjourn until the quorum is obtained. Judges *ad hoc* shall not be taken into account for the calculation of the quorum.

ART. 31. The Court shall sit in private to deliberate upon the decision of any case or upon any advisory opinion; also, when dealing with any administrative matter.

During the deliberation referred to in the preceding paragraph, only persons authorized to take part in the deliberation and the Registrar or, in his absence, the Deputy-Registrar, shall be present. No other person shall be admitted except by virtue of a special decision taken by the Court, having regard to exceptional circumstances.

Every member of the Court who is present at the deliberation shall state his opinion together with the reasons on which it is based.

The decision of the Court shall be based upon the conclusions adopted after final discussion by a majority of the members voting in an order inverse to the order of precedence established by Article 2.

Any member of the Court may request that a question which is to be voted upon shall be drawn up in precise terms in both the official languages and distributed to the Court. A request to this effect shall be complied with.

No detailed minutes shall be prepared of the Court's private meetings for deliberation upon judgments or advisory opinions; such minutes, which are to be considered as confidential, shall record only the subject of the debates, votes taken, with the names of those voting for and against a motion, and statements expressly made for insertion in the minutes.

Subject to a contrary decision by the Court, the same procedure shall apply to private meetings for deliberation upon administrative matters.

After the final vote taken on a judgment or advisory opinion, any judge who desires to set forth his individual opinion must do so in accordance with Article 57 of the Statute.

CHAPTER II. PROCEDURE

HEADING 1. CONTENTIOUS PROCEDURE

Section A. General Provisions

Art. 32. The rules contained under this heading shall in no way preclude the adoption by the Court of such other rules as may be jointly proposed by the parties concerned, due regard being paid to the particular circumstances of each case.

Art. 33. The Court shall fix time limits in each case by assigning a definite date for the completion of the various acts of procedure, having regard as far as possible to any agreement between the parties.

The Court may extend time limits which it has fixed. It may likewise decide in certain circumstances that any proceeding taken after the expiration of a time limit shall be considered as valid.

If the Court is not sitting, the powers conferred upon it by this Article shall be exercised by the President, subject to any subsequent decision of the Court.

Art. 34. The originals of all documents of the written proceedings submitted to the Court shall be signed by the agent or agents duly appointed; they shall be dated.

The original shall be accompanied by ten copies certified as correct. Subject to any contrary arrangement between the Registrar and the agent or agents, it shall likewise be accompanied by a further forty printed copies.

The President may order additional printed copies to be supplied.

Section B. Procedure before the Court and before the Special Chambers (Articles 26 and 27 of the Statute)

I. Institution of Proceedings

Art. 35. (1) When a case is brought before the Court by means of a special agreement, the latter, or the document notifying the Court of the agreement, shall mention:

(a) The names of the agents appointed by the respective parties for the purposes of the case;

(b) The permanent addresses at the seat of the Court to which notices and communications intended for the respective parties are to be sent.

In all other cases in which the Court has jurisdiction, the application, in addition to the specification of the subject of the dispute and the names of the parties concerned, a succinct statement of facts, and an indication of the claim, shall include:

(a) The name or names of the agent or agents appointed for the purposes of the case;

(*b*) The permanent addresses at the seat of the Court to which subsequent notices and communications in regard to the case are to be sent.

Should proceedings be instituted by means of an application, the first document sent in reply thereto shall likewise mention the name or names of the agent or agents and the addresses at the seat of the Court.

Whenever possible, the agents should remain at the seat of the Court pending the trial and determination of the case.

(2) The declaration provided for in the Resolution of the Council of the League of Nations of May 17, 1922 (*Annex*[1]), shall, when it is required under Article 35 of the Statute, be filed with the Registry not later than the time fixed for the deposit of the first document of the written procedure.

[1] ANNEX TO ART. 35. *Resolution adopted by the Council on May 17, 1922.*

The Council of the League of Nations, in virtue of the powers conferred upon it by Article 35, paragraph 2, of the Statute of the Permanent Court of International Justice, and subject to the provisions of that article,

RESOLVES:

1. The Permanent Court of International Justice shall be open to a State which is not a Member of the League of Nations or mentioned in the Annex to the Covenant of the League, upon the following condition, namely: that such State shall previously have deposited with the Registrar of the Court a declaration by which it accepts the jurisdiction of the Court, in accordance with the Covenant of the League of Nations and with the terms and subject to the conditions of the Statute and Rules of the Court, and undertakes to carry out in full good faith the decision or decisions of the Court and not to resort to war against a state complying therewith.

2. Such declaration may be either particular or general.

A particular declaration is one accepting the jurisdiction of the Court in respect only of a particular dispute or disputes which have already arisen.

A general declaration is one accepting the jurisdiction generally in respect of all disputes or of a particular class or classes of disputes which have already arisen or which may arise in the future.

A State in making such a general declaration may accept the jurisdiction of the Court as compulsory, *ipso facto*, and without special convention, in conformity with Article 36 of the Statute of the Court; but such acceptance may not, without special convention, be relied upon vis-à-vis Members of the League or States mentioned in the Annex to the Covenant which have signed or may hereafter sign the "optional clause" provided for by the additional protocol of December 16th, 1920.

3. The original declarations made under the terms of this Resolution shall be kept in the custody of the Registrar of the Court, in accordance with the practice of the Court. Certified true copies thereof shall be transmitted, in accordance with the practice of the Court, to all Members of the League of Nations, and States mentioned in the Annex to the Covenant, and to such other States as the Court may determine, and to the Secretary-General of the League of Nations.

4. The Council of the League of Nations reserves the right to rescind or amend this Resolution by a Resolution which shall be communicated to the Court; and on the receipt of such communication and to the extent determined by the new Resolution, existing declarations shall cease to be effective except in regard to disputes which are already before the Court.

5. All questions as to the validity or the effect of a declaration made under the terms of this Resolution shall be decided by the Court.

(3) Should the notice of a special agreement, or the application, contain a request that the case be referred to one of the special Chambers mentioned in Articles 26 and 27 of the Statute, such request shall be complied with, provided that the parties are in agreement.

Similarly, a request to the effect that technical assessors be attached to the Court, in accordance with Article 27 of the Statute, or that the case be referred to the Chamber for Summary Procedure shall also be granted; compliance with the latter request is, however, subject to the condition that the case does not relate to the matters dealt with in Articles 26 and 27 of the Statute.

ART. 36. The Registrar shall forthwith communicate to all members of the Court special agreements or applications which have been notified to him.

He shall also transmit them through the channels provided for in the Statute or by special arrangement, as the case may be, to all Members of the League of Nations and to all states not Members of the League entitled to appear before the Court.

II. WRITTEN PROCEEDINGS

ART. 37. Should the parties agree that the proceedings shall be conducted in French or in English, the documents constituting the written procedure shall be submitted only in the language adopted by the parties.

In the absence of an agreement with regard to the language to be employed, documents shall be submitted in French or in English.

Should the use of a language other than French or English be authorised, a translation into French or into English shall be attached to the original of each document submitted.

The Registrar shall not be bound to make translations of documents submitted in accordance with the above rules.

In the case of voluminous documents the Court, or the President if the Court is not sitting, may, at the request of the party concerned, sanction the submission of translations of portions of documents only.

ART. 38. When proceedings are begun by means of an application, any preliminary objection shall be filed after the filing of the case by the applicant and within the time fixed for the filing of the counter-case.

The document submitting the objection shall contain a statement of facts and of law on which the plea is based, a statement of conclusions and a list of the documents in support; these documents shall be attached; it shall mention the evidence which the party may desire to produce.

Upon receipt by the Registrar of the document submitting the objection, the Court, or the President if the Court is not sitting, shall fix the time within which the party against whom the plea is directed may submit a written statement of its observations and conclusions; documents in support shall be attached and evidence which it is proposed to produce shall be mentioned.

Unless otherwise decided by the Court, the further proceedings shall be oral. The provisions of paragraphs 4 and 5 of Article 69 of the Rules shall apply.

ART. 39. In cases in which proceedings have been instituted by means of a special agreement, the following documents may be presented in the order stated below, provided that no agreement to the contrary has been concluded between the parties :

a case, submitted by each party within the same limit of time ;

a counter-case, submitted by each party within the same limit of time ;

a reply, submitted by each party within the same limit of time.

When proceedings are instituted by means of an application, failing any agreement to the contrary between the parties, the documents shall be presented in the order stated below :

the case by the applicant ;

the counter-case by the respondent ;

the reply by the applicant ;

the rejoinder by the respondent.

ART. 40. Cases shall contain :

1. A statement of the facts on which the claim is based ;

2. A statement of law ;

3. A statement of conclusions ;

4. A list of the documents in support ; these documents shall be attached to the case.

Counter-cases shall contain :

1. The affirmation or contestation of the facts stated in the case ;

2. A statement of additional facts, if any ;

3. A statement of law ;

4. Conclusions based on the facts stated ; these conclusions may include counter-claims, in so far as the latter come within the jurisdiction of the Court ;

5. A list of the documents in support ; these documents shall be attached to the counter-case.

ART. 41. Upon the termination of the written proceedings the President shall fix a date for the commencement of the oral proceedings.

ART 42. The Registrar shall forward to each of the members of the Court, and to the parties, a copy or copies of all documents in the case as he receives them.

The Court, or the President if the Court is not sitting, may, after hearing the parties, order the Registrar to hold the cases and counter-cases of each suit at the disposal of the government of any state which is entitled to appear before the Court.

III. ORAL PROCEEDINGS

ART. 43. In the case of a public sitting, the Registrar shall publish in the Press all necessary information as to the date and hour fixed.

ART. 44. The Registrar shall arrange for the interpretation from French into English and from English into French of all statements, questions and answers which the Court may direct to be so interpreted.

Whenever a language other than French or English is employed, either under the terms of the third paragraph of Article 39 of the Statute or in a particular instance, the necessary arrangements for translation into one of the two official languages shall be made by the party concerned. In the case of witnesses or experts who appear at the instance of the Court, these arrangements shall be made by the Registrar.

ART. 45. The Court shall determine in each case whether the representatives of the parties shall address the Court before or after the production of the evidence; the parties shall, however, retain the right to comment on the evidence given.

ART. 46. The order in which the agents, advocates or counsel shall be called upon to speak shall be determined by the Court, failing an agreement between the parties on the subject.

ART. 47. In sufficient time before the opening of the oral proceedings, each party shall inform the Court and the other parties of all evidence which it intends to produce, together with the names, Christian names, description and residence of witnesses whom it desires to be heard.

It shall further give a general indication of the point or points to which the evidence is to refer.

ART. 48. The Court may, subject to the provisions of Article 44 of the Statute, invite the parties to call witnesses, or may call for the production of any other evidence on points of fact in regard to which the parties are not in agreement.

ART. 49. The Court, or the President, should the Court not be sitting, shall, at the request of one of the parties or on its own initiative, take the necessary steps for the examination of witnesses out of Court.

ART. 50. Each witness shall make the following solemn declaration before giving his evidence in Court:

"I solemnly declare upon my honour and conscience that I will speak the truth, the whole truth and nothing but the truth."

ART. 51. Witnesses shall be examined by the representatives of the parties under the control of the President. Questions may be put to them by the President and afterwards by the judges.

ART. 52. The indemnities of witnesses who appear at the instance of the Court shall be paid out of the funds of the Court.

ART. 53. Any report or record of any enquiry carried out at the request of the Court, under the terms of Article 50 of the Statute, and reports furnished to the Court by experts, in accordance with the same Article, shall be forthwith communicated to the parties.

ART 54. A verbatim record shall be made of the oral proceedings, including the evidence taken, under the supervision of the Registrar.

The report of the evidence of each witness shall be read to him in order that, subject to the direction of the Court, any mistakes may be corrected.

The report of statements made by agents, advocates or counsel shall be communicated to them for their correction or revision, subject to the direction of the Court.

ART. 55. The minutes mentioned in Article 47 of the Statute shall in particular include:

1. The names of the judges;
2. The names of the agents, advocates and counsel;
3. The names, Christian names, description and residence of witnesses heard;
4. A specification of other evidence produced;
5. Any declarations made by the parties;
6. All decisions taken by the Court during the hearing.

The minutes of public sittings shall be printed and published.

ART 56. The party in whose favor an order for the payment of costs has been made may present his bill of costs after judgment has been delivered.

IV. INTERIM PROTECTION

ART. 57. When the Court is not sitting, any measures for the preservation in the meantime of the respective rights of the parties shall be indicated by the President.

Any refusal by the parties to conform to the suggestions of the Court or of the President, with regard to such measures, shall be placed on record.

V. INTERVENTION

ART. 58. An application for permission to intervene, under the terms of Article 62 of the Statute, must be communicated to the Registrar at latest before the commencement of the oral proceedings.

Nevertheless the Court may, in exceptional circumstances, consider an application submitted at a later stage.

ART. 59. The application referred to in the preceding Article shall contain:

1. A specification of the case in which the applicant desires to intervene;

2. A statement of law and of fact justifying intervention;

3. A list of the documents in support of the application; these documents shall be attached.

Such application shall be immediately communicated to the parties, who shall send to the Registrar any observations which they may desire to make within a period to be fixed by the Court, or by the President, should the Court not be sitting.

Such observations shall be communicated to the state desiring to intervene and to all parties. The intervener and the original parties may comment thereon in Court; for this purpose the matter shall be placed on the agenda for a hearing the date and hour of which shall be notified to all concerned. The Court will give its decision on the application in the form of a judgment.

If the application is not contested, the President, if the Court is not sitting, may, subject to any subsequent decision of the Court as regards the admissibility of the application, fix, at the request of the state by which the application is made, time limits within which such state is authorized to file a case on the merits and within which the other parties may file their counter-cases. These time limits, however, may not extend beyond the beginning of the session in the course of which the case shall be heard.

ART. 60. The notification provided for in Article 63 of the Statute shall be sent to every state or Member of the League of Nations which is a party to the convention relied upon in the special agreement or in the application as governing the case submitted to the Court.

The Court, or the President if the Court is not sitting, shall fix the times within which states desiring to intervene are to file any cases.

The Registrar shall take the necessary steps to enable the intervening state to inspect the documents in the case, in so far as they relate to the interpretation of the convention in question, and to submit its observations thereon to the Court. Such observations shall be communicated to the parties, who may comment thereon in Court. The Court may authorize the intervening state to reply.

VI. Agreement

ART. 61. If the parties conclude an agreement regarding the settlement of the dispute and give written notice of such agreement to the Court before the close of the proceedings, the Court shall officially record the conclusion of the agreement.

Should the parties by mutual agreement notify the Court in writing that they intend to break off proceedings, the Court shall officially record the fact and proceedings shall be terminated.

VII. Judgment

ART. 62. The judgment shall contain:

1. The date on which it is pronounced;
2. The names of the judges participating;
3. The names and style of the parties;
4. The names of the agents of the parties;
5. The conclusions of the parties;
6. The matters of fact;
7. The reasons in point of law;
8. The operative provisions of the judgment;
9. The decision, if any, referred to in Article 64 of the Statute.
10. The number of the judges constituting the majority contemplated in Article 55 of the Statute.

Dissenting judges may, if they so desire, attach to the judgment either an exposition of their individual opinion or the statement of their dissent.

ART. 63. When the judgment has been read in public, duly signed and sealed copies thereof shall be forwarded to the parties.

This text shall forthwith be communicated by the Registrar, through the channels agreed upon, to Members of the League of Nations and to states entitled to appear before the Court.

ART. 64. The judgment shall be regarded as taking effect on the day on which it is read in open Court, in accordance with Article 58 of the Statute.

ART. 65. A collection of the judgments of the Court shall be printed and published under the responsibility of the Registrar.

VIII. Revision and Interpretation

ART. 66. 1. Application for revision shall be made in the same form as the application mentioned in Article 40 of the Statute.

It shall contain:

(a) A specification of the judgment impeached;

(b) The facts upon which the application is based;

(c) A list of the supporting documents; these documents shall be attached to the application.

It shall be the duty of the Registrar to give immediate notice of an application for revision to the other parties concerned. The latter may submit observations within a time limit to be fixed by the Court, or by the President should the Court not be sitting.

If the Court, under the third paragraph of Article 61 of the Statute, by a special judgment makes the admission of the application conditional upon previous compliance with the terms of the judgment impeached, this condition shall be immediately communicated to the applicant by the Registrar, and proceedings in revision shall be stayed pending receipt by the Registrar of proof of previous compliance with the original judgment and until such proof shall have been accepted by the Court.

2. A request to the Court to construe a judgment which it has given may be made either by the notification of a special agreement between all the parties or by an application by one or more of the parties.

The agreement or application shall contain:

(a) A specification of the judgment the interpretation of which is requested;

(b) An indication of the precise point or points in dispute.

If the request for interpretation is made by means of an application, it shall be the duty of the Registrar to give immediate notice of such application to the other parties, and the latter may submit observations within a time limit to be fixed by the Court or by the President, as the case may be.

The Court may, whether the request be made by agreement or by application, invite the parties to furnish further written or oral explanations.

3. If the judgment impeached or to be construed was pronounced by the full Court, the application for revision or the request for interpretation shall also be dealt with by the full Court. If the judgment was pronounced by one of the Chambers mentioned in Articles 26, 27, or 29 of the Statute, the application for revision or the request for interpretation shall be dealt with by the same Chamber. The provisions of Article 13 of the Statute shall apply in all cases.

4. Objections to the Court's jurisdiction to revise or to construe a judgment, or other similar preliminary objections, shall be dealt with according to the procedure laid down in Article 38 of the present Rules.

5. The Court's decision on requests for revision or interpretation shall be given in the form of a judgment.

Section C. Summary Procedure

Art. 67. Except as provided under the present section the rules for procedure before the full Court shall apply to summary procedure.

Art. 68. Upon receipt by the Registrar of the document instituting proceedings in a case which, by virtue of an agreement between the parties, is to be dealt with by summary procedure, the President of the Court shall, as soon as possible, notify the members of the Chamber referred to in Article 29 of the Statute. The Chamber or, if it is not in session, its President, shall fix the time within which the first document of the written procedure, provided for in the following article, shall be filed.

The President shall convene the Chamber at the earliest date that may be required by the circumstances of the case.

Art. 69. Summary proceedings are opened by the presentation of cases according to the provisions of Article 39, paragraph 1, of the present Rules. If a case is presented by one party only, the other party or parties shall present a counter-case. In the event of the simultaneous presentation of cases by the parties, the Chamber may invite the presentation, under the same conditions, of counter-cases.

The cases and counter-cases, which shall be communicated by the Registrar to the members of the Chamber and to opposing parties, shall mention all evidence which the parties may desire to produce.

Should the Chamber consider that the documents do not furnish adequate information, it may, in the absence of an agreement to the contrary between the parties, institute oral proceedings. It shall fix a date for the commencement of the oral proceedings.

At the hearing, the Chamber shall call upon the parties to supply oral explanations. It may sanction the production of any evidence mentioned in the documents.

If it is desired that witnesses or experts whose names are mentioned in the documents should be heard, such witnesses or experts must be available to appear before the Chamber when required.

ART. 70. The judgment is the judgment of the Court rendered in the Chamber of Summary Procedure. It shall be read at a public sitting of the Chamber.

HEADING 2. ADVISORY PROCEDURE

ART. 71. Advisory opinions shall be given after deliberation by the full Court. They shall mention the number of the judges constituting the majority.

On a question relating to an existing dispute between two or more states or Members of the League of Nations, Article 31 of the Statute shall apply. In case of doubt the Court shall decide.[2]

Dissenting judges may, if they so desire, attach to the opinion of the Court either an exposition of their individual opinion or the statement of their dissent.

ART. 72. Questions upon which the advisory opinion of the Court is asked shall be laid before the Court by means of a written request, signed either by the President of the Assembly or the President of the Council of the League of Nations, or by the Secretary-General of the League under instructions from the Assembly or the Council.

The request shall contain an exact statement of the question upon which an opinion is required, and shall be accompanied by all documents likely to throw light upon the question.

ART. 73. 1. The Registrar shall forthwith give notice of the request for an advisory opinion to the members of the Court, to the Members of the League of Nations, through the Secretary-General of the League, and to any states entitled to appear before the Court.

The Registrar shall also, by means of a special and direct communication, notify any Member of the League or state admitted to appear before the Court or international organization considered by the Court (or, should it not be sitting, by the President) as likely to be able to furnish information on the question, that the Court will be prepared to receive, within a time limit to be fixed by the President, written statements, or to hear, at a public sitting to be held for the purpose, oral statements relating to the question.

Should any state or Member referred to in the first paragraph have failed to receive the communication specified above, such state or Member may express a desire to submit a written statement, or to be heard; and the Court will decide.

---

[2] This paragraph was added by amendment by the Court on September 7, 1927.

2. States, Members, and organizations having presented written or oral statements or both shall be admitted to comment on the statements made by other states, Members, or organizations, in the form, to the extent, and within the time limits which the Court, or, should it not be sitting, the President shall decide in each particular case. Accordingly, the Registrar shall in due time communicate any such written statements to states, Members, and organizations having submitted similar statements.

ART. 74. Advisory opinions shall be read in open Court, notice having been given to the Secretary-General of the League of Nations and to the representatives of states, of Members of the League, and of international organizations immediately concerned. The Registrar shall take the necessary steps in order to insure that the text of the advisory opinion is in the hands of the Secretary-General at the seat of the League at the date and hour fixed for the meeting held for the reading of the opinion.

Signed and sealed original copies of advisory opinions shall be placed in the archives of the Court and of the Secretariat of the League. Certified copies thereof shall be transmitted by the Registrar to States, to Members of the League, and to international organizations immediately concerned.

Any advisory opinion which may be given by the Court, and the request in response to which it is given, shall be printed and published in a special collection for which the Registrar shall be responsible.

HEADING 3. ERRORS

ART. 75. The Court, or the President if the Court is not sitting, shall be entitled to correct an error in any order, judgment, or opinion, arising from a slip or accidental omission.

Done at The Hague, the thirty-first day of July, one thousand nine hundred and twenty-six.

(Signed)   MAX HUBER
President
(Signed)   A. HAMMARSKJÖLD
Registrar

BIBLIOGRAPHY

Acremant, Albert. *La procédure dans les arbitrages internationaux*. Sueur-Charruey, Paris, 1905.

Administrative Decisions and Opinions of a General Nature and Opinions in Individual Lusitania Claims and Other Cases to July 30th, 1925. Mixed Claims Commission, United States and Germany. Government Printing Office, Washington, D.C.

Alaska Boundary Commission. Senate Document 165, 58th Congress, 2d Session. Government Printing Office, Washington, D.C.

American and British Claims Commission Report, F. K. Nielsen, American Agent. Government Printing Office, Washington, D.C., 1926.

American Journal of International Law, 1907—. Baker-Voorhis & Co., New York.

American Society of International Law. *Proceedings of 1907*. Washington, D.C.

American Society for Judicial Settlement of International Disputes. *Proceedings 1910–1916*. Baltimore.

Anales de la Corte de Justicia Centroamericana, 5 volumes. San José de Costa Rica, 1907–1917.

André, A. *De l'arbitrage obligatoire dans les rapports internationaux*. Douai, 1903.

Annuaire de l'Institut de droit international, 1873–1927. A. Pedone, Paris.

Arbitration and the United States, World Peace Foundation Pamphlets, Vol. 9. Boston, 1926.

Audry, Léon. *La révision de la sentence arbitrale*. Duchemin, Paris, 1914.

Baker, Ray Stannard. *Woodrow Wilson and World Settlement*, 3 volumes. Doubleday, Page, Garden City, 1922.

Bello, Andrés. *Principios de derecho internacional*, 4th edition. Garnier, Paris, 1882.

Bluntschli, J. C. *Droit international codifié*. Paris, 1895.

Bokanowski, Maurice. *Les commissions internationales d'enquête*. Pedone, Paris, 1908.

Bonfils, Henry. *Manuel de droit international public*, 4th edition. Rousseau, Paris, 1905.

Borchard, Edward M. *The Diplomatic Protection of Citizens Abroad*. Banks Law Publishing Company, New York, 1915.

Boutwell, George S. *Report of French-American Claims Commission*. House Executive Document 235, 48th Congress, 2d Session. Government Printing Office, Washington, D.C., 1873.

British-American Claims Commission under Treaty of 1853, Report of. Senate Executive Document 103, 34th Congress, 1st Session. Government Printing Office, Washington, D.C., 1855.

British and Foreign State Papers. Foreign Office, London.

Bustamante, Antonio Sanchez de. *The World Court*. The Macmillan Company, New York, 1925.

Calvo, Charles, *Le droit international,* 6 volumes, 5th edition. Rousseau, Paris, 1896.

Conferencia de Paz Centroamericana, Actas y Documentos. Government Printing Office, Washington, D.C., 1907.

Darby, W. Evans. *International Tribunals,* 4th edition. London, 1904.

D'Armstrong, Thomas de St. Georges. *De l'utilité de l'arbitrage.* Larose et Forcel, Paris, 1890.

De Card, M. E. Rouard. *L'arbitrage international dans le passé, le présent et l'avenir.* Durand et Pedone, Paris, 1877.

Descamps, E. E., and Renault, Louis. *Recueil international des traités du XXᵉ siècle.* Paris, 1901, 1904.

Despagnet, Frantz. *Cours de droit international public,* 2d edition. Larose, Paris, 1899.

Dreyfus, Ferdinand. *L'arbitrage international.* Paris, 1892.

Dumas, Jacques. *Les sanctions de l'arbitrage international.* Pedone, Paris, 1905.

Eagleton, Clyde. *The Responsibility of States in International Law.* New York University Press, New York, 1928.

Edmunds, Sterling E. *The Lawless Law of Nations.* John Byrne & Co., Washington, D.C., 1925.

Fenwick, Charles G. *International Law.* The Century Co., New York, 1924.

Field, David Dudley. *Draft Outlines of an International Code.* New York, 1876.

Fiore, Pasquale. *Nouveau droit international public.* Translated by Pradier-Fodéré, 2 volumes. Pedone, Paris, 1868.

Foreign Relations of the United States. Government Printing Office, Washington, D.C.

Fur Seal Arbitrations, 15 volumes. Senate Executive Document 177, 53d Congress, 2d Session. Government Printing Office, Washington, D.C., 1893.

Grotius, Hugo. *Le droit de la guerre et de la paix.* Translated by Jean Barbeyrac, 2 volumes. Amsterdam, 1729.

Hackett, F. W. *Reminiscences of the Geneva Tribunal.* Boston, 1911.

Haines, Charles G. and Bertha M. *Principles and Problems of Government.* New York, 1921.

Hale, Robert S. Report of American Agent British-American Claims Commission, in *Foreign Relations of 1873.* Part III. House Executive Document, 43d Congress, 1st Session. Government Printing Office, Washington, D.C., 1874.

Hall, William E. *A Treatise on International Law,* 4th edition. Stevens & Son, London, 1895.

Heffter, A. W. and Geffcken, F. H. *Das europäische Völkerrecht der Gegenwart,* 8th edition. Berlin, 1888.

Hertslet's Treaties—Hertslet, L. and E.,; etc. *Commercial Treaties.* London, 1835.

Holls, Frederick W. *The Peace Conference at The Hague.* Macmillan, New York, 1900.

Howard, Henry. Report of British Agent, *British-American Claims Commission.*

Hudson, Manley O. *The Permanent Court of International Justice.* Harvard University Press, Cambridge, Mass., 1925.

Hudson, Manley O. *The Work of the Permanent Court of International Justice during Four Years.* World Peace Foundation Pamphlets, Vol. 9. Boston, 1926.

Hyde, Charles Cheney. *International Law,* 2 volumes. Little, Brown & Co., Boston, 1922.

International Conferences of American States. Reports.

> *First Conference,* Senate Document 224, 51st Congress, 1st Session, 1890, and *International American Conference,* 1890.
>
> *Second Conference,* Senate Document 330, 57th Congress, 1st Session, 1902.
>
> *Third Conference,* 1907.
>
> *Fourth Conference,* Senate Document 744, 61st Congress, 3d Session, 1911.
>
> *Fifth Conference,* 1923.
>
> *Sixth Conference,* 1928.
>
> Government Printing Office, Washington, D.C.

International Law Association. *Reports of Conferences.* Sweet & Marwell, London, 1873—.

Jay, William. *War and Peace; the Evils of the First and a Plan for Preserving the Last.* Oxford University Press, New York, 1919.

Journal du droit international privé, 1874—. Marchal et Billard, Paris.

Kamarowsky, L. *Le tribunal international.* Pedone, Paris, 1887.

Kant, Immanuel. *Perpetual Peace, Trueblood's Translation.* American Peace Society, Washington, D.C., 1897.

King, L. W., and Hall, H. R. *Egypt and Western Asia.*

Ladd, William. *Essay on a Congress of Nations without Resort to Arms.* Oxford University Press, New York, 1916.

La Fontaine, H. *Pasicrisie internationale; Histoire documentaire des arbitrages internationaux.* Berne, 1902.

Lange, Chr. L. *L'histoire de l'internationalisme.* Publications of the Norwegian Nobel Institute, Christiania, 1919.

Laurent, François. *Principes de droit civil,* 33 volumes. Brussels, 1869–78.

Lauterpacht, H. *Private Law Sources and Analogies of International Law.* Longmans, Green & Co., London, 1927.

Lawrence, Thomas J. *The Principles of International Law.* London, 1910.

Laveleye, Emile de. *Des causes actuelles de guerre en Europe et de l'arbitrage.* Guillaumin & Cie, Paris, 1873.

Le Ray, André. *Les commissions internationales d'enquête au XX⁰ siècle.* Paul Godet, Saumur, 1910.

Lobo, Helio. *Report of Brazilian-Bolivian Claims Tribunal* (Manuscript).

Lockey, Joseph B. *Pan-Americanism: Its Beginnings.* The Macmillan Company, New York, 1920.

Loria, Achille. *Les bases économiques de la justice internationale.* Publications of the Norwegian Nobel Institute, Christiania, 1912.

Malauzat, Auguste. *La cour de justice arbitrale.* Edward Duchemin, Paris, 1914.

Malloy, William M. *Treaties, Conventions, International Acts, Protocols and Agreements between the United States of America and Other Powers, 1776–1909.* Senate Document, 357, 61st Congress, 2d Session, 2 volumes. Government Printing Office, Washington, D.C., 1910; 3d volume, Senate Document, 348, 67th Congress, 4th Session. Government Printing Office, Washington, D.C., 1923.

Manning, William R. *Arbitration Treaties among the American Nations to the Close of the Year 1910.* Oxford University Press, New York, 1924.

Mérignhac, A. *Traité théorique et pratique de l'arbitrage international.* Larose, Paris, 1895.

Moore, John Bassett. *A Digest of International Law,* 8 volumes, House Document 551, 56th Congress, 2d Session. Government Printing Office, Washington, D.C., 1906.

Moore, John Bassett. *American Diplomacy.* Harper & Brothers, New York, 1905.

Moore, John Bassett. *History and Digest of the International Arbitrations to Which the United States Has Been a Party,* 6 volumes. Government Printing Office, Washington, D.C., 1898.

Moore, John Bassett. *International Law and Some Current Illusions.* Macmillan Company, New York, 1924.

Monicault, M. de. *L'arbitrage international.* Monaco, 1899.

Morris, Robert C. *Report of United States and Venezuela Claims Commission.* Senate Document 317, 58th Congress, 2d Session.

Nicaragua Mixed Claims Commission. Report of President Otto Schoenrich, Washington, 1915.

North Atlantic Coast Fisheries, 12 volumes. Senate Document 870, 51st Congress, 3d Session. Government Printing Office, Washington D.C., 1912.

Novacovitch, Mileta. *Les compromis et les arbitrages internationaux du XII° au XV° siècle.* Pedone, Paris, 1905.

Ottoman Annuities Case, Opinion and Decision of M. Borel. Geneva, 1925.

Peirce, H. H. D. "Whaling Claims Arbitration," *Report,* Appendix I, *Foreign Relations of 1902.* Government Printing Office, Washington, D.C., 1902.

Pella, V. V. *La criminalité collective des états.* Bucharest, 1926.

Penfield, William L. *Report of the Venezuelan Arbitration before the Hague Tribunal.* Government Printing Office, Washington, D.C., 1905.

Pergler, Charles. *Judicial Interpretation of International Law in the United States.* Macmillan Co., 1928.

Permanent Court of International Justice, Judgments, Series A; *Advisory Opinions,* Series B. A. W. Sijthoff, Leyden.

Phillimore, R. J. *Commentaries upon International Law,* 4 volumes. London, 1879–89.

Phillipson, Coleman. *The International Law and Custom of Ancient Greece and Rome.* 2 volumes. Macmillan, London, 1911.

Politis, N. *La justice internationale.* Hachette, Paris, 1924.

Radulesco, Pierre. *Les solutions pacifiques internationales.* Jouvé et Cie, Paris, 1922.

Raeder, A. *L'arbitrage international chez les Hellènes.* Publication of the Norwegian Nobel Institute, Christiania, 1912.

Ralston, Jackson H. *American Agent's Report, Pious Fund Case, United States vs. Mexico.* Senate Document 28, 57th Congress, 2d Session. Government Printing Office, Washington, D.C., 1902.

Ralston, Jackson H. *Democracy's International Law.* John Byrne & Co., Washington, D.C., 1922.

Ralston, Jackson H. *The Law and Procedure of International Tribunals.* Stanford University Press, Stanford University, California, 1926.

Ralston, Jackson H. *Report of French-Venezuelan Mixed Claims Commission of 1902.* Government Printing Office, Washington, D.C., 1906.

Ralston, Jackson H. *Venezuelan Arbitrations of 1903.* Senate Document 316, 58th Congress, 2d Session. Government Printing Office, Washington, D.C., 1904.

Reclamaciones Presentadas al Tribunal Anglo-Chileno, 5 volumes. Santiago de Chile.

Recueil des arbitrages internationaux, Tome I, 1798–1855. 1905; Tome II, 1856–1872. By A. de Lapradelle and N. Politis. Pedone, Paris, 1924.

Recueil des décisions des tribunaux arbitraux mixtes institutés par les traités de paix. Tomes I–V. Société du Recueil Sirey, Paris, 1922–27.

Revon, Michel. *L'arbitrage international.* Rousseau, Paris, 1892.

Revue de droit international et de législation comparée, 1869—. Brussels.

Revue générale de droit international public, 1894—. Pedone, Paris.

Rivier, A. *Principes du droit des gens,* 2 volumes. Paris, 1896.

Roquefort, Ch. de Mougins de. *De la solution des conflits internationaux.* Paris, 1889.

Sax, B. *Histoire de l'arbitrage permanent.* Paris.

Scott, James Brown. *Arbitrations and Diplomatic Settlements of the United States.* Carnegie Endowment for International Peace, Washington, D.C., 1914.

Scott, James Brown. *The Hague Peace Conferences of 1899 and 1907,* 2 volumes. Johns Hopkins Press, Baltimore, 1909.

Scott, James Brown. *Instructions to the American Delegates to the Hague Peace Conferences and their Official Reports.* Oxford University Press, New York, 1916.

Scott, James Brown. *James Madison's Notes of Debates in the Federal Convention of 1787.* Oxford University Press, New York, 1918.

Scott, James Brown. *Peace through Justice.* Oxford University Press, New York, 1917.

Scott, James Brown. *The Recommendations of Habana Concerning International Organization.* Oxford University Press, New York, 1917.

Scott, James Brown. *Sovereign States and Suits before Arbitral Tribunals and Courts of Justice.* New York University Press, 1925.

Scott, James Brown. *The Spanish Origins of International Law.* Georgetown University, Washington, D.C., 1927.

Seijas, R. F. *Derecho Internacional Hispano-Americano,* 6 volumes. Caracas, 1884.

Sentence arbitrale du conseil fédéral suisse entre la Colombie et le Vénézuéla. Neuchatel, 1922.

Stoykovitch, Slavco. *De l'autorité de la sentence arbitrale en droit international public.* Sagot et Cie, Paris, 1924.

Sully, Duke of. *Grand Design of Henry IV* (Grotius Society Publications). Sweet & Maxwell, London, 1921.

Tchernoff, J. *Protection des nationaux résidant à l'étranger.* Pedone, Paris, 1899.

Thayer, W. R. *Life of John Hay.* Houghton, Mifflin. New York, 1915.

Tod, Marcus Niebuhr. *International Arbitration amongst the Greeks.* Oxford University Press, Oxford, 1913.

Treaties of Peace, 1919–1923, 2 volumes. Carnegie Endowment for International Peace, Washington, D.C., 1924.

Tribunal arbitral Franco-Chilien. Opinion. Lausanne, 1900.

United States and Mexico, Opinions of General Claims Commission (Pamphlet Reports).

United States and Venezuelan Claims Commission of 1885, Report of.

Urrutia, Francisco José. *La evolución del principio de arbitraje en America.* Editorial-America, Madrid, 1920.

Van Blokland, C. H. Beelaerts. *Internationale arbitrage.* Jiunta d'Albani, The Hague, 1875.

Vattel, Emer de. *Le droit des gens ou principes de la loi naturelle,* 2 volumes. Neuchatel, 1777.

Venezuela en el Centenario del Congreso de Panama. Caracas, 1926.

White, Andrew D. *Autobiography of Andrew D. White.* Century, New York, 1905.

Whitney, Edson L. *The American Peace Society—a Centennial History.* American Peace Society, Washington, D.C., 1928.

Woolf, L. S. *International Government.* Brentano, New York, 1916.

INDEX

INDEX

403